Islands in Transition

Islands in Transition

THE PAST, PRESENT, AND FUTURE OF HAWAII'S ECONOMY

BY

THOMAS KEMPER HITCH

EDITED BY ROBERT M. KAMINS

First Hawaiian Bank
Honolulu

Library of Congress Cataloging-in-Publication Data
Hitch, Thomas Kemper, 1912–
Islands in transition : the past, present, and future of Hawaii's
economy / by Thomas Kemper Hitch : edited by Robert M. Kamins.
p.   cm.
Includes bibliographical references and index.
ISBN 0–8248–1498–3 (alk. paper)
1. Hawaii—Economic conditions.   I. Kamins, Robe-t M.   II. Title.
HC107.H3H58   1992
330.9969–dc20   92–26343
CIP

Design and manufacture of this book were through
the production services program of the
University of Hawaii Press.

This book is printed on acid-free paper and meets the guidelines
for permanence and durability of the Council on Library Resources.

The opinions expressed in this book are those
of Thomas Kemper Hitch and may not reflect the
opinions of the First Hawaiian Bank.

Designed by Kenneth Miyamoto

Distributed by
University of Hawaii Press
Order Department
2840 Kolowalu Street
Honolulu, Hawaii 96822

Contents

List of Figures

List of Tables

Foreword

UNTIL THE PUBLICATION of this book, there has been a void in the literature on Hawaii. This has been the absence of a comprehensive study of
the Hawaiian economy. The only other major book on this subject,
Theodore Morgan's *Hawaii: A Century of Economic Change*, was published nearly fifty years ago and covered only the period from Captain
Cook's arrival in 1778 to the Reciprocity Treaty with the United States
in 1876.

Thomas Hitch has filled that void. This book describes, analyzes, and
evaluates economic developments from the time of the original settling
of Hawaii by Polynesians from the Marquesas Islands to the present,
with a series of thoughtful observations about economic issues that currently face us and other issues that will probably confront us in the
future.

A broad analysis such as Dr. Hitch has undertaken requires a
uniquely qualified individual. Indeed, Tom brought exceptional talents
and experiences to the task.

When Tom came to Hawaii forty years ago, he was already a nationally prominent economist. With his undergraduate degree from Stanford
(Phi Beta Kappa) and with his doctorate from the London School of
Economics, he had been a college professor, a coeditor of the U.S.
Department of Commerce's *Survey of Current Business*, and a military
government officer in the Navy during World War II. During the war he
trained officers at Princeton University for military government assign-
ments in the Pacific, at the end of the war he helped draft the administrative plans for the Trust Territory of the Pacific, and immediately after
the war he and Dr. Felix Keesing prepared the curriculum for a naval
school at Stanford to train officers for Trust Territory duty. From 1946
to 1950 he was a staff member of the President's Council of Economic
Advisers in Washington.

Having become familiar with and interested in the Pacific islands during the war, he came to Hawaii in 1950 to organize a research program
for the then new Hawaii Employers Council. The first request he got
from the council's board of governors was to prepare a comprehensive
analysis of the current state of the Hawaiian economy and what economic developments should be expected in the future. It is a fair statement that he spent the next third of a century on one or another aspect
of that kind of assignment, first with the council and then for nearly
twenty-five years as director of the economic research division of First
Hawaiian Bank—a division that he founded. In addition to directing the
research division and publishing a monthly report on the Hawaiian
economy for more than two decades, Tom also saw service as organizer
and director of the bank's international division and of its planning division.

Tom's extensive public service activities were invaluable in giving him
additional insights into how the Hawaiian economy works. He was
chairman of both a governor's and a mayor's finance advisory committee, chairman for many years of the research committee of the Hawaii
Visitor's Bureau, chairman of the committee on taxation and finance of
Hawaii's 1968 Constitutional Convention, vice-chairman of both the
territory's Economic Planning and Coordinating Authority and the
state's Board of Economic Development, president of the Tax Foundation of Hawaii, chairman of the board of directors of the Chamber of
Commerce of Hawaii, and a member of the board of directors of a number of major companies, including Matson Navigation Company, the
Hawaiian Telephone Company, American Factors, and several sugar
plantation companies. He told me that his two most satisfying public
service activities were founding and nurturing Hawaii's economic education program (the Joint Council on Economic Education) and chairing
the citizen's committee that in 1969 caused Hawaii's leprosy treatment
program to stop isolating patients and to start treating them like victims
of any other disease. Tom's accomplishments were recognized by his
being listed in *Who's Who in America* from 1952 and in *Who's Who in the
World* from 1975 until his death in 1989.

With this exceptional background, Tom was able to produce a reveal-
ing and provocative study for anyone who lives in Hawaii and would
like to be knowledgeable concerning economic realities and trends. As a
relative newcomer to these islands, I find the material presented in the
chapters on Hawaii's earlier history interesting, but I do not believe that

I am appropriately qualified to comment further upon them. As an economist myself, however, I found the chapters dealing with Hawaii's development since 1930 particularly enlightening. These chapters draw on Tom's many years of experience and demonstrate his great understanding of how Hawaii's economy operates and what historical imperatives it has been following.

Tom's special insight into Hawaii's economic history resulted from his personal involvement in the forces that have shaped our lives today. I believe that anyone spending time with this very readable book will gain a much better awareness of modern Hawaii.

Albert J. Simone
Former President,
University of Hawaii

Preface

SEVERAL YEARS AGO I embarked on a research program to make me better informed about the economic history of Hawaii and to improve my comprehension of the early economic development of the Hawaiian Islands. As I progressed with this study of how these islands leaped from the Stone Age to one of the most advanced economies of the modern world in less than two centuries, it occurred to me that what I had learned and concluded might be of interest to others; hence this book. Adding an analysis of the present economy was relatively easy because I had been very much a part of its development for nearly forty years.

In this study I have given considerable attention to the social and political impacts of economic development. I have always considered economic activity and its rewards to be only a means to an end, the end being the happiness and well-being of the greatest possible number of people. And since economic activity plays an important part in determining social and political developments and conditions, I tend to use the latter to judge the efficacy of the former.

This book deals not only with what happened but also with why developments occurred and what their effects have been. One dramatic development was Hawaii's Westernization, which had a serious impact on the native Hawaiian people, some of whom today express scorn for the Western system of economic, social, and political organization that displaced the Polynesian society that Captain James Cook chanced upon in 1778. While I understand this viewpoint and appreciate the difficulty that many Hawaiians had in adjusting to a different economic and social organization, I am nonetheless a strong advocate of private capitalism in a democratic society, in spite of its faults. I know that there are many ways in which economies and societies have been organized, and I can understand how various people at various times under various circumstances have thought that one or another was superior to all others. But my conclusion, based on long study and observation, is that in the long run a private capitalistic system of economic organization, kept in check by being both democratic and pluralistic, will provide more benefits and satisfactions to more people than any other form of socio-economic organization.

Acknowledgments

MANY PEOPLE helped me with this book by reading drafts of the manuscript to catch errors of omission or commission. They deserve a great deal of credit for whatever merit the book has, but since I have not taken all the advice I have been given, they bear no blame for any of the book's weaknesses. Others were of great help in assisting me in locating elusive information. The following persons, listed alphabetically and with retirees being identified by their preretirement affiliation, were particularly helpful.

Edward M. Barnet, School of Travel Industry Management, University of Hawaii (UH); Karl Berg, Hawaii Sugar Planters' Association (HSPA); David Bess, School of Business Administration, UH; Helen Bevens, Research Division, First Hawaiian Bank; Mary Blewitt, Gross State Product Accounts, State Department of Business and Economic Development (DBED); Gladys Brandt, Board of Regents, UH; John Brogan, Sheraton Hotels; Kenneth Brown, businessman; Robert L. Brown, Regional Economic Analysis, U.S. Department of Commerce; J. W. A. Buyers, C. Brewer & Co.; George Chaplin, *Honolulu Advertiser*; Hung Wai Ching, businessman; Henry Clark, Castle & Cooke; Agnes Conrad, State Archivist; Robert Cushing, Pineapple Research Institute and HSPA; James deBates, U.S. Immigration and Naturalization Service; Walter Dods, First Hawaiian Bank; Donald Duckworth, Bishop Museum; Mark Egan, Hawaii Visitors Bureau (HVB); John Farias, State Department of Agriculture; Ben Finney, Department of Anthropology, UH; Sherl Franklin, Kamehameha Schools; Robert Fujimoto, HPM Building Supply; Wallace Fujiyama, attorney; Chuck Gee, School of Travel Industry Management, UH; Wytze Gorter, Department of Economics, UH; Earl Greathouse, Community Relations, CINCPAC; Jackie Gulisao, Library, Hawaiian Telephone Co.; Joe Hartley, Maui

Pineapple Co.; Connie Hastert, Research Department, Hawaii Employers Council (HEC); Ronald J. Hays, CINCPAC; Howard Hiroki, accountant; Betty Hirozawa, HEC; Charles J. Hitch, University of California; Mae M. Hitch, Research Division, First Hawaiian Bank; Stanley Hong, HVB; Ralph Hook, Center for Economic Education, UH; Robert Hughes, HSPA; Harriet Iwai, Library, HSPA; David Judge, Edmund E. Judge & Sons; Ernest Kai, attorney; Robert Kamins, Department of Economics, UH; George Kanahele, businessman; Alvin Katahara, Research Department, HVB; Keiji Kawakami, Iolani Sportswear; Noel Kefford, Department of Agriculture, UH; John W. Kendrick, Department of Economics, George Washington University; Pauline King, Department of History, UH; Richard Kosaki, Governor's Office; Bob Krauss, *Honolulu Advertiser*; Sumner La Croix, Department of Economics, UH; Aaron Levine, Oahu Development Conference; Jack Magoon, Hawaiian Airlines; James Mak, Department of Economics, UH; George Mason, *Pacific Business News*; Fujio Matsuda, UH; Chuck Mau, attorney; Homer Maxey, Foreign Trade Zones, DBED; Buddy McGuire, *Hokule'a*; Robert Midkiff, American Trust Company of Hawaii; Mark Miller, Matson Navigation Company; John Murphy, Castle & Cooke; Seiji Naya, Resource Systems Institute, East–West Center, and Department of Economics, UH; Jim Nikkel, Pacific Aerospace Museum; Eleanor Nordyke, Population Institute, East–West Center; Janet Norwood, Commissioner for the Bureau of Labor Statistics; Perry Philipp, Department of Agriculture, UH; Hebden Porteus, attorney; Richard Post, United Airlines; M. C. Rip Riddle, Dillingham Corporation; Joyce Roberts, Pineapple Growers Association (PGA); Robert Robinson, Chamber of Commerce of Hawaii; Mike Roeder, First Hawaiian Bank; William Rowland, Oceanic Institute; Winona Rubin, State Department of Human Services; Robert Schmitt, Statistics Branch, DBED; Victor Seely, Boeing Museum of Flight; Barry Shapiro, U.S. Office of Personnel Management; Wendy Shimoda, secretary, First Hawaiian Bank; Robert Shore, Economic Analysis Branch, DBED; John Shupe, U.S. Department of Energy; Y. Sinoto, Department of Anthropology, Bishop Museum; Michael Sklarz, Research, Locations, Inc.; Kit Smith, *Honolulu Advertiser*; Adam A. Bud Smyser, *Honolulu Star-Bulletin*; Dwight Steele, HEC; Fred Stindt, Matson Navigation Company; Newton Sue, Legislative Auditor; Jan TenBruggencate, *Honolulu Advertiser*; John Tolan, PGA; Raymond Torkildson, attorney; Tommy Trask, International Longshoremen's and Warehousemen's Union (ILWU); Sonja

Tyau, Library, HEC; Linda Uchida, Library, First Hawaiian Bank; Roger Ulveling, DBED; Henry Walker, Amfac; Herbert Weaver, Department of Psychology, UH; Earl Westfall, Pacific Maritime Association; Herbert E. Wolff, First Hawaiian Bank; Edwin S. N. Wong, Alexander & Baldwin.

I also want to acknowledge the help that First Hawaiian Bank gave me by providing an office and other assistance. Anything that eases the burden of a long, tough job is most appreciated.

Editor's Note

TOM HITCH died in 1989 after this book was virtually completed. Despite his valorous attempts during his illness to put the manuscript into final form for publication, it still required some revision of the kind an author makes after receiving the comments of those chosen to read his next-to-final draft.

I was asked to make the revision, perhaps because of my long acquaintance with Tom, and despite the fact that my views of matters economic and political sometimes differed markedly from his. I accepted, agreeing to make ready for publication a piece of writing that—as noted in the foreword—is much too valuable to be left unpublished.

In revising the manuscript, I have been careful to retain all of Tom's analyses and opinions. Particularly in the second part of the book, entitled "As I Saw It," the account of Tom's own participation in Hawaii's economic development gives vivacity to his record of history. Tom's voice speaks from those pages, undistorted by editorial interference.

Robert M. Kamins
Honolulu, 28 May 1991

Abbreviations

In ADDITION to the commonly-understood abbreviations, the following appear in this book.

A&B	Alexander & Baldwin, Ltd.
AFL	American Federation of Labor
AJA	American(s) of Japanese Ancestry
BLS	(U.S.) Bureau of Labor Statistics
CC-OTEC	Closed-cycle ocean thermal energy conversion
CINCPAC	(U.S.) commander in chief, Pacific
CIO	Congress of Industrial Organizations
COLA	Cost of living allowance
CPI	Consumer-price index
C&H	California & Hawaii Sugar Refining Company
DBED	(State) Department of Business and Economic Development (successor to DPED, July 1987)
EPCA	(Territorial) Economic Planning and Coordination Authority
FSCC	Federal Surplus Commodities Corporation
GSP	Gross State Product
HEC	Hawaii Employers Council
HFCS	High-fructose corn syrup
HHSS	Hawaii health surveillance surveys
HVB	Hawaii Visitors Bureau
HSPA	Hawaiian Sugar Planters' Association
ILA	International Longshoremen's Association
ILO	International Labour Office
ILWU	International Longshoremen's and Warehousemen's Union

IPR	Institute of Pacific Relations
IRAC	(Territorial) Industrial Research Advisory Council
NASA	National Aeronautical and Space Administration
NIRA	National Industrial Recovery Act
NLRB	National Labor Relations Board
NRA	National Recovery Administration
OC-OTEC	Open-cycle ocean thermal energy conversion
OMG	Office of Military Government
OPM	(U.S.) Office of Personnel Management (formerly Federal Civil Service Commission)
OTEC	Ocean thermal energy conversion
PICHTR	Pacific International Center for High Technology Research
PGA	Pineapple Growers Association (of Hawaii)
PRI	Pineapple Research Institute
STOP	Shipping Tie-ups Over Permanently
TH	Territory of Hawaii
UCAPAWA	United Cannery, Agricultural, Packing, and Allied Workers of America
UH	University of Hawaii
WPA	(U.S.) Works Progress Administration

Part 1

FROM THE RECORD

CHAPTER 1

The Polynesian Economy, Sixth Century to Mid-Nineteenth Century

WHEN CAPTAIN JAMES COOK chanced upon the Hawaiian Islands in 1778, he encountered a people with arguably the highest standard of living in Oceania. The Hawaiians occupied an isolated land area of no considerable size, as measured against other island areas of Oceania, such as the Bismarck Archipelago, New Caledonia, and especially New Zealand. Nevertheless, the economy of the Hawaiian Islands sustained a population upward of a quarter million, a tenth or more of all the Polynesians, Micronesians, and Melanesians alive when Cook and other Western explorers first met them.[1]

Hawaiians enjoyed the "most varied cuisine" in Oceania. That, a salubrious climate, and the cordon of distance from the infectious diseases that plagued the populous continents helped sustain a vigorous population. Such island people, with a culture termed merely Stone Age because of the absence of metals, had achieved a living standard of adequate, if not abundant, means. How did they achieve this?

The Economic Base

PEOPLE

Archeological evidence indicates that the ancestors of the Polynesian people moved out of Southeast Asia many thousands of years ago on an eastward migration that passed through Fiji and reached Tonga and Samoa around 1500 B.C. There they settled, and it was in this Polynesian homeland that they developed their distinctive language, culture, and physical characteristics.[2]

NOTE: Except for Hawaiian place names, which are spelled without diacritics, Hawaiian words are spelled with diacritics the first time they appear in the text and thereafter written without diacritics.

At about the time of Christ, these Polynesians found and settled the Marquesas Islands far to the east. Within a few hundred years the Marquesans in Tuan found and settled the Hawaiian Islands to the northwest, Easter Island to the southeast, and the Society Islands to the southwest. From the Society Islands they settled New Zealand around 1000 A.D.

Except for New Zealand, Hawaii was the last significant land area of the world to be discovered and settled by *Homo sapiens*. This is not surprising because these islands are isolated in the middle of a vast ocean that stretches at least 2,000 miles in all directions before any major land area is reached. For more than 150 years after Magellan had crossed the Pacific, Portuguese, Spanish, British, French, and Dutch ships crisscrossed the Pacific Ocean before Captain Cook came upon Hawaii. The Polynesians roamed the Pacific in their large double-hulled canoes and returned home on course without benefit of compass or sextant after voyages of a thousand miles or more. And when they settled Hawaii, they developed one of the most advanced and productive Stone Age economies the world has seen. Instead of getting their food by gathering and hunting, as did most Stone Age peoples, they tilled the land, built irrigation systems, terraced hillsides, conditioned the soil, rotated crops, and raised domesticated animals. Moreover, to supplement the fish they caught with great skill, they were advanced aquaculturalists who raised fish in ingeniously constructed ponds.

To the Marquesan discoverers of Hawaii, these islands must have been a tremendous find. The Marquesas, settled perhaps five centuries before Hawaii, are a group of eleven volcanic islands with a total land area of less than 400 square miles. Moreover, most of this land is extremely rugged, with mountain ridges running down to the sea; and, with neither extensive coastal plains nor flat uplands, the only cultivable land was to be found in the valleys between the mountain ridges. The discovery of Hawaii, comprising more than 6,000 square miles of land, opened a great new frontier.

Hawaii offered many variations in climate, which created the capability of supporting a wide range of tropical and temperate zone plants and animals. Peaks rose nearly 14,000 feet high on the biggest island (Hawaii), over 10,000 feet on Maui, over 5,000 feet on Kauai and Molokai, over 4,000 feet on Oahu, over 3,000 feet on Lanai, and over 1,000 feet on Niihau and Kahoolawe—so that the climate ranged from tropical at sea level to temperate or even alpine at higher elevations. Prevalent

northeast trade winds gave windward areas climatic differences from leeward areas. And there were both coastal plains and upland plains as well
as fertile valleys. But despite these natural advantages, a productive self-
sufficient economy required the importation of foodstuffs. As first
encountered by the Marquesans, Hawaii had a meager variety of indigenous flora and fauna owing to the biological barrier presented by the
Pacific Ocean against the migration of plants and animals from the surrounding continents.

INDIGENOUS RESOURCES

The most abundant food resource in aboriginal Hawaii was marine life—
reef and inshore fish, crustaceans, deep-sea fish, and edible seaweed.[3]
Although there were a number of wild birds—including the *nēnē* or
Hawaiian goose, the *'alae* or mudhen, the *ka'upu* or booby, the *kōlea* or
Alaskan plover which wintered in Hawaii, and numerous small birds—
the only land animals were a few small species of lizards and bats.

Plant life to sustain mankind was equally scarce. The few edible plants
consisted of berries (a raspberry, a strawberry, and berries from the
'ohelo, the *ulei*, and the *popolo* plants); seeds from the fan palm tree; three
types of fern whose young, curled leaves could be eaten; the *'āheahea*
plant, whose leaves could be eaten when cooked; and two types of leaves
from which tea could be brewed, the *ko'oko'olau* and the *māmaki*.

Resources to meet other human wants were somewhat greater. For
building shelters there were a number of indigenous trees that provided
good house posts (the *hala*, the *'ōhia*, the *'a'ali'i*, the *lama*, and the
māmane); two good thatching materials (*pili* grass and the leaves of the
fan palm); and the false sandalwood for the main timbers of the house.

Material for clothing was more limited. Only the mamaki, a small tree
whose bark fibers could be beaten into a *kapa* cloth, and the smooth flat
sedge, whose thin stems could be plaited into soft mats for use as loin
cloths, skirts, and bedding material, were available.

For the many utensils, tools, and artifacts needed for work and play,
the early settlers had a fair selection of materials. Baskets, mats, canoe
sails, and sandals could be woven from the leaves of the hala tree; the
koa made fine canoes, paddles, and surfboards; the light *wiliwili* wood
was good for outrigger canoe floats (*ama*), surfboards, and fishnet floats;
the ohia tree was usable for spears, poi-pounding boards, and canoe gun-
wale stakes; the plectronia tree's hard wood made digging sticks (the
hō'o'o); the *kauila*, or buckthorn, with a very hard wood had many uses,

for example as digging sticks, musical bows, vaulting poles, darts, arrow tips, needles, and fish spears; the mamane tree was used for digging sticks and sled runners; and the *uhiuhi* was cut into kapa-beating sticks. For cordage needed for fish lines and fishnets, for the fiber base of capes and cloaks, and for tying things together, there were good fibers from the *olonā* shrub, the bark of the *ʻakia* tree, and the *ʻieʻie*.

From an abundance of volcanic rock, stones, and seashells, adzes and cutting tools were fashioned. However, aside from a few flowers, sandal-wood prized for its fragrance, a few medicinal plants, and some poison-ous plants that could be used to stun fish, these resources were about all that Hawaii had to offer the arriving Marquesans—not much upon which to build a viable economy.

POLYNESIAN IMPORTS

When the first settlers looked at Hawaii's meager inventory of flora and fauna, they must have been thankful for their foresight in bringing with them seeds, plant material, and domestic animals that would more amply sustain human life. The necessity of taking along plants and ani-mals on their voyages of discovery must have been learned on previous migrations when they had encountered barren islands.

The large number of plants brought to Hawaii from southern Polyne-sia strongly suggests that return trips were made to obtain material not brought on the original voyage. Not only do Hawaiian legends tell of such trips, but also the voyages in later years between Hawaii and east-ern Polynesia must have been so numerous that the channel between the islands of Lanai and Kahoolawe leading south from Maui was given the name Kealaikahiki—which means "the road to Tahiti."[4]

Even a partial listing of the plants and animals introduced into Hawaii by the ancient Polynesians reveals how much the aboriginal settlers enriched the biological basis of their economic life.

For food they brought the coconut, banana, breadfruit, mountain apple, taro, yam, sweet potato, sugarcane, arrowroot, ginger (for spice), and *ʻawa* for making the narcotic drink. Food containers were to be made from the gourds and hardwood trees *(milo, kou, kamani)* they intro-duced, and food was wrapped in leaves from the ti plant.

The bamboo they planted had many uses: lengths for fishing poles and house thatching rafters, short sections for musical instruments, sliv-ers for knives. So had the nuts of the *kukui* (candlenut tree). Oil from the nut was the principal source of artificial light; soot from the burning was used as a dye; kernels were roasted and eaten, or used as medicine; polished hard shells could be strung into leis.

Bark of the paper mulberry (*wauke*) made superior kapa cloth, and the inner fibers strong fishnets. Other cordage could be braided from the bark of the *hau* tree, whose light wood made outrigger booms, fishnet floats, and kite frames.

The Polynesians also carried with them to Hawaii their main sources of meat, the dog and the pig. These were raised as domesticated animals for food, and their teeth and certain bones were used as fish hooks, piercing instruments, and needles. The Polynesians introduced the chicken, which was used for cockfighting and for its feathers as well as for food. Their canoes also brought the Polynesian rat to Hawaii, probably as a stowaway.

These long ocean voyages, which apparently stopped around the fourteenth century, demonstrated a number of remarkable Polynesian skills and attributes.

First were marine architecture and engineering. The small round-hulled outrigger canoe, usually powered by paddles, was designed for coastal waters and short interisland trips. The V-hulled double sailing canoe was developed for ocean travel because of its greater stability and carrying capacity.[5]*

Second was ship building. The Polynesians' oceangoing canoes extended up to 100 feet in length. To build them without metal of any kind (saws, nails, screws, bolts, hammers, strapping, etc.) required highly resourceful techniques.

Third were the Polynesians' navigational skills. Despite popular legends to the contrary, Columbus knew where he was headed when he started west across the Atlantic. Most educated people in Europe at that time knew the earth was round and they knew that Asia and the Indies, lying on the other side of the world, had been reached by going east. Seeking them by sailing west was speculative and adventuresome; nonetheless the ships were headed in the right direction for a known destina-

*The successful voyages of the double-hulled voyaging canoe *Hōkūle'a*, built in 1975 as a replica of the ancient Polynesian voyaging canoe, establish without doubt the feasibility of long trips. The *Hōkūle'a* has made several round-trips between Hawaii and Tahiti. In 1987 it completed a two-year, sixteen thousand mile voyage of rediscovery that took it to most of the Polynesian islands in the South Pacific—all without the aid of modern navigational instruments.

tion. In fact, Columbus called his expedition "The Enterprise of the Indies."

In contrast to Columbus's search for a certain land, the Polynesian voyages of discovery were search parties looking for islands that the Polynesians did not know existed. In the case of Hawaii, it has been speculated that the Marquesans had reason to believe that land of some sort lay to the north because of the annual visits from that direction of the migratory Pacific golden plover. However the direction was chosen by the Marquesan voyagers, finding their way back and forth between their home islands and their new settlements in Hawaii required navigational skill quite beyond that of any Europeans until the magnetic compass was used by the Vikings centuries later. The only navigational aids available to the Polynesians were the stars, the sun, the ocean currents and swells, migratory birds, and, when close to land, island clouds, reefs, floating debris, and land birds.[6]

Nursery skills were another Polynesian attribute. Most plants brought to Hawaii from southern Polynesia were cuttings or slips rather than seeds, and given the fragility and short life of such plant material and the deadly effect of salt water on its tissues, it required that the Polynesians package it skillfully to keep it alive for the required three to four weeks of the trip. The most difficult plant material of all to bring was the breadfruit, as Captain William Bligh discovered in the late 1780s when he unsuccessfully tried to take live plants from Tahiti to Jamaica. It had to be transported as a tender young shoot and, according to legend, not until centuries after the first Polynesians had arrived in Hawaii did the Hawaiian chief Kaha'i succeed in bringing live breadfruit back to Hawaii from Raiatea in the Society Islands.[7]

A final important attribute was character. It took not only bravery to embark on such hazardous journeys, but also great strength of character for the crew and passengers (up to thirty people on a large canoe) to withstand the stresses and strains of each voyage. The emotional and mental discipline required must have been extreme, similar to that now required of astronauts.

Given their skills and abilities, it is not surprising that a visitor from Boston in the early 1820s would pay high tribute to the Polynesians. "As to their qualities of heart and mind, wrote missionary Charles S. Stewart, who lived in Hawaii from 1823 through 1825, "they in general appear to be as mild and affable in disposition, and as sprightly and active in intellect, as the inhabitants of our own country."[8]

The Ohana Economy, Sixth Century to Eleventh Century

BASIC CHARACTERISTICS

The ancient Hawaiian society that began around the sixth century and lasted until around 1000 A.D. was based on the extended family group, the *'ohana*, living and working cooperatively on the *ahupua'a* under the leadership of the most respected person in the group, the *haku*. Most members of the ohana were engaged in agriculture, some in fishing, and some were artisans who probably devoted most of their time to their crafts; undoubtedly others were all three. In this society a gender division of labor existed to some extent—men and older boys doing the farming, fishing, and cooking while women and children were weaving mats, making kapa cloth, braiding cordage, tending the domestic animals, and helping with gardening.

The ahupuaa was the basic land division, supporting one or more ohana. Each ahupuaa was "a complete estate, running from sea to the mountains, and hence providing a share of all the different products of soil and sea; fish from the seashore; taro, yams, sugarcane, breadfruit, and bananas in the fertile area of the lowlands; and further up in the forest belt, firewood, poles for houses, logs for canoes, bark for tapa cloth, olana and other plant fibers for cords and rope, and feathers."[9]

Because of this basic self-sufficiency within an ahupuaa, only a modest amount of bartering of goods took place between different ohana. No money or other medium of exchange seems to have been used. The very idea of buying and selling remained to be introduced by Westerners.

Some notion of how the early Hawaiian economy developed is provided by Craighill Handy and Elizabeth Handy:

> The true community in which sundry homesteads were integrated by socioreligious and economic ties was the dispersed community of *'ohana*. . . . In the course of native settlement, as the early *kanaka* colonizers spread from fishing sites on the shore to inland areas and fanned out over the plains and hills from original centers of settlement, households with ties of relationship became scattered. Some located on upland slopes . . . , some on the plains toward the sea . . . , and some along the shore. . . . Neighborly interdependence, the sharing of goods and services, naturally resulted in the settling of contiguous lands by a given *'ohana* rather than in a scattering over an entire district. In this way there came to be an association of particular *'ohana* with the land units later designated as *ahupua'a*.[10]

The prime characteristic of the ohana period was the essentially egalitarian nature of the society and the economy—as distinguished from the highly stratified chieftainship system that followed. Westerners would describe this situation as being one in which everybody was a commoner since there were no chiefs; but David Malo, the early Hawaiian historian, put it the other way around: "Perhaps in the earliest time all the people were *ali'i* and it was only after the lapse of several generations that a division was made into commoners and chiefs."[11]

LEVEL OF TECHNOLOGY

Given the total absence of metals for tools, the level of technological skills achieved by the Hawaiians was remarkable, arguably beyond that developed by Stone Age societies in other parts of the world. This achievement is illustrated by three examples of their technology—one drawn from farming (taro cultivation), another from the crafts (canoe construction), and the third from fishing. Some particulars of the techniques here described are probably more representative of the later alii period, but they derive from the earlier ohana society.

Wetland Taro Cultivation. Because taro was the staff of life to the ancient Hawaiians, it was a sacred plant, more sacred than the human race itself. Mankind, in Hawaiian mythology, descended from the *second* son of Wakea (Widespread Sky) and his wife, Ho'o-hoku-ka-lani (daughter of Papa, the Earth). But taro came from the *first* son of this union—a premature fetus from which, when buried, sprang the taro.[12]

Although varieties of taro have been developed that can grow in soil like most other plants, it is semiaquatic and grown best in leveled flats called *lo'i* that are kept flooded with water from irrigation ditches. This meant that fresh water for taro irrigation was an extremely valuable necessity—so valuable that the Hawaiian word for wealth (*waiwai*) is simply a duplication of the word for water (*wai*).

Taro was the chief product in Hawaiian food production. The entire taro plant is edible: the leaves, the corm, and the stalk. The corm was prepared in several ways—boiled, steamed in the *imu* (earth oven with hot stones), or, most commonly, cooked and pounded into poi. The stalks can be peeled and cooked as greens.

Taro cultivation stimulated development of a remarkable skill in building irrigation systems (dams, aqueducts, and ditches) to keep the fields flooded with fresh water. Most irrigation was fairly simple, consisting of damming a stream and running trenches to the terraced loi fields where each field could be flooded by opening a sluice gate. Where the trenches had to carry water around hillsides, the built-up embankment would be faced with stones.

Some irrigation systems, however, were major constructions for a society lacking metallic tools. Best known is the so-called Menehune Ditch, on Kauai, built around the base of a cliff that confines the Waimea River before it reaches a delta on the southeast coast. The ditch diverted water from the river to irrigate a series of loi seaward of the cliff. As Craighill and Elizabeth Handy (p. 112) describe the project,

> The problem that the builders . . . solved successfully was that of constructing a wall against the cliff face and down to the river bed that would remain intact against the force of the river when in flood. They solved the problem by cutting, on all but the inner sides, the large stones—some more than three feet long—with which the facing wall was constructed. Thus the wall offered a smooth surface to the river at all levels while the stones fitted together with precision at all points of vertical and horizontal contact. In order to make tight joints, a number of stones [were] notched to make them fit where there is a difference in height of the blocks at points of contact. Behind the wall was a fill of dirt and rocks. . . ."

Canoe Construction. The Hawaiian canoe, used primarily for fishing but also for transportation and racing, was different from most other Polynesian canoes because of its one-piece hull construction, made possible by the giant hardwood koa trees that the Marquesans found in upland areas when they settled Hawaii. It staggers the imagination to visualize the ancient Hawaiians with stone adzes felling such trees, with circumferences up to twenty feet, then carving out the hull to meet the exact shape and dimensions that their knowledge of marine architecture told them was required, and then moving it to the beach area for all the finishing work. Some thirty types of adzes were used to build a canoe—fashioned for hewing, planing, scooping, shaving, gouging, and smoothing. Several types of stone and coral rubbers did the work of modern rasps, files, and sandpaper. Finally, the hull was preserved and decorated with paints made from the flowers and buds of various plants and the inner root of the kukui tree, tinted by burnt wiliwili nut kernels.[13]

Other woods were selected for their properties. Gunnels might be fashioned from *'ōhia ha*, stern and bow of *'ahakea*, outrigger floats of wiliwili, seats of *'ulu*, mast of *'ōhia lehua*, and paddles of koa. Finally the sail, if the canoe had one, was woven of pandamus leaves. Component parts of the canoe were lashed together with sennit, a superior cordage made from the inner fibres of the coconut husk, painstakingly fashioned by the older members of the ohana into lines of various sizes and degrees of tightness depending on the use.

The canoe, despite its heavy labor costs, was essential to the life of the ancient Hawaiians, a necessity for transportation and for fishing. Its variety was enormous, designed not only for fishing, ocean travel, and along shore transportation, but also for racing, surfing, and finally for burials. It has been estimated that in the late eighteenth century there were as many as twelve thousand canoes in these islands—a ratio of about one to every twenty people.[14] One can assume much the same ratio of provision during the earlier ohana period.

Fishing. Just as taro was the prime source of carbohydrates in the diet of aboriginal Hawaiians, fish was the prime source of protein. Limited piscine populations in the surrounding ocean and shallows, and a virtual absence of rivers on the geologically young islands, made fishing a fine art using almost every conceivable technique other than rod-and-reel casting. The Hawaiians seined; netted with throw, gill, and basket nets; stunned fish with drugs; chummed; used pole, line, and baited hooks; trolled; scooped small fish by hand or with small scoop nets; and speared by daylight or torch light.[15] Their lines were spun from the olona and other plant fibers; their hooks were made of bone, sea shells, or turtle shells; their poles were made of bamboo; and their lures were cowry shells.

The early Hawaiians were adept not only at fishing but also at aquaculture. Fishponds supplied a ready catch even when storms prevented fishing at sea. All major islands in the archipelago had fishponds, some 200 to 400 in total, but the fishponds were most common on Oahu and Molokai.[16] All ponds, of course, were used to feed and fatten the resource (mostly mullet); but some, equipped with seaward gates, trapped fish brought with the incoming tides, after which the gates were closed.

Large saltwater fishponds were built by impounding several acres of water off a beach with a wall of large stones. Inland freshwater ponds, such as the many in the Waikiki district, were likely to be smaller and linked to irrigation feedlines.

The Alii Economy, Eleventh Century to Mid-Nineteenth Century

From their legends and cultural legacy to later generations, it is evident that the Hawaiians during the early ohana period had developed a simple subsistence economy, based on agriculture and fishing, which supplied a good cuisine, housing, and artifacts for production and play. This society and economy underwent a dramatic change in the eleventh or twelfth century, when a highly stratified social structure with dominant chiefs (alii) and subservient commoners replaced the essentially egalitarian society that the original settlers from the Marquesas had established. According to Samuel Kamakau, Hawaiian legends tell that the egalitarian social system lasted for fifty-three generations before the chieftainship system was established.[17]

The fact that this transformation occurred simultaneously with the arrival of immigrants from Raiatea in the Society Islands would suggest that this new form of society was introduced from without. Some credence is given to this view from the fact that the name Hawaii is the ancient name of Raiatea (Havaiki). Buck[18] and Lindo and Mower[19] state that the Raiatea invaders conquered the original settlers. The transformation could have been an evolutionary process, however, as the population increased and resources became scarcer—a process that Ben Finney[20] describes as having occurred in Tahiti and Patrick Kirch[21] speculates may have been duplicated in Hawaii. Irving Goldman[22] suggests it was probably a combination of the two. It may never be known for sure why the change occurred, but the fact is that the relatively classless and essentially communal society of the ohana period was replaced by a highly stratified system of chieftainships and commoners, which introduced what may be called the alii period.

DIFFERENCES FROM THE OHANA ECONOMY

The economies of the ohana and alii periods had major similarities and major differences. The ohana and ahupuaa remained the basic social and land units. However, decisions as to what was produced, who would produce it, when it would be produced, and how it would be shared among the population were drastically changed. In the ohana period, these basic economic decisions were made by the most respected group members, or haku, probably with the general consent of the other members of the ohana. Now, in the alii period, a new structure of authority and decision making was imposed on the ohana. Economic decisions were made by a chief or his administrator, to be carried out by the ohana.

The administrative structure that emerged was complex. Each of the major islands was a polity under control of the *ali'i nui*, or supreme chief. These chiefs controlled all land and had preemptive rights over all crops in the field, fish in the sea, water in the streams, dogs and pigs, canoes, and other artifacts. They specified the *kapu*, or taboos, and enforced them. By their authority, war was waged, lands allocated, taxes collected, fishponds and irrigation projects constructed. Their responsibility in turn, was to see that the land, the precious *'āina*, was sustained in fertility as ordained by the gods.

Under the alii nui was a network of lesser chiefs and administrators. Leading subchiefs were in charge of the *moku* into which each island was divided, and lesser alii headed the several ahupuaa in the moku. Within the ahupuaa would be further land subdivisions, such as the *ili*, each with its own chief.

At each level were administrators: *konohiki*, who ordered the work and collected the taxes; *ilāmoku*, who enforced the laws; and *kahuna*, expert practitioners, notably those who served as priests and enforced the kapu. Key to economic production, principally successful agriculture and fishing, was the ability of the konohiki, who as managers planned and supervised the taro fields, fishponds, and other enterprises of their respective ahupuaa, decided where and when various kinds of fish could be caught at sea, how much irrigation water each family could use, and how much each family must contribute to the support of the chief and his entourage. "No one could dispute his position as the central manager and prime mover of the Hawaiian economy."[23]

Technical skills were taught and practiced by the nonpriestly kahuna. Experts in their craft, they specialized in canoe building, house construction, fishing, navigation, medicine, and—far from least in importance—warfare.

The base of the social and economic pyramid, comprising most of the population, was made up of commoners—the *maka'āinana*, or people of the aina, who did most of the hard work. Below them, apparently few in number, were the outcasts, called *kauā* in the literature of early Hawaii, who, living apart as untouchables, were liable to be used when human sacrifices were required, as at the dedication of a *heiau*, or shrine.

This stratified system of social, political, and economic authoritarianism lasted until the nineteenth century, when it began to decay under Western influences. Although the alii social structure remained in place during some eight centuries, the cast of leading alii changed with frequency. Warfare between opposing chiefs was frequent, and with each new conquering chief might come a whole new regime of subchiefs and administrators. The makaainana, not bound to the soil, might arrange to find a new *kuleana* (land claim) to live on after a change of management; but there was inherent uncertainty as to their fate when the alii struggled for power or revenge.

Over the centuries a higher degree of occupational specialization evolved, such as condensing sea salt, canoe making, and fishpond operation. Regional bartering of goods became more widespread. For example, on the island of Hawaii the excellent taro of Waipio Valley was shipped to Hilo in exchange for fish, while light wood for outriggers was sent from Kau to Kona in exchange for canoe-hull trunks.[24] Most exchange, however, continued through tribute. There still was no money.

EVALUATION OF THE ALII ECONOMY

The authoritarian regime of the chiefs probably did not fulfill the economic needs of the commoners as fully as did the earlier ohana society. Improvements over time in technology—better fishhooks and adzes, more efficient irrigation methods, etc.—may have offset the need of a growing population to use less fertile lands; but critical attributes of the alii economy would have tended to lower living standards for most of the people.

First, the ruling classes generally did not engage in economically productive work, except for managerial skills of the konohiki. Chiefs, from the head of the smallest ahupuaa to the alii nui, basically lived off the labor of the makaainana, as did their courtiers, warriors, priests, administrators, policemen, servants, and hangers-on. Estimates vary as to the size of the tax burden that commoners bore to support this upper structure, ranging from more than half to about two-thirds of the fruits of the commoners' labor.[25] David Malo, who lived in the last years of this society, simply stated that "the amount of property which the chiefs obtained from the people was very great. Some of it was given in taxes, some was the fruit of robbery and extortion" (p. 85). If something in the range of one-half to two-thirds of the commoners' work product was taken for the use of the chiefs and their entourages, it follows that the standard of living of the makaainana was probably reduced from what it had been during the earlier period, when the product of each ohana was shared by its members.

A second factor that adversely affected the economy was the frequency of war. Hand-to-hand combat with slings, spears, clubs, and daggers is not greatly destructive of the physical environment. Nevertheless, the diversion of much labor into making instruments of war, plus the fact that much work time was lost when the commoners—who served as a ready reserve to support the warriors, or *koa*—were called to combat duty, must have reduced nonmilitary production considerably. At the very least, wars were, as Morgan puts it (p. 115), "disruptive of agriculture and fishing."

More pervasively, the arbitrary exercise of chiefly power over the product of labor must have adversely affected the incentive of commoners in times of peace and war. A wide range of opinion exists, however, as to the weight of this disincentive. Early Western observers were struck by the depressing effects of the chiefs' rapacity. The missionary Charles Stewart stated that commoners worked only four or five hours a day because "there is no motive for industry presented to them, beyond the fear of starvation, and a dread of displeasure by their chiefs" (p. 151). Serano Bishop reported visiting a native village where most of the pigs he saw were "miserably lean, whose scant food came from scavaging. Occasionally, a pig was fattened in a pen, but the eye of the chief's retainer was usually on such pigs, and it was likely to be snatched away after being cooked. . . . The chief cause of destitution was the ceaseless oppression of the chiefs, and the attendant shiftlessness of the people."[26] Consistent with that description was the account of William Richards: "There was no distinct dividing line by which the tenant might know and hold his own. If a man of uncommon industry brought his farm to a higher state of cultivation than his neighbor, he was not thereby sure of having more for his own use . . . no landholder considered himself safe in his possessions, and therefore even ridiculed the idea of making extensive improvements."[27]

Some latter-day historians, however, dispute such views of alii repression, dismissing them as the result of applying Western, capitalistic values to a society that *haole* (Western) observers did not understand. Edward Beechert, for example, writes that "viewed from the western wealth-accumulating perspective, the comments of . . . many early nineteenth century observers picture a rapacious society out of control. This application of a western concept of private property obscures the political function and nature of the *ali'i* system. . . . The much talked about oppression of the Hawaiians by their chiefs thus seems to misconstrue the political role of the chief."[28]

Craighill and Elizabeth Handy (p. 326) offer a similar opinion, that economic relations were not exploitive or resented by commoners—at least not prior to the nineteenth century, when the system was coming to a close:

> The relationship of the planter and his family to the high chief, and to the *ali'i* class in general, was a very personal one in which ardent affection was the prevailing feeling unless an *ali'i* was quite despicable, which was rare. . . . The annual tax collecting was actually a countryside offering of a share of the produce, not to "the government" as such, but to Father Lono, the rain god, impersonated by the ruling *ali'i*, who was himself in most instances more like a father to his people than a "despot." The quantity of produce offered was more a result of emulation and enthusiasm than it was a calculation on the part of the tax collectors."

Theodore Morgan (p. 49) summarizes the evidence in the following manner. "It is clear that there was a heavy weight of discouragement to economic effort from the lack of security of personal property, the doubtful tenure of land, and the unlimited dominance generally of the chieftain class. But the discouragement was not sufficient in the native economy to lead to idle and careless habits of life. Early voyagers are unanimous in praising the industrious habits of the natives."

From this contradictory testimony, one can conclude that Hawaiian commoners were industrious, with a deeply ingrained respect for authority that accepted a large transfer of their production to the upper classes. Nevertheless, the resulting disincentive to work inherent in the alii economy would have been a drag on productivity.

Evaluation of the Polynesian Economy

While there is reason to believe that the economic well-being of most Hawaiians of the alii period was somewhat below that of the ohana period, there is little doubt that even the commoners of the alii time were better off economically than the vast majority of their contemporaries around the world.

Today the common measure of living standards is per capita gross
national product, or some similar estimation of production or consumption. For earlier periods, for which no such data exist and when all but
the top fringe of the population had only the basic necessities of life, the
measure of physical well-being must be simple: How adequately was the
general population supplied with food, housing, and clothing and how
free was it of debilitating disease? By such a measure, the precontact
Hawaiians had a high living standard compared with the general experience of the eighteenth century.

The Hawaiian Islands then, as now, were ideal for humankind, having
fertile soil, abundant rainfall, a climate that provided good growing conditions year-round and required minimal housing and clothing, lying in
an ocean stocked with a wide variety of fish, shellfish, crustaceans, and
edible plant life. A description of rural Samoa in the 1930s may charac-
terize the condition of the Hawaiian part of Polynesia centuries earlier:
[a people] "so bountifully supplied by nature that they meet their everyday needs without hard work, and had little need to store against lean
seasons."[29]

The Polynesian diet was quite nutritious, as evidenced by the stature
of the Hawaiians and the rate of increase in their numbers. Studies of
skeletal remains show that precontact male Hawaiians averaged five feet
and seven inches in height and weighed more than 160 pounds. Comparing these averages with those of twentieth century full-blooded
Hawaiians led Charles E. Snow of the Bishop Museum to conclude that
the Stone Age population "apparently achieved virtually a maximum
size, or at least the greater part of their hereditary potential. This probably meant that the native diet . . . was as adequate for growth as the
diet of their modern descendants."[30]

Early Western visitors noted the robust physiques of the Hawaiians.
Captain James King in 1779 reported that the natives generally were
"above the middle size" of Europeans. William Ellis in 1823 also found
them to be "in general above the middle stature." All were impressed
with the size of the alii, who were usually around six feet tall. To Charles
Stewart (p. 133) they seemed "indeed in stature almost a distinct race."
This physical superiority might have been caused by selective breeding
as well as by a varied diet.

As to the test of population growth, the increase of numbers in
Hawaii during the ohana and alii periods is phenomenal by world standards of that span of time. The hundred or so Marquesan colonists who

reached Hawaii around 500 A.D. had increased to a quarter million or more by the time Captain Cook arrived some thirteen hundred years later. That was an increase averaging about 0.6 percent per year. By way of comparison, between the settlement of England around 11,000 B.C. and the invasion early in the Christian era by the Romans, who took a census and counted about two million inhabitants, it may be estimated that the annual population growth over those centuries averaged only about 0.09 percent. Had the original Marquesan settlers multiplied at the same rate as the English population, Hawaiians would have numbered only hundreds when Cook arrived, instead of hundreds of thousands.

In conclusion, then, it can be said that the precontact Hawaiian economy produced a standard of living—as indicated by the extent to which basic needs of the population were met—that must have been high by the standards of most parts of the world at that time. Although the Hawaiian Islands themselves had provided the physical potential for this level of economic well-being, it was the Polynesian settlers who realized that potential. Even the caste system of the alii period maintained living standards exceptional in Oceania, especially for the chiefs who commanded the island communities.

CHAPTER 2

The Nineteenth Century Transition Period, circa 1819–76

Contact and Unification

CAPTAIN COOK's discovery opened Hawaii to the Western world, but this opening process was prolonged. For most Hawaiians, the alii economy of the precontact Polynesian period continued in operation for two-thirds of a century—until the mid-1840s—and the transition to a Westernized economy was not completed for another third of a century.

Western influence and ideas infiltrated into Hawaii only slowly as more explorers, naval ships, and then merchantmen found their way to what the English soon called the Sandwich Islands. It was not until 1786, seven years after Cook's arrival, that the second ship from the West visited Hawaii; and as late as 1810, more than thirty years after Cook, there were only a few Western residents in Hawaii, the number estimated at no more than sixty.[1] Most of them were seamen who had jumped ship, some to work for Kamehameha I as carpenters, sailmakers, riggers, or other craftsmen helping the king ready a small fleet of Western-style ships. Others were simply enticed by a languid tropical life with a native wife.

The subsistence Polynesian economy, modified perhaps by the intrusion of foreign goods and ideas, might have continued for generations, as some other island economies in Oceania have, if radical institutional changes had not taken place. For an economy to achieve its full production potential (by Western standards), it seems necessary that people be free to do what they want, within prescribed but broad limits, and be able to retain most of the fruits of their labor. They have to be governed by established law, not by the dictates of a ruler. And they must have control over the land they work.

None of these conditions existed in the first sixty years after Cook reached Hawaii, and consequently economic change was sporadic and minimal. Further, when Hawaii did begin to develop economically, it became evident to the kingdom's rulers that the islands must become part of the outer world economic system if their resources were to be exploited fully. Changes, some deliberate, others by chance, worked to bring about this transformation.

POLITICAL UNIFICATION OF THE ISLANDS

The first important development was the cessation of internal warfare as a result of the political unification of the islands under Kamehameha the Great. The able and shrewd young chief had brought the entire island of Hawaii under his control by 1791; had conquered Maui, Molokai, and Oahu in quick succession in 1795; and peacefully brought Kauai under his rule fifteen years later. Quick to seize the advantage of Western weaponry, he had achieved these victories with the aid of cannon. Unlike earlier conquering chiefs, he was able to consolidate the islands he had gained into a governable kingdom.

Political unification of the islands had two direct economic benefits. First, the drain of warfare, limited as it had been in the time of hand-to-hand combat, was now staunched. Kamehameha retained a body of warriors and amassed his small Western-style navy to augment the fleet of war canoes, but commoners were no longer pressed into service. Second, landholdings of his subordinate chiefs became stabilized, ending the ancient practice whereby a conquering alii nui would redivide seized lands among his chieftain supporters as the spoils of victory. While all lands now remained under the control of the king, those held by lesser chiefs, on down to the kuleana of the commoners, no longer changed hands with the succession of supreme chiefs. Consequently, cultivators of the land began to feel greater confidence in their undisturbed possession—which was somewhat akin to what Americans would call "squatters' rights." Thus the later Kamehamehas on their ascension to the throne were checked from making a general redistribution by a growing expectation of continuity in land tenure.

ABOLITION OF THE KAPU SYSTEM

The second development was even more important than political unification. Shortly after the death of Kamehameha I in 1819, the kapu system was abolished by the alii nui themselves. This was a momentous action, because the kapu not only were the outward manifestation of the Hawaiian religion but also constituted a code of behavior for the people.

Kapu—a forbidden act—was derived from the Polynesian concept of nature, which deemed some things sacred or precious (life, light, things masculine) and others profane or common (death, darkness, things feminine). Kapu were decreed by the gods and enforced by the chiefs, themselves subject to the divine code. The alii nui, as the highest chiefs, bore the ultimate responsibility for the well-being of the people, which depended on observance of the kapu. Many commandments governed the relationship of commoners to their chiefs, in effect making a civil code. Others related to women, such as prohibitions against eating bananas, pork, and certain fish, and against eating with men or eating food cooked in an imu along with men's food. Some kapu were seasonal, such as the prohibition against catching certain fish at certain places at certain times, or the major commandment against warfare during the *makahiki,* or annual festival season.

In the absence of a written language, all such commandments were proclaimed orally and were variously applied. Enforcement of the kapu, according to Abraham Fornander, was "as uncertain and capricious as the will of the chief."[2] The punishment for breaking a kapu might be death.

When the kapu system was abolished shortly after Kamehameha's death, the gods who had ordained the commandments were abandoned with it, the heiau were pulled down, the idols burned, sacrifices stopped, and places of refuge no longer held to be sacrosanct. It was into this religious void that the brig *Thaddeus* carrying the first company of American missionaries to the Sandwich Islands arrived in 1820. At first cautiously, then enthusiastically received by the alii, the Congregationalists brought with them a new religion, morality, and models of social behavior that were to have profound consequences for the economic life of the islands. The pace of change in Hawaii quickened from that time.

CONTACTS WITH THE WESTERN WORLD

Along with the arrival of the Protestant work ethic came an increase in trade with foreign ships, all at first on a barter basis. When European and American vessels began visiting Hawaii, their captains wanted provisioning of fresh water, food, and firewood. In return, the alii initially demanded guns and other instruments of war, including ships that could carry small armies. The chiefs (male and female) quickly developed appetites for the beguiling variety of goods that ships carried for trade: metals and metal tools, utensils, preserved food, household furnishings, clothing, jewelry, liquor, tea. The commoners wanted much of the same, and to get it they provided such ship supplies as the alii permitted, plus the chief desire of the sailors, the warm companionship of native women. The volume of trade swelled during the 1830s.

In the early 1880s ships carrying furs from Alaska and the Pacific Northwest to China began taking on sandalwood from Hawaii, as well as provisions, and quickly the fragrant wood became the kingdom's chief export. In the absence of Hawaiian money, sandalwood became a standard measure of value for trading with foreigners. In 1817, Kamehameha bought the *Albatross*, a seventy-two-foot American ship, for 400 piculs of sandalwood (the picul, an East Asian measure of volume equalling 133.33 pounds). At that time the going rates of exchange in Honolulu were eighteen piculs of sandalwood for four large boxes of tea, four piculs for two lengths of cotton, ten piculs for two pairs of trousers, five piculs for a bed, and one picul for two parasols.[3]

Until the death of Kamehameha I in 1819, trade with the foreigners was a monopoly of the king. Under Liholiho (Kamehameha II), however, chiefs were allowed a share of the sandalwood trade, and in 1826 even commoners were allowed to cut and sell a bit of the wood on their own account.[4] Nevertheless, most of their labor in the highlands, filling with sandalwood earth pits dug to the dimension of a ship's hold, was on behalf of the chiefs, who were running up large debts with ship captains and local merchants newly established in the islands to handle the growing volume of trade.

From trade with Westerners—American, English, French, Russian, South American—Hawaiian rulers learned that if they were to get what they wanted from the foreigners, they had to supply something the haole wanted in exchange. They found that barter as a means of trading was inferior to having a medium of exchange, as the foreigners had in money.

Major Institutional Changes

Honolulu increasingly became the focus of political and economic change after Kamehameha and his immediate successors made their chief residence in the village along the harbor. The harbor itself, the only anchorage in the kingdom deep enough to accommodate large, deep-draft ships, made Honolulu the center of foreign trade and therefore the center of commerce. Here sprang up a merchant class of foreigners to serve as chandlers to the ships in the harbor, export–import agents, and general merchants for the population of the village, which had grown to a population of about five thousand by the mid-1820s. Charles Stewart reported (p. 23) that in 1823 there were four American merchant firms in Honolulu. Soon they were joined by others, mostly American but some European.

Also in Honolulu was the center of the growing American mission to the Sandwich Islands, with its church, school, and printing press. This conjunction of Hawaiian rulers, foreign businessmen, and American missionaries hastened acceptance by the sons of Kamehameha—first Liholiho and then Kauikeaouli, who reigned as Kamehameha III after 1825—of the political doctrine and economic practices of the West.

Visiting naval officers from the United States and England also indoctrinated the Hawaiian rulers with the necessity of adopting Western institutions, notably the system of land ownership. As Ralph Kuykendall notes (1:67),

> there was scarcely one of the foreign naval commanders who visited Hawaii down to 1838 who did not offer the king and his chiefs advice on some subject. The general tenor of this advice, so far as it touched on political and economic institutions of the country, was that a more systemized and liberal policy should be pursued, the people should be made secure in the possession of the land they occupied and cultivated, allowed to enjoy the fruits of their labor, to accumulate property, and not be burdened by oppressive taxation, and that just laws be enacted and published for the information and guidance of all. Even those commanders who presented demands on the king usually accompanied them with suggestions as to how the rulers might prevent a recurrence of such demands in the future.

The desirability of changes such as those the naval commanders recommended was demonstrated by the problems facing the first large business enterprise in Hawaii—the plantation operation of Ladd & Company, which was started in 1835 at Koloa, Kauai. Before then, economic activities other than the self-sufficient farming and fishing operations of the old Polynesian economy had consisted of stripping the mountains of sandalwood under a monopoly conducted by the king and his chiefs, provisioning ships first under a monopoly of the king and his chiefs and later by the merchants of Honolulu, and scattered minor agricultural operations, such as a vineyard started in 1815 at the mouth of Nuuanu

Valley of Honolulu by the Spaniard Don Francisco de Paula Marín[5] and a thirty-acre sugar operation started in Manoa Valley in 1826 by the Englishman Wilkinson.[6]

Ladd & Co., an American merchant house in Honolulu, in 1835 succeeded in leasing from Kamehameha III several thousand acres of land on Kauai, which was planted in sugar (25 acres), coffee (5,000 trees), bananas (5,000 plants), and 45 taro patches.[7] The labor required for this operation was obviously considerable, and one of the greatest difficulties the company had was hiring labor. Local commoners considered the pay satisfactory (twelve and one-half cents a day plus food), but the local chiefs considered the commoners their indentured tenants and refused to permit them to work for Ladd & Co. until the king intervened and overruled them. There was no freedom of labor except at the whim of the king, and the persistent opposition of the chiefs required the king's intervention on several occasions.[8]

David Malo, one of the Hawaiians educated at the Lahainaluna missionary school on Maui, warned Kamehameha III in a letter to his *kuhina nui* (prime minister) in 1837 that a major restructuring had to take place:

> I have been thinking that you ought to hold frequent meetings with all the chiefs . . . to seek for that which will be the greatest benefit to this country: you must not think that this is anything like olden times, that you are the only chiefs and can leave things as they are. . . . This is the reason. If a big wave comes in, large fishes will come from the dark Ocean which you never saw before, and when they see the small fishes they will eat them up; such also is the case with large animals, they will prey on the smaller ones. The ships of the white man have come, and smart people have arrived from the great countries which you have never seen before, they know our people are few in number and living in a small country; they will eat us up, such has always been the case with large countries, the small ones have been gobbled up. . . . God has made known to us through the mouths of the men of the men-of-war things that will lead us to prepare ourselves. . . .[9]

Malo's fear of being "gobbled up" was pervasive among the alii throughout this period. It was evident that, as long as total power resided in the king, any foreign nation that could displace the king would assume total power—ownership of all the land, virtual ownership of all the people, and ownership of all powers of government. Recognition of this situation led to acceptance of an idea proposed by Western

advisers, that the solution lay in the dispersion of royal and chiefly powers—establishing individual ownership of land, personal rights of the
people, and constitutional government with some authority in the
hands of a legislature. Then if Hawaii were "gobbled up," what might be
seized would not be the entire Hawaiian society, economy, and government, but only the constitutional power that resided in the personage of
the king.

A change in attitudes toward landholding was a second and fundamental factor in the reformation of Hawaiian society. As already noted,
prior to the consolidation of power in the kingdom of Kamehameha I,
changes in property tenure had been frequent, with each new conquering alii nui distributing property rights to his subordinate chiefs. Under
Kamehameha this frequent change in land tenure came to an end, and
there was no redistribution of land when Kamehameha II or Kamehameha III became king. By the mid-1830s, then, there had been no
reshuffling of landholdings for a full forty years, long enough for the
chiefs to feel comfident that they owned the land rather than merely
holding it at the pleasure of the king.

A third factor that may well have prompted examination of the structure of the Hawaiian government, society, and economy was that it was
no longer functioning well. The subsistence, communal, ohana-oriented
society was gradually disintegrating as more production was being done
for sale to foreigners, as many commoners were leaving the ahupuaa for
other work, and as the population was beginning a rapid decline under
the onslaught of introduced diseases. These developments led to declining tax revenues, a factor that Sumner La Croix and James Roumasset
conclude was a major cause of the decision to change the system.[10]

The final force for liberating Hawaii from some of the confines dictated by its Polynesian heritage was the desire of the young King Kamehameha III to assert his leadership after the death of the co-ruling regent
Kaahumanu in 1832. He wanted to reduce the power that the chiefs had
acquired under Kamehameha II and during the regency. One way to do
this was to turn the allegiance of the commoners more toward him as
king, rather than toward the chiefs as their immediate superiors. Grant-
ing commoners some rights of their own (as was done by the Bill of
Rights of 1839), giving them some voice in the government (as was done
by the Constitution of 1840), and giving them land so that they would
no longer be dependent tenants of the chiefs (as was done by the *Mahele*,
or land division, in 1848) tended to serve this purpose.[11]

The leading chiefs were also minded to consider radical reform, though not necessarily for the same ends as the king's. In 1836, a year before David Malo's warning to Kamehameha III, the Council of Chiefs (later called the House of Nobles to distinguish it from the lower legislative house composed of commoners) asked William Richards, one of the missionaries who was leaving on a trip to the United States, to find a person who would come to Hawaii and be "a teacher of the chiefs in what pertains to land, according to the practices of enlightened countries"—which Kuykendall interprets as a request for a teacher of economics and political science.[12] Richard Armstrong, another missionary who later was to serve the government for many years, wrote: "There is a wide field of usefulness here for a man acquainted with the subject of law, politics, economy & withal truly devoted to Christ. He wd. be of essential benefit to the chiefs in their management of affairs and might be the means of overcoming the present wretched administration of govt. under wh. we now live."[13]

When Richards returned to report his failure to recruit a teacher of economics and political science, he learned that the chiefs had decided that he himself was the man for the job. He was appointed "Chaplain, Teacher, and Translator" for the government in July 1838 and immediately severed formal ties with the missionary group. He wrote at the time that "they also expect from me suggestions on every subject connected with government and on their duties as rulers of the nation."[14]

Thus by the late 1830s the king and chiefs had accepted the idea that fundamental changes in the structure of government, society, and the economy were necessary if Hawaii were to remain independent in a world populated by stronger countries. They had also acquired a capable adviser in William Richards to guide them in their decisions as to what changes to make. Within the short span of ten years they adopted a bill of rights that lifted the commoners out of their centuries-long condition of complete subjugation to the chiefs, adopted a constitution that placed strict limits on the power of the king, created a lower legislative house composed of commoners, and adopted the Anglo-American legal regime of landholding in fee simple. These revolutionary acts completely undermined the old alii economy and formed the basis for a transition to a free-enterprise, capitalistic system based on Western institutions and practices.

Magna cartas to end despotisms, constitutions to end absolutisms, and land reforms to end feudalisms are developments that normally require the shedding of a great deal of blood. Hawaii's achievement of them bloodlessly on the initiative of the ruling elite is possibly unique in world history. The earlier voluntary abolition of the kapu system, which displaced a long-established religion without a religious war, was another example of the remarkable ability of the early Hawaiian leadership to take bold action when they decided that it was desirable. These acts were even more remarkable because each reduced considerably the power of the ruling group that initiated it. The bill of rights (to give the people a measured freedom to do what they chose, to retain the fruits of their labor, and to liberate them from bondage to their chiefs), the constitution (to govern Hawaii by a set of democratically enacted laws rather than by the whim of the king and to limit the power of the chiefs), and the land division (to make realty available as private property) were the basis of a new society that transformed the Hawaiian economy.

The Bill of Rights (1839)

A bill of rights for Hawaii was drafted by a native graduate of the missionary school at Lahainaluna named Boaz Mahune, revised by the Council of Chiefs, and signed by Kamehameha III in June 1839. Translated from the original Hawaiian, in part it stated: "God hath made of one blood all nations of man, to dwell on the face of the earth in unity and blessedness. God has also bestowed certain rights alike on all men, and all chiefs, and all people of all lands. These are some of the rights which he has given alike to every man and every chief—life, limb, liberty, the labor of his hands, and production of his mind."[15] Appended to the declaration of rights was a codification of the laws of Hawaii that had been proclaimed from time to time in the past, together with new guarantees to citizens of the kingdom, including the right to inherit personal property.

With the declaration of rights, the people of Hawaii were set free to work and otherwise manage their affairs as they wanted, as long as they did not violate written law, and to accumulate personal property and pass it along to their heirs. The legal basis of a free-enterprise economy had been laid. As a natural outgrowth of the bill of rights, an apprenticeship law was enacted in 1842 and a comprehensive statute governing the relationship of masters and servants (i.e., employers and employees) was passed in 1850.

THE CONSTITUTION (1840)

A Western-style constitution, drafted by the Council of Chiefs and signed by Kamehameha III and kuhina nui Kekauluohi in October 1840, gave commoners an institutional voice in the government by creating a lower house to be elected by the people.[16] Further, this house of representatives was to select a majority of the members of the new supreme court of the kingdom. Among other innovations, the constitution delineated the functions of king and kuhina nui, the body of chiefs (now called in English the House of Nobles), and the new lower house; provided for the appointment of four governors over the major islands of the kingdom to have general charge of matters of government not assigned to other officers; created a legal system headed by the supreme court; and established officials to assess and collect the taxes of Hawaii.

The importance of Hawaii's first written constitution for the future of economic development was primarily that it guaranteed a regime of law for business transactions and property holding. Enterprisers could now have greater assurance that they understood the rules of the game and that those rules would be followed.

LAND DIVISION (1848)

Acceptance of the advice so often given by Westerners to end the ancient Polynesian land tenure system, under which all land was held only provisionally and subject to redistribution by the alii nui and the king, and to replace it with an Anglo-American system of private ownership was foreshadowed in the 1839 Bill of Rights, which stated that "protection is hereby secured to the persons of all the people, together with their lands, their building lots and all their property." The Constitution of 1840 declared that the land was not the property of the king, but rather "belonged to the chiefs and people in common" and was only managed by the king. It was not until 1848, however, that Kamehameha III and 245 chiefs agreed among themselves how much land should go to the crown and how much to the chiefs. After this decision, bilingually called the Great Mahele, the king split his lands into "government" lands, which were to be held for the support of the kingdom, and "crown" lands, which were to be the property of the monarch.[17]

In 1850 the legislature instructed the recently created Board of Commissioners to Quiet Land Titles to grant fee-simple titles to native tenants for the parcels of land cultivated by them. By the time the commission had completed its work in 1853, some 10,000 kuleana grants had been made to commoners. The legislature also provided that government lands on each island should be set aside for sale in lots of up to 50 acres to natives not otherwise provided with land sufficient for their subsistence. Non-Hawaiians could also buy land in fee simple, and in larger acreage. Businessmen and missionaries appeared with alacrity before the Board of Commissioners. Natives, to whom the very idea of land ownership was baffling, lagged behind.[18]

The end result of the Great Mahele was that the government retained title to some 1.5 million acres and the crown to about 1 million acres. The chiefs received about 1.6 million acres, and the commoners (who then numbered approximately 80,000) got about 30,000 acres in all. The commoners' share was thus but a small fraction of the total; but since the kuleana lands were already improved and cultivated, they were the primary productive agricultural land of the kingdom, "considered the more valuable lands in the Islands."[19] In contrast, "extensive areas of Crown, government, and chiefs' lands were useless mountain wastes or lava strewn deserts or were covered with forests which benefited all by conserving the water supply."[20] Further, the kuleana grants put land into the hands of about two out of every three Hawaiian families, said to be "a record of fee simple ownership among natives unique in the early nineteenth century."[21] With private property rights thus established, capital could now be invested in a business enterprise without the fear that land on which the enterprise was based would be withdrawn at any time and for any reason.

The Search for Security in an Insecure World

THE PRECARIOUSNESS OF INDEPENDENT STATUS

Although the three major institutional reforms consummated during the decade of 1839–48 laid the basis for the economic development of Hawaii, one major obstacle still remained that had to be removed before Hawaii could be considered a safe place for the investment of capital. That obstacle was the precarious position of an independent Hawaii in a world filled with strong, empire-building nations, any one of which probably had the ability to annex Hawaii with the use of no more than one naval vessel. With most Pacific islands being taken over by world powers, uncertainty about Hawaii's future was intense until 1875, when Hawaii established an economic connection with the United States by negotiating a trade reciprocity treaty.

To appreciate the uncertainty surrounding Hawaii's independent status in the nineteenth century, one must realize that France, Britain, Russia, and later the United States, Japan, and Germany, were extending their domains into the Pacific at a fast, almost frantic, rate. The "new imperialism" of the nineteenth century was stimulated by the industrial revolution of western Europe and the United States, which expanded production so rapidly that entrepreneurs avidly sought foreign sources of materials and foreign markets. A psycho-political rationale for seeking economic colonies to dominate, later popularized in the Social Darwinism of Herbert Spencer, was that developed nations were inherently superior to more primitive societies, giving them a "divine mission to conquer and rule inferior races for the benefit of the conquered, the conqueror, and civilization. . . . [H]urriedly they seized regions which were of little immediate value in order to forestall their rivals or in the expectation of future benefits to be derived from them."[22]

Britain was settling Australia at the opening of the nineteenth century and New Zealand a few years later (1840). In 1828 the Dutch took control of western New Guinea (Irian Jaya). In 1842 the British acquired Hong Kong. The French acquired the Society Islands of the southeastern Pacific in 1847, New Caledonia in 1853, and much of Southeast Asia (Indochina) in the 1860s. Russia meanwhile colonized Alaska, and the United States entered the imperialism race by buying that area in 1867. Japan broke out of its seclusion and began its imperial phase by taking possession of the Bonin Islands in 1877 and of the Ryukyu Islands (Okinawa) in 1879.

Over the next twenty-five years the British acquired Fiji, Papua New Guinea, the Solomons, and a half interest in the New Hebrides (the French having joint sovereignty of the last); the Germans acquired the Marshall Islands, the Carolines, the Northern Marianas, Nauru, Western Samoa, the Admiralty Islands, the Bismark Archipelago, and part of New Guinea; Japan took Taiwan from China; and the United States acquired Eastern Samoa and captured the Philippines and Guam from Spain. Not to be outdone by the big powers, Chile took Easter Island in 1888. Although much of this expansionism happened after Hawaii had negotiated a reciprocity treaty with the United States in 1875, a great deal of it happened earlier. It was obvious that most, if not all, the islands of the Pacific would be, as David Malo had predicted in 1837, gobbled up. This nineteenth century imperialistic race, once completed, left the entire Pacific basin with only one independent nation—the Kingdom of Tonga, whose independence was less than complete because Britain handled Tonga's foreign relations.

Kamehameha I had been deeply impressed with the awesome power of Western naval vessels, having seen Cook's British men-of-war in 1778–79, La Perouse's two French naval vessels that visited Hawaii in 1786, and Vancouver's warships in 1792, 1793, and 1794. It was obvious to Kamehameha that any of these powers could conquer Hawaii with ease, and that the continued independence of his little kingdom hinged on having one of these powers as a protector. This idea fitted well with Vancouver's desire that Hawaii be a secure and reliable base for supplies and provisioning of British ships in the vast reaches of the northeastern Pacific. Because Kamehameha and Vancouver (who had gotten to know each other when Vancouver served under Captain Cook) became close friends during Vancouver's subsequent visits to Hawaii in the 1790s, a deal was struck between the two in 1794. To Vancouver, this agreement constituted a "solemn cession" of the island of Hawaii (which was all that Kamehameha controlled at the time) to Great Britain, which would own the island but would not interfere in domestic affairs.[23] But to Kamehameha and his chiefs, the compact was simply for a defensive alliance that would give them the support of the British in the event it were needed to ward off foreign enemies. The fact that the British did not take any official cognizance of this agreement between Kamehameha and Vancouver did not keep Kamehameha from feeling for the rest of his life that he had a solid defensive alliance with Great Britain. It seems a reasonable surmise that the Union Jack is incorporated in the Hawaiian flag for this reason, though the certain origin of the flag remains debatable.

Kamehameha II (Liholiho) shared his father's views on the British connection, and his visit to England in 1824 was partly to "observe the laws, customs, institutions, religion and character of the country beneath whose guardian friendship and protection they and their countrymen who remain have with confidence to place themselves."[24] Liholiho died in London before he could have an audience with King George IV, but his companion chief, Boki, on his return to Honolulu reported that the British monarch had made this promise: "I will watch over your country, I will not take possession over it for mine, but will watch over it, lest evils should come from others to the Kingdom. . . ."[25]

Over the years, the Hawaiian government had a number of encounters with foreign governments—or, more specifically, with foreign nationals who claimed to represent their governments—but the protection that King George promised was never sought. In fact, the most threatening skirmish of all was with the British themselves.

The first ominous encounter involving a foreign power was in 1816, when a Dr. Georg Scheffer was sent by the Russian American Company in Alaska to Kauai to recover cargo from a Russian ship that had sunk off the coast of Waimea in 1815. Scheffer ingratiated himself with Governor Kaumualii, the former Kauai king who still resented the dominance of Kamehameha I. Scheffer struck a deal with Kaumualii whereby he promised to provide the governor with an armed vessel and 500 men in return for which Scheffer would build a fort at Waimea, get half of Oahu after Kaumualii had defeated Kamehameha, and have a monopoly on the sandalwood trade. Kaumualii would also cede Kauai to Russia. All this came to naught when the Russian American Co. in New Archangel and the Russian government in St. Petersburg repudiated Scheffer, whereupon Kamehameha successfully ordered Kaumualii to expel him. The threat was gone but the thought remained: had the Russian government supported Scheffer, Kamehameha would have been helpless.[26]

Some historians have considered the visit of two American warships to Honolulu in 1826 a show of force to protect the interests of Americans there, but such was not the case; all contacts with the Hawaiian government and the chiefs were friendly. During his stay, Thomas ap Catesby Jones of the USS *Peacock* removed several ship jumpers undesired by the Hawaiian government and negotiated Hawaii's first written treaty with a foreign government. The treaty contained a declaration of perpetual friendship between the two countries, a commitment that the Hawaiian government would henceforth apprehend all deserters from American ships, and a most-favored-nation commercial clause that guaranteed in commerce with the United States treatment equal to that of any other nation trading with Hawaii.[27]

Further, Captain Jones succeeded in having the Hawaiian government assume responsibility for paying the debts owed to local American merchants by chiefs who had failed to supply sandalwood already paid for, an indebtedness reckoned as amounting to the equivalent of between $150,000 and $500,000. This was the origin not only of the national debt of Hawaii but also of its first Western-style tax, since "through the influence of Captain Jones an arrangement was then made by the chiefs to pay these demands in six and eight months, this was to be effected by levying a tax . . . on every native of the Sandwich Islands."[28]

The first serious show of foreign force occurred in 1839, after Kamehameha III had forbidden the preaching of the Catholic religion in Hawaii and had expelled a number of French priests. The French government dispatched to Honolulu a warship commanded by Captain Laplace to seek redress. When Laplace arrived he gave the king an ultimatum, demanding under threat of bombardment that Catholic worship henceforth be free in Hawaii, that the government give a site for a Catholic church, and that $20,000 be put in escrow to ensure compliance with these demands. Kamehameha III had no choice but to comply.[29]

The next encounter was with the British, and it was the most serious of all. In January 1843 Her Britannic Majesty's ship *Carysfort*, commanded by Captain Lord George Paulet, arrived in Honolulu to settle various grievances lodged against the Hawaiian government by traders and other Britains in Hawaii. When Paulet did not receive satisfactory settlement of his demands from the government, he announced the cession of the Sandwich Islands to Great Britain. Kamehameha's government could offer no resistence, and Paulet raised the British flag over the fort guarding Honolulu Harbor. Hawaii was thus made part of the British Empire from February to July 1843. Not until Rear Admiral Richard Thomas, commander of all British naval forces in the Pacific, was informed of his government's policy respecting Hawaiian independence and arrived to restore Hawaii's sovereignty was the Union Jack lowered.[30]

Six years later the French were again flexing their muscles in Honolulu. The French consul had compiled a list of grievances, such as the imposition of an import duty of five dollars per gallon on brandy, which the Hawaii government had not resolved to his satisfaction. In August 1849 two French frigates commanded by Admiral de Tromelin put into Honolulu, and the consul persuaded the admiral to seek satisfaction on behalf of France. When the Hawaiian government refused to take the actions demanded, de Tromelin sent his forces ashore to seize the customs house and the fort. To add further insult, the French also seized the king's personal yacht. The frigates departed a month later, however, with the demands of the admiral unsatisfied. Relations between the two countries remained so tense for the next few years that in 1851 Kamehameha III, with the agreement of his kuhina nui and the Council of Chiefs, approved a plan to raise the American flag over Honolulu if France engaged in further hostile actions and to place the islands under the protection of the United States. The American consul was informed of this arrangement and given a document that would ratify the act.[31] There was no necessity to implement the plan, and Hawaii remained independent for another half century.

Economic Alliance with the United States

Although the Hawaiian government in the 1840s was able to escape capture by any Western power, and was even able a few years later to sign formal treaties with the United States and Great Britain respecting its independence, there were too many qualifications in those documents for the rulers of Hawaii to feel that the kingdom had full recognition as a sovereign state. Kamehameha III's government became convinced of the need for a formal alliance with a major power to ensure Hawaii's safety. The United States was the obvious choice.

The American government had never pushed the Hawaiian government on behalf of its citizens as had the French and the British. Perhaps it did not need to do so, since most of the king's ministers and advisers were American, as were most of the merchants doing business in the ports of the islands. Most of Hawaii's expanding production of sugar, coffee, and other crops went to the United States. And a large number of the foreign residents in Hawaii were Americans—perhaps some 1,500 out of a total of not many more than 2,000 non-natives at mid-century.[32]

Hawaii's first move toward closer relations with the United States occurred in 1848, when an official delegation was dispatched to the new state of California with power to negotiate a trade treaty—which of course California was powerless to do under the U.S. Constitution. Hawaii then proposed to the U.S. commissioner in Hawaii that a reciprocal trade treaty be agreed to by Washington that would replace higher tariffs with a uniform 5 percent ad valorem duty on all trade items. In 1852 Hawaii proposed that flour, fish, coal, lumber, staves, and headings from the United States be admitted duty free, if the United States would reciprocate for Hawaiian sugar, syrup, molasses, and coffee. The offer was not accepted.[33]

The next year Hawaii requested outright annexation by the United States, and a treaty to that effect was negotiated in Honolulu with U.S.

Commissioner David Gregg. It provided for the admission of Hawaii as a state to the Union. Again, the federal government withheld its agreement.[34]

A decided shift in Hawaii's foreign policy came with the accession of Kamehameha IV to the throne in December 1854. He and his successors were all strongly opposed to annexation, but they also favored securing an economic treaty of trade reciprocity under which there would be essentially free trade with the United States. Such an economic connection was felt to be essential to Hawaii's prosperity; and, assured of a strong economy, Hawaii would be better able to maintain its political independence. Consequently, until a reciprocity treaty was finally signed by the United States in 1875, the main thrust of Hawaii's foreign policy was to persuade America to accept this economic alliance. One of the first acts of Kamehameha IV was to negotiate a reciprocity treaty with U.S. Secretary of State William L. Marcy in 1855, but it failed to be ratified by the Senate.[35] When Kamehameha V proposed the same treaty in 1864, the Civil War delayed consideration in Washington until 1867, when the State Department and the President agreed, but again the Senate did not.[36] Then King Lunalilo in 1873 instructed Charles Reed Bishop, minister of foreign relations, to renew the negotiation. The proposed treaty was favorably received in Washington because it now provided for the cession of Pearl Harbor to the United States.[37] Before the Senate could act, however, mounting cries in Hawaii against the cession grew so loud that the Hawaiian government withdrew the offer, nullifying the treaty effort.

The final, successful initiative for a reciprocity treaty was initiated by the government of King Kalakaua shortly after his inauguration in 1874. Hawaii Chief Justice Elisha H. Allen and U.S. Secretary of State Hamilton Fish negotiated the treaty, which President Grant approved. Kalakaua himself went to Washington to join in the persuasion, which succeeded when the Senate ratified the treaty in March 1875.[38] Enabling legislation was passed the next year to put the treaty into effect. It did not cede Pearl Harbor but did state that so long as the treaty remained in effect Hawaii would "not lease or otherwise dispose of . . . any port, harbor or other territory . . . to any other power, state or government."[39]

Under the Reciprocity Treaty, fifteen tropical products of Hawaii were admitted duty free into the United States, the most important being sugar, molasses, and rice. In return, Hawaii placed no tariffs on such American exports as agricultural equipment and other machinery, building materials, grain and breadstuffs, cotton, and woolen goods—all of which were important to the growing economy of the islands.[40]

Hawaii had at last achieved the goal of becoming a part of the immense economy of the United States. The treaty was a clear signal to all other world powers to keep their hands off the kingdom.

Economic Developments during the Transition Period

With personal, political, and property rights established respectively by the 1839 Bill of Rights, the 1840 Constitution, and the Great Mahele, and with economic union with the United States, which practically guaranteed freedom from any further British or French foreign intervention, Hawaii had completed its transition from a Polynesian economy. It was now ready to develop as a full-fledged free-enterprise, capitalistic, Westernized economy.

During the long transition period needed to effect these political and legal developments, economic forces had been at work to change profoundly the ways that the people of Hawaii earned their living. Chief among those forces were the sandalwood trade and whaling.

THE SANDALWOOD TRADE

Hawaii's first break with centuries-long economic self-sufficiency came with its sandalwood trade with China. This trade developed because Hawaii had large stands of sandalwood in its mountainous areas, the Chinese prized the wood's fragrant aroma, and freighter service was available between Hawaii and China on ships engaged in the fur trade that stopped in Hawaii on their way from the Pacific Northwest to the Orient. Sandalwood was the only major commodity at the time that could be traded in exchange for the guns, ships, and other items that Kamehameha I so avidly desired.

Sandalwood exports to China began in the early 1790s, but it was not until about 1810 that they increased to sizable proportions.[41] The volume of Hawaiian sandalwood off-loaded at the principal port of Canton in 1812–13 was reported to be 19,036 piculs.[42] Valued at around $10 a picul, that export item would gross approximately $200,000, a large sum in Hawaii's Polynesian economy. During the next decade the volume increased, reaching 30,000 piculs in 1821. After that the tonnage produced declined as the forests were depleted. The trade finally disappeared around 1840.[43]

To appreciate the magnitude of the sandalwood trade, one has to realize that 30,000 piculs are the equivalent of 4 million pounds, or 2,000 tons. That tonnage had a value of $300,000 in 1821 dollars—the equivalent in purchasing power of more than $3 million in 1989.

The sandalwood trade was well organized and stable as long as Kamehameha I lived because it was a monopoly of the king. The king or his aides bargained with the Yankee ship captains who bought the wood for sale in China. According to Kuykendall (1:83), Kamehameha was a shrewd bargainer, but always honest and fair in his dealings. Whatever he bought from the traders he paid for on the spot—almost invariably with sandalwood, which was gathered by the commoners on his command. Perhaps on balance the sandalwood trade was good for Hawaii during Kamehameha's reign because the ships and guns and other commodities he was able to obtain in exchange for it strengthened his power and contributed to political stability, and also because the personal wealth that it brought to him probably reduced his need for taxes on his chiefs and the commoners.

But after Kamehameha I's death in 1819, his son Liholiho succumbed to pressure from the chiefs and permitted them to sell sandalwood on their own account. The result was feverish activity in gathering the wood, creating a situation that a visitor described in 1822 as follows: "Instead of a divided and lawless aristocracy, the King and his Chiefs compose a united corps of peaceable merchants, whose principal object is to become rich by the pursuits of trade" [in sandalwood].[44]

The phrase "to become rich" may not be completely apposite because, while their desire to possess attractive foreign objects hitherto unknown to them must have been great, the king and his chiefs desired to keep those items out of the hands of the commoners—commoners never having been permitted to possess anything classifiable as a luxury. The combination of these two considerations meant that anything and everything that the foreigners had to sell found a ready market: ships, furniture, clothing, cloth (both plain and fancy), all kinds of utensils, uniforms, billiard tables, and so on, ad infinitum. Pratt (p. 94) tells of a Kauai chief who paid $400 (in sandalwood) for a simple mirror. Bishop (p. 26) relates that Chief Kuakini of Kailua "possessed great quantities of foreign goods stored in his warehouse, while his people went naked," adding that the chief once ordered a large double canoe "loaded with bales of broadcloth and Chinese silks and satins which had been damaged by long storage" out to sea, where the cargo was dumped. Kamehameha II's experience in trading illustrated the difficulty of selecting from the cornucopia of goods offered by the haole ship captains and merchants. In the early 1820s he purchased two ships that had so rotted that they were totally unseaworthy, one for $50,000's worth of sandal-wood and the other for $90,000.[45]

The inevitable result of the buying frenzy was that many chiefs began to buy on credit whatever they were offered before the sandalwood needed for payment had been harvested. It is estimated that by 1826 the chiefs had outstanding IOUs valued at well over $100,000.[46] The last of these debts was not settled until 1843.[47]

To stimulate the felling of sandalwood, Kamehameha III and his chiefs in 1826 did for the commoners what the king had done for the chiefs a few years earlier—cut them into the sandalwood trade and profits. As already noted, Hawaii's first written tax law was levied to pay off the debts of the alii to traders, following the visit of Captain Thomas ap Catesby Jones. The tax required each man to supply one-half picul of sandalwood annually, in return for which he was permitted to keep half of any additional amount that he cut. (Every woman had to bring a mat, a piece of kapa, or a Spanish dollar, the coin most commonly introduced by visiting ships.)

"The promulgation of this law resulted in a renewed and more vigor-ous assault on the sandalwood forests"[48] and consequently less regard for the taro and sweet potato patches and for fishing. A missionary at that time wrote that food on Oahu was scarce because the people were largely "engaged in cutting sandalwood, and have of course neglected the cultivation of the land. Vegetables are sold at a very dear rate."[49] Complaints about the high cost of living in Hawaii were to echo down the years.

The main effects of the sandalwood trade after the death of Kameha-meha I were, first, a massive diversion of labor away from the historic Polynesian economy to the cutting and transporting of wood, and with this a decline in the production of the necessities of life; second, the spending by the king and his chiefs of the proceeds from the sale of the wood on a vast array of items desired more for conspicuous consump-tion than for any intrinsic utility; and, third, a serious decline in the health and well-being of the commoners, who were pushed to their limit in the gathering of the wood.

According to Morgan (p. 72), commoners were sent as conscripted labor without pay on "sandalwood expeditions into the rugged upland regions where for weeks at a time, hundreds or thousands underwent wet and cold weather and arduous work, with inadequate food and next to no clothing or shelter. Their resistance to exposure was the less because they were used to the congenial temperature and moderate work of the coast." He concludes that this had "an enfeebling" effect on the health of the entire nation. Kuykendall (1:89) agrees: "All this resulted in the pitiless exploitation not merely of the sandalwood but of the labor and vitality of the common people."

Hawaii's first venture into world trade was thus a disaster—particularly after the death of Kamehameha I, when the avarice of the new king was shared by many of the chiefs. The result was that the islands were stripped of their sandalwood forests, the commoners weakened by brutal overwork, and the basis of the native subsistence economy pushed into a permanent decline—all to enable the king and his chiefs to enjoy a brief buying spree in which they purchased almost everything the Western traders had to offer, with little to show for it when the party was over.

Servicing the Pacific Whaling Fleet

As the ships carrying off the sandalwood of Hawaii disappeared, a new kind of vessel began arriving in the ports of the kingdom. This was the ugly but profitable whaling ship, a floating factory-warehouse that on its deck rendered out oil from blubber and stored it in its hold. Each ship required substantial provisions for its long sweeps of the whaling grounds. Prices of whale oil, particularly the favored sperm oil, were high enough to make the ships good customers of suppliers ashore.

From early days, the sailors of New England had hunted whales to light the lamps of America, venturing first off shore and then further into the reaches of the Atlantic Ocean, in competition with the British and French. As these whaling grounds were depleted, the search for new whale populations brought the New England ships around the Horn into the Pacific Ocean. When the whaling industry reached its peak in the mid-nineteenth century, six-sevenths of the American fleet was operating in the Pacific.[50]

The first Pacific whaling grounds were in the south, but by 1820 the well-populated waters off Japan had been discovered and in the 1830s Alaskan waters started to be exploited. In the closing decades of large-scale whaling (the 1850s–70s) Arctic seas beyond the Bering Strait were the most productive fields.[51]

The typical whaler in the Pacific in the 1840s would be away from its home port for three to four years, would fish "the line" (i.e., equatorial waters) in the winter, come to Hawaii for a couple of months in the spring for refitting and recreation, then move to the northern grounds in the summer, returning to Hawaii for a couple of months in the fall before repeating the routine.[52] So, unlike the sandalwood traders who were in port just long enough to take on cargo, the whaling ships spent perhaps four or five months a year anchored in Hawaiian waters. Being away from home port for such extended periods, the whalers had to be supplied periodically—with fresh water, large amounts of firewood, beef, pork, salt, and vegetables. The ships were in frequent need of repair, which laid the basis for a sizable ship-repair business in Hawaii. (The oldest firm in Hawaii is McWayne Marine Supply Company, which dates back to 1823.)

Each time a whaler visited a Hawaiian port, its owners, officers, or crew spent an average of about $700 or $800. Soon the whale trade became more profitable and more dependable than the sandalwood export had ever been—as long as the Pacific whaling fleet endured.[53]

The first two American whalers to put into Honolulu came in 1819,[54] and the number thereafter increased rapidly, to 60 in 1822, 138 in 1826, 198 in 1832, and 596 in 1846.[55] Until the Civil War largely stopped American whaling, some 300 to 500 ships would put into Honolulu or Lahaina (less often, into Hilo) each year. Whaling never made a significant recovery after the Civil War because by then the petroleum that had been discovered in Pennsylvania was found to be a better and cheaper fuel than whale oil. The end of the whaling era for Hawaii was hastened in September 1871 by the loss of 34 ships, caught and crushed by the ice in Arctic waters, where they had sought the vanishing pods of the cetaceans.

For the small Hawaiian economy that existed in the mid-nineteenth century, to supply firewood to hundreds of whaling ships annually and food for the 10,000 to 15,000 sailors who manned those ships made it necessary to divert a good portion of the kingdom's resources to the task. In 1844, at the peak of the whaling trade, Robert C. Wyllie, later Hawaii's long-time foreign minister, wrote: ". . . it is obvious that the prosperity of these islands has depended, and does depend, mainly upon the whaleships that annually flock to these ports. . . . Were the whale fishery to fall off . . . or were the vessels engaged in it to abandon these islands for some others in this ocean, or for ports on the Main, the Sandwich Islands would relapse into their primitive insignificance."[56]

Despite the prosperity that the whaling trade brought to Hawaii's merchants and chiefs (who took two-thirds of the receipts of any sale by a commoner to a whaler), the replenishing of the ships had a number of economic disadvantages to Hawaii. The most obvious was that it diverted labor from the production of food for local consumption to the production of items for sale to the ships. Since proceeds of these sales went primarily to the merchants and chiefs, the standard of living of commoners may have been further reduced from that experienced during the years of the sandalwood trade. Offsetting this loss quantitatively, if not qualitatively, was cash earned by native women aboard ship or ashore when the whaling fleet was in. The income from their sexual favors helped develop a lively trade in consumer goods in the local retail stores that sprang up along the waterfronts of the ports.

A second shortcoming of the whaling trade was that it was a boom and bust activity. Not only was the business highly seasonal, but also each ship returned to its home port in New England when filled with oil. Consequently, the number of vessels that stayed in the Pacific and visited Hawaii each year varied greatly. The record number of 596 that called in 1846 fell to 274 in 1849, but then rose back to more than 500 for several years in the 1850s.[57]

A third disadvantage, to quote Morgan (p. 85), was that "it helped to develop further the tastes of the chiefs toward foreign goods, beyond the point to which the sandalwood trade had carried them. By providing new ways to consume conspicuously, it gave them incentive to heavier taxes at a time when both the social situation and the productive routine could less well support even the old taxes."

The whaling trade also postponed the day when Hawaii would turn its energies and resources to the production of staple crops and commodities for export to more dependable markets.

Probably the worst economic impact of the whaling era, however, was on the social structure of the Hawaiian community, a matter of economic importance because a society that places drunkenness and debauchery high on its scale of values is not going to achieve an advanced level of economic productivity. With some 10,000 or more sailors in port every spring and fall, the social impact on the native population was devastating. The prime interest of most of the sailors was in the grog shop and the brothel—to the point that Morgan (p. 84) concludes that the "influence of these men was without alleviation destructive of the native social order" and Kuykendall (1:311) concurs that "from a moral

standpoint, the semi-annual visits of thousands of these seamen had a most pernicious influence."

Theophilus H. Davies, a Honolulu merchant during the whaling era, recorded the qualms he and other members of the merchant community had on watching the saturnalia when the ships came in and the hungry crewmen came ashore. "Then the crimps get hold of poor Jack, and give him cash in advance at frightful premiums, and minister to his wants and fancies. Then the harpies pounce upon him and poor Jack is held in bondage of sin for six weeks and finds his 'lay' has been spent, and he has to get a heavy advance against the next season. . . . Troops of Hawaiian maidens come from country homes to Honolulu . . . and few of them ever return. . . ."[58]

If Hawaii's first foray into world trade with sandalwood exports was an almost total disaster, her second venture, supplying and refitting the Pacific whaling fleet, was no better.

Other Economic Developments

Other, more modest, economic developments of the transition period proved to be more constructive. These included the production of sugar, rice, coffee, and salt; ranching; miscellaneous commodity exports; visitors; and banking.

Sugar. The Polynesians had grown sugarcane for centuries, but they merely chewed it for its sweetness without crushing it and extracting the juice for sugar. Near the beginning of the nineteenth century Hawaii had several small-scale sugar-grinding operations, the earliest probably being the one started on the island of Lanai in 1802 by a Chinese; but the first commercial sugar mill was constructed in 1835 at Koloa, Kauai, by Ladd & Co., a Honolulu trading firm.[59]

Although the Koloa operation has a prominent place in Hawaiian history as the first sugar plantation, it was not primarily a sugar producer at its inception. In its first year of operations, only 25 acres were planted in cane.

The surprising thing about Koloa Plantation was that it ever started any operations, given the massive roadblocks to business enterprise that still existed in the 1830s. Since all land in Hawaii was under the control of the king, Kamehameha III had to be persuaded that this operation would be good for him and for his people before he would lease the land to Ladd & Co.[60] It was necessary for the plantation to hire native labor;

but the local chiefs on Kauai considered the commoners to be their personal vassals, who should work only for them. They threw roadblock after roadblock in the path of the plantation operation, including a refusal to sell seed cane (from which sugarcane is started) to the company.[61]

And there were all the physical problems of starting a relatively complex operation like this in a primitive environment. The only tool for land preparation was the *hōʻōʻō* (Hawaiian digging stick). There were few draft animals. Labor was totally unaccustomed to the type of work to be performed. Rollers for crushing the cane had to be formed from wooden logs. Nonetheless, two tons of raw sugar were produced with the first harvest and four tons the next year.

In spite of all the problems, the plantation survived, and in the next few years the sugar industry expanded rapidly. Throughout the 1840s Hawaii exported an average of about 250 tons of raw sugar a year, this figure rising to more than 700 tons per year in the 1850s—with, of course, considerable fluctuation from year to year.[62]

The U.S. Civil War, which cut the North off from its normal supply of sugar from Louisiana, gave the Hawaiian industry a tremendous boost. Suddenly, instead of trying to sell sugar for about six cents a pound wherever in the world a market could be found, Hawaii sugar producers found the nearby American market opened wide with war-inflated prices that got as high as seventeen cents per pound in 1864. As a consequence, sugar in Hawaii boomed and exports rose from 700 tons in 1860 to 7,500 tons in 1865 and to 9,000 tons in 1870.[63] By then, the whaling fleet had practically disappeared and sugar was King—a role that the industry kept for a full century. In the spring of 1865 the *Pacific Commercial Advertiser* stated: "Fortunately for these islands, they are not dependent on the whaling fleets as formerly, and our sugar plantations alone are now worth to us five times more than ever the former were, and give to our people a more steady, healthful and lucrative employment."[64]

Sugar was not the only "steady, healthful and lucrative employment" that got started during the transition period. Besides growing food for local consumption, agricultural enterprises developed several new crops for export.

Rice. The most important of these new export crops was rice.[65] Unsuccessful efforts to grow rice had been made as early as 1838, but by 1860 several circumstances combined to start a veritable rice boom in Hawaii.

The Royal Hawaiian Agricultural Society in 1858 had demonstrated in an experimental field in Nuuanu Valley that rice could be grown successfully in Hawaii. In 1860 Dr. S. P. Ford grew a small field that produced more than 7,000 pounds of rice per acre. By 1860 about 700 Chinese were living in Hawaii who had fulfilled their contract periods on the sugar plantations, were knowledgeable about growing rice, and wanted it in their diet. Moreover, by then California had some 35,000 Chinese immigrants, who provided a ready market for Hawaiian rice. Finally, during the Civil War most of the American whaling fleet disappeared and much agricultural land that had been used to produce food for the whalers was available for other uses. Hawaii had wetland and old taro patches that were ideal for rice cultivation.

This combination of factors resulted in a tremendous growth in rice cultivation in the 1860s. As Kuykendall (2:150) summarized the development, "a veritable craze for rice growing swept over Oahu and parts of the other islands" in the early 1860s. As a result, exports of rice and paddy (unhulled rice) exceeded 1 million pounds in 1867, and about the same amount was consumed in the islands. Production continued to expand and in 1880 exports exceeded 6 million pounds.

Coffee. Coffee was grown in Hawaii as early as 1817 by the Spaniard Don Francisco de Paulo Marín. By the 1830s many small growers and a few large growers were in production on most of the islands. Ten thousand pounds were exported in 1845, and thereafter the growth of coffee was considerable; but it always proved to be a difficult crop. Fluctuating weather, resulting in many bad seasons with low production, susceptibility to disease which from time to time ravished the trees, and high labor requirements for picking the berries all combined to make coffee a risky venture. For several decades, until much coffee land was converted to sugar after the Reciprocity Treaty of 1875, coffee exports were considerable, ranging from a low of around 50,000 pounds to highs of 300,000 to 400,000 pounds in the late 1860s.[66]

Salt. Salt was Hawaii's first export, carried by some of the early ships in the fur trade back to the Pacific Northwest for curing furs. Another early market was provided by the Russian settlements in Alaska; records show a cargo of salt going to Kamchatka in 1819. Early salt production was made by natural evaporation of seawater in tidal ponds, but later commercial salt was mined from the bottom of Moanalua Lake, near

Honolulu, and produced by evaporation from special reservoirs. Salt exports ran to around 2,000 to 3,000 barrels a year in the 1830s, reached 15,000 barrels in 1847, and thereafter declined gradually until exports ceased in the 1880s.[67]

Ranching. Vancouver had introduced cattle and sheep in the early 1790s, and these, together with later imports from other parts of the world, laid the basis for Hawaii's livestock industry. Although many of the animals ran wild and did considerable damage for some decades before fencing came into common use, they nonetheless gave Hawaii a source of meat for domestic consumption and also a surplus that could be sold to the ships in the fur and sandalwood trades and later to the whalers. From the early days (figures start in 1836) cattle hides and goat skins were exported in fair volume: 6,000 cattle hides and 20,000 goat skins in 1836, and the figures rising to some 20,000 cattle hides and 50,000 goat skins annually in the 1860s and 1870s. Wool exports attained significant volume during the U.S. Civil War and reached some 500,000 pounds annually during the 1870s.[68]

Miscellaneous Commodity Exports. During and after the Civil War three other products were shipped in fair quantity to California. Banana exports rose from 100 bunches in 1861 to nearly 20,000 bunches in 1880. The export of *pulu*, a soft, glossy substance that envelops the fronds of the tree fern and was dried to be used for stuffing mattresses and pillows, was considerable during the 1860s and 1870s, averaging nearly 400,000 pounds a year. Finally, a fungus called *pepeiao akua*, which was gathered from the decaying trunks and limbs of felled kukui nut trees, was a favorite food of the Chinese in California, and 100,000 pounds per year were shipped during its brief trade life in the 1860s.[69] Given that Hawaii's population in the 1860s and 1870s numbered fewer than 70,000 people, the quantities of pulu and pepeiao akua gathered by native families in the forests is astounding. Morgan (p. 172) says that on these collection trips, which might last for weeks at a time, the gatherers were "undergoing privations reminiscent of sandalwood days."

In the search for other crops to export, a number of efforts were undertaken that failed. Silk production looked like a possibility in the 1830s, and by 1840 100,000 mulberry trees were growing to feed the worms. But plant diseases, insects, drought, and heavy trade winds put an end to that effort.[70] Cotton was grown in small amounts throughout the nineteenth century, and during the Civil War, when cotton prices soared, some was exported to America; but the revival of production in the American South after the war stopped that trade.[71] Efforts were also made to grow tobacco and arrowroot, but the quantities were never consequential.

Visitors. It is rather remarkable that during this early period tourism was already recognized as having a potential for Hawaii's economic development. The islands had been host to tens of thousands of what were mostly undesirable "tourists" during the whaling-fleet days, when most of the seamen would stay ashore in hotels that generally also served as brothels and grog shops. After the U.S. Civil War a more desirable type of visitor was coming to Hawaii—not just from California, where the population had grown to more than half a million, but also occasionally from the East Coast after the transcontinental railroad was completed in 1869. By 1870, when steamer service between San Francisco and Honolulu had been established, an estimated two thousand visitors from the mainland were coming to Hawaii annually and a first-class hostelry was needed. With urgings from local businessmen, King Kamehameha V persuaded the legislature to appropriate funds for such a facility; and in 1871 the Hawaiian Hotel was built at the *mauka* Ewa (northwest) corner of Hotel and Richards Streets, where the Armed Services YMCA was later located. Later, when King Kalakaua permanently reserved a suite in the hotel for his personal use, the hotel became known as the Royal Hawaiian Hotel. This was a first-class establishment, with gas lights, indoor plumbing, and room keys—as fine in its day as the second Royal Hawaiian Hotel was when it opened in Waikiki in 1927.[72]

Banking. The growing business community of Honolulu had long felt that a bank was necessary for economic development; and in 1852 Robert Crichton Wyllie, Kamehameha III's minister of foreign affairs, presented to the Royal Hawaiian Agricultural Society a report, "On Capital and Banking," in which he detailed the importance to Hawaii of having a savings bank. Wyllie had spoken briefly to the society the year before on the same subject, and he opened his 1852 report as follows:

> When I had the honor to address you, at one of your meetings last year, I stated my fears that a severe crisis in the money market was approaching, and that some of your number would have to succumb under its pressure, from the want of that Banking accommodation, which, in other countries, enables the man of enterprise and good character to command cash, so long as he can give good security for it. Unfortunately, my predictions

have proved to be true. Since that period, several industrious and well deserving men, largely engaged in planting, have been unable to meet their liabilities, though possessed of assets greatly exceeding the amount of those engagements. As the best prevention of such evils, in the interest of the planters, I suggested to the meeting, the urgent necessity of establishing a Bank in Honolulu, with branches in the principal islands."[73]

Wyllie then went on to list the many valuable functions a bank could perform in a community such as Hawaii besides loans to distressed plantations, and to sketch how such a bank could be organized, financed, and managed. The secretary and treasurer of the Royal Hawaiian Agricultural Society at that time was Charles Reed Bishop, who had come to Hawaii six years earlier from upstate New York and had married Bernice Pauahi Paki, one of the last surviving members of the Kamehameha dynasty. Bishop apparently took Wyllie's arguments seriously, because in 1858 he founded a bank. Bishop & Company, as it was called, is still doing business as First Hawaiian Bank—Hawaii's oldest bank by a quarter of a century.

Although Hawaii acquired a bank during the transition period, it was not until 1883 that it issued its own coinage. In the early years of the nineteenth century, barter had still been the standard method of exchange, and during the sandalwood period that commodity was the common standard in which values were expressed. It was not until the 1820s that any significant amount of currency was in circulation, and this was mainly Spanish silver dollars.[74] Bills of exchange were used as early as 1823 to pay for goods purchased from local merchants by the Sandwich Islands Mission. As barter diminished and cash transactions became more standard, other currencies (British, American, etc.) entered into circulation. But there was still such a scarcity of currency that when Ladd & Co. started the Koloa Plantation in 1835 and had to meet a daily payroll, it printed its own currency (script) on cardboard, redeemable in merchandise at the company store.[75] When the Reciprocity Treaty with the United States went into effect in 1876, the Hawaiian government decreed U.S. currency to be the legal tender of Hawaii.[76] Finally, in 1883, it had its own coins minted.[77]

Summary of the Transition Period

The Polynesian society and economy of the precontact era were doomed the day that Captain Cook arrived on the south coast of Kauai in January 1778. No nonwestern society and economy has remained unchanged after contact with the West, and always the period of transition from precontact conditions to Westernized conditions has been long and hard —and frequently devastating to the people involved. If Hawaii were to be strong enough to withstand outright conquest by the new world that Cook opened up to it, and if it were to acquire the many marvelous goods that Western people had—and these two objectives were uppermost in the minds of Hawaii's leaders in the decades after contact—the old Polynesian society and economy had to change, and the changes pressed on the alii by advisors and circumstances necessitated adopting Western values and practices.

Hawaiian leaders showed a remarkable willingness to make such changes, starting with the dramatic abolition of the kapu system in 1819. Next came the recognition that people had to be free—free to do what they wanted and to retain in their possession the fruits of their labor—out of which came the Hawaii Bill of Rights. Then came the complementary recognition that their economy could not function effectively if everything that everyone did was subject to arbitrary control by the king and chiefs, and this in turn resulted in the creation of a constitutional monarchy to replace the absolutism of the precontact era. Finally came the recognition of the need for citizens to own land, the primary factor of production in Hawaii's agricultural economy. Unless one could be secure in the possesssion and use of land, production would never approach its potential—hence the land division called the Great Mahele.

Prior to these dramatic changes made in the short span of 1839–48, the only significant economic development in Hawaii was that thrust upon the island kingdom from the outside, by fur traders who discovered that Hawaii had sandalwood that could be sold in China along with their furs, and by whalers who put into the most convenient port for rest and refitting as they hunted alternately in northern Pacific and equatorial waters. These economic activities were short-lived and probably did Hawaii more harm than good. After the adoption of a bill of rights, a constitution, and a Western system of land tenure, however, economic activities of a more lasting and productive nature—activities that provided what the *Pacific Commercial Advertiser* later called "steady, healthful and lucrative employment"—were able to come into existence and begin to lay the basis for the strong Hawaiian economy that ultimately developed.

The troubled history of Koloa Plantation, already briefly noted, deserves a fuller account as an example of the checks on enterprise that existed before these three critical institutional changes were made. In 1835, when Ladd & Co. began sugar operations, the king controlled all land in Hawaii, so that the company had to persuade him that making acreage available to it would be desirable for the kingdom. According to Arthur Alexander's history of Koloa, "The wholehearted endorsement of their enterprise by the missionaries undoubtedly helped the partners in obtaining their lands, for it was not easily obtained."[78]

Persuading the king to lease the land was not enough because the chiefs in the Koloa area had occupied and controlled the lands for generations and, while they could not challenge the authority of the king, they nonetheless felt aggrieved that "their" lands had been taken from them. "The jealousy of the petty chiefs, in seeing their lands thus alienated, proved, for some time, a great obstacle to their success," wrote James Jarves, who was at Koloa at the time. "They carried their opposition so far as to forbid all sale of provisions, from their people to the agent, who repaired here to commence operations, and he was well nigh starved into a retreat."[79] Later the chiefs placed a kapu on the sale of seed cane to William Hooper, the plantation manager, and then the paramount chief (governor) of Kauai refused to let Koloa Plantation build a dam to provide water power for its mill. This obstruction was so serious that Hooper persuaded the king to send a personal emissary to Kauai to straighten matters out. The dam was built, but then the governor forbade Hooper to send men into the forests to collect firewood. Hooper responded by refusing to harvest cane grown by the chiefs until all restrictions were lifted.[80] At one point, Hooper believed that the chiefs on Kauai resented him so much that his life was in danger. "I know enough of them to feel that they would not be very particular as to the means employed in removing obnoxious persons," he wrote in 1838.[81]

Since labor was no freer than the land, Hooper also had trouble with the chiefs over his work force. The chiefs believed that they controlled the commoners, as traditionally they had, so that in addition to paying his workers a daily wage of twelve and one-half cents, he had to pay each commoner's chief two dollars per month for having the commoner "allotted" to him.[82]

But to Hooper the greatest obstacle was the inefficiency of the native laborers because of "their repugnance to regular and protracted labor, and their utter ignorance of tools." In 1838 he wrote: "I consider that the results of the experiment we have been making for three years past . . . prove the complete worthlessness of Sandwich Islanders as laborers on a farm."[83] Such opinions were later to shape the immigration policy of the kingdom. What Hooper, fresh off the boat from Boston in 1833 and speaking no Hawaiian, did not realize was that the idea of working by the clock for payment in paper script redeemable at the company store was totally alien to the Polynesian. With proper motivation, Hawaiians worked as hard as anybody.

Finally, with no bank in Hawaii, when Koloa Plantation ran into hard times and needed money to keep going, there was no place to turn to for funds, even though Ladd & Co.'s assets probably would have made a loan secure.

In sum, it is not surprising that the plantation, Hawaii's first large-scale agricultural free enterprise, went bankrupt within a decade, sold at a sheriff's auction. Hooper blamed his troubles on the Hawaiians. "I had had more annoyance from the chiefs and difficulties with the natives . . . than I ever thought it possible for a white man to bear," he wrote.[84]

Fundamental to Koloa's failure, however, was the lack of freedom in the uses of productive means. Neither king, chiefs, nor commoners were yet attuned to an economic system that combined land, labor, and capital to form an enterprise run for profit. Success of the system from the West required adjustment by the native population to a whole new way of life, with different rules and practices—an adjustment long and difficult, and perhaps not yet completed for all Hawaiians today.

Nor, considering the full impact of Western forces on Hawaii during the transformation from a traditional to a market economy, is that resistance, voiced by some contemporary Hawaiian nationalists, surprising. The following section attempts to summarize the adverse effects of Westernizing the society and economy of these islands and to consider if any of the adversities could have been avoided—and if so, at what cost.

Impact of the Transition on the Hawaiian People

Western contact with Hawaii and the ensuing Westernization of the society was in several ways a disaster for the Hawaiian race and its culture. The hundred years of transition was a century of decay in the physical, religious, cultural, social, and moral stature of the native Polynesians. The fact that the same thing happened in many other parts of the world as native cultures came into contact with the West does not diminish the devastating effects on Hawaii; it simply shows that something of this sort almost always happens and raises the question of whether those negative effects could have been averted had the Hawaiian leadership tried to resist Westernization rather than to emulate it. Before attempting to answer this question, it is necessary to consider the adverse effects themselves.

DISEASE

The native Hawaiians, who came into contact with Captain Cook and his crew and with tens of thousands of other Westerners later on, had practically no immunity to any of the Western diseases—the immunity (or relative immunity) that builds up in the human body through countless generations of contact with a disease. As a result, diseases considered mild because of the immunities Westerners had built up against them— such as chicken pox, whooping cough, and measles—were absolutely deadly to the Polynesians, whose ancestors had had no contact with the diseases. Syphilis and gonorrhea take their toll on people of all races, but these diseases were particularly virulent among the Hawaiians. Later, when leprosy was introduced into Hawaii in the mid-nineteenth century, the Polynesians contracted the disease on a much vaster scale than did the Caucasians or the Orientals.

As a result of Western diseases, the Hawaiian population declined precipitously for more than a hundred years after 1778, to the point that it appeared that the native population might in time become extinct. It is generally thought by demographers that the native population of Hawaii numbered around 250,000 at the time of contact, but had dropped to fewer than 150,000 by the early 1820s and was 130,000 when the first census was taken in 1831–32.[85] By 1850 the total population of Hawaii was down to 84,000 (of whom some 1,500 were foreigners), and by 1860 it had fallen to 70,000. It reached a low point in the 1870s, when the total population dropped to about 54,000, with the native Hawaiians numbering fewer than 50,000. Although epidemics made drastic inroads in the population during some years (cholera in 1804, influenza in 1826, mumps in 1839, measles and whooping cough in 1848–49, and small pox in 1853), the death rate during all those years was consistently high. Furthermore, the birth rate was consistently low, probably because syphilis caused stillbirths and gonorrhea caused sterility. Thus Hawaii had its native population reduced by 80 percent in the first hundred years after new diseases were introduced by Westerners, producing the first, most dramatic, and most drastic impact of Western contact.

RELIGION

The Polynesians were a religious people, not just in Hawaii but in the rest of Polynesia as well. Religion is beyond the scope of this book; but in noting the devastating impact of Westernization on the native culture, it may be observed that when a religious people suddenly lose their religion, they are stripped of one of the foundations of their society and are, so to speak, set adrift without sail or compass. Furthermore, in Hawaii this happened suddenly, when in 1819 the new king (Liholiho), the queen regent or kuhina nui (Kaahumanu), and the new king's mother (Keopuolani) decided to abolish the kapu system and with it the entire Hawaiian religion. Immediately thereafter the heiau were destroyed, the images were burned, and the kapu that had governed every aspect of life and conduct were suddenly abandoned. This sudden change might not have caused any problems for Liholiho, Kaahumanu, or Keopuolani, but to the commoners out on the ahupuaa it must have been like a great earthquake, destroying the foundations of their society.

MORALS

Whereas the alii socialized with the sea captains, the missionaries, the merchants, and the naval commanders, the commoners' contact with Westerners was mainly with the crews of the sandalwood and whaling ships—some of whom had jumped ship to live in Hawaii and others of whom were simply in port from time to time, even for extended stays during the whaling season. These men were generally rough and tough, boisterous and uneducated, and troublesome enough even when at home with their families and neighbors. When they rounded the tip of South America and entered the Pacific, they "hung their conscience on the Horn," and when in port they were generally interested only in grog and women. Although there were undoubtedly many exceptions to this generalization, most of the Westerners with whom the commoners came into contact were about the worst elements of Western society on their worst behavior. In a period when Hawaiians were by necessity and by the example of their leaders trying to emulate the West, the example of the majority of the Westerners coming to Hawaii was probably the worst imaginable.

FREEDOM

Under the alii system, the commoners were to all intents and purposes the property of the chiefs, on whom they relied for support, guidance, orders—and everything else. The alii exercised absolute power over every aspect of life. When people have lived under this kind of a system for centuries and know nothing else, freedom is a difficult condition to adjust to. It can take them a long time to develop a sense of their independence and a corollary sense of responsibility. The Bill of Rights that was proclaimed by Kamehameha III in 1839 established in Hawaii the principle of freedom, but it would take generations for many of the commoners to become, in fact and by their behavior and their thinking, free people. Again, they were, so to speak, cast adrift.

INDIVIDUALISM

Equally difficult to adjust to was the Western concept of the supremacy of the individual, which contrasted with the Polynesian concept of the supremacy of the group, or ohana. The group identity of the Polynesian under the conditions that existed in precontact Hawaii was perhaps more suitable than the individualism introduced by the Westerners. It suffices to say that when the group breaks down and each person is left on his own as an individual, he has to make a tremendous adjustment in his way of thinking and acting before he becomes comfortable in the new system and a productive and functioning member of it. As with the adjustment to personal freedom, this adjustment can take generations.

LAND

At present the strongest and most persistent complaint by native Hawaiians against the changes wrought by Westernization is that the process has left them a landless people. This complaint is hard for many Westerners to understand because prior to the Great Mahele of 1848 and the subsequent distribution of kuleana lands, all land in Hawaii was vested in the king, with the chiefs, subchiefs, and commoners occupying and using the land only at the (sometimes fickle) pleasure of the alii nui. After the Great Mahele the lands of Hawaii were almost exclusively in native hands—those of the government, the king, the chiefs, and the commoners. Thereafter, much of the private land of the chiefs and the commoners was lost by abandonment, foreclosure for nonpayment of debt or taxes, or sale to Westerners who understood the new law and the benefits of private property, including the economic advantage of land ownership, far better than did most Hawaiians.

But to many Hawaiians this view overlooks the fact that in ancient Hawaiian culture land was considered the sacred source of life, and that while "title" to all the land may have been in the king, he held it (at least in theory) in trust for the chiefs and the commoners. Dr. Noa Emmett Aluli, a prominent spokesman for the Hawaiian movement, says that *"Aloha 'Āina"* is more than a popular slogan of present-day Hawaiians; a tenet of the movement is that the land is the religion and the culture of Hawaiians. "Native Hawaiians descend from a tradition and genealogy of nature deities: Wakea, Papa, Ho'ohokuikalani, Hina, Kane, Kanaloa, Lono, and Pele: the sky, the earth, the stars, the moon, the water, the sea, natural phenomenon as rain and steam: and from natural plants and animals. . . . The land is religion. It is alive, respected, treasured, praised and even worshipped."[86]

CONCLUSION

One can only conclude that the process of Westernization that started in 1778 and lasted for a full century was extremely hard on the Hawaiian people, who were weakened and drastically reduced in number by new diseases, had their religious foundations suddenly uprooted, were demoralized by the example set for them by the dregs of Western society, had been thrust into a society in which freedom and individualism were the bases of behavior and thinking rather than the extended family and clan, and had seen their ancient land tenure system changed abruptly.

In the last century the Hawaiians have become Westernized, but a good many of them still have a considerable way to go before achieving full social and economic equality in the Westernized, modern society that Hawaii is today. Some Hawaiian activists, however, do not seek that kind of "progress" for the Hawaiians. Instead, they would prefer to establish a separate Hawaiian nation in which Hawaiians could live a life similar to that of their ancestors, in consonance with their Polynesian heritage.

So back to the question posed earlier: Could the negative effects of Westernization have been avoided? To answer that question, it is helpful to consider separately each of the adverse effects already discussed.

Disease: Disease could never have been kept out except by keeping all Westerners from landing in Hawaii—which would have been impossible.

Loss of religion: The ancient Hawaiian religion was abandoned by the monarchy before there was any significant Western influence in Hawaii. The record of the rest of Polynesia is that Christianity sooner or later displaced native religions, and therefore it is reasonable to conclude that the Hawaiian religion would have been superseded sooner or later.

Morals: Like the Hawaiians' exposure to Western diseases, the negative moral example set by visiting seamen could have been avoided only by keeping the seamen out in the first place—which would have been impossible.

Sudden freedom: Commoners would probably have been freed sooner or later from at least most of their bondage to their chiefs and king, even if the basic social, political, and economic structure of precontact Hawaii had been kept intact. Most opinion today is strongly opposed to the type of bondage in which the makaainana were held by the alii prior to the adoption of the 1839 Bill of Rights—as it is strongly opposed to many of the practices of Americans 150 years ago, such as slavery in the South and the twelve-hour work day for children in the New England textile mills. Some degree of freedom was bound to come to Hawaiians as world opinion ceased to tolerate gross forms of human oppression.

So the first four adverse impacts were unavoidable. They were bound to be felt regardless of the policies that the Hawaiian leadership followed after contact. This leaves the last two aspects of Hawaiian life affected by contact, collectivism and communal land holding, as the only ones that might have conceivably been kept intact.

For the Hawaiians to continue to identify with the group, the extended family, or ohana, would have had to remain intact, and the only way the ohana could have remained intact was to avoid the economic developments that dispersed the extended family. In short, it would have been necessary for the subsistence farming and fishing economy of the ahupuaa to continue. This would have required maintaining the old land tenure system. Thus these last two aspects of impact were closely related.

If the ohana and communal system of land tenure had not been displaced, the Hawaiian economy and society would be much the same today as it was 150 years ago. In that case, Hawaii would not be the only place in the world that had stopped the clock for a century and a half. Tonga today has a society and economy very much like what it was 150 years ago and strikingly similar to the Hawaii of the 1840s. Like Hawaii then, Tonga has a king who governs with a House of Nobles composed of his chiefs and a lower house elected by the commoners; all land is owned by the crown; only about 2 percent of the one hundred thousand inhabitants are foreigners; Tongan society is still based on the extended family; and the economy is still based essentially on small-scale subsistence agriculture and fishing, producing the standard Polynesian diet of fish, taro, and yams.

It is extremely unlikely that Hawaii, with its strategic location and much larger size, could have kept the Westerners out. But if its leaders had pursued a keep-Hawaii-intact policy and if the world powers had permitted them to do it, the two kingdoms would have much in common today, including their standards of living and employment opportunities.

In 1983 Tonga's per capita gross national product was barely $700, whereas Hawaii's per capita gross product was in excess of $14,000— twenty times greater than Tonga's. By world income standards, Hawaii is close to the top and Tonga is close to the bottom.

Tonga's lack of technological development and its inability to produce exports of any consequence has meant a lack of growth in jobs, so that for decades it has been plagued with high levels of unemployment, relieved only by heavy out-migration as its surplus population seeks employment abroad that will produce a decent level of living. By contrast, Hawaii has been a net importer of labor during most periods for more than a hundred years. By world employment-opportunity standards, Hawaii is close to the top and Tonga is close to the bottom.

These two measures constitute a rough estimate of what the cost would have been of keeping the ohana intact to maintain the ancient Hawaiian culture and of keeping the ownership of all land out of private hands—had this scenario been possible.

Since the first four of the devastating impacts of Western contact could not have been avoided in any case, and since avoiding the last two would have condemned Hawaii to economic poverty, there seems to be little doubt but that the adaptive policies followed by Hawaii's leaders in the nineteenth century were vastly better, even for native Hawaiians, than the policies of preserving Polynesian customs followed by Tonga's leaders.

CHAPTER 3

The Plantation Economy,
circa 1876–1941

Rapid Demographic and Economic Growth

WITH THE RECIPROCITY TREATY finally in effect in 1876, the vast U.S. market was opened to Hawaii for duty-free entry of its sugar and other agricultural products. Security from hostile action by any of the other world powers that were busily carving up the Pacific was assured. The American connection propelled Hawaii into a period of rapid economic growth. By the time the United States entered World War II in 1941, the Hawaiian economy had developed from insignificance to what was one of the biggest plantation economies in the world, producing 4 percent of the world's sugar supply and 60 percent of the world's commercial pineapple pack. The basis of that success was a plantation agriculture by far the most productive and efficient in the world.

The phenomenal growth of Hawaii's population during this two-thirds of a century—starting when the islands' population had dropped to 54,000, its lowest point in recorded history—may be gauged by comparing it with that of the United States during the same period. In 1876 the United States consisted of only thirty-six states, with much of the West still to be won. The nation was just beginning to leave the sailing-ship era, the first transcontinental railway had been completed only a few years earlier, long-distance communication was by post or telegraph, local transportation was by horse and buggy, and houses were still lighted by oil lamps. In the next two-thirds of a century, until 1941, the country grew rapidly in population, with a vast immigration from Europe, and became the most powerful economy in the world.

Yet during the same span of time, while the U.S. population and labor force were increasing threefold, the population and labor force of Hawaii increased eightfold! The Hawaiian economy during the plantation era grew nearly three times as fast as the rapidly expanding U.S. economy.[1] By 1940, per capita personal income in Hawaii approximated that of the mainland United States, by far the world's wealthiest country: $577 in Hawaii and $592 for the entire country.[2] This extraordinary rise in income and the productivity that generated it was almost entirely the work of the sugar and pineapple plantations.

Sugar was already the main crop in Hawaii in 1876, but the Reciprocity Treaty led to a sustained expansion of production. At the time of the treaty the plantations were receiving gross returns on sugar sold in the United States that averaged about 6.5 cents per pound. The U.S. duty, deducted from the gross, averaged just over 3 cents per pound, thus cutting net returns by almost half. By freeing Hawaiian exports from American tariffs, reciprocity had the effect of almost doubling profits of the plantations.

Rising profits on the American market stimulated a rapid expansion of sugar acreage during the next sixty-five years, from 15,000 acres in 1876 to 238,000 acres in 1941—a nearly sixteenfold increase. And with higher productivity, the output of raw sugar rose from 13,000 tons to 947,000 tons, up nearly seventy-three-fold.

During this period, land planted in pineapple grew from practically nothing to 48,600 acres, and the 1940–41 pack amounted to more than 20 million cases—12 million cases of fruits and 8.5 million cases of juice.

In contrast to the 250,000 acres planted in sugarcane and pineapple, all other agriculture in Hawaii at the end of the period (excluding pasture land) used only about 12,000 acres—some 8,600 acres in coffee; about 1,000 each in papaya, macadamia nuts, and vegetables; some 600 in taro; and about 500 in rice.[3]

In 1941 one out of every three employed persons in Hawaii was on the payroll of a sugar or pineapple company,[4] and many in the rest of the civilian work force owed their jobs directly or indirectly to purchases of goods and services by the sugar and pineapple companies or their employees. With gross revenues of sugar and pineapple plantation companies in 1941 exceeding $135 million and with all the rest of agriculture and manufacturing combined generating only an estimated $35 million of product,[5] Hawaii's civilian economy was overwhelmingly dominated by the plantations. Only the expansion of the military in the last half of the 1930s kept the whole economy from being almost entirely based on sugar and pineapple. This chapter describes how this situation came about and analyzes its ramifications.

Sugar

CANE SUGAR AND ITS PRODUCTION

Throughout history, sugar has been a prized food, both for its sweet taste and for its high energy content. Until the blockade of Europe by the British during the Napoleonic wars forced development of the sugar beet, which grows in temperate zones, the prime source of sugar was sugarcane, which grows only in tropical and subtropical zones—honeys and edible syrups being of minor consequence. Sugar's historical importance is indicated by the fact that over 90 percent of the taxes collected in colonial America by the British came from the tariff on imported sugar, and until the introduction of personal and corporate income taxes in the United States early in the twentieth century, nearly half of all federal government revenues were derived from tariffs on imported commodities, the larger part of which were paid on sugar.[6]

In the mid-nineteenth century, when Hawaii's sugar industry was in its infancy, the demand–supply relationships in sugar were such that the price was extremely high compared with other prices, including those of land and labor. From around 1840 to the 1875 Reciprocity Treaty between Hawaii and the United States, the U.S. price of raw sugar was in the range of six to seven cents a pound, and was considerably higher during the Civil War, when supplies from Louisiana were cut off from the North.[7] In modern equivalents—using the national price indexes for the conversion—the price of raw sugar then was, at the price level of the 1980s, in the range of 60 to 70 cents a pound, whereas Civil War prices were around $1.70 a pound.

Sustained technological improvement made a large-scale sugar industry possible. Before mechanization of the industry, the production of cane sugar required an immense amount of hand labor—to prepare the fields, plant the cane, cultivate it through a long growing period, cut it, move it to the factory, and process it. Another requirement of sugar is an immense amount of water, calculated prior to World War II at about two tons of water for every pound of sugar produced.[8] This meant that a major factor in cane cultivation, in all but a few areas where there was very heavy rainfall, was an irrigation system that would bring copious amounts of water to the fields. These two needs—large amounts of labor and, for most plantations, extensive irrigation systems—gave a competitive advantage to large plantations over small, independent farmers.

Milling requirements also favored large plantations. Mills to crush juice from the cane require major capital investments. If a mill is to be well utilized, instead of lying idle much of the time, the fields must be planted on a schedule to produce fairly continuous harvesting. Such considerations make it advantageous to have the mill and the fields under one management in a vertically integrated industry. Only large mills can be cost-efficient, again dictating large-scale operations on the plantation.[9]

The word "plantation" connotes an agricultural colony. Historically, when a people colonized an area and started planting crops, that place was called a plantation. The term implied that those involved lived as a colony in some degree of self-sufficiency. Thus some of the British colonies in North America were known as plantations; in fact the official name of Rhode Island is "The State of Rhode Island and Providence Plantation." Southern cotton plantations were true plantations, with the owners and their slaves forming a colony that was largely self-sufficient—all living on the large estate and planting, growing, and harvesting the crop. When Hawaii's large sugar plantations developed, they also were true plantations.

In this sense, Koloa Plantation was not true to its name. Ladd & Co. went to Koloa, which was already a settled community, put up a mill, and hired local labor to plant and work the fields and to operate the mill. Many of the early sugar operations in Hawaii were simply mills that crushed the cane of local growers on a contract basis. Thus the 1843 contract between Governor Kuakini of Hawaii Island and A. H. Fayerweather, who had a sugar mill in Waimea, read as follows:

> That Kuakini shall plant sugarcane at Waimea and when the same shall be ripe, shall carry or cause the same to be carried to the Sugar Mill of A. H. Fayerweather at Waimea, and shall furnish men to do all the labor for same including the grinding, and shall furnish firewood for boiling the same. That A. H. Fayerweather shall furnish a mill for grinding the aforenamed cane, a Sugar Maker, and all the tools for making the sugar and molasses; and the sugar and molasses proceeds of the aforementioned cane shall be shared equally between said Kuakini and A. H. Fayerweather, one half to each."[10]

Over time, the integrated, full-scale plantation developed in Hawaii for the reasons mentioned. By 1882 the islands had fifty-two vertically integrated plantations, and also nine independent mills and twenty-six farms that grew only cane. By 1900 there remained only one independent mill and four farming-only operations.[11] Furthermore, economies of scale dictated that plantations become larger and larger. In 1880

Hawaiian sugar plantations averaged 413 acres, but with each passing decade that average increased by about 1,000 acres, so that by 1940 the average size of the thirty-eight Hawaiian sugar plantations was over 6,000 acres. In 1989 the average exceeds 14,000 acres.

Improvements in transporting cane from the field to the mill have been a major factor in the increased scale of operations, with the bullock carts of the mid-nineteenth century replaced, first by railroads on the irrigated plantations and by flumes on the unirrigated plantations, and then by huge trucks which ultimately took over the job everywhere.

LABOR SUPPLY

During most of the period from the start of commercial sugar cultivation in 1835 until the end of World War II more than a century later, Hawaiian plantations faced chronic labor shortages of serious proportions. The importation of workers required as field hands and the consequent repopulation of the islands with people from around the world had a profound impact on Hawaii, bringing together the most polyglot mixture of races.

The Local Labor Supply. William Hooper's experience at Koloa proved to him that native Hawaiians early in the nineteenth century were totally unskilled and unadapted to plantation work. As the years went by, however, they acquired the necessary skills and adapted to plantation work as their supervisors learned better methods of supervision, particularly when work by the task rather than by time (*ukupau*) was introduced in the 1850s.[12] In fact, "by the 1860s the native Hawaiian had lived down his reputation of being a wretched worker, and was conceded superior to imported labor."[13]

But native Hawaiians were in limited supply and their numbers were decreasing every year. Hawaii's population had dropped to 100,000 by the early 1840s, to 80,000 by the early 1850s, to 70,000 by 1860, to 60,000 by 1870, and to a low point of 54,000 in 1876, when the Reciprocity Treaty propelled the sugar industry into a period of rapid expansion. The only solution to the labor supply problem of the plantations was to import workers from overseas.

The Importation of Labor. From 1852 (when the Royal Hawaiian Agricultural Society brought the first 180 Chinese to Hawaii under contracts that provided that they work for five years at three dollars a month plus free food, housing, clothing, and medical care), until 1946 (when the Hawaiian Sugar Planters' Association in cooperation with the Pineapple Growers Association brought in a final 6,000 Filipinos), the total number of immigrant laborers recruited to Hawaii in organized groups amounted to an estimated 350,000.[14] Many of them returned home after their contracted time on the plantations and many others migrated on to the mainland United States or to Canada, but most stayed in Hawaii.

The organized importation of labor into Hawaii falls into three periods, depending upon the source of the immigrants. From 1851 to 1885 most of the laborers (about 30,000) were Chinese. In addition, some 2,500 South Sea islanders were recruited, plus around 600 Norwegians and more than 1,000 Germans. During this period a few Portuguese from the Madeiras were also recruited and one group of about 150 Japanese came in 1868. The Japanese, recruited in Yokohama, had many arguments about the terms of their contracts when they arrived in Hawaii; some returned home with the help of Charles Reed Bishop, founder of the predecessor of First Hawaiian Bank, for which he was awarded the Order of the Rising Sun, First Class, by Emperor Meiji.

From 1885 to 1908 most of the immigrants, some 140,000 in all, were Japanese, although there continued to be considerable Chinese immigration until annexation in 1898, when the Chinese Exclusion Act of the United States prohibited Chinese from entering the territory of Hawaii. In addition, during that period some 15,000 immigrants came from the Madeiras, 5,000 from Puerto Rico, 7,000 from Korea, 2,000 from Spain, and a sprinkling of Russians from Siberia, Hindus from India, African Americans from Tennessee, and Caucasians from New York and San Francisco.

The nature of the labor contract changed when Hawaii became a territory of the United States. The Thirteenth Amendment to the Constitution prohibited any form of involuntary servitude, thereby invalidating the standard Hawaiian labor contracts that required a multiyear period of service. To emphasize the ban, Congress in 1900 passed an act specifically prohibiting the importation into Hawaii of "foreigners or aliens under contract agreement to perform labor."[15] All laborers imported after annexation were therefore free to leave their jobs at will. About one-half of the 350,000 plantation laborers imported into Hawaii came in under these free-labor contracts.

The Hawaii Immigration Board, formed to administer overseas recruitment, then concentrated its efforts on Caucasian workers, but with only limited success. In 1909–10 some 2,000 more Russians from Manchuria and nearly 1,000 Iberians arrived—not nearly enough to fill the labor needs of the plantations. Because federal law barred the importation of Chinese and Japanese, that left the Philippines as "the only available source of a permanent labor supply."[16] The Hawaiian Sugar Planters' Association (HSPA) established a recruiting office in Manila and a Division of Filipino Affairs in Hawaii to get arriving laborers to the plantation, arrange to bring in their wives and up to two children, if desired, to provide return passage after completion of the work contract, and to make other arrangements.[17] Between 1909 and 1934, when the Philippines Independence Act stopped further Filipino migration to the United States, 118,449 Filipino workers were brought to Hawaii by the HSPA.[18] A specific exemption permitted a final group of some 6,000 to come to Hawaii in 1946 to help meet the critical labor shortage created by World War II.[19]

In addition to the organized importation of labor into Hawaii for work on the plantations, a large but unrecorded number of workers came on their own. Some of these, such as Chinese in the nineteenth century and Filipinos in the twentieth, came primarily for unskilled jobs, but many other people migrated to Hawaii for skilled jobs on the plantations. The skilled workers included a number of Scottish engineers and bookkeepers (many of whom later became managers) and several German sugar chemists who came to supervise the delicate operation of boiling the cane juice into sugar.

The overall success of plantation labor recruitment, and its consequences, can be illustrated in many ways. Briefly, more people were on sugar plantation payrolls in 1928 than there had resided in all of Hawaii fifty years earlier, when large-scale labor immigration was getting under way. And those 56,000 sugar employees in 1928 had approximately 50,000 dependents, raising the plantation population to more than 100,000—almost a third of the entire civilian population of the territory.

Evaluation of Hawaii's Labor Importation Practices. There is continuing debate in Hawaii as to how well the public and private authorities responsible for overseas labor recruitment were able to avoid the inhumanities that through the ages have been associated with trafficking in common labor, particularly when that labor is indentured. Pondering this issue, I have come to the following conclusions:

1. The Board of Immigration tried hard to avoid such inhumanities.

2. Under the circumstances, however, there was no practical way that the indentured laborers who were brought to Hawaii to work on the sugar plantations could have been effectively protected from mistreatment by insensitive employers or overseers.

3. The fact that the laborers were indentured instead of free undoubtedly encouraged insensitivity to them and mistreatment of them by the employer class.

4. Although both the Hawaiian government and the sugar industry leaders were convinced that the penal labor contract was necessary, both would probably have been better served if it had never been in Hawaiian law.

5. In spite of all this and as bad as working conditions were on some of the plantations, the immigrant laborers who came to Hawaii for contract work were generally better off in the short run than their fellow workers who stayed home, and most of them were certainly far better off in the long run.

The initial large-scale recruitment, from 1864 to 1909 under the Hawaii Board of Immigration, was mandated by Kamehameha V to follow "the dictates of humanity." The smaller importation of Chinese that preceded the board's existence was managed by the Royal Hawaiian Agricultural Society, whose founder, first president, and most influential member was William L. Lee, chief justice of the Hawaiian Supreme Court, a man presumably of high humanitarian standards.[20]

Contracts governing the employer–employee relationship were set by the government rather than by the employer and had as their basis the Masters and Servants Act of the kingdom, which provided basic protections for the worker. "In keeping with the liberal spirit of the Hawaiian constitution, a number of provisions designed to prevent the abuses characteristic of bound service were written into the Masters and Servants Act of 1850," comments labor historian Edward Beechert.

Contract employees were entitled to the full protection of their civil liberties by the judicial system. In contracts made with adults in Hawaii and in those made with persons in a foreign country, "cruelty, misusage, or violation of the terms of the contract" served to invalidate the contract after a hearing before any district magistrate (sec. 1423). A fine ranging from five to one hundred dollars could be levied against the master (sec. 1423). . . . No contract could be written outside of Hawaii which contravened the laws of Hawaii, and such contracts were limited to a maximum of ten years, the period of service to begin on the day of arrival in Hawaii (sec. 1418). In practice, contracts were most often written for three-year terms, occasionally for five years, regardless of where the contract was signed.[21]

The Masters and Servants Act was significantly amended in 1872 to humanize it in ways detailed in the 1903 report of the U.S. commissioner of labor on labor conditions in Hawaii:

> The amendments of 1872 greatly improved the legal status of contract men. Though the courts condemned the practice as illegal, the old ship custom of flogging laborers for disorder or disobedience still obtained on some plantations. It was impossible to secure the conviction of the guilty parties in such cases, because the flogging was not done in the presence of witnesses. The first of the amendments . . . made the complainant—i.e., the laborer—a competent witness . . . and provided for his discharge from his contract and for fining and imprisoning the employer if he proved his case. A second amendment rendered a contract by a married woman invalid. . . . The third amendment provided that when a servant was sentenced by a court to make up time lost by desertion, he should be paid for such time at the rate stipulated by the contract. The fourth amendment, which was evidently intended to prevent peonage, prohibited masters from holding a servant to work beyond the expiration of his regular term of service for any debt or advance made during the period of the contract.[22]

Labor recruits from Japan were under at least the nominal supervision of the Japanese government. Under the terms of an 1885 convention with Hawaii, Japan maintained an inspector of immigration in the islands to see that employers abided by the contract terms previously approved by Tokyo. The Hawaii Board of Immigration in 1886 appointed its own inspector general over contract labor, assigning inspectors and interpreters to each plantation island. Laborers were told to make any complaints to these inspectors, who visited each plantation at least once every six months. During inspections, the quality of housing, clothing, food, and medical attention were to be examined. The board "reminded the planters that the law forbade any employer or overseer to strike or lay hands upon any contract laborer who was imported under the Bureau of Immigration regulations. Apart from being counterproductive, such actions were illegal and when confirmed would be grounds for the withdrawal of all labor assigned to such persons."[23] In its 1886

report the board claimed that this system would "secure the cordial com-
mendation, not only of the several governments interested, but of all
enlightened nations everywhere."[24]

Safeguards devised by the Hawaii legislature and the Board of Immigration to insure humane treatment of immigrant labor looked good on
paper but were apparently largely ineffectual in practice. Prior to 1886,
when the inspection system was established, contract provisions were
enforced through the twenty-four district courts; and access to the
courts was almost the exclusive prerogative of the employer. As a result,
thousands of cases of desertion were brought before the courts by
employers[25] but few cases of mistreatment were brought by workers.
This imbalance was due not to the absence of mistreatment by overseers
on some of the plantations, but rather to the fact that the only way
a worker could file a complaint with the court was to absent himself
from his work—and this would lay him open to the serious charge of
desertion.[26]

The government inspection system, together with the inspections
made by Japanese and Portuguese inspectors, was apparently almost
equally ineffective. When the new system was announced, planters notified the Board of Immigration that they were strongly opposed to it and
thought it to be "uncalled for, extrajudicial, and unconstitutional";[27]
but after some experience with it the Hilo Planters' Association notified
the board that the inspectors were "unassuming, prudent, just and useful."[28] Doubtless, the planters were able to show the inspectors only
what they wanted them to see and the workers were probably too intimi-
dated to make complaints in front of their overseers. As a result, the
inspectors (who were fed, housed, and entertained by the managers on
their inspection trips) tended to side with management. For example, in
1889 the Japanese inspector found that although there had been a hundred desertions in one area, only thirty deserters had been apprehended,
and he therefore recommended that the legislature "change the law so as
to make the act of deserting by contract laborers more heavily punish-
able."[29] The 1890 report of the Hawaii inspector general stated that
there was no sugar-growing country in the world where plantation labor
was better treated than in Hawaii.

The statement of the inspector general was probably true, partly
because of the regulations of the Board of Immigration, but more importantly because a large part of the plantation work force consisted of free

labor, which had to be treated with respect and which tended to set the pattern for treatment of all labor. The 1903 report of the U.S. commissioner of labor makes this point:

> It must be remembered that the free or day laborers were nearly as numerous as those under contract; that both classes were working side by side in the field, and that the same manner of handling must be used with both to a large extent. Furthermore, the cost of importing new men was very heavy, and consequently every farsighted manager was studying to maintain such conditions among his employees as would make his day laborers remain and lead as many as possible of his contract men to "reship" with him when their period of service was over. More than 45 percent of the 23,000 field hands on Hawaiian plantations in 1897, the year before annexation, were day men, and the policy of managers in relations with their laborers could hardly fail to be guided by this fact.
>
> There seems no ground, therefore, for believing that the former contract system in Hawaii was a system of quasi-servitude for laborers after the reforms of 1872, or that it was marked by extreme injustice or brutality. Europeans who have worked under it seem to regard it with no special antipathy. A man who had himself risen from the position of field cultivator to the highest rank of plantation administration, stated that he had seen more abuse of men in a single watch upon an American sailing vessel that in 21 years of life in the Hawaiian cane fields. It was not a system that an American would care to work under, or one that it would be practical to revive, but it ought not to go down in history burdened with any particular odium.[30]

Nonetheless there is no doubt that some of the overseers on some of the plantations were hard on workers and that brutal corporal punishment, while strictly forbidden by law and by regulation, was resorted to on occasion. This was due partly to the very nature of a system of bound service, which invites and encourages abuse. Free labor can respond to mistreatment in various ways, the mildest being to walk off the job and not come back. But an indentured laborer, unless he can obtain redress through some channel, has to stay and take the mistreatment. Further, since the labor contract was also binding on the employer, this removed his normal response when a worker turned out to be unsatisfactory—dismissing him. What was a manager to do if a field hand was lazy, inept, uncooperative, or insubordinate, as inevitably some of the immigrant workers proved to be? Or what was to be done if the employer's rough and ready, drill-sergeant style of management outraged a worker who under better management might be a fine employee? The answer is that if the manager could not get rid of him, he tended to get tough with him. Getting tough generally meant mistreatment and physical abuse.

An example of how a manager might be led to use illegal methods of punishment was related in the 1903 report on Hawaii of the U.S. commissioner of labor:

> A manager . . . related a personal experience of this character [dealing with an employee who was "unusually refractory"] which may be taken as typical of what occurred at times without exciting much comment. Among a lot of recently arrived contract laborers he received two Japanese who were apparently from the criminal class of their own country. These men, whose passage money had been advanced by the plantation, refused to work as agreed in their contracts, and deserted repeatedly, so that the rewards and court charges for their apprehension and restoration to the plantation amounted in a short time to a sum considerably greater than their services promised ever to compensate. When the men were brought back one evening by a police officer after their last desertion, the manager, who had heretofore used only strictly legal methods with the men, took them back of his house and gave each a sound horsewhipping, and then ordered his own cook to give them a good meal in his own kitchen. After the men had finished their supper they both voluntarily came around to the veranda where the manager was sitting, salaamed profoundly, expressed their thanks, and went to their quarters. One remained on the plantation until his contract expired three years later, and the other worked for eight years—five years after his contract was out —for the same manager. Neither ever gave him the least trouble afterwards. This was the whipping that settled the school on that plantation, but, as the manager himself admitted, there were ten chances of failure to one of success in adopting such a policy.[31]

Mistreatment, unsuitability for plantation labor, failure to adjust to a totally different way of life, and other factors persuaded many workers to take the drastic and illegal action of leaving their jobs. Desertions were remarkably frequent; between 1875 and 1900 more than 42 thousand cases of desertion were brought before the district courts. The conviction rate ran about 85 percent.[32]

Nevertheless, according to Beechert, who has studied the history of plantation labor with great thoroughness and who viewed what he saw through the eyes of a former labor union man, "many of the immigrant workers found the general situation reasonably satisfactory" and that "indeed, a majority of those imported remained as sugar workers beyond their initial term, usually as free workers" (p. 325).

This contradictory outcome of the system—with tens of thousands of contract workers so dissatisfied that they deserted their jobs knowing that in all probability they would be hauled into court and forced back to the plantation, and other tens of thousands sufficiently satisfied with their jobs to remain on the plantation after their initial contracts had expired—strongly suggests that the workers, the employers, and the government would all have been better off if there had been no such thing as bound labor in Hawaii. Instead of bringing in immigrant labor under a criminally enforceable contract, the Board of Immigration and the plantations would have been wiser to have given much more care to the selection of the workers imported. As a case in point, one of the first groups recruited by the board comprised the 149 Japanese who came in 1868, selected by the Hawaiian consul general in Japan, Eugene Van Reed. When the workers proved to be unsatisfactory and discontented, he explained that they had had no agricultural work experience and that they were "mere laborers who had been picked out of the streets of Yokohama, sick, exhausted, and filthy and without clothing to cover decency."[33] A careful selection of the immigrant workers to be brought to Hawaii, and bringing them in as free workers, would certainly have given the plantations a far more productive work force than they got under the indentured labor contract system. The experience of the HSPA in doing just that with its recruitment of some 118 thousand Filipino workers between 1909 and 1934 proves the point.

Another example of bad recruitment occurred in 1884 when, in an effort to Europeanize the Hawaiian population, some 600 Norwegians were recruited—blond people who had spent their lives close to the Arctic Circle, eminently unsuited for ten-hour days under the tropical sun. To compound the difficulty of adjustment, these Norwegian recruits were unemployed artisans and craftsmen from metropolitan areas. Predictably, they found plantation work life totally unacceptable. The complaining letters they wrote home were so persuasive that Sweden (which then included Norway) sent its foreign minister to investigate. Minister Anton Grip found the Norwegians' complaints largely ill-founded. In his opinion, their working conditions, food, and housing were all acceptable. His conclusion was that the problems were caused by the fact that the immigrants were townspeople, unsuited by their background, training, and experience for agricultural work.[34]

According to Beechert, Grip's conclusion was in accord with that reached by other diplomats who came to Hawaii to investigate complaints of immigrants, and who generally found them to be largely without foundation.[35] Again, the careful selection of Filipinos by the Manila office of the HSPA after 1909, when it recruited free labor to work on the plantations, showed that for plantation work, as for any other kind, it is essential to recruit the right type of person for the job. Haphazardly picking out bodies, as the Board of Immigration apparently did, led to disastrous results.

Blame for mistreatment of plantation workers rests in large part on the undeveloped state at that time of the art of industrial psychology. Not until close to the end of the nineteenth century were new concepts of individual differences applied to industry. The idea that individual differences suit different people for different kinds of work, at low-level jobs as well as high, was a concept totally unknown during Hawaii's penal contract labor period. Any young and healthy body would do.

Another part of the blame must be borne by the drafters of the Masters and Servants Act. At mid-century, when it was adopted, there was little thought of using it for immigrant labor; it was enacted primarily to provide an apprenticeship system and to enforce some work discipline on native Hawaiians. At that time the typical working-class Hawaiian would far prefer to spend a few hours a day raising his taro and sweet potatoes and catching his fish than to work from dawn to dusk for money. It was thought that without the Masters and Servants Act to force him to stay on the job, the Hawaiian would continue to be "lazy." When a few years later the time came to import labor for plantation work, this was the accepted form of labor contract in Hawaii—and there were no industrial psychologists to explain that it would have been far better to recruit free immigrant labor.

Many people in Hawaii objected to the indentured labor contract, but on moral grounds (because it condoned involuntary servitude) rather than for the practical reason that it was an inefficient and costly way to organize a work force. No one argued that free labor would outproduce bound labor by a wide margin.

One more observation may be made about Hawaii's program to import labor. A government objective of replacing the declining native population sometimes got in the way of the plantations' labor-supply objective. Islanders from the New Hebrides, the Gilberts, and other areas of the South Seas were no more suited to work on the plantations than city dwellers from Norway. But both South Sea islanders and Europeans were recruited because it was thought that they would restock and improve Hawaii's depleted population.

In this search for a genetic and cultural diversity of people to inhabit Hawaii, the government was right. Repopulated from the four corners of the earth instead of from a single nation, Hawaii got a population mixture in which no ethnic group constitutes anything close to a majority. This, combined with the cultural heritage of the racially tolerant Hawaiian, has made Hawaii a unique place. We are indebted to the Board of Immigration for repopulating Hawaii with a wide diversity of people, but have to fault it for not selecting the immigrants on the basis of their suitability for agricultural work and for not bringing them in as free workers.

Although many of the immigrant laborers were unsuited for the work they were assigned in Hawaii and although life on some of the plantations must have been unsatisfactory for many of them, as a group the workers were better off than if they had stayed home. Many found success on the plantations as they moved up the occupational and economic ladder. A study of the racial distribution of supervisory and skilled jobs on the sugar plantations in 1899 showed that of the 791 overseers, fewer than half (362) were American or European, the majority being Hawaiian, Portuguese, Japanese, and Chinese, in that order. Nearly half the bookkeepers and sugar boilers were non-Caucasian, and in the skilled trades of carpentry, masonry, and blacksmithing more than half the total were Japanese. The only skilled jobs in which the Caucasians were clearly dominant were those of harness maker and chemist—and, of course, the plantation manager himself.[36]

Even for the majority who stayed on the plantations in unskilled work, "the standard of living of the Hawaiian plantation family was no doubt considerably higher than that of the agricultural worker in Japan,"[37] and unquestionably higher than that of the agricultural worker in China. The 1903 report on labor conditions in Hawaii by the U.S. commissioner of labor stated that a Japanese plantation worker "can save as much from his wages in a year in Hawaii as in the better part of a lifetime in some of the rural districts of his own country."[38] And the 1911 report stated that immigrant plantation workers in Hawaii were sending home in excess of one million dollars a year.[39]

But the big advantage of coming to Hawaii was the promise for the future. After three years on the plantation, the immigrant worker became a free laborer who could move up the occupational ladder as high as his efforts and abilities permitted him—granted that until after World War II some jobs might have been closed to him. Many first-generation immigrants went far; even more importantly, their children were American citizens, eligible for a free education through high school. An impressively large number of immigrant laborers, even when drawing pay as unskilled plantation workers, were able to save enough to send their children to college. Many a wealthy and educated resident of Hawaii of oriental ancestry has traveled back to Japan or China and, observing the poor agricultural peasant tending his rice field, has said quietly to himself, "There, but for my grandfather, go I."

PRODUCTIVITY

The most outstanding characteristic of the Hawaiian sugar industry throughout the century and a half of its existence has been its initiative in finding ways to increase productivity, year after year and decade after decade.

William Hooper at Koloa planted 25 acres in cane in 1835 and with a work force of 400 people succeeded in producing two tons of sugar when he harvested his first crop in 1837, or about one-twelfth of a ton of sugar per acre. On the assumption that half his employees worked in sugar, that yield was equivalent to about one ton of sugar for 100 sugar workers. In 1843, after Charles Burnham, who knew something about sugar cultivation and grinding, had replaced Hooper and after a new mill had been built, Koloa averaged three-fourths ton of sugar per acre.[40]

By 1874, a third of a century later, the Hawaiian sugar industry was producing 12,000 tons of sugar on 12,000 acres in cane, or one ton per acre. And with total sugar employment at under 4,000, it was averaging three tons for every worker.[41]

By 1941, two-thirds of a century later, the industry was annually producing just under a million tons of sugar on 238,000 acres—almost four tons per cultivated acre. It was doing this with a work force of 36,000, which meant that workers averaged 27 tons per year.[42]

Today, a half century later, production remains about a million tons a year; but the land in cane has dropped to 187,000 acres, yielding about five and a half tons per cultivated acre, and the work force has decreased to about 7,000, which translates into nearly 143 tons per employee per year.[43]

The average daily wage for sugar workers in 1835 was 12.5 cents; for

1874 it is estimated at 45 cents; for 1941, $2.18; and in 1986 it was $68.72, with an additional $35.40 in fringe benefits—all figures being in current dollars.[44] The Hawaiian sugar industry now pays an average worker more than $100 a day. To afford a wage of that level, when most other sugar workers in the tropics make only a few dollars a day, Hawaii has to have the most efficient sugar industry in the world.

That productivity has long been recognized. A 1917 study by the U.S. Department of Commerce on the cane sugar industry stated that in Hawaii "the most scientific and intensive system of cultivation is practiced. . . . Hawaii represents the best efforts of the United States . . . in the cultivation of sugarcane and in the manufacture of sugar."[45] The U.S. Department of Agriculture has frequently compared the geographic areas of the American sugar industry with respect to productivity. Its findings in 1965 are typical: the number of man-hours required to produce a ton of sugar were 12.50 in Hawaii, 25.80 in Florida, 37.50 in Louisiana, and 81.40 in Puerto Rico.[46]

Attaining such eminence in production required the application of scientific methods of growing and milling sugar. Starting in the mid-nineteenth century from a primitive base of technology—using neither fertilizers nor irrigation, grinding the cane between homemade wooden rollers turned by a horse or bullock trodding in a circle, boiling the juice over open fires in the "try pots" used by whalers to render blubber—the infant Hawaiian industry produced a sugar of such dubious quality that it sometimes fetched only a losing price in the California market.[47]

When the Royal Hawaiian Agricultural Society was formed in 1850, one of its first committees stated in a report on sugar production in the islands:

> It is a fact worthy of remark that . . . all the sugar plantations that have been commenced at these islands have been so commenced by persons possessing neither experience . . . nor the requisite capital and knowledge of the soil, to carry it through to a successful result. Large sums of money have been thrown away, experiments which the experience of persons acquainted with the business would have enabled them to avoid, and no system of intercourse between the planters has been established by which the experience of one could be rendered available to another. . . . To meet these difficulties, to provide for these wants, to render the experience of other countries available to this, to supply by a combined action, facilities and information *to all*, which cannot be procured by individuals, to encourage and foster agricultural operations in every form, are the main objects of the proposed association.[48]

After that decisive effort was made to organize the industry for the mutual advantage of the plantations, processes and procedures in the growing and milling of sugarcane in Hawaii improved continually, to the point that the local sugar industry became the model for the world to emulate. Even an abridged history of its technological advances is impressive.

The first big breakthrough was development of the centrifugal machine for separating the sugar crystals from the molasses. The centrifugal effectively separated sugar from molasses in minutes, in contrast to the crude method it replaced which had taken weeks. It was brought to Hawaii in 1853 and was greatly improved by David M. Watson, who later founded the foundry and machine shop that became the Honolulu Iron Works, a firm that over the next hundred years developed a great deal of machinery for both the sugar and the pineapple industries.

The next landmark was the introduction of a better variety of cane, called the "Lahaina." A Maui planter in 1854 imported some sugarcane cuttings from Tahiti[49] which proved to be far superior to the old Hawaiian variety. Lahaina was the main variety of cane used commercially for the next half century.

Irrigation of cane fields started at Lihue Plantation on Kauai in 1856, when Father Rice built a ditch at the cost of $7,000 to tap the Hanamaulu stream near its source to bring water some eleven miles to his fields.[50]

As soon as railroad transportation became feasible, it replaced the draft animal for moving cane from the fields to the mill. The first plantation rail systems were built in the early 1870s, and by the end of the 1930s the islands had thirty-nine complete railway systems—thirty-two on the plantations and seven independent ones that were used mainly to haul sugar. These rail systems had more than 1,200 miles of permanent track and another 300 miles of portable track for getting deep into the fields during the harvesting.[51]

Steam power for the mill, introduced at Lihue in 1853, rapidly replaced the bullock and horse and in time replaced the water wheel.[52] Likewise, the steam plow replaced the mule-drawn plow on most level fields.

The vacuum pan, invented in England in 1813, was first used at the Kaupakuea Plantation (later called Pepeekeo) on the Big Island in 1861— a development that rivaled the centrifuge in its value to the industry. Boiling the cane juice in a partial vacuum at temperatures much lower than 212 degrees, the pan diminished chances of scorching the sugar while increasing both the quality and the quantity of the sugar recovered.[53]

Nor was this all. A 1926 pamphlet of the Hawaiian Sugar Planters' Association listed fifteen local inventions for producing cane sugar that have been of world importance. Named after their inventors, all of whom worked in the Hawaiian sugar industry, were such devices as the Messchaert Juice Grooves in rollers, the Searby Shredder, the Ewart Bagasse Conveyor, the Ramsay Maceration Scraper, the Meinecke Chutes, Peck's Revolving Juice Screen, and the Hind Hubless Knife for leveling sugarcane in the carrier.[54]

The new mechanical devices and improved scientific procedures were generally first tried at one plantation and then rapidly adopted by the others. Throughout their history, the plantations have been cooperative and open rather than competitive and secretive. This is manifest in the development through the HSPA's experiment station, established in 1895, of a host of scientific procedures and processes, only a few of which are described in the following sections.

New Plant Varieties. Early in the twentieth century the commonly planted Lahaina variety of cane began to be affected by a root rot disease that threatened the very existence of the industry. Other varieties were quickly imported, but none was successful under Hawaiian soil and weather conditions. The industry then turned to crossbreeding a new variety that would combine the high sugar content of the Lahaina with the disease resistance of other varieties. The HSPA experiment station quickly developed the famous H-109 strain, which was planted widely in the first decades of the century.

But H-109 was not suited to all Hawaiian soil and weather conditions, and like all cane varieties it tended to become less productive over the years as it was replanted for successive crops. The experiment station therefore continued its breeding program, producing about one million new seedlings a year, out of which one or two might assume commercial importance.[55]

Insect Control. Hawaii's sugar industry suffered no serious problems from insect damage during the nineteenth century because the local cane originally used on the plantations, grown over a long period by native growers, had a genetic resistance to local insects. So had the new Lahaina variety from Tahiti, but the continued importation of plant material from around the world, without a quarantine, inevitably brought in exotic bugs, some of which proved troublesome.[56] One, the sugarcane leaf hopper, was found on Oahu in 1900 and quickly spread to all the islands. Multiplying by the billions, the insects could be heard swarming from afar. Descending on a field, they would soon kill the cane, leaving it blackened and withered. Pahala Plantation on the Big Island was hit particularly hard. It harvested 18,888 tons in 1903, but only 1,620 tons in 1905 and 826 tons in 1906.

The HSPA experiment station sent entomologists to the sugar fields of Queensland, Australia, where they collected specimens of a tiny parasite that, laying its eggs in the leaf hopper, checked its monstrous reproduction. Introduced in the Hawaii fields, the parasite reduced the leaf hopper plague to manageable size. That success was repeated over the decades in checking other insect invaders, notably the importation of the New Guinea Tachinid fly to parasitize the highly destructive sugarcane borer.

The establishment in Hawaii of a strict plant quarantine system in 1903 further limited, but could never eliminate, insect damage to the sugarcane. For the most part the sugar plantations have continued to rely on methods of biological control, rather than turning to chemical poisons, which in the twentieth century have become the fix of most American agriculture—quick and easy, but polluting and in the long run more expensive.

Irrigation. Sugarcane grows best when it gets abundant sun and water, and nature provides few areas that supply both. Although at one time or another the northeastern coasts of all the major Hawaiian islands had sugar plantations, the many days of overcast made operations uneconomical and ultimately all failed. The roughly 40 percent of Hawaii's cane land that receives adequate rainfall does not get enough sunshine to make those plantations high producers.

The ideal location is sunny, which usually means that the cane will not receive the annual rainfall of ten feet that it needs. With some 60 percent of Hawaii's cane land having insufficient rainfall, there has been a strong emphasis on irrigation since Lihue Plantation put in the first system in 1856. Hawaii's sugar plantations then developed irrigation systems unequalled in any other sugar growing area of the world.

These systems ingeniously tap the three sources of fresh water in Hawaii: mountain streams; water perched in impervious basalt catchments on mountainsides, called dikes; and the basal water table under each island. Examples of systems using each of the three sources for sugar-field irrigation are the Hamakua Ditch (tapping mountain streams), the Waiahole water system (tapping dikes), and the Hawaiian Commercial and Sugar Company "Pump 7" (bringing water to the surface from the fresh water lens underground).

The Hamakua Ditch on Maui is famous because it was the first major irrigation system that did more than divert water from a nearby stream, demonstrating that large areas of dry, worthless land could be made highly productive if sufficient quantities of water could be brought to them.[57] It also demonstrated the vision, perseverance, and energy of the New England Yankees—merchant traders, former sea captains, and descendants of early missionaries—who were largely responsible for the early development of the sugar industry here.

In 1870 Samuel T. Alexander and Henry P. Baldwin, sons of missionaries, started a sugar plantation in the northern end of the dry central valley that lies between Maui's two mountain ranges. Although the rainfall was greater than in the central part of the valley, it was insufficient for good cane culture and subject to periodic droughts. When the Reciprocity Treaty with the United States was negotiated, the two young men decided the future of sugar looked so good that it would be worth the expense to bring upland water from the slopes of Haleakala down to their fields. They persuaded their Honolulu agents, Castle & Cooke, to lend them $25,000 to construct what was called the Big Ditch. Work started in September 1876 and was completed two years later, creating a seventeen-mile aqueduct, partly open ditch, partly tunnel, and partly iron pipe, that moved 40 million gallons of water a day to their plantation. Some 200 workmen were involved in the project, and Henry Baldwin supervised it from start to finish—even though shortly before its start he lost his right arm in an accident at his sugar mill.

Vandercook describes the ditch as being "beautifully successful and immensely profitable."[58] A correspondent at the time called it a "watery Bonanza." The fact that it ended up costing $80,000 instead of the planned $25,000 did not matter.[59] It would have been a bargain at twice the cost.

The Waiahole irrigation system is a good example of how dike water has been tapped. The Oahu Sugar Company fields on the arid central leeward plains of Oahu near Pearl Harbor required an immense amount of irrigation. Plans to provide the water were started in 1905, construction began in 1913, and the system was completed in 1916. Twenty-two miles long, it links forty-five tunnels in the Koolau Mountains that wind from the mountains' windward side down from an elevation of about 800 feet to exit in leeward Oahu in the vicinity of Wahiawa. This system carries an average of 40 million gallons of water a day, and in rainy periods as much as 125 million gallons.

The basal fresh water lens underlying Oahu was first tapped by James Campbell at his cattle ranch on the dry Ewa plain just west of Pearl Harbor in 1879. Campbell had already made a fortune with his Pioneer Mill sugar plantation at Lahaina, Maui, and could afford to bring a well driller from San Francisco to see if water could be found in Ewa. The drilling was successful and tapped artesian water which, from internal pressure, forced its way to the surface without being pumped.[60] Most basal water in Hawaii lacks this artesian pressure and has to be pumped to the surface. Pratt lists 347 wells that were drilled by sugar companies in Hawaii between 1883 and 1933, an average of almost seven a year over fifty years.[61]

Once irrigation water—from mountain streams, dikes, or the basal water table—reaches the field, various distribution methods, improved over the years, take it to the growing plants. In the pre–World War II era, distribution was generally by furrows trenched in the ground. Water was directed to the plants about every two weeks, enough to soak the soil to about fourteen inches. After the war many fields were irrigated by overhead sprinklers, but the major innovation was the "drip" or "trickle" method, turned to by many plantations in the early 1970s. In this technique, small pipes perforated with tiny holes are laid between rows of cane at the time of planting. They deliver the irrigation water about every other day directly to the roots of the growing cane. The plastic pipes have to be replaced with each new planting of cane, but they are cheap and efficient, saving water by reducing evaporation, and saving both labor and fertilizer by delivering water-soluble chemicals to the roots. The industry's average yield rose to 12.5 tons of sugar per harvested acre by 1986, with some drip-irrigated fields producing up to 20 tons. By world standards, these are astonishingly high yields.

Plowing the Fields and Transporting the Cane. The use by island plantations of steam plows for tilling the soil and of railroads for transporting the cane from the fields to the mill were outstanding successes in the application of mechanical power to replace animal power in agriculture.

When Hawaii's shipments of raw sugar to the United States in 1887 exceeded 100,000 tons for the first time, *Harper's Weekly* was prompted to send a correspondent to the "Sandwich Islands" to investigate its sugar industry. The reporter, Lee Meriwether, was familiar with cane sugar operations in Louisiana and drew comparisons to illustrate the high level of technology used by the sugar industry in Hawaii at that time. "[T]he Spreckels plantation on Maui [now the Hawaiian Commercial and Sugar Co.] is on so vast a scale that the methods in vogue on Louisiana plantations would be entirely inadequate," Meriwether wrote.

> The huge steam ploughs that go bowling over the miles of fields on Maui turn over more ground in a day than ordinary ploughs on other plantations turn in a week. With oxen it would take a month to bring to the mills the cane that the Spreckels plantation railroads bring in a single day. Forty miles of railroad traverse the fields, and four locomotives with long trains of cars transport the cane to the mills. In addition to the regular lines of railroad, sections of portable track are thrown in various directions as needed . . . thus enabling the cane to be brought by rail to the mills from the most remote parts of the plantation.[62]

Cutting and Loading the Cane. Historically, the hardest, most back-breaking, most labor-intensive, and costliest jobs in the production of cane sugar have been cutting the ripe cane and loading it onto the vehicle that would take it to the mill for grinding. Until the 1930s practically all this was done by hand, as, half a century later, it still is in many Third World tropical countries.

Loading the cut cane was the first part of this operation to be mechanized. Grab hooks were put in use by the Hawaii sugar industry to pick up the cane in the fields and pile it into railroad cars or trucks. The model introduced was uneconomically small, and so the local industry developed much larger grabs that were attached to crawler cranes.[63] At about the same time "piling rakes" were developed to collect the cut cane into piles for the grab hooks to pick up. By the end of the 1930s, mechanized piling and loading of cane were standard practice throughout the Hawaiian sugar industry.

Mechanizing the cane-cutting operation presented more difficulties. Here is how Vandercook (p. 29) describes the problem:

> A mature cane field is a tangled mess. A certain superficial resemblance to a field of standing corn vanishes on closer examination. Corn stands up. Cane, half of it, sprawls down, lies every which way. Some stalks,

growing to a length of twenty or even thirty feet, will reach along the ground for two-thirds of their length, then perk up in a final right angle. Many cane fields are littered with stones. Some of the best cane land in Hawaii is on steep hillsides. Fields fifty yards apart are divided by gorges so sheer that the effective journey between them is one of miles. . . . [Mechanizing the cutting operation] has long been a problem that has baffled the skill of engineers.

The first mechanical harvesting of cane in Hawaii came in 1937, when it was found that the hook used in loading could, with some modification, grab a bunch of standing cane which would then break off where the stalks connected with the roots. This method eliminated cutting and piling, but it introduced vast amounts of soil, trash, and stones to the mill and made the cleaning operation much more difficult.

The next innovation, an invention of Herbert Watson of Waialua, was introduced in 1938—the "Waialua Rake."[64] This device consisted of a rake attached by steel cables to two tractors which pulled it through the field, breaking the cane off at the roots and leaving it in piles for loading. Again, the rake introduced much trash into the mill.

By the end of the 1930s about a fifth of the fields were being harvested mechanically, while the rest were still being hand cut but mechanically piled and loaded.[65] And the HSPA experiment station was still hard at work on the problem.

The Continuous Planting, Growing, and Harvesting Cycle. Paradoxically, another factor that has helped raise the productivity of Hawaii's sugar industry above other cane areas of the world is that in Hawaii the cane takes an average of nearly two years to reach maturity, about double the growing time needed elsewhere in the tropics. Hawaii's climate, not truly tropical although the islands lie just below the Tropic of Cancer, is modified by winter storms that move across the northern Pacific Ocean to bring abundant rain in the cooler months of the year. A truly tropical climate is just the reverse, bringing heavy moisture to the cane during the heat of the summer and therefore causing it to grow much more rapidly.

A two-year crop offers a double advantage. First, the longer growing period produces a thicker, taller plant that yields disproportionately more juice and sugar than sugarcane that matures after only nine months or so. For example, in 1940 the average yield of cane per acre harvested in Hawaii was 65.5 tons and produced 14,500 pounds of sugar, whereas in Florida the cane tonnage per acre was only 29 and produced only 6,000 pounds of sugar. In Louisiana the cane harvested was a mere 13.8 tons per acre and produced only 2,200 pounds of sugar. Doubling the sugar produced in Florida and Louisiana (to allow for the two crops taken there while Hawaii was taking only one) yields 12,000 pounds of sugar per acre in Florida and 4,400 pounds in Louisiana, compared with Hawaii's 14,500 pounds. Further, the costs of raising two crops are much greater than those of raising one.

The second advantage is that with cane growing throughout the roughly two-year period, fields can be planted in rotation so that there is year-round planting and year-round harvesting. This schedule utilizes the mill and other plantation machinery more efficiently than if all cane were planted in the early spring and then harvested in the late fall.

Summary of Productivity. The outstandingly high productivity of the Hawaiian sugar industry is the result of an innovative, scientific approach to farming that overcame the high costs of land, labor, and transportation that have prevailed in the islands. Efficiency has enabled the plantations to compete in a world where most cane sugar is heavily subsidized by governments to provide jobs and secure foreign exchange. The United States has not paid its sugar producers cash subsidies (except during the years of the McKinley Tariff, 1892–94), so that the survival of the industry in Hawaii, as elsewhere in the United States, has depended on high levels of productivity—along with federal protection against the dumping of subsidized foreign sugar.

THE PATERNALISTIC PLANTATION SYSTEM

Particular conditions determined the formation and operation of the Hawaii sugar plantation system. The nature of sugarcane production dictated both a large-scale farming operation and an integration between agricultural work in the field and manufacturing work in the mill. The nature of the labor force, composed largely of immigrant labor coming to a strange country and to an isolated rural setting, dictated that the enterprise be a "plantation," something of a self-contained community distinct from the rest of society, under the paternalistic supervision of the plantation manager.

The immigrant sugar worker arriving in Hawaii, unlike the European immigrant arriving at Ellis Island, already had a job. But he generally had no money, and no contacts other than the immigration official and the plantation to which he would be assigned for work. When the worker arrived at the plantation, he needed almost everything—food, housing, medical care, clothing. Because there was no ready alternative for providing him with these things in nineteenth-century rural Hawaii, his contract said that they would be supplied by the employer.

In the isolated plantation community of several hundred or even several thousand people, the plantation manager was supreme. He provided the job, the pay, housing, and many necessities and non-necessities of life. He ran the company store, the fire department, and what was in effect a police department. Management supplied the infirmary and hospital, organized the cultural, recreational, and social affairs of the community, and served as the prime social service agency, permeating almost every respect of life on the plantation. Management saw to it that churches and schools were built and that recreational facilities were provided. Conversely, the plantation system demanded that everybody live by the code laid down by management.

In this setting, the plantation manager was much like the Hawaiian chief of the eighteenth century, his assistants like the lay kahuna, and his workers like the makaainana, or commoners. Theodore Morgan (p. 173) was struck by the fact that in the century covered by his book (1778 to 1876), Hawaii had "come full circle," with a rigid, all-embracing, paternalistic authoritarianism replacing the rigid, all-embracing feudalism of the alii society. The major difference was that on the plantation, in contrast to the ahupuaa, everyone worked hard, including the manager.

That the plantation manager before World War II was substantially the equivalent of the alii nui of precontact days was brought home to me shortly after I arrived in Hawaii in 1950 as director of research for the Hawaii Employers Council. One of my responsibilities was to keep abreast of changes in wage control regulations instituted in 1950 after the United States became involved in the Korean War. One day the distinguished attorney Alfred Castle of the old firm of Robertson, Castle, and Anthony telephoned me to ask if he could bring Mr. Sinclair Robinson around to see me about a wage control problem. Sinclair Robinson was the patriarch of the family that owned the island of Niihau and the Gay and Robinson Sugar Plantation at Pakala (now Makaweli) on Kauai. The Gay and Robinson plantation was totally paternalistic, the only plantation in Hawaii never organized by a union. Niihau had been kept off-limits to all visitors since the last century. In the 1950s the plantation and the island remained essentially unchanged since the nineteenth century.

When Mr. Castle and Mr. Robinson entered the offices of the Hawaii Employers Council, they walked past the desk of the receptionist—a woman of Japanese ancestry who had grown up on the Gay and Robinson plantation and to whom Mr. Robinson was nearly divine. After my guests had left, she staggered into my office and told me how cold chills had run through her body, how she had had difficulty breathing, how she had almost fainted when she suddenly found herself in the immediate presence of Mr. Sinclair Robinson. It was as if she were a devout Catholic and had suddenly found herself in the presence of the Pope.

Plantation paternalism had to change when Hawaii was annexed by the United States in 1898. Under American law, the labor contract under which imported labor served was illegal and imported labor was now free to leave the plantation at any time. Managers who previously had provided housing and other perquisites to their workers because it was required by contract had to continue these benefits after annexation because discontented workers could walk off the job with impunity. Under this impetus, housing standards were improved, health and recreational activities were stepped up, wages were increased, and the plantation managers, in their own self-interest, developed a concern for the welfare and contentment of their work forces.

This later paternalism is exemplified by the experience of my wife's mother at Kekaha Plantation on the island of Kauai. In 1906 her husband came from Okinawa to the plantation, where he worked until retirement. She joined him in 1909, found that the Kekaha community (which was largely Japanese and Okinawan) had no source of tofu, and started a small commercial tofu-making operation at their home.

The manager thought this was a good idea because, he reasoned, immigrants supplied with their ethnic foods are more content. To encourage her, he had a small tofu plant built next to her house with concrete floors and walls. For its use, the plantation charged one dollar a year. The manager also provided, gratis, millstones to grind the soybeans, and, when electricity came in, free power to turn them. This operation continued for forty-five years, most successfully.

Despite the concern that the average plantation manager of the twentieth century had for the welfare of his plantation "family," the paternalistic plantation system contained two faults that would inevitably destroy it.

The first fault was that it put far too much control over the lives of the plantation community into the hands of the manager. Most people in developed countries in the twentieth century place a high value on personal freedom and resent being dictated to. Authoritarian management may have worked in the monarchy of the 1880s, when most plantation employees were immigrants, but not in the Hawaii of the twentieth century, after most sugar workers had lived in America for many years. The desire for free choice and doing things one's own way has resulted in the destruction of every "company town" that the captains of American industry created at about the time the sugar plantations were developing in Hawaii. Plantation camp or company town, it was bound to go.

The second fault of the paternalistic plantation system is that it virtually guaranteed that everyone living on the plantation had some grievance against the boss. If *anything* went wrong, the manager would be blamed because he was responsible for *everything*—what Clark Kerr labeled the "mass grievance." In the normal employment situation, workers blame the boss only if something goes wrong on the job, but not so on the plantation. If something goes wrong with the house, they blame the boss because he is the landlord. If they think they paid too high a price for something at the store, they blame the boss because he runs the company store. If some foul-up has occurred at the gymnasium, they blame the boss because he is in charge of recreation.

When union organizers began to sign up sugar workers in the late 1930s, they found plantations where nearly everybody had a gripe against the plantation manager. The luck of the organizers resembled that of the missionaries in 1820, who arrived just after the native religious system had been overthrown. In both instances there was a void to be filled.

It was a tribute to the intelligence, good sense, and humanity of some managers that the organizers found plantations where the employees were not at all inclined to sign up with the union. The second sugar-plantation representation election held in Hawaii was at Kekaha, a superbly managed plantation, and the union lost by a vote of 136 to 60.[66] But this was not the usual situation.

WORKING CONDITIONS AND PAY

Plantation work was heavy and hard before the machines came. The work day started before dawn. After a few hours there was a short break for breakfast, then more work until the noon break for a box lunch taken to the field by each worker, and then more backbreaking work until quitting time (*pa'u hana*) in mid-afternoon. This ten-hour work day continued Monday through Saturday, with only Sunday for rest and recreation.

The work pattern hardly changed during the era of the plantations' dominance before World War II, except that in the 1930s an eight-hour day became fairly standard for workers on time pay. By then many workers had short-term contracts, being paid for the job done rather than for the hours spent doing it. This arrangement attracted the more ambitious and more capable workers, and they frequently worked a longer day than those on hourly pay.

Pay consisted of a cash salary plus perquisites—basically housing, utilities (including cooking fuel), and medical care. In addition, the plantation continued to provide schools and churches, recreational facilities, transportation to community events, etc. A 1939 survey showed that all plantations maintained tennis courts, with over 80 percent of those lighted for night play; nearly one-third had swimming pools; 94 percent had basketball courts; 55 percent had community centers; and more than half had mountain recreation houses or plantation clubhouses.[67] Many companies maintained informal, unfunded, noncontributory pension plans.

Facilities of the late 1930s were far superior to those of earlier decades. Despite complaints about the quality of those perquisites down through the years, by the end of the plantation era prior to World War II, there was general agreement that, the hard work aside, life on a sugar plantation in Hawaii was fairly comfortable.

Cash rates of pay also improved as productivity rose.[68] In 1866, before the large-scale importation of contract labor, unskilled Hawaii sugar workers averaged just over $9 a month, compared with $15.50 for hired farm workers in the United States. This put Hawaii at about 60 percent of the U.S. average. In 1890, when most of the plantation workers were immigrants, Hawaii's rate was $16.90, compared with $19.50—putting Hawaii's rate at about 85 percent of the U.S. average. In 1915 the difference was still about the same, with Hawaii at $25.20 and the mainland U.S. at $30. Hawaii's pay rates reached 98 percent of mainland rates by 1924 ($47.83 vs. $49) and thereafter exceeded the mainland's by a fair margin through World War II.

Hawaii's virtually year-round sugar work brought the annual earnings of plantation workers far above the average of mainland farm workers because sugar production in Hawaii was, and still is, practically non-seasonal. For example, in 1983 the adult hired farm workers of America averaged only 3.5 months of work during the year and only 16 percent of them worked full time year round.[69] Differences in seasonality probably raised annual earnings of Hawaii's sugar workers well above those of mainland farm hands, even back in the nineteenth century.

James Shoemaker, in his study of labor in Hawaii for the U.S. Bureau of Labor Statistics, thus summarized his findings on the compensation of sugar workers in Hawaii during the late 1930s:

> [C]ontrary to popular opinion, Hawaiian plantation labor receives higher monthly wages than the general average of farm labor or the average of mainland cane-sugar workers. Because of the advantage of climate, irrigation, and a continuous cycle of growth, the stability of employment and economic security of the average plantation worker in Hawaii is far greater than that of the farm or plantation worker on the mainland. For the same reasons, the average annual earnings of Hawaiian plantation labor amounts to far more than the average annual earnings of farm labor on the mainland.[70]

THE SUGAR FACTORS

Just as the immigrant worker arriving at a distant plantation in rural Hawaii depended on the plantation to supply almost everything, so the plantation itself, physically isolated from direct contact with the outside world, needed to have many things provided for it. A manager one hundred years ago—whether on a plantation at Kohala at the northern tip of the island of Hawaii, or at Pioneer Mill in west Maui, or at Waialua on the north shore of Oahu, or at any other place in rural Hawaii—was isolated from any source of supply. Ground transportation was by foot, draft-drawn wagon, or carriage. Sea transportation, when available, was by sailing ship. Honolulu was days away, San Francisco was weeks away, and New York was months away. Communications were by written post.

Under these conditions, how would the manager arrange to get the labor he needed from China, Japan, Madeira, or wherever? How would he get needed mill machinery from Glasgow or Pittsburgh? How would he obtain jute bags from India to hold his sugar? How would he find a market for his sugar, whether it were in Valparaiso, Sydney, or San Francisco? How would he arrange to ship this sugar after he found a buyer? How would he obtain insurance to cover the cargo? Who would finance him until he was paid? How would he secure lumber to build houses for his employes? How would he recruit a doctor for the plantation hospital?

The answer was always the same: the manager had to have an agent in Honolulu with worldwide contacts to handle these things for him. His job of growing the cane and grinding it, together with watching after all the myriad aspects of the plantation and its community, was enough for any manager. Consequently, from the very beginning, sugar plantations affiliated themselves with one of the merchant trading houses in Honolulu. These firms acted on behalf of the plantation in many ways. The Honolulu companies that represented the plantations were called sometimes "agencies" but more commonly "factors." "Factoring" has the specific meaning of financing a business by purchasing its accounts receivable, but it also has the general meaning of conducting business transactions for some other company. The sugar factors generally did both.

Jacob Adler, in his biography of Claus Spreckels, who dominated the Hawaiian sugar scene in the last quarter of the nineteenth century, writes (p. 13):

> The agency system as it was practiced in the islands has no close parallel elsewhere. The sugar factors or agencies grew out of the merchandising houses established in the early years of the nineteenth century to provision the whaling fleets. The merchant predecessors of the agencies were exporters, importers, financiers—experienced businessmen in a kingdom where "business" in the western sense, was almost unknown until after 1800.
>
> The transition from merchant to sugar agent was a natural one. With the decline of whaling after 1850, those merchandising houses which had prospered now looked more and more to the young sugar industry. The struggling planters had enough trouble merely growing cane. For financing, warehousing, marketing, purchase of supplies and equipment, the planters turned to the Honolulu merchants. Here they could get help—for a price. The agency system grew out of the need for specialization and division of labor which had to be developed if both agent and planter were to prosper.

Financial relationships between the agency and the plantation have varied over time, generally growing closer as the decades passed. In the nineteenth century ownership of the plantations was usually separate from that of their Honolulu agency; but in the twentieth century the factors tended to become owners of much of the stock of the plantation companies, and after World War II most of the plantations became wholly-owned subsidiaries of the agencies.

Ladd & Co., serving as agent for (and owner of) Koloa Plantation, was the first sugar factor. Two other early sugar factors were H. Hackfeld and Company (now Amfac), which took over the Koloa agency in 1853,[71] and Janion, Green and Company, the predecessor of Theo. H. Davies & Company. One of the largest sugar agencies in the early 1860s was Walker, Allen and Company, which served a dozen plantations and mill companies until it went bankrupt because of falling sugar prices after the Civil War.[72] William G. Irwin & Company, which was the agency for Claus Spreckels's plantations among others, was dominant in the closing years of the nineteenth century.

Other companies have been in the sugar factoring business at various times. Bishop & Co., predecessor of First Hawaiian Bank, represented Olaa Plantation for some years early in the twentieth century.[73] The Chinese firm of Chun-Hoon & Company served as a sugar factor briefly,[74] as did Bishop Trust Company, F. L. Waldron, and F. A. Schaefer & Company.[75]

But the sugar factors that survived and prospered were what have been known for two-thirds of a century as "the Big Five"—C. Brewer & Company; Theo. H. Davies & Co.; American Factors; Castle & Cooke; and Alexander & Baldwin.[76] Brewer was founded in 1826 by James Hunnewell, a New England sea captain, and did a general merchandising business. It took the name of C. Brewer & Co. in 1843 and started serving as agent for sugar plantations in the early 1860s. It became a major sugar factor when it took over William G. Irwin & Co. in 1910.

Davies started in 1845 as a British merchant trading house, originally called Starkey, Janion & Company. One of its employees, Theophilus H. Davies, took it over in 1867 and immediately directed its activities to sugar.

The predecessor of American Factors (Amfac) was H. Hackfeld, a merchandise house founded by a German sea captain in 1849. Still owned by Germans in 1917, when America entered World War I, Hackfeld was taken over by the Alien Property Custodian and sold to a group of Hawaii businessmen in 1918. It was given the patriotic name of American Factors, and its main retail store, which had gone under the name of B. F. Ehlers, was renamed Liberty House.

Castle & Cooke was founded by two missionaries, Samuel Northrup

Castle and Amos Starr Cooke, who had arrived in Hawaii in 1837 as members of the eighth company of missionaries sent out by the American Board of Commissioners for Foreign Missions in Boston. In 1849 the board decided that the Hawaii mission should become self-supporting and withdrew its financial support. This prompted Messrs. Castle and Cooke in 1851 to start their merchandising house "and to get a part of our support, and finally the whole from our own resources."[77] Its first agency relationship was with Kohala Plantation in 1863, probably because Kohala's founder was an ex-missionary, Elias Bond. Reverend Bond had started the plantation at the northern end of the Big Island "to create jobs for the Hawaiians living in the remote Kohala district.[78]

Alexander & Baldwin differed in several respects from the other four in that it was founded much later (in 1894) by two local men (Samuel T. Alexander and Henry P. Baldwin, both sons of missionaries), started off as a factor to represent the sugar plantations that the two partners had built on Maui, and had its original office in San Francisco.

Toward the end of the plantation era shortly before World War II, the Big Five collectively were the power center of Hawaii—the center of economic power, political power, and social power all rolled into one. Economically, they represented most of the sugar industry, and three of them controlled most of the pineapple industry as well. Four of them controlled Matson Navigation Company, which was not only the main common carrier operating between the mainland and Hawaii but also the owner-operator of Hawaii's two largest hotels—at a time when the territory had only a dozen tourist-class hotels. Most of the Big Five were also involved in merchandising, supplying stores and shops throughout Hawaii. One of the Big Five owned the main foundry and machine shop (the Honolulu Iron Works), and others were engaged in stevedoring, railroading, water supply, and representing steamship lines other than Matson.

In addition to running their own firms, Big Five officers held commanding posts in most of the other large businesses in Hawaii. A network of interlocking directorships made the whole business community, when the chips were down, all members of one family. This network as of 1939 was charted by James Shoemaker. Board members of the Big Five were shown in the center of the chart, and the directors of seventy other major Hawaiian companies were printed around its periphery. Wherever a Big Five director also appeared as a board member of one or more of the seventy companies, lines connected the names. The result was a chart resembling an immense, tightly-woven spider web. While this interlocking resulted partly from the small size and the isolated location of the Hawaiian community, the inevitable result was an emphasis on cooperation rather than on competition and a solid front by almost the entire business community in the face of any threat to its security or its supremacy. Most of such interlocks were abolished by Hawaii's anti-trust law of 1961.

Virtually the only major companies in prewar Hawaii outside the Big Five network were the national companies whose branches in the territory constituted the local pineapple industry—California Packing Corporation (now Del Monte); Libby, McNeil & Libby; and the American Can Company, which supplied them. These firms all operated in Hawaii for decades, long enough to do business alongside—though only marginally in competition with—the Big Five. The opening of a large Sears Roebuck retail store in Honolulu in 1941, over the opposition, it was said, of the Big Five, broke the pattern and presaged the new order that was to come after Hawaii became a state.

At the outbreak of World War II, however, overseas business firms in the territory, other than those just listed, were few. Aside from one advertising agency (N. W. Ayer), three general merchandise stores (Kress, Ben Franklin, and Mitsukoshi), a stockbroker (Dean Witter), two Japanese banks (Sumitomo and Yokohama Specie), some insurance and oil companies, three cable companies (Globe, Mackay, and RCA), several shipping lines, and Pan American Airways, all enterprises were Hawaii-owned.

Cooperative Marketing

One of the main things the plantations relied on their agencies for was marketing their sugar. Early on, Ladd & Co. sent Koloa's sugar incredible distances from Hawaii—to Sydney (Australia), Valparaiso (Chile), and around South America to the East Coast of the United States.[79] In the 1830s no significant market yet existed on the sparsely settled West Coast of North America. With the rapid growth of California after the gold rush of 1849 and the settlement of the Oregon country, however, the West Coast of the United States became the prime market for Hawaiian sugar. The Honolulu agencies frequently established relations with West Coast firms to assist in marketing, financing, and other business matters. Thus one of the main sugar factors in Honolulu during the Civil War days was Walker, Allen and Co., which was closely affiliated with the San Francisco firm of Charles W. Brooks and Company.[80]

Until Claus Spreckels established the Bay Sugar Refinery in San Francisco in 1863,[81] the West Coast had only one small refinery. Hawaiian raw sugar, unrefined, was generally sold directly to the consumer.

It was initially important therefore for Hawaii's plantations to improve the quality of their product so that they could supply a grade of raw sugar, called "grocery grade," that consumers would buy. By 1867, however, four refineries had operations in San Francisco, and from then on most consumers demanded refined white sugar.[82]

Raw sugar thenceforth was sold to a West Coast refinery, since the cost of shipping it all the way around the Horn to the Atlantic Coast was prohibitive. This put Hawaii's plantations at the mercy of San Francisco, and for the last two decades of the nineteenth century the problem was accentuated by the virtual monopoly on West Coast refining that Claus Spreckels gained in 1881.[83] Hawaiian suppliers had to sell to Spreckels on his terms. This made no difficulty for Spreckels's plantations in Hawaii, but for the other plantations and agencies it was doubly galling because the Sugar King's activities in Hawaii had been conducted in so heavy-handed a manner that most of the business community disliked him personally.[84] The solution, ultimately, was for the Hawaiian sugar industry to market its own sugar cooperatively, refining in its own refinery on the West Coast the amount of sugar that could be sold profitably there and then selling the surplus as raw sugar to Gulf or East Coast refineries—with these sales being handled by the industry-owned marketing cooperative.

It took several decades to accomplish the solution. In 1884 the Alexander & Baldwin plantations on Maui bought a part interest in a small refinery in San Francisco (The American Refinery);[85] and in 1899 Colonel Z. S. Spalding of Makee Sugar Company on Kauai, together with Castle & Cooke and C. Brewer, bought a small sugar beet factory at Crockett, California, just northeast of San Francisco. Later that year, Alexander & Baldwin joined the others in this venture.[86] A few years later, most of the sugar plantations and agencies in Hawaii (all but the Spreckels–Irwin group) formed a marketing company called Sugar Factors, which in 1905 took over the Crockett refinery and renamed it the California and Hawaiian Sugar Refining Company (C&H).[87] This cooperative handled more than 80 percent of Hawaii's sugar; and when William G. Irwin & Co. merged with C. Brewer in 1910, the entire Hawaiian sugar crop was marketed through C&H. At last "the Hawaiian agencies had gained control of Hawaiian sugar refining."[88] By 1925 the C&H refinery at Crockett was the largest sugar refinery in the world.[89]

Land and Capital

Since the beginning of commercial sugar cultivation in Hawaii, a large part of the land in sugar has been leased by the plantations, not owned in fee. In the mid-1930s, of 248,000 acres then in cane, some 123,000 acres were owned by the plantations and 125,000 acres were leased— from individuals, landed estates, companies, and mostly the territorial government. Leases typically provided for a minimum cash rent, plus a share of the plantations' revenues. Government leases were granted to the highest bidder.[90] A 1976 study showed that 55 percent of the land then in sugar was owned by the plantations, the remainder being leased.[91]

As for capital, the chief source of funds for plantation development has been the reinvested profits of the industry—again a somewhat unusual situation. As the sugar plantations developed, their capital needs were tremendous—for mills, irrigation systems, railways, pumps and other equipment. In the first couple of decades after the Reciprocity Treaty of 1875, tens of millions of dollars were invested in sugar. An 1879 study showed the "value of sugar estates" to be $9 million and a similar study in 1883 calculated the figure at $16 million. In 1889, the Planters' Labor & Supply Company's journal, the *Planters' Monthly*, placed the "aggregate capital stock" of the incorporated plantations plus the estimated value of the unincorporated plantations at $30 million. This figure had risen to $40 million by the time of annexation in 1898. (In 1896, the Republic of Hawaii valued the sugar estates for tax purposes at $19 million.[92] Compared with that amount, the total annual expenditures of the Hawaiian government in those years averaged only about $2 million.[93])

Kuykendall (3:54) notes the disappointment of Hawaii's business community in the failure of American capital to flow into the local sugar companies:

> It is safe to say that the greater part of the money that went into the Hawaiian sugar industry came out of that industry; it was simply profits plowed back into the industry by men who had the spirit of business

adventure and the courage to back up their faith and judgment against the known and the unknown risks. It had been expected that the opportunities for profit opened up by the Reciprocity Treaty would induce American capitalists to invest substantial amounts in Hawaiian enterprises. But with one notable and a few minor exceptions, those moneyed gentlemen either did not see the opportunities or were not impressed by them. At the end of 1877 the American minister to Hawaii, General J. M. Comly, disturbed by the failure of American capitalists and manufacturers to take advantage of the opportunities existing in Hawaii, wrote a dispatch on the subject and Secretary of State Evarts gave to the press a full abstract of Comly's letter. But there was not much response from the American business community."

Despite the opportunity for making money in Hawaii, U.S. "capitalists large and small do not take advantage of it," complained Charles Reed Bishop, head of Hawaii's only bank, in 1880. "Hundreds might have come here with money, strong hands and clear heads and started plantations, thus getting every advantage that the treaty offers equally with those who were here, but instead of doing so they have most of them kept away, croaking, growling and threatening, while the people here have put in every dollar they had or could borrow—having faith in the honor and good will of the U.S. Govt. and Congress pledged in the treaty, in the honesty of their purposes and in our virgin soil and fine climate." Bishop went on to point out that a good bit of San Francisco money had been loaned to Hawaii planters and merchants on short term but that this was simply to tide them over a period of financial stringency and was not investment capital.[94]

The "one notable" exception that Kuykendall refers to was Claus Spreckels, who started his sugar operations in Hawaii immediately after the Reciprocity Treaty came into effect and financed his operations largely with capital he brought with him. According to his biographer, Jacob Adler (p. 9), "the treaty brought about some direct investment by Californians in Hawaii plantations. By far the most important of these foreign 'interlopers' was Claus Spreckels." But Adler concludes that "there can be little doubt that over the years the plantations have received a large share of their financing from retained earnings."

The several minor exceptions that Kuykendall refers to were three small plantations incorporated in San Francisco and financed largely with California money—Hakalau Plantation Company, Hutchinson Sugar Plantation Company, and the Hana Plantation Company.[95]

In 1939 Vandercook (p. 156) summed up the sources of plantation capital in the following manner:

> [I]t is a source of almost smug satisfaction in Hawaii that, almost alone among American industrialists, they [the plantation owners] took advantage of the rich years to do away with bonds. Heavy capitalization had been necessary to establish island sugar growing. . . . But when the war years with their attendant high sugar prices came along, bonds seemed to be an unnecessary burden. . . . So all but a few of the bonds were amortized. In the boom period, when other corporations were spending their profits on riotous living, the sugar men got themselves completely out of debt.

Fat Years, Lean Years

The "rich years" that Vandercook refers to were by no means always there for Hawaii's sugar industry. Although it has experienced many years of prosperity, there have also been many years of deep depression during which individual companies failed and the future of the entire industry was in doubt.

This has been true over the full century and a half of the industry's existence. The early plantations produced sugar of such poor quality that, as Dr. Wood, who took over Koloa Plantation from Ladd & Co., said in 1850, "The sugars produced from that estate [Koloa Plantation] previously to the year 1842 would now be considered scarcely merchantable."[96] The nascent industry found itself in a recession in 1851 when the San Francisco market turned against Hawaiian sugar because of the low quality of the 1850 exports. With sugar from China, the Philippines, and Batavia favored over Hawaiian sugar, the industry was depressed during most of the 1850s. Serious sugar shortages and high prices caused by the U.S. Civil War resulted in a rapid expansion of the Hawaiian industry, but falling prices after the war caused the failure of several plantations.[97] In the early 1870s Hawaii's growers had serious trouble because of labor shortages, high transportation costs, and the high U.S. tariff.[98]

The Reciprocity Treaty brought an immense boom to the industry, but in its exuberance sugar expanded so rapidly that large debts were incurred, and the years 1879 and 1880 were years of financial crisis. The banker Charles Reed Bishop had to borrow $250,000 from the Hawaiian government to tide some of the plantations over that stringent period. In 1884–85 prices fell to around five cents from the prior six- to seven-cent level, creating another depressed period. Then in 1891 the McKinley Tariff permitted all foreign sugar to enter the U.S. market duty free (paying domestic producers a bounty of two cents a pound). The day the tariff went into effect the price of sugar fell from five and three-quarters cents to three and one-half cents, and there was no recovery until about 1896.[99]

Annexation and the Spanish-American War brought recovery for a number of years, but as a result of the war Philippine and Puerto Rican sugar was allowed to enter the United States duty free and Cuba was given preferential tariff treatment. In 1913 the Cuban crop was extremely large, causing U.S. prices to fall below four cents; but during the boom years of World War I and the great sugar-price inflation of 1920, prices rose to over twenty-three cents.[100] The collapse of this balloon left the world sugar industry in serious trouble throughout the 1920s. The Great Depression of the 1930s did not hurt sugar as much as it did most industries, but a world surplus of sugar led the Congress to place domestic production controls and foreign import controls on sugar to stabilize the industry. Under this program, Hawaii's production of sugar was ordered cut by 10 percent,[101] a more severe restriction than that placed on the forty-eight states. This federally mandated reduction in sugar production in Hawaii deserves attention because it was a major reason why the Hawaiian sugar industry strongly supported statehood for Hawaii—and statehood had a tremendous impact on the economy.

In addition to the ups and downs of the market, sugar has been subject to all the problems that nature creates for any farming operation. And poor management can turn what otherwise would be a profitable company into a bankrupt one. Consequently, there have been many failures of Hawaiian sugar plantations since Koloa had to be sold at a sheriff's auction in 1845. But the plantations have experienced far more successes than failures; and before the bombs falling on Pearl Harbor in 1941 heralded the end of the plantation era, Hawaii's sugar plantations, together with the expanding pineapple industry, were almost totally responsible for the remarkable health and prosperity of the Hawaiian economy.

Table 3.1 identifies Hawaii's 38 sugar companies in 1941 by agency affiliation and island. It also shows their acreage, production of sugar, and volume of sugar produced per acre harvested. For the industry as a whole, total production was nearly 950,000 tons, and average production per acre harvested was 7.24 tons.

Table 3.1   Hawaii's sugar crop, 1941

AGENT, COMPANY, AND ISLAND	AREA IN CANE (ACRES)	SUGAR MADE (TONS 96° RAW VALUE)	TONS OF SUGAR PER ACRE HARVESTED
American Factors, Ltd.			
Grove Farm Co., Ltd. (Kauai)	3,799	13,191	6.50
Kekaha Sugar Co., Ltd. (Kauai)	7,021	41,601	9.50
Kipu Plantation (Kauai)	1,192	4,068	4.48
Koloa Sugar Co., The (Kauai)	3,737	15,540	6.81
Lihue Plantation Co., The (Kauai)	13,615	62,435	7.19
Oahu Sugar Co., Ltd. (Oahu)	11,096	60,678	9.25
Olaa Sugar Co., Ltd. (Hawaii)	15,394	45,676	5.57
Pioneer Mill Co., Ltd. (Maui)	10,099	47,101	8.26
Waianae Co. (Oahu)	1,297	6,495	8.12
Waimea Sugar Mill Co., The (Kauai)	647	3,566	9.41
	67,897	300,351	
C. Brewer and Co., Ltd.			
Hakalau Plantation Co. (Hawaii)	6,232	17,998	5.91
Hawaiian Agricultural Co. (Hawaii)	9,028	30,999	7.03
Hilo Sugar Co. (Hawaii)	7,807	26,898	6.54
Honolulu Plantation Co. (Oahu)[a]	4,796	25,774	6.20
Honomu Sugar Co. (Hawaii)	3,027	10,407	6.22
Hutchinson Sugar Plantation Co. (Hawaii)	4,892	13,237	6.86
Kaeleku Sugar Co., Ltd. (Maui)	3,476	5,392	2.51
Kilauea Sugar Plantation Co. (Kauai)	3,967	12,654	4.39
Onomea Sugar Co. (Hawaii)	7,895	23,978	5.50
Paauhau Sugar Plantation Co. (Hawaii)	4,163	15,429	6.77
Pepeekeo Sugar Co. (Hawaii)	3,842	14,629	6.00
Wailuku Sugar Co. (Maui)	4,399	21,803	6.98
Waimanalo Sugar Co. (Oahu)[b]	2,601	9,454	4.86
	66,125	228,652	
Alexander & Baldwin, Ltd.			
Hawaiian Commercial & Sugar Co. (Maui)	13,886	78,595	10.69
Hawaiian Sugar Co. (Kauai)[c]	6,246	19,384	6.66
Kahuku Plantation Co. (Oahu)	4,310	21,587	7.61
Maui Agricultural Co. (Maui)	8,306	39,821	9.37
McBryde Sugar Co., Ltd. (Kauai)	4,766	23,066	7.54
	37,514	182,453	

continued

Table 3.1 *(continued)*

AGENT, COMPANY, AND ISLAND	AREA IN CANE (ACRES)	SUGAR MADE (TONS 96° RAW VALUE)	TONS OF SUGAR PER ACRE HARVESTED
Castle & Cooke, Ltd.			
Ewa Plantation Co. (Oahu)	8,874	50,108	10.14
Kohala Sugar Co. (Hawaii)	12,593	34,457	5.98
Waialua Agricultural Co. (Oahu)	9,925	58,479	11.27
	31,392	143,044	
Theo. H. Davies & Co., Ltd.			
Hamakua Mill Co. (Hawaii)	5,819	15,436	6.59
Kaiwiki Sugar Co., Ltd. (Hawaii)	4,377	11,164	6.29
Laupahoehoe Sugar Co. (Hawaii)	6,221	18,251	5.72
Waiakea Mill Co. (Hawaii)	5,612	15,024	4.74
	22,029	59,875	
F. A. Schaefer & Co., Ltd.			
Honokaa Sugar Co. (Hawaii)	9,015	19,074	4.85
Bishop Trust Co., Ltd.			
Gay & Robinson (Kauai)	2,406	8,860	7.55
F. L. Waldron, Ltd.			
Wailea Milling Co. (Hawaii)	1,733	4,881	5.56
Industry total	238,111	947,190	7.24
Islands			
Hawaii	107,650	317,538	5.89
Maui	40,166	192,712	8.53
Oahu	42,899	232,575	9.16
Kauai	47,396	204,365	7.08
Industry total	238,111	947,190	7.24

SOURCE: HSPA, unpublished data.

a. Honolulu Plantation Co.: 25,774 tons 96° raw value sugar manufactured into 24,088 tons refined sugar.

b. Waimanalo Sugar Co.: 9,454 tons 96°raw value sugar manufactured into 8,836 tons refined sugar.

c. Hawaiian Sugar Co. was not able to renew its lease in 1941 and therefore took out its last crop that year. The successor company that took over the land and the mill was Olokele Sugar Co., which was affiliated with C. Brewer & Co.

Pineapple

Development of the Pineapple Industry to 1941

Pineapple, the "king of fruits," has been grown in Hawaii for at least the last 175 years. "This day," wrote Don Francisco de Paula Marín in his diary on 21 January 1813, "I planted pineapples."[102] It has frequently been said that Marín probably introduced the fruit to Hawaii by having it brought from Mexico or South America, but Marín casually mentions planting it and his biographer states that Marín did not introduce the fruit to Hawaii.[103] There is some slight evidence that pineapple was grown in the Marquesas long before Western explorers discovered the Hawaiian Islands, and therefore the Marquesans might have introduced it into Hawaii long before Captain Cook's arrival.[104] Old Hawaiian stories suggest that pineapple came to the islands in the sixteenth century.[105] To confuse the issue further, the Hawaiian word for pineapple is *hala kahiki*, which implies that the fruit was introduced by foreigners because *hala* refers to the pandanus, which has fruit that looks like a pineapple, and *kahiki* means foreign.[106] In any event, when the missionaries arrived in 1820, they found pineapple growing in family gardens.

As with sugarcane, the cultivation of pineapple went through a radical development before the product of the islands merited recognition for its superiority. The early Hawaiian pineapple was a small fibrous fruit of a variety called Wild Kailua. It briefly entered commerce in the early 1850s when the Gold Rush population of California needed food imports and many crops were shipped from Hawaii, including some 21,000 pineapples in 1850–51. The fruit originated mainly in Lahaina, Maui, but also came from Waimea, Kauai, and Hilo.[107]

The next appearance of pineapple as a commercial crop occurred in 1882, when two men in North Kona named Ackerman and Muller packed a few cases in homemade cans and shipped them to Theo. H. Davies in Honolulu. Davies could not sell them, so that ended that venture.[108] That same year, however, a British sea captain and horticulturalist named John Kidwell came to Hawaii, and by 1885 he had some five acres in pineapple in Manoa Valley where the University of Hawaii is now located and was shipping fresh fruit to the United States. It arrived in such poor condition that he decided that pineapple must be canned. By 1892 he had, with the help of a plumber named John Emmeluth, built a small cannery. He had also imported the greatly preferred Smooth Cayene variety from Jamaica[109] and had moved his fields to

Pearl Harbor near his cannery. By 1896 the Kidwell–Emmeluth company (Hawaiian Fruit and Packing) was producing 5 thousand cases of pineapple a year.[110] The U.S. duty on canned pineapple was 35 percent, however, and Kidwell decided he could make more money in sugar, so he gave up pineapple and converted his fields to sugar in 1898.[111]

This was remarkably poor timing because Hawaii was annexed by the United States in 1898 and annexation did for pineapple what the Reciprocity Treaty had done for sugar. Canned pineapple (like all other Hawaiian products) then began to enter the United States duty free. Lorrin A. Thurston had earlier stated that the high U.S. tariff "was the one barrier to the [pineapple] industry['s] becoming one of the leading articles of export."[112] Developments proved him right.

When the tariff was lifted in 1898, Oahu land desirable for growing pineapple became available. Eighteen lots, ranging in size from 50 to 150 acres, were opened for homesteading in the Wahiawa area. A number of homesteaders started growing pineapple, getting their slips for planting from the abandoned plants of Kidwell in Ewa. One of these Wahiawa homestead pineapple pioneers was Byron Clark, who organized the Hawaiian Fruit and Plant Company.[113] Another was Alfred W. Eames, who started the Hawaiian Islands Packing Company.[114]

The third new entrant was James D. Dole, second cousin to Sanford Dole, who was then serving as the first governor of the territory of Hawaii. James Dole came to Hawaii in 1899 fresh out of Harvard, purchased 60 acres from a Wahiawa homesteader in August 1900, and started growing pineapple.[115] Clark and Eames were successful, and Dole was spectacularly so. His Hawaiian Pineapple Company began in 1901 with a capitalization of $20,000, using cannery machinery purchased from a defunct packing plant in Baltimore.[116] During this early period, according to Gus Oehm's history of the pineapple industry in Hawaii (p. 112), some of the new companies ran into financial trouble, but "the Bank of Bishop and Co. [predecessor of First Hawaiian Bank] had confidence in the new industry as it was being developed by this courageous group and offered financial aid on more than one occasion."

Between 1903, when the Wahiawa homesteaders packed their first harvest of 1,893 cases, until 1930, when the industry attained its prewar maximum, the pineapple industry in Hawaii had phenomenal growth. The number of cases packed had jumped to 75,000 by 1906. It rose to 350,000 in 1908, to 726,000 in 1911, to 1.7 million in 1913, to more than

3 million in 1918, to 6 million in 1923—and then doubled again to nearly 13 million cases by 1930.[117]

The Great Depression hit pineapple much harder than it hit sugar, partly because the fruit was considered a luxury compared with sugar and partly because the crop years of 1930 and 1931 had been phenomenally large, exceeding any previous year by more than 3.5 million cases. Producing that amount of canned pineapple at the bottom of the Depression served only to fill warehouses with unsold inventory. As a result, production was cut back considerably from 1932 to 1934, but by the end of the 1930s it was back to about where it had been at the beginning of the decade.[118]

Early efforts to market pineapple juice had failed. It was first thought that consumers would accept juice only if it were free of sediment, and so the juice was put through a process that made it a clear liquid but also deprived it of flavor. Next came a scheme to concentrate the juice by partial evaporation so as to produce a heavy liquor-like product that could be diluted for use as a fountain drink. That was no more successful. Finally, in the early 1930s, the industry tried simply canning the natural juice, sediment and all, and found good market acceptance.[119] By 1940–41, almost as many cases of juice were being packed and sold as cases of fruit.

Selling the juice meant that the entire pineapple was being sold, with nothing going to waste. The good slices were canned as sliced pineapple; the broken slices were canned as chunks, tidbits, or crushed pineapple; and the core of the fruit was crushed for its juice, with its residual fiber being added to the shell and marketed as a stock food called "pineapple bran." Nonpotable juice was used to make citric acid, vinegar, or alcohol. During World War II, a local brand of gin called Five Islands was made from pineapple alcohol.

Throughout this period, a limited amount of fresh fruit was shipped to the mainland. Joseph King Goodrich states that in the years before World War I about 1,000 tons of fruit were being shipped fresh annually;[120] and according to Crawford (*Hawaii's Crop Parade*, p. 203) in a typical year during the 1930s nearly 2,000 tons would be shipped. These figures contrast with about 115,000 tons of fresh pineapple going to the mainland from Hawaii annually at the present time (late 1980s) under controlled refrigeration.

Over the first two decades of the century, new firms continued to be attracted by the potential of the Hawaiian pineapple industry—some sixty plantations and canneries in all.[121] Most failed, or otherwise disappeared.[122] Several were forced out by depressed market conditions on the mainland in 1907 and 1912. Some were located in areas where weather conditions were not suitable for pineapple culture, such as windward Oahu and North Kohala and Kona on the island of Hawaii. Others were hit by plant disease or insects. Some company names disappeared as a result of merger or sale. Some were mismanaged. When the first industry association was formed in 1908, it had seven member companies, but only one of them still existed twenty-five years later.[123]

Unlike sugar, which expanded rapidly after the Reciprocity Treaty but failed to attract much business interest from the United States (with the notable exception of Claus Spreckels), the expansion of the pineapple industry after annexation brought several major mainland companies to Hawaii. The first was the American Can Co., which opened branch factories in Hawaii in 1906. It not only relieved the pineapple companies of the expense of bringing in empty cans from the mainland, but also introduced to the industry the practice of sealing the lid of the can by simply rolling and crimping it ("double sealing") instead of using solder.[124] In 1910 Libby, McNeill & Libby started operations on Oahu, later adding fields on Molokai and Maui and a cannery on Maui.[125] In 1917 California Packing Corp. (Calpac, now Del Monte) bought out A. W. Eames's Hawaiian Islands Packing Co. on Oahu and later established a plantation on Molokai. Calpac opened a cannery on Maui in 1925–26 but sold it to Maui Pineapple Company in 1934.[126] A major expansion of the industry occurred in 1922, when Dole's Hawaiian Pineapple Company purchased the island of Lanai and made it the largest pineapple plantation in the world.

On the eve of World War II the industry had 48,000 acres planted in pineapple and annually packed 12 million cases of fruit and 8.5 million cases of juice. Membership included eight pineapple companies with twelve plantations and nine canneries, as follows: Hawaiian Pineapple Co., with plantations on Oahu and Lanai and the world's largest pineapple cannery in Honolulu; Libby, McNeill & Libby, with plantations on Oahu, Molokai, and Maui and canneries in Honolulu and on Maui; California Packing Corp., with plantations on Oahu and Molokai and a cannery in Honolulu; Maui Pineapple Co., with a plantation and cannery on Maui; Baldwin Packers, with a plantation and cannery on Maui; Kauai Pineapple Company, with a plantation and cannery on

Kauai; Hawaiian Canneries Company, with a plantation and cannery on Kauai; Hawaiian Fruit Packers, with a plantation and cannery on Kauai.

Of these companies, Hawaiian Pineapple Co. was by far the largest, accounting for nearly 40 percent of total production. Libby, McNeill & Libby and California Packing Corp. each accounted for about 20 percent, and the other five smaller companies produced the rest.[127] These eight firms dominated the world market in the years before World War II, packing well over half (59 percent) of all pineapple canned in Hawaii.

Problems of the Industry and Solutions

Marketing. When Hawaii started shipping pineapple to the U.S. mainland, the fruit was an exotic, expensive novelty. As long as the Hawaiian pineapple industry was exporting only a few thousand cases of fruit a year, its output could be sold. But with a rapid growth in production, Hawaiian shipments had increased to 168,000 cases by 1907. In that year the American economy was in recession and sales declined as supplies soared. Faced with this glut, seven of the eight local pineapple companies, led by James Dole, formed the Hawaiian Pineapple Growers Association in 1908 and embarked on a $50,000 advertising program designed to introduce Hawaiian pineapple to the American public. This "was one of the first nationwide consumer advertising campaigns in America,"[128] and it proved remarkably effective, setting the pattern for continued cooperative promotion. It was also a big gamble, because the combined *gross* sales of all Hawaiian pineapple companies the year before had amounted to only $268,000.

A more severe marketing crisis occurred between 1931 and 1934. With output having mounted to the highest level the industry had known as the American economy was sinking into the worst depression of its history, Hawaii's growers were unable to sell their huge volume of pineapple even at tumbling prices. In 1931, Hawaiian Pineapple Co. had a net loss of $3.9 million, and two of the industry's canneries closed. In the words of Gus Oehm in his history of the pineapple industry in Hawaii, "The industry descended from zenith to nadir" (p. 128).

Reacting, the companies in 1932 formed the Pineapple Producers' Cooperative Association to administer a marketing agreement and, under authorization of the federal Cooperative Marketing Act of 1922, embarked upon a drastic program to cut production and launched an ambitious marketing program."[129] For the latter purpose, the financially depressed companies appropriated the substantial sum of $1.5 million for the 1932–33 year.

Again, industry cooperation worked: the surplus inventory was completely disposed of within a year. Thereafter, the association gave each company a production quota based on its past production record. The success of the effort was trumpeted in an article about the Hawaiian pineapple industry in the June 1934 *Western Canner & Packer*: "Bright indeed should be the future. Production is held in line with consumption; the quality of the fruit is uniquely high; competition from the rest of the world is negligible; cooperative merchandising is proving successful; both sales and prices are climbing back to normal. . . . It is reported that every company is out of the red and operating in the black again."[130]

The statement underscores the almost monopolistic position that the Hawaiian pineapple industry had before World War II. In the 1930s it was producing well over half of all the world's canned pineapple.[131] The major competition to Hawaiian pineapple in the U.S. market was from peaches, pears, and apricots, with citrus juices the main competitor to pineapple juice. If in any year a late spring frost reduced the peach and citrus crops appreciably, Hawaii would benefit by a sympathetic rise in the price of canned pineapple products.

Labor Supply. Although securing an adequate labor force presented some problems to the pineapple industry, those problems were much less severe than they had been in sugar. There were several reasons for this.

First was the pineapple industry's later development. By 1910, when it was emerging from its infancy and beginning to need large numbers of employees, the population of Hawaii had risen to 193,000 and included many former sugar workers who were ready to try pineapple work.

A second reason was that pineapple did not require nearly as many workers as did sugar. Even in the late 1930s, when the total value of pineapple production had risen to a level almost equal that of sugar, full-time equivalent employment in pineapple was only about one-third of that in sugar.[132] This difference was due primarily to the fact that a large part of the value of canned pineapple was created by firms outside the industry. Other firms made the cans, the labels, and the cases in which the cans were packed, whereas sugar was marketed simply in inexpensive bags. And pineapple bought the energy it needed to run the cannery, whereas sugar generated its own mill energy by burning bagasse. Moreover, pineapple used more chemical spraying for insect control than did sugar.

Third, approximately half of all pineapple employment was in the cannery, and the canneries were mainly located in towns such as Honolulu on Oahu and Kahului on Maui, where labor was far more plentiful than in isolated rural areas. Furthermore, cannery employment was seasonal and intermittent, encouraging many women to enter the labor market.

Finally, with the main harvesting and canning season occurring in the summer months when schools were out, the industry found a sizable source of labor among high school and college students who were available for temporary employment.

For all these reasons, pineapple was never the importer of workers that sugar was. What overseas labor the pineapple industry recruited came through the Hawaiian Sugar Planters' Association on a fee basis.[133] The only exception was the last group of immigrants brought from the Philippines in 1946 to meet the severe labor shortage created by World War II. In that instance the Hawaiian Sugar Planters' Association and the Pineapple Growers Association jointly organized the project.

Productivity. The Hawaiian pineapple industry would never have achieved its growth and success without the extensive application of research and science to its problems. As Dr. Auchter observed in 1950, "had it not been for science and research, the pineapple industry might not be in Hawaii today."[134] For an agricultural activity to succeed, it not only has to produce a better product more efficiently than its competitors, but also must protect itself from the many insects and diseases that can destroy it.

When a single crop in an area is replanted over many years without rotation to other crops, problems with insects, disease, and nutrition are bound to develop. From its early days the pineapple industry sought scientific solutions to this problem, relying initially on individuals in the major companies and scientists in the HSPA's experiment station who were willing to help the fledgling industry. In 1914 the Hawaiian Pineapple Packers Association reached a formal agreement with the HSPA for its experiment station to do research for the industry, and several years later the HSPA experiment station established a pineapple department.[135] In 1923 the pineapple industry formed its own cooperative experiment station at Wahiawa and a year later added a research station at the University of Hawaii with the president of the university, Dr.

A. L. Dean, as an active participant. He became director of the station a few years later, and in 1941 its name was changed to the Pineapple Research Institute.[136]

The first quantum leap in pineapple productivity, as in sugar, came with the development of a processing machine. For sugar it was the centrifugal for separating the sugar crystals from the molasses. For pineapple it was a machine for peeling and coring the pineapple, invented in 1913 by Henry Gabriel Ginaca, a young mechanical draftsman hired by James Dole to develop such a device.[137] Displacing the time-consuming and labor-intensive chore of hand-peeling and coring the pineapple, the Ginaca machine accepted the pineapple from a conveyor belt, centered it in the machine, removed the top and bottom from the fruit, cut out the round central core, and then removed the shell from the outside—all in one operation, without requiring a machine operator, and handling forty to fifty pineapples per minute.[138]

A year after the Ginaca machine was invented, John L. Whitmore of Hawaiian Pineapple Co. came up with an idea that saved an immense amount of field labor—to lay down mulch paper (a heavy paper impregnated with asphalt) at the time of planting. Mulch paper for weed control had already been developed by Charles Eckhardt of Olaa Sugar Company,[139] but Whitmore recognized that it would have even greater advantages for pineapple, not only by suppressing weed growth but also by conserving moisture in the soil, preventing the leaching of fertilizer, and increasing soil temperature, which would serve to increase the activity of nitrifying bacteria.[140] The result was to reduce labor costs, improve plant growth, and increase yields.

A serious problem in the early years was the severe chlorosis (yellowing of the leaves) that pineapple plants experienced, the immature fruit turning a reddish pink and developing cracks in its shell. At first it was thought that the cause was the high magnesium content of Hawaii's soils and the problem was diagnosed as "magnesium poisoning." But in 1916 Maxwell Johnson of the Hawaii experiment station determined that magnesium was only the indirect cause—it kept the plant from absorbing the iron in the soil. The real problem was a deficiency of iron, which was cured by spraying the plants with iron sulfate.[141]

"Wilt" or "blight" was for years a serious pineapple disease, causing the root system to rot. After considerable research, it was discovered that the cause was the mealy bug (a small, white, waxy insect) and that the ant carried and spread the mealy bug. By 1930, with the use of a high-pressure oil emulsion spray, the wilt problem was largely solved, but the industry probably will be working on ant control for the rest of time.[142]

Another chronic threat was the nematode—a tiny worm in one variety or another found throughout the world. The nematode burrows into the roots of plants that are susceptible to it, and there it develops a blockage of the flow of moisture and nutrients. Nematode root-galls were found in Hawaiian pineapple as early as 1910, but it was not until the 1930s that a satisfactory, but expensive, way of killing nematodes by fumigating the soil before each planting was developed.[143] A better solution was discovered in 1940 by Dr. Walter Carter of the pineapple experiment station, who found that dichloropropene-dichloropropane (D-D) was an efficient and inexpensive soil fumigant for nematodes.[144] The fumigation method he developed was patented "in the name of the American people" and thus made available to growers everywhere. All the Hawaii pineapple industry wanted to do was to keep someone else from patenting it and denying its use to Hawaii.[145]

As in sugar production, in the pineapple industry the most labor-intensive and costly job is harvesting the crop. As a result, in pineapple as in sugar, mechanization of the harvesting operation had a high priority. In the late 1930s several companies developed machines to aid in harvesting which consisted of conveyor belts stretched on long booms out over the field. Workers would walk behind each boom, picking the ripe fruit and placing it on the conveyor belt. The belt would carry the pineapple to a tractor at the edge of the field, where the crown would be removed and the fruit dropped into a lug box for hauling to the cannery.[146]

Not only did this "boom harvester" save immense amounts of labor, it also did a better job than humans could do alone. A study in 1939, when the harvester was introduced, reported that only 2 percent of mechanically harvested fruit was bruised, as against 12 percent of hand-harvested fruit.[147]

These few examples illustrate the application of science to solving the problems of the industry. Many others occurred during the pre–World War II plantation era, and more since then. They make the basic point that in pineapple, as in sugar, cooperation to mobilize scientific problem solving characterized the industry. This approach to problem solving is common in business today; but it was rare sixty years ago when the Hawaiian pineapple industry established its cooperative experiment station, and it was almost unique nearly a century ago when sugar created its experiment station. Sugar set a high standard that pineapple followed, and both industries thereby became world leaders in scientific agriculture.

THE PINEAPPLE INDUSTRY'S PLACE IN THE BIG-FIVE POWER STRUCTURE

Pineapple never was the symbol of concentrated economic, political, and social power in Hawaii that sugar was, even though its biggest company, Hawaiian Pineapple Co. (now Dole), was larger than any sugar company except for Hawaiian Commercial and Sugar Co. on Maui. Part of the reason was that an image of concentrated economic power in Hawaii developed in the latter nineteenth and early twentieth centuries before pineapple amounted to much. Pineapple was a johnny-come-lately that tagged onto sugar's coattails for such things as labor recruitment and research. Sugar was clearly Number One, and in the popular mind it is easier to have a single symbol of power than to have it dispersed among several industries.

But the main reason for the perceived difference between the sugar and pineapple industries was that the Big Five were basically sugar agencies and not pineapple agencies. Before 1932 (when the plantation era was nearing its end), only a small fraction of the pineapple industry was tied in with any of the Big Five, and after that only slightly more than half had Big Five connections. This can be seen by a brief review of the pineapple activities of the sugar factors.

Theo. Davies purchased the Pearl City Fruit Company in 1906 and also the old Kidwell cannery near Pearl Harbor; this company lasted until 1928, when it was disincorporated.[148] American Factors' only pineapple facility was Hawaiian Canneries on Kauai. C. Brewer was never involved in the pineapple business. Castle & Cooke took over the depression-wracked Hawaiian Pineapple Co. in 1932—whether to save the firm from going bankrupt, as the company claimed[149] or to ensure that it would ship on Castle & Cooke's Matson Line, as was rumored, or for both reasons, is not clear.[150]

Alexander & Baldwin was the only Big Five company that got into pineapple directly and on purpose. In 1909 A&B became agent for McBryde Sugar Company and collaterally for the Kauai Fruit and Land Company, started in 1908 by some McBryde employees. By 1928 the pineapple company was wholly owned by A&B and renamed Kauai

Pineapple Co., Ltd. On Maui, two A&B companies, Maui Agriculture and Haleakala Ranch, planted pineapple in 1924, and in 1934 their production, along with a cannery bought from California Packing Corp., were merged into the Maui Pineapple Co.[151]

Less than two-thirds of the islands' pineapple industry prior to World War II was locally owned. About 40 percent was in the hands of Libby, McNeill & Libby and the California Packing Corp. Hawaiian Fruit Packers, though Hawaii-owned before the war, was never affiliated with any of the Big Five.

In sum, pineapple, though big in the prewar Hawaiian economy, was not seen as being at the center of concentrated economic and political power. The Big Five were thought of primarily as sugar factors. Pineapple, along with the banks, the utility companies, and other large firms, were part of the business oligarchy, but not of its core.

Other Economic Developments

Sugar and pineapple were the dominant industries of the prewar Hawaiian economy, providing the largest portion of employment and purchasing power, but other enterprises also played an essential role, as indeed they continue to do. These critical sectors are the export, and to a lesser extent the import-replacement, sectors of the economy.

Hawaii is so small and has such limited resources that it would be economically if not physically impossible for the islands to produce most of the goods that their people need for more than a subsistence standard of living. The standard raw materials for manufacturing, the metallic ores, are nonexistent and the standard energy sources, coal and oil, are equally absent. Hawaii has no great stands of timber, no great deposits of clay or of anything else that could be the basis for the development of an industrial economy. It is little exaggeration to say that if a product cannot be made out of lava, coral, air, water, or semitropical plants, then the chances are good that Hawaii must import it.

It is therefore critically important for the island economy to include export activities that will generate income from overseas to pay for imports. The vitality of the entire economy hinges on exports—including such "invisible" exports as tourism. As exports grow, the income of Hawaii's residents grows. This in turn forms the basis for growth in the non-export areas of wholesale and retail trade; finance, insurance, and real estate; construction; public utilities, communications, and transportation; and the entire service area—all of which would be at much lower levels if dependent on a self-contained island economy.

For exports to raise the standard of living of the people, they must be produced by industries that are so efficient and so productive that they can pay good wages and salaries to their employees without relying on government intervention. Hawaii was fortunate that its prime export industries during the plantation era were sufficiently efficient and productive to pay wages that were high, not only by world standards, but by U.S. standards as well. If Hawaii had lacked such export industries and if all its workers had devoted themselves, so to speak, to taking in each others' laundry, they would have been able to buy few items from overseas. Life would have resembled the self-sufficient days of the Polynesian economy, when only the basic needs for food, clothing, and shelter could be satisfied.

It was possible to reduce reliance on exports by producing some things that otherwise would have had to be imported. However, except for growing a portion of the food shipped in, import-substitution activities on any substantial scale were not considered feasible until after World War II.

DIVERSIFIED MANUFACTURING

During the plantation era almost all diversified manufacturing in Hawaii revolved around the sugar and pineapple industries. At the end of the period, firms responsible for those satellite manufacturing activities included the American Can Co., which annually made millions of cans for the pineapple companies; the Honolulu Iron Works and Hilo Iron Works, foundries and machine shops that served chiefly the sugar and pineapple companies; and the Hawaiian Cane Products Company in Hilo, which manufactured wallboard from bagasse, the fiber that is left after the cane has been ground.[152]

The only other manufacturing activities were a small tuna-packing plant in Honolulu and the printing and publishing industry. The main printing activity was publishing local newspapers, but Hawaii also had one of the first regional magazines in the world—*Paradise of the Pacific*, founded in 1887. This magazine, now called *Honolulu Magazine*, was dedicated to telling the world how great Hawaii was, partly with the idea of attracting tourists.

The dearth of manufacturing in Hawaii prior to World War II was due not only to the lack of raw materials, but also to the tiny size of the local market, based on a territorial population of only some 400,000, including the military, or about half of Oahu's population in the late 1980s. Furthermore, purchasing power per capita was only about one-fourth that of today. Consequently, Hawaii's total purchasing power amounted to only about one-eighth that of the residents of Oahu today—not enough to support much manufacturing for local consumption.

DIVERSIFIED AGRICULTURE

In sharp contrast to the attitude toward manufacturing, the conventional wisdom in Hawaii throughout the nineteenth century and well into the twentieth was that its economic future, like its past, lay in agriculture. According to that view, Hawaii not only could grow its own food but also could increase its wealth by growing agricultural products for overseas markets. Success with sugar and pineapple proved that with agriculture Hawaii could provide full employment at income levels high by world standards.

The belief persisted that much could be done in diversified agriculture, both for home consumption and for export. It was this conviction that led to the organization of the Royal Hawaiian Agricultural Society, whose main objective, in the words of its founders, was "to encourage and foster agricultural operations in every form."[153] This conviction stemmed from the fact that Hawaii's climate not only permitted year-round growing but also made possible the culture of tropical-zone plants at lower altitudes and some temperate zone plants at higher altitudes. It was also recognized that the island economy would be more stable if it were based on many products rather than on just a few. And if Hawaii grew the food it needed, supplies would be assured if shipping were disrupted by war. The American dream of a society based on small, independent farmers was popular in Hawaii, with its dominant citizenry composed largely of transplanted New Englanders. The territorial legislature established a homestead land program to stimulate family farming. Such views even permeated the sugar and pineapple industries, and as a result the Hawaiian Sugar Planters' Association experiment station and the Pineapple Producers' Cooperative Association experiment station devoted considerable research effort to testing various crops for possible commercial development.[154]

When Hawaii was annexed by the United States at the turn of the century, the U.S. Department of Agriculture "noted the excessive preeminence of the sugar industry and, mindful of the unfortunate results of overspecialization in the cotton belt of the southern states, advocated very strongly the diversification of agriculture."[155] As a result, the federal government established the Hawaii Experiment Station on the outskirts of Honolulu in 1901. This station "devoted itself to the investigation of potential new crops and industries for this newly annexed Territory. While a large number of possibilities were explored during the ensuing years, chief emphasis was placed on a few which seemed to offer the best promise, notably tobacco, rice, rubber and starch; also, several fruits received a good deal of attention, especially the orange, avocado, pineapple, mango, banana, and papaya and several vegetable crops."[156] The Hawaii Experiment Station was merged into the University of Hawaii in 1928, by which time the university had established a comprehensive agricultural extension service to assist farmers in coping with their problems.

Diversified agriculture did not fail to become a great success for lack of trying. David Livingston Crawford, president of the University of Hawaii, reviewed the effort put into "Hawaii's Crop Parade." Thirty export agricultural plants (of which only sugar and pineapple were very successful), were experimented with, along with some seventy-five agricultural crops raised for local consumption, which met with varying degrees of success, and some fifty other plants, introduced for export or local consumption, which never reached the commercial stage.[157]

A few new exports, such as rice, coffee, tobacco, and sisal, showed great promise; and others, such as goat skins, cattle hides, bananas, and honey, though of limited potential, brought in significant overseas income at one time or another. Other products found small export markets for a while and then died out. Examples are arrowroot, ostrich feathers, cotton, rubber, and Irish potatoes.

For local consumption, improvements were tried in the production of vegetables, fruits, and livestock. Most innovations enjoyed some success, but some dropped out entirely after a while, such as wheat for flour, and rabbits and squabs for hotel and restaurant tables.

Among the complete commercial failures were a large number of new products that seemed worth pursuing, but which, in Crawford's words, "joined the limbo of forgotten crops."[158] These included silk culture, allspice, buckwheat, cacao, apricots, cloves, cinchona for quinine, date palms, flax, hemp, indigo, cashew nuts, chaulmoogra oil for the treatment of leprosy, various sedges and rushes for matting, nutmeg, olives, millet, mushrooms, tea, vanilla, sunflower, soybean, and the wattle tree for the tannin in its bark.

Despite all this effort during the plantation era, Hawaii did not develop any really important and lasting agricultural exports other than sugar and pineapple. In 1941, when sugar exports amounted to $74 million and pineapple to $63 million,[159] exports of all other agricultural products earned less than $1 million. Coffee and bananas were the main nonplantation export crops at that time.[160]

The goal of agricultural self-sufficiency also remained elusive. Sketchy data indicate that in 1941 Hawaii produced just over half of its fresh vegetables and about 62 percent of its beef and veal.[161] Since almost all processed foods were imported, it is probable that, overall, Hawaii produced about half its food supply and imported the other half.

The extremely limited success of diversified agriculture in Hawaii has long puzzled those concerned with its economic development. What has sometimes escaped notice is that Hawaii's advantages in agriculture, while obvious, are limited, whereas the disadvantages, perhaps less obvious, are numerous. This discrepancy in perception has led many astray in their thinking about Hawaii's agricultural potential.

Optimistic innovators were encouraged by the fact that Hawaii has fairly large amounts of agricultural land and supplies of water. Moreover, with its great variations in elevation and temperature it can grow almost anything, and does so on a year-round basis. Given its physical ability to grow crops and raise livestock of all kinds, and given the desirability of not only raising its own food supplies but of exporting agricultural products as well, many residents have shared the impression that a broadly diversified agriculture must succeed.

That sanguine view omits the obstacles. Whether for local consumption or for export, almost all agricultural inputs other than land, labor, and water have to be imported at considerable expense—fertilizers, feeds, insecticides, and fungicides, as well as tools, equipment, machinery, and the energy to run them. Furthermore, as illustrated by the local history of both sugar and pineapple, insects and fungi introduced into Hawaii without their natural enemies can multiply rapidly and devastate crops. In the 1850s, when cotton, coffee, and sugar all held about equal promise of becoming Hawaii's main crop, the pink bollworm destroyed the cotton plants and a fungus blight eliminated coffee from most areas except the Kona districts of the Big Island.[162]

As to citrus fruits, Crawford reported that "many kinds of insects and fungus enemies were lying in wait for the citrus fruit grower and if he did not wage expensive warfare against them they took most of his crop. It was much easier to buy California oranges and lemons."[163] In 1910 the dread Mediterranean fruit fly arrived in Hawaii, later to be joined by the melon fly, the Oriental fruit fly, and most recently the Malaysian fruit fly. They are all still here, alive and active.

Another important disadvantage to Hawaiian agriculture is that tropical crops can generally be produced better or cheaper in tropical areas of the world and temperate zone crops can generally be produced better or cheaper in truly temperate climates than in Hawaii. Most tropical areas of the world have labor costs that are much lower than Hawaii's. And only at higher altitudes does Hawaii have a temperate climate; although some temperate zone plants do well in the islands, most do not. For example, the local sugar industry has tried growing sugar beets, to find that while the leaves are magnificent, the beets are much smaller than those grown in the mainland. As another example, apples and peaches can be grown in up-country areas, but the fruit is small and emaciated compared with the mainland product.

According to Harold L. Lyon, for many years head of the HSPA experiment station, "Hawaii is tropical and its fields are not suitable to the culture of temperate zone crops."[164] Dr. Lyon chaired a committee on diversified crops which in 1935 studied how Hawaii could feed itself if blockaded in wartime. The committee's report concluded that it could be done, but at great expense. "[After the emergency is over,] anyone undertaking the production of truck crops in Hawaii on a scale sufficient to satisfy the local demand for these crops is embarking on a course that will lead to financial disaster."[165]

Hawaii's geography as a chain of islands is an important disadvantage to its becoming more self-sufficient in food production. For crops grown on the neighbor islands and consumed on Oahu, the cost of getting the product from the grower to the consumer is almost as great as it would be if the grower were in California, where production costs are generally much lower. If the product is for export, it has to be shipped several thousand miles to get to market, and if it is for local consumption it faces the problems of being sold in a small-volume "pocket" market.

Before World War II, the Hawaiian market was so small and isolated that one good-sized mechanized farm could produce all of a food item that would be locally consumed. But no farmer would produce on that scale for a pocket market. If he did and if another farmer planted the same crop, the market would be flooded and prices would plummet. As a result, the pattern that has emerged has been one of a large number of small farmers producing for the local market and jointly aiming to meet

only a fraction of the local market demand. Compared with the industrialized agriculture of places like California, inefficiencies are great and
production costs high—so that imported fresh vegetables, fruits, and
meats can frequently undersell the local product in spite of the transportation costs.

In spite of all the difficulties, four crops at one time or another gave
promise of becoming mainstays of Hawaii's export economy: rice, coffee,
rubber, and sisal. Only coffee was able to sustain its growth; the other
three joined "the limbo of forgotten crops."

Rice production was for a considerable time a major agricultural
industry in Hawaii, achieving exports of nearly 14 million pounds in
1887. It still ranked second only to sugar in the early years of the twentieth century, with around 35 to 40 million pounds produced annually, of
which several million pounds were exported.[166] But rice production in
Hawaii never progressed beyond the small-farm stage in which the growers, mostly Chinese, used methods similar to those of their ancestors in
China. They competed with California rice growing, which had become
large-scale and industrialized as early as in the 1930s—seeding the fields
by airplane and harvesting the crop with combines. A study at that time
showed that rice growing and harvesting in Butte County, California,
required an average of thirteen man-hours per acre compared with 488
man-hours in Hawaii.[167] Under this competition, Hawaii's rice industry
declined drastically, dropping to 7 million pounds in 1930 and to less
than 2 million pounds in 1940, with none of it exported.[168]

Coffee is another export industry that frequently held great promise
for growth but has been plagued by high costs and inefficiencies inherent in being organized generally on a small-scale, family basis. It has also
suffered from the gyrations of the world coffee market. As a result,
Crawford commented in 1937, after coffee had been produced locally for
more than 100 years, that it had been "only indifferently successful."[169]
It had grown into a fairly sizable industry by the time of the Reciprocity
Treaty (153,000 pounds of exports in 1876), but the treaty hurt coffee as
much as it helped sugar because it removed the Hawaiian tariff on
imported coffee from the United States, flooding the local market with
coffee imported through the United States. Hawaii's coffee exports
dropped to less than 2,000 pounds by 1885.[170]

The world coffee market then rose substantially, and around the turn
of the century Hawaii was exporting from 300,000 to 800,000 pounds
annually. From then until the early 1930s, when exports peaked at about

8 million pounds a year, the industry grew by fits and starts—with exports up to 2 million pounds in 1906 but back to 1 million in 1907, up to 4 million in 1914 but back to 2 million in 1917, and up to 7 million in 1919 but down to 3 million in 1924.[171]

Coffee production in Hawaii was thought to be "a good crop for the 'little fellow' to handle, but not worthy of attention by the big concerns."[172] Consequently, even when the industry peaked in the early 1930s, "compared with the sugar and pineapple industries, coffee production [was] still in a primitive state of development."[173] Perhaps the possible efficiencies of large-scale, scientific coffee growing could counterbalance high labor costs in Hawaii, but it has never been tried.

In the case of rubber, it was not possible to increase labor productivity enough to overcome the vast difference in wage rates between Hawaii and truly tropical areas. When the automobile went into mass production, the demand for rubber for tires skyrocketed, and the price rose to over one dollar a pound. Quickly three rubber plantations were started in Hawaii (on Oahu, Maui, and the Big Island), each with tens of thousands of trees.[174] Although tapping the trees and harvesting the latex was a labor-intensive activity that did not lend itself to any form of mechanization, the three companies did fairly well as long as the price stayed around one dollar a pound. But just as Hawaii started large-scale plantings to meet the new demand, so did many tropical countries where labor could be hired for a few cents a day; and by 1915 Hawaii's experiment with rubber was finished.

The promising sisal industry failed for a different reason. New technology made the product obsolete, just as the automobile killed the buggy whip industry. Most sisal cordage was used for binder twine in bundling sheaves of wheat at harvest time. Hawaii's sisal industry, which had started just before the turn of the century, grew to the point that exports in 1919 exceeded $200,000.[175] But then along with the tractor and the truck came the mechanical harvester, and wheat was no longer bound into sheaves. By the late 1920s the sisal industry was dead. It collapsed as fast as did Hawaii's ostrich plume industry of the 1890s, when the Gibson girl era with its plumes and boas came to an end.[176]

In the decades since World War II, Hawaii's agricultural scientists and entrepreneurs have combined to develop several crops to the point that they make modest but significant contributions to the economy, in spite of Hawaii's inherent agricultural disadvantages. Outstanding among these are papayas, macadamia nuts, and flower and foliage products. They will be discussed in Part 2.

VISITORS

From 1872, when the Hawaiian Hotel (later called the Royal Hawaiian) opened its ornate doors, until annexation in 1898, Hawaii's tourism was stable at about 2,000 overseas visitors a year.[177] In spite of colorful writing about Hawaii by such literary visitors as Mark Twain, Robert Louis Stevenson, Jack London, Herman Melville, and Charles Nordhoff, Hawaii was little known to world travelers, of whom there were few in any case. As a consequence, the Hawaiian Hotel in downtown Honolulu and a few minor hostelries were able to accommodate all the visitors who came. Apparently the only other hotels built before annexation were the small Seaside Hotel and the even smaller Waikiki Villa, both in Waikiki at the approximate location of the present Royal Hawaiian Hotel.[178]

Annexation as an incorporated territory of the United States brought Hawaii to the attention of the entire country. The islands suddenly became as much a part of the United States as Oklahoma, New Mexico, and Arizona—sister territories. National awareness of Hawaii in the Pacific was further stimulated when the United States acquired Guam and the Philippines as a result of winning the Spanish-American War in 1898. The linkage was strengthened after 1903, when completion of a transpacific telegraph cable reduced communication time between Hawaii and the mainland from a week or more to a matter of seconds.

More Americans had money for traveling to Hawaii. The combined population of California, Oregon, and Washington, only 675,000 in 1870, by 1900 neared 2 million.[179] In those three decades the nation's per capita gross national product doubled. Especially important for tourism, in that era of unregulated capitalism, before the income tax, many Americans were amassing fortunes large enough to afford long, expensive vacations.

To carry them to Hawaii, steamships were replacing sailing vessels, cutting travel time in half. Shipboard accommodations for passengers aboard freighters (until passenger ships were put into service) improved as the number of travelers began to grow.

Hawaii first got regular steamship transportation in the 1870s, when the North Pacific Transportation Company of Australia inaugurated its San Francisco–Australia service via Honolulu. Then in 1881 Claus Spreckels, who already had several sailing ships to carry his sugar from Hawaii to San Francisco, founded the Oceanic Steamship Company. When the *Mariposa* and the *Alameda* were built in 1883, Spreckels

started regular steamship service between San Francisco and Honolulu.[180] These ships were basically freighters, but they were built "with
special attention to passengers by making them suitable for tropical voyages."[181] Later adding the *Sierra*, the *Sonoma*, and the *Ventura* to the run,
Oceanic dominated shipping between California and Hawaii during the
latter part of the nineteenth century and the early years of the twentieth.[182]

The Hawaii government aided the introduction of new deep-draft
steamships. From the mid-nineteenth century, public funds had been
appropriated to improve Honolulu Harbor by dredging and installing
piers, wharves, a lighthouse, and other navigational aids. In 1857 the old
fort at the foot of the growing downtown business district, the fort plun-
dered by the French and occupied by the British in the brief occupations
of the preceding decade, was leveled and its rubble used to fill up the
reefs fringing the deepened harbor.[183]

To hasten the coming of steamships, the governments of kings Lunalilo and Kalakaua subsidized the North Pacific and Oceanic lines, Kalakaua's financial support continuing until the monarchy was overthrown
in 1893.[184] To provide a first-class hotel (the Royal Hawaiian), the Kalakaua government issued bonds of $116,000 to pay for the land, building,
and furnishings. In time, the hotel passed into private hands.[185]

Increasingly, the business community and the government looked to
tourism as an activity that might bring in substantial sums of money. In
1899 Benjamin F. Dillingham, having run his railroad from Honolulu to
the far northwestern end of Oahu, built a hotel at Haleiwa primarily for
tourists.[186] The Moana Hotel went up in Waikiki in 1901 and the downtown Alexander Young opened the next year. Also in 1902, the Chamber of Commerce and the Merchants' Association sent O. C. Weedon, a
Honolulu businessman, on a six-month tour of the mainland to adver-
tise Hawaii with a series of lectures illustrated with tinted scenes shown
on his stereopticon.[187] In 1903, the Chamber of Commerce created a
permanent organization to promote tourism, jointly funded—as it still is
—by the Hawaii government and the business community. This Hawaii
Promotion Committee, with $15,000 in its first year from the legislature
to supplement private funds, began advertising Hawaii in mainland pub-
lications and printed guides, pamphlets, and other literature about
Hawaii. Its name was changed to the Hawaii Tourist Bureau in 1919, to
the Hawaii Travel Bureau in 1944, and to the Hawaii Visitors Bureau in
1945.[188]

Encouraged by these developments in Hawaii tourism, Matson Navigation Co. in 1908 built its first passenger freighter, the *Lurline*. The *Lurline* was followed the next year by the *Wilhelmina*, a more elegant steamer, first to cater to the tourist trade and capable of carrying 146 passengers on "the fanciest piece of marine hardware that had ever been seen in the Pacific."[189] Two even larger passenger ships were added shortly thereafter, the *Matsonia* in 1913 and the *Maui* in 1917.[190]

A major question facing Hawaii's infant visitor industry was, Where in Hawaii do visitors want to stay? As already mentioned, in 1899 Dillingham bet on Oahu's north shore and built his hotel at Haleiwa. In 1901 developers of the Moana Hotel bet on Waikiki, a mile and a half from Honolulu Harbor. In 1902 Alexander Young bet on downtown Honolulu, close to the harbor and the Hawaiian Hotel, a business area where most of Hawaii's earlier small hostelries had been located.

Waikiki was a risky bet, plagued with mosquitoes which bred in its many duck ponds, rice paddies, and taro patches. But this was where Kamehameha V had built a seaside bungalow that *Paradise of the Pacific* magazine called "the most notable grass hut in Hawaii Nei,"[191] where the Seaside Hotel and the Waikiki Villa had been built in the 1890s,[192] and where the downtown Hawaiian Hotel maintained a "beach annex" bathhouse for its guests who wanted to use the ocean. More importantly, visitors then as now wanted to be on the beach and did not want the long train ride to Haleiwa. In 1917 Clifford Kimball, manager of the Haleiwa Hotel, decided to abandon the north shore in favor of Waikiki. He converted a large residence on the beach there into the Halekulani Hotel.[193] That same year the old Hawaiian Hotel in downtown Honolulu ceased operations and was converted into a YMCA for the Army and Navy.[194] Finally, in the 1920s, Waikiki's swampy condition was cured by dredging the Ala Wai Canal.[195] After that, Waikiki was clearly the tourists' choice.

Hawaii's tourism, which then catered only to the carriage trade, got a boost in 1920 when the popular Prince of Wales and young Louis Mountbatten twice visited Honolulu, thereby letting the elite of the world know that Honolulu was a highly respectable place in which to vacation.[196] The number of visitors to Hawaii, estimated at only about 5,000 in 1910, increased to 8,000 in 1921, to 12,000 in 1923, and to more than 15,000 in 1925.[197]

Hawaii's tourist industry now prepared to compete with Europe and the Mediterranean as a preferred travel destination for wealthy Americans. William P. Roth, general manager of Matson Navigation Co., and Edward D. Tenney, president of Castle & Cooke (Matson's agent in Honolulu) and also of Matson, devised what they called a "grand scheme" to make Hawaii preeminent in luxury resort travel. The scheme was to build the world's finest luxury ocean liner to carry the elite from the West Coast to Hawaii and to build the world's finest luxury hotel on the beach at Waikiki, with tennis courts, a golf course, and everything else that the heart might desire. Everything was to be made first class.[198]

The liner was the *Malolo*, at 17,000 tons and designed to carry 650 passengers, almost double the size of the largest of the five Matson passenger ships. The *Malolo* was not only big but was also the fastest, safest, most expensive, and most luxurious ship ever built in the United States up to that time.

The hotel was the Royal Hawaiian. Neither Matson nor Castle & Cooke had any experience with hotels, so that at this juncture the Territorial Hotel Company, headed by Conrad C. von Hamm, was brought into partnership. Territorial owned the Moana Hotel and the lease on the nearby Seaside Hotel in Waikiki, as well as the Alexander Young Hotel in downtown Honolulu. To make Territorial Hotel Co. a full partner in the grand scheme, the company was reorganized in 1925, with both Castle & Cooke and Matson as major stockholders and with Edward Tenney as president.

The Territorial Hotel Co. proceeded with the design and building of the $3.5 million, 400-room Royal Hawaiian Hotel, engaging a nationally renowned architectural firm (Warren & Wetmore), a local contractor (Ralph Woolley), a famous landscape architect (R. T. Stevens), and a nationally known advertising firm (N. W. Ayer) to spread the great news about the Royal Hawaiian and the *Malolo*. The hotel was opened on 1 February 1927 in one of the most gala events in Hawaii's history.

The golf course, Waialae, lay just beyond Diamond Head near Waikiki. Since it was to be an adjunct to the Royal Hawaiian Hotel, its construction was the responsibility of the Territorial Hotel Co. Seth Raynor, one of the country's most noted golf course architects, was selected to design what at the time was sometimes referred to as the Royal Hawaiian Hotel Course. Its clubhouse was used by the hotel for lunches, dinners, and dancing.

The grand scheme—the SS *Malolo*, the Royal Hawaiian Hotel, and Waialae Golf Course—was a success at first. The number of visitors to Hawaii rose from 17,500 in 1927 to 20,000 in 1928 and to over 22,000 in 1929. But with the stock market crash of October 1929 and the Great

Depression that followed, the bottom dropped out. The number of visitors to Hawaii in 1932 and 1933 was less than half the 1929 total, and the Territorial Hotel Co. ran into such hard times that it was dissolved in 1933. Matson took over the Royal, the Moana, and Waialae to protect its investments in the *Malolo* and in the new *Lurline*, which was under construction. According to the official biography of Castle & Cooke, "In the long run, the Royal was a financial flop, and Castle & Cooke lost every cent it invested."[199]

The *Malolo* did not fare much better. While under construction she suffered fire damage and when launched in 1926 was stranded on a mud bank. On her trial run, she was in a collision that sent her back to the shipyard for extensive repairs and delayed her entering the Hawaiian service until ten months after the Royal Hawaiian had opened.

The grand scheme may have been a financial failure for its backers, but it achieved its goal for Hawaii by giving the islands a reputation as one of the finest resort areas in the world. For decades the Royal was thought of by millions of travelers as the epitome of a grand hotel, and the *Malolo* had a glamour that no other ship in the Pacific ever attained. Waialae Golf Course, the third and smallest spoke in the grand scheme wheel, has done much to promote Hawaii as a tourist resort by hosting golf's greatest players.

As the nation pulled out of the Depression in the late 1930s, the number of visitors to Hawaii began to increase again. By 1941, when the United States' entry into World War II stopped all vacation travel, the number of visitor arrivals had climbed to 31,000. In that period, however, no new large tourist hotels were built on Oahu, except for the rebuilding of the Halekulani in 1930. Enough visitors were traveling to the neighbor islands to support several establishments. Hilo had the Naniloa and Hilo hotels, Kona the Kona Inn, the volcano area Volcano House; Kauai had the Lihue Hotel; and Maui had the Pioneer Inn at Lahaina. All the islands possessed a few small commercial hotels, but these did not cater to overseas visitors.

Matson built no new passenger ships after the new *Lurline* was launched in 1933. The big innovation in passenger transportation occurred in the mid-1930s, when Pan American started flights across the Pacific. The first commercial flight from San Francisco to Honolulu (en route to Manila) took place on 21 October 1936. This landmark crossing took almost twenty hours and cost each passenger $360—the equivalent of about $3,000 in 1987 dollars.

It was 1950 before more travelers came to Hawaii by plane than by ship; but the Matson company, foreseeing an expansion of aviation traffic, in the 1930s drew up a plan whereby it, the Inter-Island Steam Navigation Company (which had started interisland flights in 1929), and Pan American would form a company to specialize in air traffic between Hawaii and the West Coast. The project was vetoed by the Civil Aeronautics Board.[200]

Inter-Island Steam Navigation had more success in expanding its connections between Honolulu and the neighbor islands, increasingly sought by tourists. Passage across Hawaii's rough channels on the company's small freighter-passenger ships was seldom relished by visitors, but they would be ready to fly the short distances between islands. After months of comparison among aircraft by company president Stanley C. Kennedy, Inter-Island started service in late 1929 with eight-passenger Sikorsky amphibian planes, cruising at 95 miles per hour.[201] After a few years the DC-3 displaced them in operations for what was now called Hawaiian Airlines. The air age had begun in earnest for Hawaii's tourist industry.

DEFENSE

Although America's interest in bringing Hawaii into her sphere of influence was primarily military, the 1875 Reciprocity Treaty did not give the United States any military rights in Hawaii. When the treaty came up for renewal in 1883, the U.S. Senate insisted upon securing rights to the use of Pearl Harbor. The Hawaiian king and government, however, were adamantly opposed, and it was not until 1888 that a deal was struck that resulted in the treaty being renewed for another seven years.* The agreement was that although the new treaty gave the United States the right to establish a coaling and naval repair station at Pearl Harbor and to enlarge the harbor entrance, President Cleveland assured the Hawaiian government that he had no intention of doing so.[202] His secretary of state, Thomas Bayard, told the Hawaiian government in writing that the provisions of the treaty relating to Pearl Harbor made "no subtraction from the Hawaiian sovereignty over the harbor."[203] Diplomatic language thus eased Hawaii's fears and the treaty was signed.

Indeed, the United States did nothing about Pearl Harbor until after

*Hawaii agreed to cede Pearl Harbor after the revolution of 1887, led by members of Honolulu's business and professional classes, overthrew a government opposed to the deal. King Kalakaua capitulated on the cession. (Kuykendall, 3:345 ff., 396–397; Daws, 243 ff; Joesting, 218–221.)

annexation in 1898, and even then the buildup of military strength in Hawaii was slow. Four days after annexation 1,300 troops of the 1st New York Volunteer Infantry Regiment and the 3rd Battalion, 2nd U.S. Volunteer Engineers, landed and set up Camp McKinley in Waikiki near Diamond Head.[204] This force must have been reduced in size shortly thereafter, because the U.S. census of 1900 counted only 245 military personnel in Hawaii.

In 1900 Congress appropriated $100,000 to dredge the entrance to Pearl Harbor, which was blocked by a coral rock formation. A California company got the job but was unable to complete it after losing its dredge in a storm. The work was subcontracted to a local company named Cotton Brothers & Company, which leased a dredge from Dillingham's Oahu Railway and Land Company.[205] This dredging was completed in August 1903 but created a channel that was only thirty feet deep and 200 feet wide.[206]

Slowly a midpacific military bastion was created. In 1899 a U.S. Navy coal depot was established at the Diamond Head entrance to Honolulu Harbor, apparently near where Pier 1 is now located;[207] in 1900 its name was changed to "naval station." Around 1905 it was moved to land at Pearl Harbor the Navy had purchased for $134,000.[208]

The United States government bought Diamond Head in 1904 and fortified it at a cost of $3,300.[209] In that same year a detachment of forty-nine marines was stationed in Honolulu for duty as a guard force, and in 1905 the Army established Fort Shafter.[210]

In 1906 the Navy set up a radio station in Honolulu, with a transmission range of 225 miles and a receiving range of 140 miles. It was not until 1916 that a high-power station was established, able to communicate with Washington, D.C.[211]

The federal government in 1908 decided to make Pearl Harbor a major naval base, and the military presence in Hawaii was stepped up significantly. Between 1908 and 1911 a system of gun emplacements was erected along the southern coast of Oahu—at Forts Kamehameha and Weaver to protect the entrance to Pearl Harbor, at Fort Ruger to protect Diamond Head, at Fort DeRussy to cover the waters off Waikiki, and at Fort Armstrong to protect Honolulu Harbor. Schofield Barracks was also constructed at that time.[212]

At Pearl Harbor, work was started in 1908 on three major projects: establishing a naval yard, dredging the harbor entrance to a depth of thirty-five feet, and building a large dry dock.[213] The last job was not completed until 1919, three decades after the second Reciprocity Treaty had given the United States the right to use Pearl Harbor.

Military aviation came to Hawaii in 1918, when the Army Signal Corps, then responsible for the operation of aircraft, established a field on Ford Island, in Pearl Harbor, and stationed the Sixth Aero Unit there. The larger Wheeler Field was built between 1921 and 1923. Honolulu's John Rodgers Airport, shared with the Hickam Air Force Base, was constructed in the 1930s.

There were few acts of war in the Pacific after America entered World War I in 1917, and none involved Hawaii—except for the confiscation of eight German ships that earlier had sought sanctuary in Honolulu Harbor. The heaviest adverse effect of the war upon the territorial economy was the shipping shortage caused by the diversion of freighters to more lucrative routes, as the wartime demand caused cargo rates to skyrocket. The transpacific cargo rate to the Orient rose from five dollars per ton in 1914 to sixty dollars, and Atlantic rates increased in similar measure. Hawaii was then chiefly served by twenty-five ships of the American-Hawaiian Steamship Company, but by 1916 all had been sent elsewhere.[214] Matson, with its Big Five connections, kept its eight ships running to Hawaii and its cargo rates at the prewar level.

The U.S. Shipping Board Emergency Fleet Corporation (USSB) took over American merchant ships in 1917 and made Matson its managing agent for Pacific shipping. By this arrangement, the backlog of shipping to and from Hawaii was largely wiped out, as the USSB assigned "just about everything that floated to the trade; sailing ships, schooners, wooden ships and iron and steel vessels of all descriptions."[215] Having abandoned Hawaii during the war, and with the German firm of H. Hackfeld & Co. as its Honolulu agent, the American-Hawaiian Steamship Co. did not try to get back into the Hawaiian trade after the war. When it purchased Spreckels's Oceanic Steamship Co. in 1926, Matson Navigation Co. became the primary surface connection between Hawaii and the rest of the nation, both for cargo and for tourism.

The United States emerged from World War I as a great power, increasingly concerned with the Pacific as well as the Atlantic. In the early 1920s, confronting a Soviet Union arched along the northern Pacific toward Alaska and a Japan that had taken possession of parts of Micronesia during the war, the War Department increased the number of servicemen stationed in Hawaii to about 17,000.[216] It remained at that level until the early 1930s, when Japan's annexation of Manchuria caused a further buildup of American military strength in the Pacific. When Japan invaded North China in 1937, that buildup was intensified. By early 1940 there were nearly 30,000 soldiers and sailors in Hawaii, and the number rose to 48,000 after Japan, Germany, and Italy signed their Tripartite Pact in September 1940 (Figure 3.1). In addition, almost 14,000 civilians in 1941 were serving the Army and Navy in Hawaii,[217]

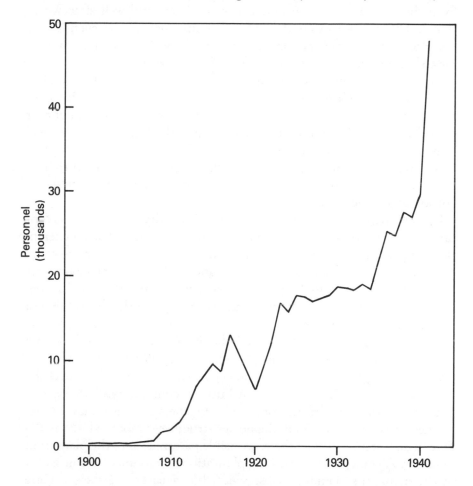

Figure 3.1 Armed Service personnel stationed or home-ported in Hawaii, 1900–41

Source: Schmitt, *Historical Statistics of Hawaii*, 10.

making total military employment amount to more than 60,000. By way of comparison, the sugar industry then employed just over 36,000 and the pineapple industry just under 16,000. The handwriting was on the wall.

TAXATION

Politically, Hawaii's business leaders were Republican. The Republican Party controlled both houses of the territorial legislature every session, from the first election after annexation in 1898 until well after World War II. Labor unions were then of little consequence; and even if they had not been, most of their members were aliens, by federal law ineligible to become citizens and vote prior to World War II.

Under these political conditions it might have been expected that legislation enacted during the plantation era would have been archly conservative, but this was not so. In fact, some of the tax legislation of that period was remarkably progressive. Although the bulk of the tax revenues for Hawaii's central and local governments came from property taxes and Hawaii had a poll tax (its tax system was similar to that of most U.S. states at the time), it led the nation in adopting personal and corporate income taxes.[218]*

In 1896 the Republic of Hawaii enacted a law that placed a 1 percent tax on net corporate and personal income, providing a $2,000 exemption for persons with gross incomes of $4,000 or less. The supreme court of the republic declared the income tax unconstitutional, but soon after annexation by the United States the new territory in 1901 passed a similar measure, with a rate of 2 percent. By exempting the first $1,000 of income, the tax was effectively limited to those in the upper income classes. This fiscal law came a decade before Wisconsin's, the first state to adopt a modern income tax. Similarly, Hawaii's inheritance taxes were first adopted by the provisional government that succeeded the monarchy, a government close to the business community.[219]

Such self-taxation by the dominant business interests may be explained by the paternalism of the power structure symbolized by the Big Five, which stemmed from the responsible paternalism of the plantation manager. A worker who joined the plantation community became a part of the manager's "family"—subservient, but a part nevertheless. Care was to be taken of those who obeyed the rules of the plantation. That

---

*In 1901 only Virginia had a personal net income tax in force.

mind set, spread to Honolulu and the government, set limits on economic self-gratification by the empowered business class, here expressed in tax policy.

The Emergence of Labor Unions

The history of labor union development in Hawaii was fairly similar in most respects to that in the mainland United States, except that development in Hawaii came later and, in the beginning, was considerably more modest.

The history of the American labor movement, both in Hawaii and on the mainland, falls into two distinct periods, pre– and post–New Deal. Prior to President Franklin Roosevelt's New Deal program of the mid-1930s, almost all labor unions in the United States and Hawaii were craft unions, most of them affiliated with the American Federation of Labor. They represented the skilled trades—carpenters, bricklayers, electricians, machinists, typographers, meat cutters, etc.—the elite of the blue-collar class. Although their incomes were generally not as high as those of most businessmen and professional people, they were a part of the great middle class and had no basic quarrel with society. Politically conservative for the most part, the craft unions had as their main goal to improve the economic well-being of their members and their status on the job through organized procedures for settling grievances—by insisting on fair treatment of workers, placing limits on the disciplinary power of employers, etc. They were "business unions"; their leaders were not promoting a class struggle between the "haves" and the "have-nots."

Hawaii's first union, established in 1884, represented the typographers. It was followed by unions representing the boilermakers in 1899; the bricklayers, the iron molders, the machinists, and the electrical workers in 1900; the plumbers in 1901; the blacksmiths and carpenters in 1902; and the hackmen (teamsters) and longshoremen in 1903.[220] The unions at that time had only small success in achieving even their modest goals. Few were recognized as bargaining agents by employers, the strikes they called were generally lost, and from time to time many of them were inactive. They greatly limited their effectiveness by restricting their membership to Caucasians. With most of the work force thus ineligible for membership, and given the tiny volume of business and industry in Hawaii at the time, they simply did not amount to much.

This situation did not change until the 1930s. A report on labor conditions in Hawaii prepared by the U.S. Department of Labor covering the period 1929–30 stated that said "labor organizations in the Hawaiian Islands are few in number, small in membership, and, with the exception of the barbers' union, have no agreements with the employers."[221] Beechert (p. 248) points out that even the barbers' union, which of course excluded persons of Asian ancestry, had only a handful of members in six barber shops, whereas ninety-one other barber shops were manned by 300 nonunion Japanese barbers. Schmitt records that in all there were an estimated 500 union members in Hawaii in 1935.[222]

Throughout the pre–New Deal era, labor unions had no help from the government in their efforts to organize workers and to gain recognition by employers. If they could muster enough strength to force an employer to recognize them, then they might become the bargaining agent for his employees. But no laws specified when a union had to be recognized, what issues were bargainable, or what constituted nonunion activities of employers.

When Franklin Roosevelt became president in March 1933, the American economy was in the worst economic condition it had ever experienced. Probably one-fourth of the labor force was unemployed, more workers were becoming unemployed every day, and the unemployed had no place to turn to for help because public and private welfare programs were practically nonexistent in the early 1930s. Roosevelt pledged a "new deal," and many New Deal programs were enacted during the first months of his presidency. The New Deal consisted of three major thrusts—relief for the unemployed; recovery for business, industry, and agriculture; and reform for the economy in general so that the Great Depression would not be repeated. Labor unions figured prominently in the last two parts of the three-part program.

Relief for the unemployed consisted primarily of make-work projects administered by the Works Progress Administration, the Civilian Conservation Corps, the Federal Emergency Relief Administration, and the Civil Works Administration. Relief was also provided from foreclosures on homes through the Home Owners Loan Corporation.

The 1935 Wagner Act, which guaranteed workers the right to organize unions and to bargain the terms of their employment with employers, gave a boost to the labor unions. Labor–management agreements were to be supervised and enforced by the new National Labor Relations Board. Any time a union represented a majority of the employees of a business, the employer had to recognize and bargain with it. The act also specified a large number of "unfair labor practices" that employers were forbidden to engage in. The Wagner Act covered all activities that affected commerce, but Congress in appropriating funds for the National Labor Relations Board consistently excluded agriculture.

Industrial unions were quickly organized under the new law, including in their membership the unskilled and semiskilled, as well as the skilled workers not already in craft unions. Industrial unions, as Hawaii was to learn, by and large had a broader and more radical perspective of labor's goals than did craft unions. Basically representing less skilled workers, they represented the "have-nots" of society. It was not uncommon for the leadership of the industrial unions to see the labor movement more as a class struggle than as just a way to increase wages and improve working conditions. Some of the more socially conscious industrial unions born during the Great Depression took a political stance that was more closely allied with socialism and communism than with capitalism. This was not surprising, since in their leaders' opinion the Great Depression showed that capitalism had inherent weaknesses that kept it from being an effective way to organize the factors of production.

Much of what was happening on the mainland also started to happen in Hawaii in the late 1930s. In earlier decades, workers on the Hawaiian sugar plantations had attempted to organize on an industry-wide basis. Their efforts resulted in several strikes—at Waialua Sugar Co. on Oahu in 1905, at Waipahu in 1906, at most of the Oahu sugar plantations in 1909, at most of the plantations on all islands in 1920, and at some Oahu plantations in 1925.[223] The labor organizations behind these efforts were formed along ethnic lines, being confined to workers of the Japanese race in the strikes of 1905, 1906, and 1909, and to Filipino organizations in 1925. Both groups joined in the 1920 strike. Most of these strikes failed, partly because the organizers did not yet have the protection of the law that the New Deal was to introduce, and partly because each organization was confined to a single race and hence as a group the unions were far weaker than if they had represented the entire work force.

The labor history of longshoremen in Hawaii requires special note. Dockworkers the world over have always been a tough labor group. In fact the first "job action" in Hawaii was taken by unorganized longshoremen in 1867 who refused to load a ship in Honolulu Harbor unless their wages were increased; other "disturbances" occurred on the waterfront in Hawaii in 1869, 1880, 1886, and 1889.[224] Hawaii's longshoremen joined the International Longshoremen's Association (ILA) in 1903, and this union staged a major Honolulu waterfront strike in 1916.[225]

By the mid-1930s, the Hawaii longshoremen's unions had dropped their affiliation with the ILA; and in May 1937 the Pacific Coast district of the ILA, which was run by Harry Bridges, broke away to form the International Longshoremen's and Warehousemen's Union (ILWU), an industrial union that included warehousemen as well as longshoremen and which promptly joined the Congress of Industrial Organizations—the CIO.[226] In 1937 the ILWU issued charters to the as yet unrecognized longshoremen's unions in the Hawaii ports. One of the important things that the ILWU brought to Hawaii—both for its own success as a union and for the long-range benefit of the people of Hawaii—was a policy of racial integration. It set itself apart from the other unions at the time by drawing no ethnic lines.

By the end of 1937 the ILWU and the CIO were established in Hawaii and the National Labor Relations Board (NLRB) had an office in Honolulu prepared to conduct representation elections among employees whenever a union claimed that it had a majority in its membership. It took only four years for the ILWU to win recognition elections in all of Hawaii's ports.[227]

At about the same time, the United Cannery, Agricultural, Packing, and Allied Workers of America (UCAPAWA, a CIO affiliate) issued a charter to a local on Kauai. Jack Hall was one of a four-man committee charged with organizing the plantation workers.[228] By the time Japan attacked Pearl Harbor four years later, the UCAPAWA had initiated two NLRB-conducted representation elections on Kauai, winning representation of the sugar mill workers at McBryde Plantation in October 1940[229] and losing an election at Kekaha in October 1941. It lost at Kekaha partly because of "a long history of good relations between management and workers" under Kekaha manager Lindsay Faye.[230] Commenting on this election, Beechert (p. 281) states that "it was clear that the workers did not yet see the union as a suitable alternative to paternalistic management." The reverse could have been said about the vote at McBryde.

Thus, by 7 December 1941, when the Japanese attacked Pearl Harbor and civilian activities such as union organizing came to an end in Hawaii under military government rule, a powerful industrial union affiliated with the CIO (the ILWU) had already established itself as the bargaining agent in all Hawaii's ports, and its sister CIO union, the UCAPAWA, had organized one sugar plantation and was working hard on others with great confidence that in time they would represent them all. Labor unions had finally emerged in Hawaii and were poised to start their major organizational drive as soon as military government controls were lifted. But by the time that happened, the UCAPAWA had become inactive in Hawaii and the ILWU had taken over its contracts.[231]

The Economy at the End of the Plantation Era

Although the heyday of the plantation era was the two decades between the world wars, during that period the two industries that would dominate the economy in the post–World War II period—the visitor industry and the defense establishment—developed a significant presence in Hawaii. The question I turn to now is, What was the relative importance of sugar, pineapple, the military, and the visitor industry in the total Hawaiian economy at the end of the plantation era? One or more of these industrial sectors, all export activities bringing outside money into Hawaii, have been the primary source of income to the Hawaiian economy for well over 100 years. An analysis of their relative importance to the total economy at the end of the plantation era gives a rounded picture of the Hawaiian economy at that time.[232]

The question that immediately arises is what figure to use to represent the size of the total economy. Nationally, gross national product is the standard used; but, although the Department of Planning and Economic Development developed a comparable gross state product figure for Hawaii, it starts only in 1958. The best measure prior to 1958 is the total personal income figure developed by the U.S. Department of Commerce, and that is the one used here.

Hawaii's total personal income is the sum of all the income received by residents of Hawaii from all sources—wages and salaries, proprietors' income, individuals' rental income, dividends, personal interest income, and net transfer payments from the government—to mention the main sources. In current dollars, Hawaii's total personal income was $218 million in 1939, $246 million in 1940, and $341 million in 1941.

The Department of Commerce study calculated an estimate of gross territorial product for 1952. It found that personal income amounted to more than 82 percent of gross product in Hawaii.[233] The main difference between total personal income and gross product is implied by their names. Total personal income is the sum of all income received by indi-

viduals, whereas gross product is the sum of everything produced. Portions of values of goods and services produced are not distributed to persons (e.g., corporate income tax liabilities, undistributed corporate profits, and depreciation and depletion allowances), so that it is necessary to
add these to personal income to arrive at a gross product figure. Or, conversely, they are subtracted from gross product to arrive at a personal
income figure. Other minor differences distinguish the two figures, but
these are the main ones.

If one takes the figure for total personal income to represent the total
Hawaiian economy, the research question is, How much of that total is
created by sugar operations, how much by pineapple operations, how
much by defense activities, and how much by visitor spending? I
answered this question for 1960 in a study published by First Hawaiian
Bank in 1962.[234] The methodology used is explained in section 1 of the
Appendix. Briefly, export industries create income for people in Hawaii
in three measurable ways. The first is by a direct distribution of some of
the money received from overseas buyers in the form of wages, salaries,
and dividends. The second is by an indirect distribution of some of that
money through the exporters' purchase of goods and services from local
firms, which in turn redistribute some of it in wages, salaries, and dividends. The third is from the multiplier effect of the direct and indirect
income noted above when it is spent and respent, thereby creating more
income throughout the economy.

I found that the money distributed by the export industries, directly
and indirectly, amounted to the following percentages of their total revenues from export sales (in the case of sugar and pineapple) and of their
total expenditures in Hawaii (in the case of visitors and the defense agencies): defense, 70 percent; sugar, 67 percent; visitors, 54 percent; and
pineapple, 53 percent. The figure for the defense agencies is high because
so much of their expenditures is in payroll. The percentage for sugar is
higher than for pineapple because most pineapple is put into imported
cans. The visitor percentage is low because, outside of expenditures for
hotel rooms and tips, many visitor expenditures are for imported commodities.

Applying this methodology to the prewar data developed by the U.S.
Department of Commerce, one can estimate the contribution made by
each of the four major export industries to the total personal income of
Hawaii. This is shown for 1939, 1940, and 1941 in Table 3.2. It reveals
that in 1939 the sugar and pineapple industries created—directly, indi-

Table 3.2 Personal income created by Hawaii's major export industries, 1939–41

YEAR AND INDUSTRY	REVENUES OR EXPENDITURES ($ MILLION) (1)	% BECOMING PERSONAL INCOME TO HAWAII RESIDENTS (2)	HAWAII PERSONAL INCOME CREATED DIRECTLY AND INDIRECTLY ($ MILLION) (3)	MULTIPLIER (4)	TOTAL PERSONAL INCOME CREATED BY THE INDUSTRY ($ MILLION) (5)	HAWAII'S TOTAL PERSONAL INCOME ($ MILLION) (6)	% OF HAWAII'S TOTAL PERSONAL INCOME CREATED BY THE INDUSTRY (7)
1939							
Sugar industry revenues	69.3	67	46.4	1.72	79.9	218	36
Pineapple industry revenues	51	53	27.0	1.72	46.5	218	21
Federal defense expenditures	35	79	27.7	1.72	47.6	218	22
Visitor expenditures	11	54	6.0	1.72	10.2	218	5
1940							
Sugar industry revenues	64.3	67	43.1	1.72	74.1	246	30
Pineapple industry revenues	46	53	24.4	1.72	41.9	246	17
Federal defense expenditures	45	79	35.6	1.72	61.1	246	25
Visitor expenditures	12	54	6.5	1.72	11.2	246	4
1941							
Sugar industry revenues	73.8	67	47.4	1.72	85.0	341	25
Pineapple industry revenues	63	53	33.4	1.72	57.4	341	17
Federal defense expenditures	85	79	67.5	1.72	116.1	341	34
Visitor expenditures	16.4	54	8.9	1.72	15.2	341	4

SOURCE: Column 1, Schmitt, *Historical Statistics of Hawaii*, 165, with government payments added to sugar revenues. Column 6, Schmitt, ibid., 167.

rectly, and through the multiplier effect—well over half the total income received by residents of Hawaii. The military establishment, with its pay of servicemen and civilians and its purchase of goods and services, accounted for slightly more than one-fifth, and the visitor industry accounted for about one-twentieth. Had data been available for the previous decade, before the significant buildup of the military in the 1930s, sugar and pineapple would of course have been considerably more important as a percentage of the total and the military would have been much less important.

Defense expenditures rose rapidly in 1940 and 1941, so that the military portion of the total economy increased considerably for those years —although sugar and pineapple were not getting smaller and the visitor industry was expanding. By 1940 the military accounted for one-fourth of Hawaii's total personal income and by 1941 for one-third. As a fraction of the total Hawaiian economy, the military had overtaken pineapple by 1939 and sugar by 1941.

Meantime, the visitor industry was still largely dependent on the few elite travelers who had the time and money to travel by train and ocean liner. Little did those in the industry suspect that the tiny (and expensive) Pan Am Clippers would be followed by successive generations of aircraft that would cut travel time and costs dramatically—first the big propeller planes of the 1940s, then the giant propeller planes of the 1950s, next the jets of the 1960s, and most recently the wide-bodied jets introduced in the 1970s. Nor did the visitor industry anticipate that the productivity of the nation (and of much of the industrialized world) would increase to the point that the carriage trade would become only a small segment of the long-distance traveling public, as tens of millions of everyday people began taking overseas trips each year.

And little did most people in Hawaii realize, as World War II approached, that after two-thirds of a century the plantation era was rapidly drawing to a close.

CHAPTER 4

The World War II Transition Period, 1941–45

General Economic Developments and Conditions

BY ANY STANDARD measure of economic growth—in output, income, or jobs—the Hawaiian economy expanded during the war years at a rate far faster than ever before or since. A real growth rate for a nation or a region of 3 or 4 percent per year is considered quite good, and a rate of 6 or 7 percent is remarkable if sustained over any extended period of time. Yet, from the base year of 1940 to the peak year of the war effort in 1944, total real personal income in Hawaii increased at an average annual rate of 36 percent.[1] This contrasted with an average annual growth rate, also measured in real gross product, for the United States as a whole over the same four years of just over 12 percent.[2] An economic boom of such proportions guaranteed that when servicemen and war workers left Hawaii there would be a severe contraction of the economy as it returned to something closer to its prewar size.

The rapid wartime rate of growth was based primarily on three factors. First, many workers came to Hawaii to staff military installations, raising total federal civilian employment from an average of 22,000 in 1940 to an average of 78,000 in 1944.[3] Second, extremely large numbers of military personnel came to Hawaii for training and staging before moving out to action. Their average annual numbers increased from 28,000 in 1940 to more than 378,000 in 1944.[4] As a result of the influx of civilian war workers and of uniformed military personnel, total employment (civilian and military) increased more than threefold, from 184,000 to 591,000, and the total de facto population doubled between 1940 and 1944, from 429,000 to 858,000.[5] Third, local residents made contributions to the war effort, giving a considerable boost to the economy. Every able-bodied man worked, so that unemployment was reduced to zero. Thousands of women who had never worked for pay before took jobs. Almost all children of ages twelve and up did some type of part-time work. Not only was the workweek extended to forty-four and in some cases forty-eight hours, but also many adults held part-time jobs in addition to their full-time jobs. The employment rate was probably at least 125 percent of the normal labor force. From December 1942 through October 1945, not a single person on Oahu drew unemployment insurance benefits.[6]

The economic boom affected various industries differently. To cite a few examples, interisland shipping was closed down in the early days of the war, but interisland air transportation expanded to take its place. Construction employment quadrupled between 1940 and 1942 but slacked off drastically in the later war years.[7] The fishing fleet was given patrol duty, and so Hawaiian Tuna Packers converted its cannery to an assembly plant for aircraft equipment, its shipyard to a repair facility for the Navy, and its cold-storage warehouse to an Army cold-storage facility.[8] Liquor stores were closed for the first several months after the attack on Pearl Harbor and were open only intermittently thereafter as supplies arrived from the mainland or were produced locally. One report stated that "Hawaii has gone dry and wet probably more times than any other spot in the country. The dry and wet spells have come and gone with the convoys."[9] Whereas alcoholic beverages had low shipping priority, the production of soft drinks was encouraged and the output of the local Coca-Cola plant rose from 57,000 cases in 1939 to 6 million cases in 1944.[10]

The variable impact of the war on different segments of the Hawaiian economy was not so much the result of market forces as of military decisions. On 7 December 1941, even before all the Japanese bombers had returned to their aircraft carriers, Governor Poindexter invoked Hawaii's "M-Day Act," which the legislature had passed at a special session in September 1941, giving unprecedented powers to the governor.[11] Minutes later, after consulting with Secretary of the Interior Harold Ickes by telephone, he acceded to the request of Major General Walter Short and declared a state of martial law, which turned most government functions, including the operation of the courts, over to the military. General Short, head of the Army's Hawaii Department and the ranking Army officer in the islands, promptly appointed his aide, Colonel Green, to the post of military governor, and Colonel Green set up his office in Iolani Palace.[12]

Although some government functions, including the basic functions of the legislature, were left in civilian hands and some others were returned to civilian agencies on 10 March 1943, the basic economic decisions—what was to be produced and sold locally and at what price, what could be exported, who worked where and at what wage, and so on— were made by the military until the government was returned to civilian control on 24 October 1944. Hawaii's economy was not merely reoriented during those three years from peacetime pursuits to winning the war; it was an economy under the direction of the military in practically every way. Because the civilian courts were replaced by military courts, enforcement of the orders by the military governor and his staff agencies was also in the hands of the military.[13] It should be noted that after the war, in February 1946, the U.S. Supreme Court held that the substitution of military courts for civil courts in Hawaii during the war had been unconstitutional. The military's authority to control employment, production, prices, and other such economic matters, however, was not seriously questioned.

Island businesses faced four basic problems in continuing to operate during the war: coping with a flood of economic control orders; replenishing stocks as they became depleted; making a profit when the prices they could charge were controlled but many of their costs were not; and, most difficult of all, finding workers in the tightest labor market in the entire country.

Problems of complying with control orders are described in Gwenfread Allen's *Hawaii's War Years, 1941–1945.*

> [In the early days of the war] orders flooded from various offices, one order sometimes covering several subjects. There were 151 "defense act rules" from the territorial governor, somewhat more than 100 "directives" from the territorial director of civil defense, and innumerable regulations from miscellaneous executives. In addition, there were 181 "old series" general orders from the military governor before March 10, 1943, and 70 of the "new series" between that date and October, 1944, plus 12 "security orders" and 12 "special orders" from the office of Internal Security after October, 1944.
>
> Many orders were worded to cover the territory, but in practice they applied only to Oahu unless they were reissued by authorities on each island. . . . some of the orders written under stress had to be corrected. (p. 167)

Although most of these orders and regulations applied to the behavior of individuals rather than of enterprises, figuring out what could be done so as not to be hauled into a military court for violation was a serious problem for all business people. According to the 1944 report of one Hawaii corporation to its stockholders, "the almost complete indifference of one government agency to the rules and regulations issued by another agency is as difficult to cope with as is their indifference to the fundamental problems of production."[14] Earlier in the war the same company had complained that it seemed "as though the winning of the war had become a secondary matter in the welter of questionnaires, regulations, rulings, and interpretations hurled at us. It is utterly impossible to keep pace with all of them."[15]

As most merchandise, supplies, and equipment came from the mainland, the wartime interruption of commercial shipping created tremendous problems for every business. All shipping was taken over by the government for the duration of the war and, in fact, until some six months after it was over—until the spring of 1946.[16]

For all of 1942 and well into 1943, all imports were controlled by the materials and supplies section of the Office of the Military Governor, which processed some thousand applications for imports each month. Nonmilitary cargo space for shipments to Hawaii was limited by a joint military transportation committee in Washington to 85,000 tons a month—50,000 tons of food and the rest for general cargo. Despite the planned allocation, the unpredictable availability of shipping caused the actual tonnage of civilian cargo coming to Hawaii monthly to vary from 50,000 to 124,000 tons—in contrast with average monthly arrivals of 200,000 tons of civilian cargo per month in the first nine months of 1941. Under those conditions, few firms got as much as they wanted. After April 1943, the procurement of mainland supplies for Hawaii was controlled by the War Production Board, and by 1944 about 100,000 tons of civilian cargo was arriving in Hawaii monthly, which was still only about half the 1941 tonnage.[17]

With the supply of civilian goods severely limited and with huge military payrolls and huge war-worker payrolls added to enlarged civilian payrolls, the potential for inflation in Hawaii was immense. The Office of the Military Governor established control over food prices on Oahu in January 1942 and in May of that year froze other prices at their highest April level. Similar price controls were established by military commanders on the neighbor islands.[18] Base prices frequently did not reflect the higher costs of wartime conditions, and as a result there were hundreds of appeals for price relief. In March 1943, when some governmental functions were returned to civilian agencies, price control was turned over to the Office of Price Administration and thereafter functioned somewhat more efficiently. Price controls were not lifted until June 1946.[19]

While controls laid down by the military governor were ubiquitous and confusing, supplies inadequate, and price controls rigid, the biggest problem most Hawaiian businesses faced during the war was their inability to find workers. Although tens of thousands of civilians came to Hawaii to work for the Army and the Navy, thousands of local workers left their civilian jobs to take war-related work, probably out of both patriotic and economic considerations.

To ensure that war-related and essential civilian services were staffed, one of the first orders of the Office of the Military Governor froze on their jobs all governmental employees, workers of private companies with government contracts, and employees of hospitals, utilities, stevedoring firms, dairies, and laundries. Furthermore, anyone who had been employed by any of these high-priority organizations on December 7 and who had since left, was ordered back to his job. Any unauthorized absenteeism was subject to fine or imprisonment by a military court.[20] This General Order 18 also abolished all union contracts and suspended the operation of the National Labor Relations Act, the Fair Labor Standards Act, and the National Wage Stabilization Program. Finally, it froze the wages of workers in the essential organizations at their 7 December 1941 levels.[21]

In January 1942 all unemployed men were required to register with the U.S. Employment Service, and they (some five thousand) were assigned to jobs on a priority basis.[22] In November 1942 all women were required to register, and most who did not have a job but were able to work took positions for fear that if unemployed they would be required to leave the territory. At the time of the registration, it was found that 53 percent of all women in Honolulu held jobs and that most of those not employed were unable to work either because they had small children at home or because they were physically disabled.[23]

Whereas labor and employment controls were quite effective, wage controls were not. To assist in recruiting workers from the mainland, wages for war-connected work were revised upward in May 1942, and in the fall white-collar workers in the federal Civil Service received two increases—a general pay raise and then a 25 percent bonus, which was later applied to all Civil Service employees.[24] This was the beginning of the cost-of-living-allowance, or COLA, thereafter embedded in federal pay schedules applicable in Hawaii.

As wages were unfrozen, inflation was uncorked, "with many persons receiving as much in a week as they previously earned in a month."[25] In 1943 the Office of Price Administration (OPA) reported that "there was probably no population in the world with so much money per capita, and whose sole object seemed to be to get rid of it quickly. Free spending, lack of wage freeze, and shortage of labor sent wages spiraling and threatened the success of the OPA."[26] Finally, in June 1944 general wage controls, which had been in effect on the mainland since October 1942, were extended to Hawaii with the Internal Revenue Service given control of salaries of $5,000 and more and the War Labor Board given control of wages under $5,000. All wage controls were dropped immediately after V-J Day.[27]

The Impact of the War on the Plantations

Hawaii's military governor considered the sugar and pineapple industries important to the war effort—not as important as the organizations that were included in his General Order 38 of 20 December 1941, but more critical than the economic sectors omitted from the order, such as wholesale and retail trade, finance, insurance, real estate, and most service industries.[28] The continued production of sugar was deemed important because U.S. sugar imports from much of the world were interrupted by the war. Sugar, in short supply nationally, was one of the first commodities rationed. The continued production of pineapple was considered important because it was a food item greatly favored by the troops. Local production in what was almost a combat zone gave the military an accessible source of supply. In one war year the military took two-thirds of Hawaii's entire pineapple pack.[29]

Further, the sugar and pineapple companies were so big and had such a large supply of manpower, materials, equipment, and skills that they were considered essential to the military as it struggled to get prepared in the early part of the war. As a consequence, while workers on Oahu's plantations were not frozen to their jobs, the military followed a policy of not hiring plantation workers who might apply for jobs and, on the neighbor islands, local military commanders generally issued job-freeze orders for the plantations.[30]

Immediately after the bombing of Pearl Harbor, the military embarked on a construction program in Hawaii that would enable it to accommodate ten times more military personnel than were stationed in the islands in 1941, and twenty times more than had been stationed in the territory in 1939. This meant building airfields, roads, barracks, training facilities, warehouses, oil storage facilities, and everything else needed to handle up to 400,000 soldiers, sailors, and marines. In the months following the attack, when an invasion of Hawaii was a possibility, beaches were covered with barbed wire, open fields booby-trapped to eliminate the possibility of enemy aircraft landing, gun emplacements erected to protect possible beach-landing areas, etc. Not only did local building and construction firms pitch in feverishly (construction employment rose from an annual average of about 8,000 in 1940 to 20,000 in 1941 and soared to nearly 38,000 in 1942[31]), but the plantations were called upon to supply an immense amount of labor for these projects as well. The sugar industry alone provided the military with 66,000 man-days of labor in the last three weeks of December 1941 and another 390,000 in 1942. The plantations also provided trucks, tractors, medical supplies, water, and electricity to military installations; repaired much equipment in their shops; and fabricated such armaments as tank barriers, gun mounts, and fuel storage tanks. Ewa Plantation's machine shop in 1942 devoted 37 percent of its time to work on military contracts.[32] Hawaiian Pineapple Co., continuing to can fruit, also became a major producer of candy bars for the military, producing more than 100 million candy bars with such wartime labels as Midway, Coral Sea, Ack-Ack, and B-17.[33]

Although plantation jobs on the neighbor islands were generally frozen and the military would not knowingly hire plantation laborers on Oahu, many employees left sugar and pineapple for more remunerative work. Sugar employment had already dropped 20 percent between 1939 and 1941, and it fell another 21 percent between 1941 and 1945, so that the industry had fewer than two-thirds as many employees in 1945 as in 1939. Furthermore, the military took much cane land to use as airfields, bases, gun emplacements, roads, and storage depots. Total cane acreage dropped 11 percent—from 238,000 in 1941 to 211,000 in 1945. Finally, there were many interferences with production during the war, one being the inability to harvest at night because of blackout requirements. Nonetheless, the industry was able to maintain production at reasonably high levels, with 1945 production being only 14 percent below that of 1941.[34] This was made possible to a large extent by the wartime child labor noted earlier. During the four years of the war, students on abbreviated school schedules put in more than eight million hours of plantation work "and saved much sugar and pineapple from going to waste."[35]

Employment and production in pineapple were not very different. Between 1941 and 1945 the industry lost about 14 percent of its work force,[36] and total production of canned fruit and juice declined by about 17 percent.[37]

A final involvement of the plantations in the war economy was the production of vegetables for the local population. Leaders of both the sugar and pineapple industries had planned, prior to the war, to play a major role in food production. The HSPA's diversified crop committee had worked since 1935 on plans for food production in the event of an emergency. The Pineapple Producers' Cooperative Association had for years maintained with the Army a schedule of pineapple land that could be used for food production. And by 1940 both sugar and pineapple plantations had set out experimental vegetable plots.[38]

But prewar plans had assumed that Hawaii would be blockaded and that sugar and pineapple would therefore cease production so that full attention could be devoted to diversified food production. These assumptions, of course, turned out to be wrong. Instead, as already noted, the first call by the military for help from the plantations was for manpower, supplies, and the repair of damaged military equipment. Furthermore, Congress quickly created a $35 million revolving fund to enable the Federal Surplus Commodities Corporation (FSCC) to establish a food reserve in Hawaii. The FSCC loaded its first shipment of food for Hawaii in San Francisco on 20 December 1941; it included a year's supply of sardines and 180 tons of cheddar cheese![39] The supply was stored in a warehouse built for that purpose by Hawaiian Pineapple Co. in 1941. Later shipments of food were "stored in plumbing shops, furniture stores, basements and any other place it [the FSCC] could obtain."[40] According to Gwenfread Allen (p. 154), "the FSCC had built up a satisfactory inventory on Oahu by June, 1942, and by January 1, 1943 there was probably as much as 150 percent more food and feed in the territory than a year before. . . . The storage plan, originally designed to fill the gap until the first harvest of emergency crops, was so successful that it was gradually accepted as a substitute for the production plan rather than an adjunct to it."

Nonetheless, homeowners planted some 15,000 "victory gardens,"[41] which provided green vegetables not available in the market, and two of

Honolulu's public parks were turned into victory garden plots for apartment dwellers. Many organizations, including Central Union Church, planted their entire grounds in vegetables. Truck farmers expanded production and raised 60 million pounds of their main truck crops in 1945, compared with 37 million pounds in 1941.[42] The plantations proceeded, on a modest scale as manpower and equipment permitted, to plant various food crops.

As with everything else during the early war years, plantation plantings were made as directed by the military governor, acting through his director of food production. Plantings were planned to yield crops in volume and in variety that would replace the imports of 1941.[43] Although some plantings were successful (Oahu Sugar Co., for example, produced more than ten million pounds of potatoes during the war[44]), Allen (p. 156) reports that "the planters experienced every woe which besets the farmer."

> Potatoes were wiped out by drought, and carrots were eaten by bugs. Planting of insufficient seed resulted in poor stands, and some crops were planted in areas where weeds outgrew the vegetables. Because vegetables require a much more carefully prepared seed bed than sugar or pineapples, the plantations lacked machinery and labor to prepare the soil properly and consequently fell behind in their assignments. Of all the crops set out in those early months, lima beans alone came up to expectations, and these presented such difficulties in harvesting and threshing that some went to waste. . . . Military authorities, admitting the failure of the program, appointed an advisory committee for food crop production. One of the advisors reported: "The sad state of the plantation plantings is almost entirely a result of ignorance in regard to vegetable production methods. Plantation personnel know that they do not understand the technique of handling these crops. Therefore the ultimate blame cannot be placed upon them, but upon those who are responsible for the entire organization of the food crop program."

One agriculturalist complained that "the Generals don't know that you can't order a plant to grow the way you order a soldier to march."[45]

Assigned plantings were discontinued in the fall of 1942. A civilian was put in charge of food production,[46] and the Army started two vegetable farms on Oahu, one at Kipapa and the other at Waialua, on 181 acres of irrigated land and with labor provided by the plantations.[47] These proved to be moderately successful.

Hawaii was fortunate not to have to cope with a blockade. Undoubt-

edly, the plantations could have mastered the technique of growing vegetables in time, but there would have been a lot of hungry soldiers, sailors, and civilians in the interim. As it turned out, food supplies were sufficient to avoid formal rationing, although critical shortages of some
items required informal rationing—such as the sale of meat only after 1
P.M. so that workers who could shop only after work would have a
chance at the limited supply, and a limit for a time on Kauai of one-quar-
ter pound of butter per week to each customer.

That the plantations cooperated with the military to the fullest extent
to aid the war effort was testified to by Admiral Chester W. Nimitz,
commander-in-chief of the Pacific Ocean Area during the war, who said
in reference to American Factors that "during World War II the company, led by President Walker, made its land available for military installations, loaned its equipment to help in their construction, diverted
sugar land to the production of food, made available to the military government the services of its organization from the President on down,
and, in short, cooperated wholeheartedly and patriotically to the fullest
degree with the armed services in the conduct of the war in the
Pacific."[48] Nimitz made this statement on the occasion of the celebration
of American Factors' 100th anniversary in 1949. Undoubtedly, he
would have said much the same about the other four sugar agencies.

Developments Leading to a Pluralistic Modern Economy
ACCEPTANCE OF HAWAII'S JAPANESE AS LOYAL AMERICANS

Perhaps the most important long-lasting impact of the war on Hawaii
was the emancipation of local Orientals and the establishment of the
loyalty of Hawaii's ethnic Japanese to America, thereby paving the way
for their entrance into what previously had been haole-dominated businesses and social organizations and making possible statehood for
Hawaii. As will be seen in Part 2, Hawaii's admission to the Union as a
state created so much overseas interest and investment in Hawaii that it
alone would have changed the economic power structure of the islands.

Uncertainty as to how local Japanese would behave in the event of a
war between the United States and Japan was a most nagging question
in Hawaii throughout the 1930s, when Japan was fashioning its "Greater
East Asia Coprosperity Sphere" by military force. In Washington,
doubts as to the loyalty of the Japanese were at least as great as in
Hawaii, as evidenced by the fact that in all Congressional hearings on

the issue of statehood the question of the loyalty of the Japanese was always an insurmountable stumbling block. The Army and Navy were worried about the behavior of Japanese residents and of Americans of Japanese ancestry (AJAs) in a war with Nippon. In the 1920s and early 1930s the Army was reported to have seriously considered interning all Japanese in Hawaii in the event of war, but gave up the idea as impracticable.[49]

In 1941 some 159,000 persons of Japanese ancestry were living in Hawaii, of whom about one-fourth were older aliens who had migrated to Hawaii. The other three-fourths had been born in Hawaii and were therefore American citizens. Even Hawaii, which had a long record of interracial marriages, shared national prejudices against non-Caucasians. The perception that local Japanese and AJAs were different from the dominant haole population may have been fed by the ties with Japan and its culture that many families maintained, for example by sending their children to Japanese language schools in the islands or sending their sons off to Japan for their education. The Tokyo government claimed all Japanese born in Hawaii as Japanese citizens, unless they renounced that dual citizenship before the Japanese consul. Few Japanese born in Hawaii did so.

Whatever were the causes of racial suspicions in Hawaii, those doubts were swept away by the actions of the local population of Japanese and the AJAs during World War II. Despite initial barriers against their enlistment in the American armed forces, AJAs enthusiastically volunteered in large numbers, and later in the war others were drafted. Their numbers included the Army's 100th Infantry Battalion and 442d Regimental Combat Team, which became the most decorated units in the entire U.S. military service during World War II.

Among the civilian population, Japanese did what everybody else did in wartime Hawaii, took jobs if able to work and volunteered for wartime tasks—clearing groves of *kiawe* trees for military construction, stringing barbed wire, rolling bandages, tending victory gardens, knitting, giving blood, etc. Few were interned. Whereas in the western states some 110,000 mainland Japanese were herded into concentration camps, in Hawaii only a few hundred were sent to the camps—in an unnecessary and inhumane act, but one made with relative restraint by the federal authorities.

As to disloyalty, there is the evidence of Ensign Takeo Yoshikawa of the Japanese Navy, who was sent to Honolulu in early 1941 to covertly gather information on Pearl Harbor. According to Yoshikawa, "I held high hopes of *nisei* cooperation when I was first assigned to Hawaii, but these hopes never came to fruition." (Nisei are second-generation Japanese Americans—that is, Americans whose parents were born in Japan.) He found Hawaii's Japanese "so distressingly loyal to the U.S." that he had to work entirely alone.[50]

In only four years the performance record of Hawaii's Japanese, both in uniform and on the home front, resulted in their no longer being regarded by most mainlanders and by many people in Hawaii as a foreign, second-class, unassimilable, coolie-type labor group. During that brief period they emerged as full-scale members of American society.

ASCENDANCY OF THE MILITARY OVER THE BIG FIVE

When military government displaced Hawaii's civilian government on 7 December 1941, the military assumed not only governmental power but economic power as well. The decision about what a plantation would grow was not one for the plantation manager or his agency in Honolulu to make; it was a command decision. Whether a plantation worker would stay on the plantation or work somewhere else was likewise decided by military authority. Matson Navigation Co., owned jointly by four of the Big Five, was taken over by the government. The Inter-Island Steam Navigation Co. took orders from the military. Mutual (now Hawaiian) Telephone Company was under the control of the Army. And so it went throughout the economy. The plantation oligarchy was instantly, and totally, eclipsed. The initials OMG stood for two names, but both had the same meaning: Office of Military Government and One Mighty God.

The elite class of men who had run the plantation oligarchy became in some ways commoners themselves. Like everyone else, they stood in line to be fingerprinted, inoculated, and issued their ID cards; they queued up to get their gas masks and gasoline ration cards; they paid their parking tickets instead of having them fixed; and many of their wives began doing housework, as their servants left for more attractive employment. When people of different classes are forced to rub shoulders together in a crisis situation, class differences tend to disappear. One could say that the mighty were symbolically dethroned.

Stanley Porteus tells the story of how a Big Island plantation manager was brought down to size by one of his workers. Immediately after the attack on Pearl Harbor, the worker had been commissioned as an emergency policeman and assigned the job of guarding a bridge on the Hamakua Coast Road. The manager, Porteus relates, "had been brought up the hard way and believed that that was the only way that should be trodden by all his subordinates."

> He did not hold with the application of the Golden Rule as much as the brass ruler. Suddenly, at one of the bridges, he found himself confronted by one Joe Souza, armed with a double-barreled shotgun. In all Joe's life he had never had such an opportunity. He knew he would never have it again.
>
> "Git out an' be recognized," Joe ordered. "You know damn well who I am, Joe Souza," the boss complained testily, and he crawled out of the front seat of the car. But this made no difference to the guard who kept his lethal weapon cocked and pointed directly at the manager's plump belly. "Don' geeve me no bullsheet, Mister," warned Joe. "How the 'ell I know you no goddam Japanese spy, huh?"[51]

Not only did the Big Five lose control over their companies, but also their plantation economy was largely overshadowed by the immensity of the war economy that was added to it. Hawaii's construction industry, of little consequence before the war, had more employees than the entire sugar industry by 1942. Most businesses regarded military contracts as far more important than contracts with the plantations. Nonplantation diversified manufacturing, practically nonexistent before the war, blossomed into a significant industry with the war work that was available. The consumer market reoriented itself to demands of soldiers, sailors, and war workers, who held most of the purchasing power. "The hordes of servicemen and war workers gave each restaurant, bar, laundry, hotel, barber shop, and store more business than it could handle," reports Allen. Service people accounted for 70 to 90 percent of retail and restaurant sales during most of the war. . . . New businesses took the place of those which closed their doors, until in 1945 there were 37,000 establishments as compared with 30,000 in 1942.[52]

In short, the Big Five were pushed out of the driver's seat and onto the back seat, where they quietly spent the years 1941–45. This is evidenced by the fact that Gwenfread Allen in her 400-page book *Hawaii's War Years, 1941–1945* completely ignores C. Brewer, American Factors, Theo. Davies, and Alexander & Baldwin. The only mention of Castle & Cooke records that "early in the war, the Army Transport Service rented the center section of the ground floor space of Castle & Cooke, Ltd.; the Maritime Commission and the Civilian Evacuation Committee used other parts of the first floor; the Navy occupied some offices on the third floor; and the Army personnel division used a large part of the basement for tabulating work."[53]

With the end of the war, demobilization of the armed forces, the departure of tens of thousands of war workers, and the ending of military government, the military presence in Hawaii diminished drastically. It reached a low point in 1950, when only about 20,000 armed forces personnel were stationed in Hawaii. But that was considerably more than had been in the territory before the massive buildup in the late 1930s. Since 1950 the military establishment in Hawaii has remained larger than it was in 1941, when the economic importance of the military first outstripped that of both sugar and pineapple.

The military importance of Hawaii to the nation stems from its being considered America's best headquarters base for the military in the Pacific. Possible alternative sites farther west would be vulnerable to possible enemy action, and other island areas such as Guam or American Samoa are too small. Therefore, when the services were unified by the Military Security Act of 1947 and the post of commander in chief of the Pacific (CINCPAC), to whom all branches of the service report, was created, his headquarters were located in Hawaii, as were those of the Pacific area commanders of the Army, Navy, Air Force, and Marines. CINCPAC's domain, which stretches from the west coast of the Americas to the east coast of Africa, is the largest of all American military commands. More active flag and general officers are stationed in Hawaii than at any one place outside the Washington, D.C., area.

DEVELOPMENTS LEADING TO POSTWAR TOURISM AND OVERSEAS INVESTMENT

One of the important things that World War II did to (or for) Hawaii was to bring it out of its relative isolation from the rest of the world, which had resultant impacts of great magnitude on the economy. The prewar economy had been almost completely Hawaiian-owned and controlled. Recently, a writer for a local business magazine quipped that the Big Five in Hawaii now consist of Japan, Hong Kong, the United Kingdom, Australia, and Canada. The reason is that those countries have invested some $4 billion in Hawaii since the 1950s.[54]

Hawaii emerged from isolation not primarily because the world became aware of it and Pearl Harbor on 7 December 1941. Nor was the reason simply that several million soldiers, sailors, marines, and war workers came to or through Hawaii during the war. And it was not just because Hawaii played a central role in the Pacific war.

These factors were important, but they would all be forgotten in a few years. The real reason why World War II brought Hawaii into the world economy was the development during the war of technologies that in time practically eliminated distance as a factor in the isolation of any part of the world. Hawaii remains 2,410 miles southwest of San Francisco, but in economic terms it has been moved much closer to the mainland. To travel to California in 1940 took five days on a ship, or twenty hours on an airplane. That same flight today takes four and a half hours and costs (in real or constant-value dollars) only about one-twentieth of what it did in 1940.

In the field of communications, much the same thing happened. It is true that in the 1930s long-distance telephone service was available by wireless transmission, which was effective only when sunspot activity, which would blank out the signals, was relatively low; but the cost was prohibitive. In 1940 the cheapest phone call from Honolulu to San Francisco cost nine dollars, which, adjusted for a half-century of inflation, is the equivalent of about sixty-seven dollars today. In 1989 the charge per minute for telephoning San Francisco is only a few cents—less than it costs to have a secretary write and post a letter. Many technological advances, notably the communications satellite, made possible this revolutionary improvement in Hawaii's day-to-day linkage to the rest of the world.

Other developments, such as the big propeller airplane and later the jet airliner, with its low fares and large seating capacity, also resulted directly from technological improvements made in World War II. These aeronautical advances had critical importance to the Hawaiian economy. Shrinking distance and reduced travel costs have induced millions of overseas visitors to vacation in Hawaii every year, spending billions of dollars, and they have led to the investment in Hawaii of billions of dollars of overseas capital. Technological improvements of this nature probably would have come in time without the impetus of World War II, but they came the faster because the war gave a life-or-death urgency to their development.

THE RISE OF LABOR UNIONS

Labor unions were on the verge of takeoff in Hawaii when America's involvement in World War II intervened. For the first year and a half of the war, Hawaii's military governor closed down many civilian government functions, including the National Labor Relations Board, and for the duration of the war unions were handicapped because staging strikes was deemed disloyal. The CIO early in the war gave President Roosevelt a pledge of no strikes for the duration of the war, and the ILWU was bound by that pledge.[55]

In March 1943 some functions of government that had been taken over by the military on 7 December 1941 were given back to civilian hands, including jurisdiction of the civil courts over all violations of civil law. Relaxation of military controls put the Honolulu office of the National Labor Relations Board back in operation, and union organizing drives got under way in full force. Prewar unionizing efforts at sugar plantations had been confined to Kauai and had been conducted by the United Cannery, Agricultural, Packing, and Allied Workers. That union had become inactive in Hawaii, however, and its place was taken by the ILWU, which made Jack Hall its regional representative in June 1944. In 1943 the ILWU began to open organizing drives at sugar plantations on all the islands, and by November 1945 it had won elections at all but one of the thirty-four sugar companies. In addition, it had won recognition from the pineapple companies and from railroading, longshoring, and a number of miscellaneous industries.[56]

In addition to the ILWU and the AFL craft unions, which had also resumed activity, a third union force had emerged by 1945 under the leadership of Arthur Rutledge. Rutledge had come to Hawaii in 1938 with no union experience other than being a member of the San Francisco Bartenders Local 41, but by 1945 he had gathered together under the umbrella he called Unity House a group of unions (some independent, others affiliated with the AFL) that he headed. Besides the Teamsters and the Hotel Workers, it included unions representing workers in a wide range of industries—dairies, breweries, quarries, warehouses, and the gas company.[57] The non-Rutledge AFL unions had contracts in the building trades, printing and publishing industry, entertainment industry, and machine shops and foundries.

Thus, among the ILWU, Rutledge, and the AFL, by the end of 1945 Hawaii business and industry had suddenly become extensively unionized. The U.S. Department of Labor in 1947 reported that Hawaii was "one of the most highly unionized areas in the United States."[58] This raises the question, Why were the ILWU and the other unions so successful so quickly in their organizing efforts?

One factor was the resentment that plantation workers had felt at being frozen in their jobs during World War II while friends and neighbors went off to Honolulu or Pearl Harbor for better paid jobs. Although they were fixed to their jobs by the military rather than by plantation managers, they still believed that they had been discriminated against. And when they were loaned to the military for emergency work, they believed that the plantations were pocketing part of their pay. The general base rate of sugar plantation workers at that time was about forty cents an hour, with perquisites valued at about nine cents an hour. The military paid the plantation sixty-two cents for each hour a plantation laborer worked, forty-one cents going to the worker and the rest to the plantation to cover costs of perquisites, overhead, administration, and taxes, and to compensate for sugar production lost because of the diversion of the labor force.[59] But for the worker, who knew that the plantation was getting sixty-two cents for each hour that he worked for the military but was passing on to him only forty-one cents, this seemed a rank injustice. With some 500,000 workdays of plantation labor loaned to the military, resentment must have been widespread throughout the plantation work force.

More important was the "mass grievance" that was an inevitable part of the paternalistic plantation system, as discussed in the preceding chapter. On the plantations, where the company was responsible for providing virtually all of the workers' needs, if anything went wrong, it created a grievance against the company—a grievance that the employer often was helpless to do much about. The accumulation of mass grievances was a major reason why the ILWU was able to sign up plantation workers as members.

Many workers also believed they had been treated unfairly by the military government. Like everyone else, they had cooperated fully with the military in the early months of the war when it was thought that Hawaii might become a battlefield at any moment. But after the decisive Battle of Midway in June 1942 removed the threat of invasion, and particularly after many military government controls were relaxed in March 1943, workers in Hawaii believed that they should be treated like workers on the mainland. Instead, essential workers were kept frozen to their jobs, their wages continued to be rigidly controlled, suspension of the U.S. Fair Labor Standards Act continued, and the stringent regulations that made it possible for military courts to fine or imprison workers for absenteeism were kept in place. According to a U.S. Department of Labor report in 1947, "Labor [during the war] believed that its position and its interest were being virtually ignored. It was the view of labor leaders that military government tended to be sympathetic to management and antagonistic to labor organizations. . . . This resentment gradually grew to explosive proportions between 1942 and 1944 and was a primary reason for the sudden unionization of all important industries as soon as restrictions were lifted."[60]

Another important factor was the change that had gradually taken place in the composition of the work force. Immigrant alien workers were being replaced by second-generation Hawaii-born and Hawaii-educated young adult citizens, who had American views about individual freedom, the abuses of autocratic power, and paternalism. By 1941 more than half the Japanese in the plantation work force were American-born, and every year that fraction increased as *issei* (first-generation Japanese Americans) died out and were replaced by young nisei.[61] Discontent rose when these young plantation workers were loaned to the military on emergency projects and worked side by side with mainlanders who had union backgrounds.

Education also played an important role in readying Hawaii's labor force for unionization. By 1945 most of the work force, although predominantly Oriental in background, had been raised and educated in Hawaii schools, which had instilled in them the ideals of democracy, equality, and freedom and had prepared them for work better than cutting sugarcane or picking pineapples.

Many plantation managers realized that educating the children of the immigrant plantation workers would someday lead to the downfall of the plantation system; but education was encouraged anyway, despite concerns that haole teachers from the mainland were teaching subjects unneeded and inappropriate for future field hands.[62] To the descendents of the missionaries, education was good in and of itself—and these were the people in agency headquarters in Honolulu who then largely determined policy. A good example was Henry P. Baldwin of Maui. One of the most powerful persons in Hawaii, in 1913 he told plantation managers, who were complaining that educating the immigrants' children would destroy them, that Hawaii must eventually become a first-rate American community and that this meant education came before all else.[63]

Another assist to unionization of the plantations came from the passage of Hawaii's "Little Wagner Act" in the spring of 1945. This was the

Hawaii Employment Relations Act, which gave agricultural workers the same union rights and protections that industrial workers had under federal law. Enactment was by the Republican-dominated legislature, reflecting a change in policy concerning labor unions in the business community that occurred in the closing years of the war.

Hawaii's history of labor relations prior to World War II was one of intense and active opposition of employers to unions of any kind and the employers' use of whatever weapon they had to fight them. Employers considered unions un-Hawaiian and unsuited to Hawaii's economic system of paternalism. As described in the previous chapter, they kept Hawaii almost completely nonunion until the mid-1930s, when the ILWU got a foothold on the docks and at one plantation.

The reversal in management's policy on unionization was dramatic. It was not based on a shift in fundamental attitudes toward unions or a willingness to share economic power with them. Hawaii's employers were probably as strongly anti-union in 1943 as they had been in 1933, but by 1943 they saw the handwriting on the wall. The Wagner Act had made many of their tactics in opposing unions illegal. They saw how unionization had swept the mainland in the last half of the 1930s like a tidal wave. They saw how that tsunami had built up in Hawaii, only to be stopped dead on 7 December 1941. They knew that the moment military government controls were relaxed enough for unions to start organizing, management would be faced with union problems of a magnitude and complexity it had never seen before. And they were smart enough to know that if they fought the unions as they had in the past, the fight would be ineffective, counterproductive in its effect on long-range relations with their employees, and under the Wagner Act very possibly illegal.

Wartime military controls had given Hawaii's employers time to ponder these imminent problems. Not knowing what to do, they got the best professional industrial relations expert they could find to come to Hawaii to advise them. In 1943 they organized the Hawaii Employers Council (HEC) and persuaded James P. Blaisdell, a prominent San Francisco industrial relations lawyer, to head the council. At that time Blaisdell was the Northern California director of the War Manpower Commission.

Because the prospect of unionization faced all employers and there would be great advantages to management if all employers followed the same policies with respect to union issues, the HEC was set up as a terri-

tory-wide, industry-wide organization with all the major companies in
Hawaii as its charter members—all of sugar, including the Big Five; all of
pineapple, including the two mainland-based firms of Calpac and Libby;
the major hotels; stevedoring companies; banks and trust companies;
public utilities; transportation companies; wholesale and retail trade
firms, including the Retail Board of the Honolulu Chamber of Commerce; major construction firms; newspapers; radio stations; and so on.
To all intents and purposes, the HEC represented the entire Hawaiian
business community. Furthermore, its board of governors was composed
of the chief executive officers of the major companies, not merely some
vice presidents who had nothing else to do. In its early years the HEC
was the most powerful business forum in Hawaii.

An early policy decision of the HEC was that member companies
should recognize a union as the legitimate bargaining agent for employees as soon as—but not until—it had established, normally by secret bal-
lot of employees, that it represented a majority of them. This meant that
unions could get recognition if they won a government-conducted representation election and would not have to force recognition by a strike.
Another policy was to settle contract disputes by negotiation—and work
stoppage if necessary—but never by arbitration, on the theory that no
outside party should be given the power to set the terms of work. A
third policy was to refuse to bargain away critical rights of management
concerning promotion, grievance handling, and disciplinary action. A
fourth policy was to insist on guarantees of no work stoppages during
the life of a contract—a no-strike, no-lockout provision.

HEC members agreed upon three other policies that they insisted be
incorporated into all collective bargaining agreements. One was a
mutual assurance: the union would not coerce an employee into joining
the union; the employer would not discriminate against any employee
for union activity. Another was a prohibition against interruption of
work during the life of the contract by the employer, the union, or any
employee covered by the union contract. The third provided that the
employer had a right to discharge employees for certain causes, including failure to perform work as required. The first policy ruled out any
form of compulsory union membership, including the union shop; the
irrevocable dues checkoff was the form of union security agreed to. The
second policy protected against wildcat strikes, job actions, or other
interruption of work by the union or employees. The third gave the
employer the right to discharge any employee who refused to work by

refusing to cross a picket line during the life of the contract. This put real teeth into the no-strike clause.[64]

These last three policies, called the "three clauses," were challenged by the Teamster's Union as being violations of the rights of labor under the Wagner Act, but they were upheld by the National Labor Relations Board in Washington. This case established an important principle for the NLRB, namely that the board would not mandate any term of a collective bargaining agreement. The two parties had agreed to the three clauses, and that settled the matter.

Because employers in Hawaii, through the HEC, had decided to recognize unions once the unions had won a secret election conducted among members of the proposed bargaining unit, there was no reason to oppose the Little Wagner Act before the legislature. In fact, there were reasons to support such an act if it were drafted in reasonable form, because, without the Hawaii Employment Relations Board which it created, there would be no official agency to conduct representation elections among agricultural workers.

A primary objective of the HEC was to avoid the whipsawing tactics effectively used by some mainland unions—getting a concession from one employer and then demanding it from others in the industry. For this reason, the HEC insisted on industry-wide bargaining for sugar, pineapple, and longshoring. Since practically all industries belonged to the HEC, it was generally able to prevent a union from obtaining some abnormal concession in one industry and then requiring it of all because it "set a community pattern."

Council members realized that industrial relations consisted of far more than bargaining with unions. They recognized that the administration of a union contract was as important as its terms. HEC became an educational agency, providing training for supervisory personnel, holding conferences and panel discussions to keep management abreast of developments in labor relations. It developed what was generally considered the best labor relations research department in the country under the presidency of Dwight Steele, who succeeded Blaisdell in 1947. Steele thought that the Council should lead in solving the serious economic adjustments that Hawaii faced when the military presence was reduced to peacetime proportions. By the close of 1945, that reduction was under way.

Part 2
AS I SAW IT

CHAPTER 5

The Modern Economy, since 1945

The Labor Challenge

FOR THE FIRST few years after World War II, far and away the biggest issue in the Hawaiian economy was the ILWU's challenge to the old establishment. Gavan Daws (p. 367) describes the situation well:

> [A]fter the sugar strike of 1946 people began to talk about the One Big Union and the Big Five in the same breath, as if they were evenly matched contestants for power. The ILWU would not have regarded this as any more than its due. The union's leaders had planned and carried out a brilliant attack on the Big Five, and they were confident that they had the best of things already. On the plantations and along the waterfront—at the strategic points in the capitalist network of production, distribution, and exchange—the barricades of radical unionism were erected, and the battle was joined. In the view of the union the plantation agencies had brought upon themselves a struggle they were doomed to lose. The Big Five, failing to move with the times, had fallen prisoner to history, and the keys to the future—political as well as economic—were in the hands of the ILWU.

The big question was, Would Hawaii, after having lived under the economic and political domination of the plantation oligarchy in prewar days and under the domination of the military during the war, now in the postwar era have to live under the economic and political domination of a Communist-oriented labor union?

For roughly the first half-dozen years after World War II the economic and political power of the ILWU was so manifest as to be frightening to many of Hawaii's residents who were not members of the union. In those troubled, suspicious days of the Cold War, the alleged Communist affiliation of some of the union's leaders made the situation doubly threatening.

The economic power of the union stemmed from the facts that the sugar and pineapple industries accounted for the bulk of all income generated by private business in Hawaii; that the ILWU could close down these two industries if it wanted to; that sugar and pineapple had to leave Hawaii on ships, and ILWU's longshoremen loaded and unloaded the ships in all Hawaii's ports; and that most sugar and pineapple went to the West Coast, where the ILWU controlled both the docks and the warehouses.

The ILWU early demonstrated its power. In the 1946 sugar contract negotiations, a stalemate was reached, closing down the industry for seventy-nine days. In the 1947 pineapple contract negotiations an impasse closed down the industry for a month. In 1951 Hawaii's biggest pineapple plantation (Lanai) was closed by a strike for nearly seven months. Between 1946 and 1948 shipping between Hawaii and the West Coast was interrupted by ILWU dock strikes (mostly on the West Coast) ten times—once for three months, once for nearly two months, and four times for more than two weeks.[1] Finally, in 1949, Hawaii's docks were closed for six months, from May to November, by a longshore strike—a strike that reduced the territory "almost to a state of siege." According to the Federal Mediation and Conciliation Service, "Few disputes have had such far-reaching effects upon the lifelines of an entire economy."[2] It is no exaggeration to say that if this record of disruptions to the economy had continued unabated, business in Hawaii would have had to face the fact that its continued existence was totally in the hands of, and at the pleasure of, the ILWU. The union's regional director Jack Hall was quoted as saying, "The ILWU is strong enough to enforce any demands if it did not have a sense of responsibility. . . . We could bring down the temple any day, but when we do we destroy ourselves."[3] The problem was that many people in Hawaii in the 1940s and early 1950s had serious doubts about the ILWU's sense of responsibility.

The political power of the union was almost as great as its economic power and for that reason was equally frightening to those who were not members. Jack Hall, from the very beginning on Kauai in the 1930s, put great emphasis on political activity because he knew that his union could succeed much better with a friendly government than with an unfriendly one, and that the things he could not win by collective bargaining he might win by legislative action—if the legislature were so disposed.

There was no place for Jack Hall and the ILWU in Hawaii's conservative Republican Party; but he knew that there was a place for them in the Democratic Party, and it became his objective to breathe life into that moribund party. When Hall started on the political trail, the party was insignificant in Hawaii's politics. Democrats held only one-fifth of the seats in the 1942 territorial Senate and only one-tenth in the House. But in 1944 fifteen Democrats were elected to legislative office, fourteen of them supported by the ILWU. And in 1946 the Democrats came very close to winning a majority, achieving an even split in the thirty-member House and gaining one seat short of an even split in the fifteen-member Senate.[4] Furthermore, some of the old-time Republican members were more politician than they were Republican and could see the handwriting on the wall. They preferred not to get in the bad graces of the ILWU, whose membership jumped from 900 in 1944 to 30,000 in 1947.[5]

At the 1948 Democratic Party Convention, Hall's forces made a bid to capture the party and write its platform. Only forty-seven of the several hundred delegates were ILWU members, but the old-time conservative Democrats led by Governor Ingram Stainback were "hopelessly outnumbered by the combined strength of the ILWU delegates and the several hundred delegates who, though not identified with the union, were anxious to break with the conservative past."[6] New young, liberal, independent Democrats, such as Jack Burns, Chuck Mau, Mitsuyuki Kido, Dr. Ernest Murai, and Vincent Esposito, managed to win a majority of the crucial votes.[7] In the primary elections "Democrat fought Democrat . . . enabling the Republicans to win another sweeping victory despite the fact that private Republican polls showed most voters now leaning to the Democratic party."[8] Even so, in 1948 it appeared that the Democrats would gain control of the territorial legislature in due time (which they did in 1954) and that the ILWU might control the party—which it never did, although it had great influence with it in later years.

What frightened many in Hawaii was that the ILWU leadership appeared to be Communist (surely by sympathy and probably by party membership), presenting an opportunity for Communist infiltration from within, the very treachery so many Americans both in Hawaii and on the mainland at that time feared. Its leaders had a class-warfare philosophy and hence shared many ideas with the Communist Party.

Cold War apprehensions fed distrust of left-wing unions, such as the ILWU. The United States was openly at war with communism, and it was a particularly frightening kind of war because class wars do not respect national boundaries. The enemy need not be thousands of miles away behind the Soviet border: he might be a Communist agent or sympathizer working for the electric company and in a position to pull the wrong switch.

The idea of an employee of the electric company pulling the wrong switch on purpose was no farfetched possibility in those days. Although the fear of communism undoubtedly produced a good bit of hysteria and unjustified witch-hunting, many Americans, all apparently loyal citizens, were actually found to be Communist agents—including a professional economist, whom I knew personally, who was on the staff of the Office of War Mobilization and Reconversion. In this extremely tense struggle between international communism and the free Western world, the idea that the ILWU—which by then was not only the most powerful labor union in Hawaii but also one that could close down the Hawaiian economy if it so chose—had a close affiliation with the Communist Party was enough to alarm many island people. And the evidence of Communist Party's infiltration of the ILWU (or vice versa, as the ILWU leadership argued) was quite substantial, with most of it provided by ILWU officers themselves. Those officers claimed that the ILWU was merely using the Communist Party to help its legitimate union organizing activities.

In 1947 the president of ILWU pineapple Local 152 (Robert Mookini) was suspended by the union because, he charged, he had refused to follow Communist orders.[9] Then the president of a Kauai local (Ichiro Izuka) and an ILWU unit leader and territorial senator on the Big Island (Amos Ignacio) both resigned because, they said, the union was Communist-dominated.[10] In 1950 Jack Kawano, president of the Honolulu waterfront local, defected,[11] and in 1952 Bert Nakano left Local 155 in Hilo and took nearly 400 ILWU members with him[12]—both charging Communist domination of the union. At U.S. House Un-American Activities Committee hearings held in Honolulu in mid-1951, Kawano testified that he had joined the Communist Party but then left the union because the Communist Party intended to use the union for political purposes, rather than to improve working conditions.[13]

Not only the Hawaii division of the ILWU but also the entire union was suspected of Communist affiliation. The U.S. Justice Department was convinced that Australian-born Harry Bridges, its founder and president, was a Communist and repeatedly tried to deport him. The secretary of the union, Louis Goldblatt, was frequently alleged to be a Communist Party member.[14] In 1949 and 1950 the national board of the CIO conducted an analysis of ILWU policies before expelling the union in August 1950 for unswervingly following the Soviet Union's foreign policy line.[15]

Finally, in 1951 the U.S. Department of Justice indicted seven of thirty-nine "reluctant witnesses" (who had refused to testify before the House Un-American Activities Committee hearings in Honolulu a year earlier) for violating the Smith Act, which forbade advocating the violent overthrow of the government. One of the seven was Jack Hall.[16] The seven were convicted, but their five-year prison sentences were reversed on appeal after the U.S. Supreme Court ruled that the Smith Act was unconstitutional. In his successful appeal, Hall's attorney argued that his activity in the Communist Party was never substantial, that he "held only the most lowly Party positions."[17]

The early postwar growth in union power did not continue. Instead, Hawaii's economy developed into one in which today neither the unions nor business has a dominant economic or political position. The rest of this section is devoted to an explanation of why the trends in Hawaii's labor relations were reversed.

To begin with, credit goes to Dwight Steele, then president of the Hawaii Employers Council, for his belief that these trends could be reversed. In the fall of 1949, at the end of the six-month-long Great Hawaiian Dock Strike, Steele wrote me in Washington, D.C., where I was a staff member of the President's Council of Economic Advisers, asking me to come to Hawaii to direct the research activities of the HEC. He stated that the postwar years had been difficult for labor relations in Hawaii. But now that there had been an industry-wide strike in each of Hawaii's major industries organized by the ILWU, he thought the time had come when progress could be made. The HEC needed a strong research capability so that constructive work could proceed on the basis of fact and analysis rather than by guesswork.

Steele's comments disclose an understanding of the first reason why postwar trends began to change in the early 1950s: every new union must stage at least one big strike in each of the industries that it represents to build solidarity in its membership and to show the employers that it cannot be pushed around. There simply *had* to be a sugar strike, a pineapple strike, and a longshore strike in the early years of the ILWU. After the initial strikes, they would be called only as a last resort. In the forty years since 1951, Hawaii has not had a major pineapple strike or a major longshore strike, and it has had only one industry-wide sugar strike, in 1958.

Except for the 1958 sugar strike, responsible collective bargaining on both sides has served to settle all major labor disputes involving the ILWU. In fact, the staff of the Hawaii Employers Council believes that the ILWU over the last thirty years has, despite its toughness, been a "responsible" union—meaning that its leaders keep their word and that they understand and respect the economic problems of the management they are negotiating with. On occasion, the ILWU has negotiated below-the-industry-line wage contracts with distressed plantations, and it has even accepted wage decreases when a plantation's economic position dictated such a course to keep it alive (and therefore to keep jobs for its union-member employees). Furthermore, the ILWU has been remarkably cooperative in working with the sugar, pineapple, and stevedoring companies to effect work force reductions caused by mechanization—through attrition and early retirement, so that their members would not be hurt. The Mechanization and Modernization Fund, established by the West Coast and Hawaii stevedoring companies and the ILWU in the late 1950s to handle work force reductions made necessary by the use of containers, is a model of industrial-relations cooperation.[18]

The second reason for the trend reversal was that much of the radicalism and class-warfare sentiment went out of union members and their leaders as they improved their lot. Sugar and pineapple workers, already making more money than agricultural workers anywhere else in the world before unionization, found that their pay increased dramatically with the bargaining power of the union; they became "haves" instead of "have-nots." Writing in the early 1960s, Lawrence Fuchs (p. 376) put it this way:

> The vast majority of Hawaii's laborers appear to have accepted the most crucial aspect of capitalist economics: the profit system. The very success of the labor movement in the Islands had destroyed the class struggle in Hawaii. It also limited the prospects for communism by fighting racism and economic exploitation. On the eve of statehood, Jack Hall behaved like the tough and autocratic union boss that he was, but not like a communist. Like the workers of his own union, who now enjoyed paid holidays, owned their own homes, and voted as they pleased, Hall, from all available evidence, had now joined the ranks of the bourgeoisie.

Hall and other ILWU leaders not only joined the ranks of the bourgeoisie but in time became in some ways as much a part of the "establishment" in Hawaii as the top officers of the Big Five. In due course, Hall served in various community posts, for example on the Police Commission and on the board of the Hawaii Visitors Bureau. He and his lieutenants were more welcome and respected by many legislative committees than were representatives of the Chamber of Commerce. After John A. Burns became governor in 1962, the ILWU had access to the executive branch of the state government in much the same way that the Big Five had had in prewar days.

Another factor was that over the years, as a result of the long negotiating sessions they participated in, the ILWU leaders got a liberal education in economics; and most of them were good students. Hall probably knew more about the economics of the sugar and pineapple industries than many company officers. He learned to respect and grew to like many of the people who sat across the table from him in those negotiations. Whether they were the professionals from the Hawaii Employers Council or industry representatives, they always treated him as an equal who had a job to do for his union, just as they had a job to do for their companies. It was hard to maintain the hate-the-boss attitude of the early days after personal relationships with the boss and his representatives had become friendly and mutually respectful. During his Smith Act trial, Hall asked a sugar plantation manager to testify on his behalf.[19] Such testimony proved unnecessary because his defense attorney attacked the Smith Act directly rather than arguing the innocence of the accused.

Throughout the long ideological struggle, the Hawaii Employers Council never allowed the Communist issue to interfere with its efforts to stabilize labor relations. As a result of that and other policies, labor relations in Hawaii, which had probably been the country's worst prior to World War II, were among the best by the late 1950s. In 1957 Curtis Allen of the Institute of Industrial Relations at the University of California in Berkeley stated that "conciliators and others close to the parties agree that bargaining today is as mature [in Hawaii] as anywhere in the United States."[20]

A final factor in the reversal of the destructive trends of the immediate postwar years was the apparent determination of the people of Hawaii, acting through their legislative representatives, never to permit another devastating waterfront strike like that of 1949. Toward the end of that strike the legislature passed the Dock Seizure Act, which would authorize the territorial government to take over and operate the docks if another such strike were called. With this legislation hanging over the union's head, union leaders realized that more caution in calling for strikes was in order. After 1956 the threat of longshore strikes became a dead issue because by then the local longshoremen had negotiated wage parity with the West Coast longshoremen, so that Hawaii longshore contracts automatically followed whatever agreements were reached in West Coast negotiations. Nonetheless, the ILWU continued to try (unsuccessfully) to have the act repealed.[21]

Hawaii's Dock Seizure Act of 1949 had a 1973 sequel in the U.S. Congress in which I and the First Hawaiian Bank were deeply involved and which is relevant to this discussion. Over the years mainland dock and shipping stoppages had interrupted transportation to Hawaii and seriously disrupted the Hawaiian economy, and the situation worsened dramatically in the late 1960s and early 1970s. Between the end of 1968 and the end of 1972, shipping to Hawaii was cut off from the West Coast for nearly eight months and from the East and Gulf Coasts for about four months by dock and maritime strikes—a total of one year out of the four.[22] The Hawaii community was thoroughly incensed. Surveys made of the impact of these shipping tie-ups found that practically every business in Hawaii was hurting, some to the point of closing. Many items for both consumers and businesses were frequently unobtainable. Unemployment was the highest it had been since the 1949 dock strike. Government revenues were declining. Prices were rising. Something *had* to be done.

Two newspapermen, George Mason, editor of *Pacific Business News*, and Bill Paul, advertising director of the Hawaii Press Newspapers, organized an active, community-wide committee called STOP, an acronym for Shipping Tie-Ups Over Permanently. Hawaii's congressional delegation returned to discuss strategy with local community leaders. The Merchant Marine Subcommittee of the U.S. Senate Commerce Committee came to Hawaii for extensive hearings.

What should be done? There were plenty of suggestions, such as persuading Congress to lift the Jones Act's restrictions on the use of foreign bottoms in domestic shipping, authorizing Hawaii's governor to charter ships in the event of a maritime stoppage, or getting the military to use its ships to serve Hawaii's needs when commercial shipping did not. I worked closely with our two senators and two congressmen and with the STOP committee and got agreement that we should ask Congress to enact legislation that would require partial operation of struck transportation industries to provide continuing service to Hawaii even if the rest of the industry were closed down. We thought this proposal could be jus-tified as necessary to prevent great damage, and also on de minimus grounds. We estimated that only about 2 percent of West Coast dock labor, about 7 percent of West Coast U.S. flag shipping, about 1 percent of East Coast and Gulf dock and shipping, and about 2 percent of the trunk carrier airline traffic were involved in Hawaii traffic. We argued that partial operation of these transportation sectors to provide essential service to Hawaii would not interfere with the economic pressure of the strike on either the unions or the carriers, and that it would serve an urgent public purpose.

When the bill was introduced before Congress, it received massive support not only from all segments of the Hawaiian community, includ-ing some union leaders, but also from business interests in every state of the Union, which was what Hawaii needed to get special legislation through the Congress. This was achieved in a number of ways, including extensive use of a forty-page booklet I wrote entitled Hawaii: The Most Vulnerable State in the Nation, of which First Hawaiian Bank published 15,000 copies. This booklet described how the transportation stoppages Hawaii had experienced had affected the islands and explained the rationale of the proposed legislation. First Hawaiian Bank had copies of the booklet, with a letter from its president, hand-delivered to every member of Congress and mailed more than 3,000 copies to business friends on the mainland with letters asking them to urge their Congress-men to support the bill. STOP sent the booklet with similar letters to several thousand mainland firms that were suppliers of Hawaii compa-nies, and it organized delegations to lobby members of Congress and tes-tify before Congressional committees.

The result was that the Senate, controlled by Democrats, passed the bill by a substantial majority over strong opposition from the major labor organizations of the country. Although the bill was bottled up in the House Labor Committee by its chairman, passage by a prolabor Sen-ate of the bill whose chief sponsor was prolabor Senator Daniel K. Inouye sent a clear message to the longshore and maritime industries, both unions and management: Don't tie Hawaii up any more or this leg-islation is likely to become law. The bill stood, so to speak, in the wings of the Congress, ready to be brought forward the moment Hawaii was again strangled by a major transportation tie-up.

In the postwar years prior to the consideration of this bill by the U.S. Senate (1946–72), thirty-seven dock or maritime strikes in the Pacific, each lasting for more than three days, had affected shipping between Hawaii and the West Coast for a total of 801 days—nearly twenty-seven months—thereby interrupting shipping to Hawaii for an average of one month per year.[23] In the fifteen years that followed, only one such stoppage took place, a sympathy strike in support of another union that lasted only one week.[24] There is no way of knowing whether the Inouye bill was responsible for this almost complete cessation of work stoppages, but the evidence points to it as the major factor.

It is probable that whatever ties the ILWU had had with the Communist Party were severed by the early or mid-1950s. It is my belief, from having known him pretty well, that Jack Hall was being honest when he said he used the Communist Party to help him organize workers and that his sole objective was the success of the union—instead of the Communist Party using him and the union to further its objectives. By 1950 it must have been clear to Hall and the other ILWU leaders that the public's knowledge of their Communist affiliation was harming the union. The union's Communist ties had contributed to galvanizing the public and the territorial government against the union in the 1949 dock strike, and the defection of some ILWU officers because of those ties had hurt the union. The Communist taint was indeed turning out to be a serious political handicap. Commenting on the 1950 Democratic Party Convention, Fuchs stated: "Despite the walkout [of some conservatives] the ILWU lost ground in the 1950 convention. Shocked by the revelations of Jack Kawano, such leaders as Jack Burns, Chuck Mau, and war hero nisei Daniel Inouye were determined to force a showdown with the ILWU leaders for control of the party. Aware that the Democrats could not capture the delegateship or the legislature if the party was controlled by the union or was tainted with Communism, they fought and won control of the Democratic Territorial Central Committee."[25]

Noel Kent, a University of Hawaii political scientist, dates the beginning of the end of the ILWU's Communist orientation as the fall of 1949, when the great dock strike was over. That strike, he asserts, "in retrospect . . . was the last hurrah of radicalism."[26] By the late 1950s the ILWU had settled down to being a strong, tough labor union, but without any grandiose schemes to put the proletariat in control of society.

The postwar impact of labor unions on the Hawaiian economy was not confined to the ILWU but involved the traditional AFL craft unions, the Unity House (Rutledge) group, and the government workers' unions, some AFL-affiliated and others independent. Among these four union groups, total union membership in Hawaii adds to about 150,000 workers—more than 30 percent of the employed civilian work force, as contrasted to less than 20 percent nationally.[27] The Hawaii union membership figure, however, is somewhat inflated because the Hawaii Government Employees Association, in addition to its roughly 17,500 bargaining-unit members, has some 15,000 other "members" who joined at reduced rates simply to participate in various benefit programs that are available to members at group rates well below individual rates. Eliminating these 15,000 from the membership rolls, Hawaii's total union membership, as a percentage of the employed civilian work force, drops to something over 27 percent—still nearly ten percentage points higher than the national figure. So even with this adjustment, Hawaii is obviously a highly unionized community.

One reason why Hawaii has such a large union membership is that government workers, both state and county, are highly unionized. This development occurred mostly during the last twenty years, because the right of government workers to join unions was not clearly spelled out until the 1968 State Constitutional Convention amended the constitution to guarantee persons in public employment the right to organize for purposes of collective bargaining. As a result, not only are the blue-collar and white-collar workers in the various state and county administrative departments unionized, but so are the police, firemen, public school teachers, and the academic staffs of the state university and community colleges. Nationally, about 37 percent of government workers are unionized, but the figure for Hawaii is over 55 percent.[28] The biggest union of government workers is the Hawaii Government Employees Association, an AFL affiliate whose 17,500 bargaining-unit members[29] make it second in size to the 23,000-member ILWU—and the biggest union in the state if its 15,000 non-bargaining-unit members are included.

A second reason why such a large fraction of the labor force is unionized in Hawaii is that most agricultural labor in Hawaii is organized—over 60 percent, compared with only about 3 percent nationally.[30]

The Unity House (or Rutledge) group of unions consists primarily of the Teamsters and the Hotel and Restaurant Employees Union, the Teamsters having absorbed some of the smaller unions that Rutledge controlled. The Teamsters have contracts not only in the traditional fields of transportation and warehousing, but also in such diverse fields as public utilities (The Gas Company), hospitals, concrete products, and dairies. They even have one unit representing kindergarten teachers. The union has a membership of 5,500.[31]

Arthur Rutledge showed great foresight in establishing control of the Hotel Employees and Restaurant Employees Union in the early days before the growth of tourism, for it burgeoned into one of the largest unions in Hawaii, with a membership of some 11,000.[32] Because the ILWU, which does not recognize jurisdictional lines any more than do the Teamsters, tries (with some success) to augment its declining agricultural and longshore membership with hotel workers, Art Rutledge—and now his son and successor, Tony—and the ILWU have frequently been hot contestants, both in representation elections and in raiding activities.

As noted earlier, the ILWU was expelled from the CIO in 1950 for its Communist leanings. Then in 1957 the Teamsters Union was expelled from the merged AFL-CIO after a U.S. Senate investigating committee disclosed numerous improper activities of some of its national officers. After being independents for several decades, both the Teamsters and the ILWU have been readmitted. How this will affect the central organizations of labor in Hawaii is anybody's guess. It probably will not reduce the level of conflict between unions, as the Teamsters and the ILWU seek to augment their membership wherever they can.

The Four Postwar Economic Periods

Unlike the national economy, which between the end of World War II and 1989 experienced eight periods of recession, averaging about one year, and nine periods of expansion, averaging about three and a half years each, the Hawaiian economy has traversed only four rather distinct economic periods, each one quite different from the others. The first period, 1945 to 1949, was one of drastic contraction from the inflated war economy and ended in a severe recession. During that period the average annual decline in real (i.e., deflated) total personal income was nearly 15 percent, one of the sharpest and most extended declines experienced in peacetime by any economy. The second period, which stretched for nine years from 1949 to 1958, was one of substantial expansion, with an average growth rate of nearly 4 percent per year. After that, for fifteen years, the Hawaiian economy boomed. The average growth rate of real gross state product was nearly 7 percent per year.

This probably set an all-time record for sustained high-level expansion for any state or region in the nation. The fourth period, from 1973 to the present, has been one of moderate growth, with some years better than just good and others relatively stagnant. The average for the fifteen years from 1973 to 1988 was a growth rate of about 3 percent per year. Why the Hawaiian economy did not follow the ups and downs of the national business cycle is discussed in Chapter 7.

For the four decades from 1949 (by which time the major postwar adjustments had been made) to 1988, the Hawaiian economy averaged about 5.3 percent annual growth after inflation, compared with about 3.4 percent for the entire United States. In those thirty-nine years the Hawaiian economy, as measured by real total personal income, increased more than fivefold. With the resident population doubling (511,000 to 1,080,000), real per capita personal income was about 2.6 times larger in 1988 than in 1949. This means that, after inflation, residents of Hawaii averaged about two and a half times more real purchasing power in 1988 than in 1949. Personal income during the first two postwar economic periods and gross state product during the latter two periods are plotted in Figure 5.1. The annual growth rates for the four periods are approximate and shown in billions of dollars. This is done for a number of reasons that are explained in the Appendix.

Figure 5.2 shows the changing industrial composition of the economy in the postwar period and compares it with the immediate prewar period. The only industries shown are those that bring income into Hawaii from outside the state—the export industries—because they are the ones that basically move the whole economy. The methodology used in developing Figure 5.2 is the same as that used in Table 3.1, also described in the Appendix. The figure presents my estimate of the fraction of total personal income created by each of the export sectors: some of it created directly in wages, salaries, and dividends paid out; some of it created indirectly in the local purchase of goods and services from firms that then pay part of that money out in wages and salaries; and some of it created by the multiplier effect generated by the spending and respending of the income created directly and indirectly.

Figure 5.2 shows that the sugar industry decreased from nearly 20 percent of the total economy in 1949 to just over 2 percent in 1988 (although its actual level of production remained about the same). Pineapple, which experienced a considerable decline in output, fell from about 12 percent of the economy in 1949 to about 1.2 percent in 1988.

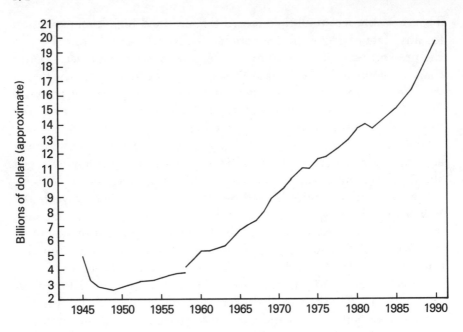

Figure 5.1 Personal income, 1945–58, and gross state product, 1958–90

(All in 1982 dollars)

Tourism, which accounted for a mere 2.4 percent of the economy in 1949, by 1988 accounted for more than one-third of Hawaii's total personal income. The military, which in 1949 represented still nearly one-third of the total economy despite the drastic cutbacks after the war, had fallen to about 7.5 percent by 1988.

The "other" category lumps together all of Hawaii's other export activities (both commodities and services). Developing an estimate for "other" exports is difficult both conceptually and statistically, for reasons explained in the Appendix.

I found that the "other" category in 1939 accounted for about 0.5 percent of total personal income in Hawaii, with the main components (listed in the order of importance) being coffee, bagasse wallboard, canned tuna, bananas, and garments. The "other" category in 1949 accounted for about 1 percent of total personal income, the main items then being coffee, flowers and foliage, bagasse wallboard, canned tuna, garments, macadamia nuts, and papayas. For 1988 I estimate the "other" category to be responsible for about 2 percent of the state's total personal income, with agricultural exports being the largest component (flowers and foliage, macadamia nuts, papayas, and a few smaller items

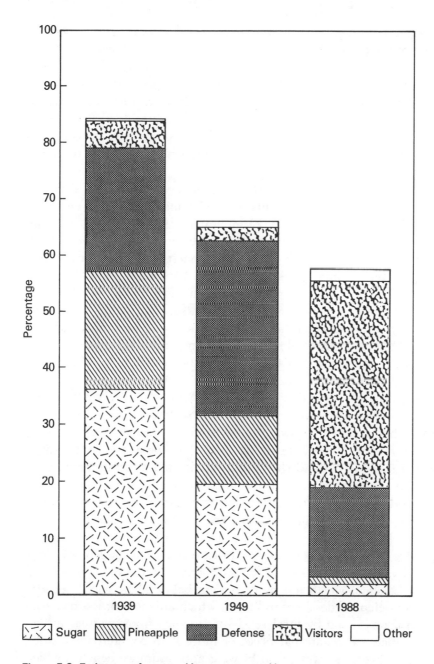

Figure 5.2 Estimates of personal income created by exports as a percentage of total Hawaii personal income: 1939, 1949, 1988

such as seed corn, ginger root, and guava) and accounting for about 30 percent of the total. The other 70 percent comes from five areas, in the following order of importance: scientific activities in the fields of astronomy and oceanography, educational programs, sports activities, movie and TV filming, manufactured items (mainly garments), and international consulting in such areas as agriculture, aquaculture, and ocean floor surveying. By 1988 "other" exports had become more important to the economy than pineapple and were approaching the size of the sugar industry.

Personal income created by "other" exports, as measured in 1989 dollars, by my estimates rose from just over $1 million in 1939 to nearly $7 million in 1949 and to over $350 million in 1988. But total personal income for these three years rose respectively from $218 million to $685 million and to $18.5 billion[33]—hence the modest increase in the percentage-of-personal-income figures of from 0.5 to 1 and to 2.

It should be noted that I omitted marijuana exports from the "other" category. I did so because, first, personal income created by marijuana exports is not included in official total personal income figures and, second, my estimate of the value of marijuana exports (discussed later in this chapter) was made only for 1981, and any estimate for 1988 could only be a guess.

Economists may note that some sizable "exports" (i.e., commodities and services for which income is received in Hawaii from out-of-state sources) that appear in Hawaii's gross state product accounts are not included in the "other" category. Some of these are commodities imported into Hawaii and then reexported, such as scrap metal, used machinery, and transportation equipment. Some (at least conceptually) are properly included in one of the Big Four export categories of sugar, pineapple, the military, and visitors. An example is a major part of the sale of aviation fuel to transpacific airlines, which as noted in the Appendix belongs largely in the visitor category. Some largely wash out and in any case are not a part of the productive economy—such as social security benefits, which are more or less balanced by social security taxes; nondefense federal expenditures, which are more or less balanced by federal taxes paid by local residents; income from overseas investments, which are counterbalanced, or more than counterbalanced, by earnings of overseas investors in Hawaii; and insurance benefits, which are more or less balanced by premium payments.

Yet another economic phenomenon disclosed by Figure 5.2 needs explanation, namely the declining portion of total personal income generated by Hawaii's export activities. This has resulted primarily from increases in the purchasing power of Hawaii's residents over the years. Real per capita income expressed in 1967 dollars increased from $1,270 in 1939 to $1,763 in 1949 and to $4,936 in 1986.

The effect of this increase in purchasing power on the structure of the economy is that as people grow wealthier they spend more of their incomes on services and less on commodities. An indicator of this change is a much more rapid growth in service employment than in commodity employment. Between 1940 and 1950, total employment in Hawaii increased by only about 10 percent. But employment in transportation, communications, and utilities increased by 64 percent; employment in finance, insurance, and real estate increased by 75 percent; employment in the service industries increased by 147 percent; and employment in state and local government increased by 55 percent.[34] When people spend their money in these areas, most of it stays at home and creates income locally—hence the growth of the "internal" (non-export) economy from 15 percent of the total in 1939 to about one-third by 1949. As the 1988 bar shows, this trend has continued, so that non-export activities account for more than 40 percent of total income in Hawaii.

Contributing to this trend in the last couple of decades has been the growth of several significant import-substitution industries, of which cement production and petroleum refining are good examples. The development of products replacing imports will be discussed later in this chapter.

CONTRACTION, 1945–49

From 1945 to 1949 a drastic contraction in the economy ended in a severe depression, creating widespread pessimism about the economic future of Hawaii. The contraction resulted from the withdrawal of the military from the Pacific after World War II. Military expenditures in Hawaii, estimated to have exceeded $400 million in 1945, dropped to $224 million in 1946 and kept declining every year until they hit bottom at $147 million in 1950.[35] Uniformed personnel in Hawaii declined from 300,000 in 1945 to 68,000 in 1946 and continued down to a low of 21,000 in 1950.[36] Civilian employees of the defense agencies were reduced from 64,000 in 1945 to 42,000 in 1946. They continued to decline until 1950, when they numbered only 17,000.[37]

Amazingly, the civilian economy continued rather strong during the first part of this period, primarily because during the preceding four war years Hawaii's residents had been making good money but were unable to spend it on all the things they wanted, such as new houses, automobiles, refrigerators, or other durable consumer goods. Business was therefore brisk in 1946 and 1947, with total nongovernment employment rising from 120,000 in 1945 to 130,000 in 1947.[38] Unemployment in those years ran at less than 2 percent of the labor force.[39] The postwar buying boom ended in 1948, however, and the unemployment rate more than doubled. Then in 1949 the economy was laid low by the strike of the ILWU longshoremen at all Hawaiian ports from May into November —six long months. The only cargo permitted to move was military cargo and essential food, feed, and medical supplies. Not only were Hawaii's docks closed, but also shipments bound to or from Hawaii were picketed as "hot cargo" in all West Coast ports where the longshoremen and warehousemen were ILWU members.

As I later explained to several congressional committees in Washington, a shipping strike to an insular state creates what amounts to a siege. When this kind of siege lasts half a year, it brings an economy to its knees. Nongovernment employment in Hawaii dropped from 128,000 in mid-1948 to 105,000 in November 1949, when the strike was finally settled.[40] The unemployment rate rose to 15 percent in November and for the year averaged over 11 percent, causing the federal government to designate Hawaii as a severely depressed labor market area.[41] Many other strikes in the late 1940s affected Hawaii adversely—sugar in 1946, pineapple in 1947, and a number of West Coast dock and maritime strikes in almost all the years—but the 1949 longshore strike made history as the Great Hawaiian Dock Strike.

Even before the dock strike, economists looking at Hawaii's economic prospects saw little cause for optimism. The U.S. Department of Labor's 1947 report to Congress on Hawaii devoted a chapter to an analysis of the economic outlook. According to the report, sugar and pineapple had reached their peak and with increases in productivity would require fewer and fewer workers; overseas tourism was a luxury trade and therefore had severe limits to its growth, although in time it might "expand to a point considerably above prewar levels" (when the biggest year, 1941, had seen only 32,000 visitors to Hawaii); the growth of most nonplantation agriculture was stymied by a lack of irrigation water; Hawaii's tuna-packing industry would probably see a "gradual expansion"; and a few minor products—such as Hawaiian handicrafts, orchids, Aloha shirts, and macadamia nuts—offered "some promise." The report concluded that the possibilities for expanding job opportunities "appear to be rather limited," and "should the rate of population growth in Hawaii continue at the rate of the past two decades, the pressure of population against subsistence resources and available employment opportunities may be expected to rise sharply."[42]

When the 1949 dock strike was superimposed on this rather dismal assessment of Hawaii's economic outlook, it is not surprising that many people in Hawaii decided to look for jobs elsewhere. As a result, although there had been practically no net in- or out-migration during the three years 1946 through 1948, in 1949 about 21,000 more civilians moved out of Hawaii than moved in. This figure rose to 22,000 in 1950 and stayed in quintuple-digit figures for the next three years. Between 1949 and 1953 a total of 87,000 more civilians left Hawaii than came.[43] Because some people (including myself) moved to Hawaii during that period, the gross out-migration was probably well in excess of 100,000— or close to 25 percent of the total civilian population. It is evident that the early postwar period was not a happy one in Hawaii's economic history.

EXPANSION 1949–58

From 1949 to 1958 the Hawaiian economy made a substantial recovery and a number of developments took place that would in time encourage further economic growth. Most, but certainly not all, of the economic growth of this period was caused by a large increase in the number of visitors and by the return of the military to Hawaii.

The visitor industry started the period with a 36 percent increase in the number of overseas visitors in 1950 over 1949, demonstrating that air travel would in time displace travel by ship. For the first time, more visitors to Hawaii came by air than by ocean travel. This high growth rate was not sustainable of course, but the number of visitors for the period 1949–58 grew annually by a whopping 20 percent.[44] This meant that Hawaii had over five times as many visitors in 1958 as it had had in 1949, and it also meant that the construction industry was kept busy building new hotels and other visitor facilities. Data on the number of hotel rooms in Hawaii are sketchy for that period, but it appears that Hawaii had somewhere around 2,000 hotel rooms in 1949 and that by 1958 the number had risen to around 6,000.[45] The main Waikiki hotels to be built during this period were the Surfrider annex to the Moana Hotel, the Edgewater and Reef hotels, the Princess Kaiulani, and the Biltmore (later removed to make way for the Hyatt Regency). By 1958 visitors were estimated to be spending over $80 million annually in Hawaii.[46]

The percentage rise in expenditures by the military during this period was not as great as for tourism, but it was nonetheless large. Renewed expansion of the armed forces in Hawaii was propelled by the war in Korea that started in June 1950 and lasted three years. In 1954 the Twenty-Fifth Division was brought back home to Schofield Barracks on Oahu. From a low in 1950, when defense expenditures in Hawaii totaled $147 million, the military enlarged its presence almost every year and by 1958 was spending over $300 million. The number of servicemen increased from 21,000 in 1950 to more than 50,000 in 1958, and these troops had with them some 57,000 dependent spouses and children.[47] The number of civilian employees of the defense agencies remained almost constant during this period, at approximately 20,000 in both 1949 and 1958. Even so, the aggregate of servicemen, dependents, civilian workers, and *their* families in 1958 approximated 200,000 persons directly dependent for their livelihood on defense employment—some 30 percent of Hawaii's total resident population.

Pineapple also contributed to the postwar expansion of the island economy. During this period the industry reached its maximum size. At its previous peak in the late 1930s, Hawaiian producers annually canned about 12 million cases of fruit. A decade later the annual pack rose to approximately 15 million cases, then continued to grow until in the mid-1950s it exceeded 18 million cases—a level that was generally maintained until the mid-1960s, when production began to decline.[48]

At the beginning of this section on the four postwar economic periods I alluded to several developments that in time did much to promote economic development in Hawaii, particularly the export of diversified agricultural and manufactured products and the development of manufacturing to replace imports. The first of these developments was the creation by the territorial legislature in 1949 of the semiautonomous Industrial Research Advisory Council (IRAC), which was succeeded in 1955 by an agency of the territorial government called the Economic Planning and Coordination Authority (EPCA). EPCA's functions were greatly expanded when it became the Department of Economic Development after statehood in 1959.

IRAC and EPCA acted to promote economic growth by appraising the potential for new industries and new agricultural products, and then aiding in solving their production and marketing problems. The county of Maui followed the lead of the territorial government by creating the Maui Economic Development Authority with many of the same functions.

Three major companies established departments to conduct economic research and to promote economic development—first the Bank of Hawaii, then Hawaiian Electric Company, and later Bishop (now First Hawaiian) Bank. Hawaiian Electric Co. retained Stanford Research Institute to conduct a study designed to identify those economic areas that seemed to offer the best opportunities for development on Oahu, and then established a department to pursue these suggestions.[49] Other major companies started asking themselves what new economic activities they could get involved in that would use their land, their capital, and their expertise to better advantage. One outcome was C. Brewer's establishment of a consulting subsidiary to market its sugar production know-how worldwide.

With the growth of several small and a few large manufacturing activities, finding industrial sites on Oahu became a problem. So Campbell Estate in the mid-1950s developed a 2,400-acre industrial park beyond Pearl Harbor where currently 135 business firms are located, ranging from feedlots to two oil refineries. More recently, a deep-water port was dredged to serve this large industrial area.

From all this activity came two things, one tangible and the other intangible but probably equally important. The tangible result was the expansion of several diversified agricultural products for export (flowers and foliage, macadamia nuts, and papayas) and a number of diversified manufacturing products for export, primarily garments. A number of import-replacement industries also developed, notably refined petroleum products, cement, furniture, and reinforcing iron bars made from ferrous scrap. The intangible result was a shift in government and business thinking from the prewar and immediate postwar pessimism about Hawaii's economy to a thoroughly optimistic attitude. In the mid-1950s the Honolulu Chamber of Commerce reflected this new optimism by organizing large trade-development conferences on four of the neighbor islands to discuss economic development opportunities with the local business representatives there.[50] In the late 1950s, when it became clear that Hawaii would need outside capital for its further economic development, EPCA organized similar meetings in mainland cities to persuade mainland business interests to include Hawaii in their development plans. This was a far cry from the plantation era, when Hawaii was generally considered off-limits to any businessman who was not a *kama'āina* —a native of the islands.

Finally, several developments in tourism in the 1950s served as a basis for more effective tourist promotion in later years. The first, in 1950, was the formation of a research committee for the Hawaii Visitors Bureau. This committee instituted basic statistical programs needed by the bureau and the many companies that constituted the visitor industry to engage in effective marketing and promotion and to insure satisfaction for visitors. These research programs developed detailed data on the demographics of visitors and information on why they selected Hawaii and what they liked or disliked about their visit.

A second development was for the HVB to become independent of the Chamber of Commerce of Honolulu. Ever since the formation of its predecessor, the Hawaii Promotion Committee, in 1903, Hawaii's visitor promotion agency had been a standing committee of the Chamber of Commerce; but in 1958 a special committee, of which I was a member, recommended that it be separated and become an independent non-profit organization. One reason was that Hawaii's legislature was being relied on more and more for the increased funding required by the bureau, and the prolabor orientation of the legislature at that time dictated that the bureau not be a part of the Chamber of Commerce.

The third development affecting tourism was the building, starting in the late 1950s, of Hawaii's first "destination resort area" at Kaanapali on West Maui. It was evident that as tourism in Hawaii grew, it would break out of the confines of Waikiki and spread to the neighbor islands. And it was evident that when a good resort site (i.e., beach area) was selected on a neighbor island it would be in a rural area with no recreational or entertainment facilities nearby. American Factors, in developing Kaanapali, therefore decided that it would take a large area of land and develop it into a self-sufficient resort, with several hotels, restaurants, and shopping centers, and with golf courses, equestrian riding facilities, tennis courts, and everything that visitors would need during an extended stay. This pattern of developing a master-planned destination resort area has largely been followed in most neighbor island tourism developments, as well as in rural Oahu. It has been an important factor in the success of the visitor industry on the neighbor islands.

BOOM, 1958–73

From 1958 to 1973, primarily as a result of statehood, the coming of the jet airplane, and the buildup of the defense establishment during the Vietnam War, the Hawaiian economy was in a state of great boom.

Statehood had tremendous economic importance to Hawaii. Before it was achieved in 1959, most people on the mainland knew little about the islands. Three personal examples of their ignorance will illustrate this point. In the early 1950s I wanted to make a change in one of my life insurance policies, and so I wrote to the head office of the insurance company in New York with my request. I was told that I would have to get a physical examination and that for that purpose I would have to see a doctor recommended by the American consul in Honolulu! Then in the mid-1950s I corresponded with my old friend Steve Saulnier, at that time chairman of the President's Council of Economic Advisers under President Eisenhower. His letters, which came to me out of the White House mail room, all had postage for a foreign destination on them. Finally, in the late 1950s I was in Boston giving a talk about the growth possibilities of Hawaii. An old friend in the audience told me, sarcastically, that there was no need for me to come back to Boston to tell the business people and investors there about Hawaii. Most of them, he said, had been down to one or more of the Caribbean islands and they already knew how natives on small islands lived.

Ignorance about Hawaii permeated most American businesses. If they were engaged in overseas trade, they almost universally put the Hawaii market in their foreign trade department. Even the U.S. Department of Commerce treated Hawaii as a foreign area until 1947, by requiring all shipments to Hawaii from the mainland to be reported by item, quantity, and value just as foreign shipments had to be reported. Of course no such requirement existed for shipments between mainland states.

Statehood was worth a billion dollars of advertising and promotion for Hawaii. Suddenly we were the fiftieth state, and thousands upon thousands of national business firms with activities all over the country began asking themselves why they were not doing business in Hawaii. Those that already had connections with Hawaii transferred the Hawaii market program out of the foreign department and put it in the domestic department.

In 1971 I spent a day briefing the board of governors of the Federal Reserve Bank of San Francisco on economic conditions in Hawaii. In preparation I had made a count of the "foreign" (i.e., overseas, mainly mainland U.S.) business firms doing business in Hawaii. As of 1955 there had been only 311 of them. By 1971 this number had increased to 1,916—a better than sixfold increase that, without statehood, would probably have taken a generation or two to achieve. Among the 1,916 were two cement companies (Hawaiian and Kaiser); one oil refinery (Standard Oil of California); two cardboard container manufacturers (Weyerhaeuser and Fibreboard); five hotel management chains (Hilton, Sheraton, Western International, Holiday Inn, and Cinerama); all the major oil distribution companies; all the major insurance companies; major U.S. airlines, including United, Pan Am, Northwest, Western, Continental, Braniff, American, and TWA; a host of supplemental and foreign air carriers; four major van lines (Bekins, Martin, Dean, and Smyth); two major milk distributors (Foremost and Beatrice Foods); leading retailers, such as Sears, J. C. Penney, Kress, Woolworth, Hart-field's, Roos-Atkins, Parkway-Gem, and Longs Drug; the major U-drives (Hertz, Avis, National); two major bakery chains (Continental and Ward Foods); a brewery (Schlitz); a supermarket chain (Safeway); and Boise-Cascade in retailing and land development. This was such a far cry from prewar Hawaii, even from prestatehood Hawaii, that I told the board of governors that Hawaii's economy had come to represent a wide spectrum of big, medium, and small businesses—some local, some mainland, and some foreign—no one of which or group of which could be said to be dominant in any sense of the word. Hawaii had become a modern, diversified, pluralistic economy.[51]

Both statehood and the jet airplane came to Hawaii in 1959. Between the two of them they gave Hawaii's tourism a tremendous boost—statehood because it brought Hawaii to the attention of the traveling public, the jet because it made flying long distances faster, more comfortable, and (most importantly) much cheaper. The gains in speed and comfort and the lower cost of the jet over the propeller plane were immense. How even the original narrow-bodied jet, as represented by the Boeing 707, put the passenger ship out of business is easily comprehended by realizing that one jet could make two round trips between San Francisco and Honolulu per day whereas the ship would take ten days to make one round-trip voyage. In ten days (twenty round trips) the jet could carry at least five to six times as many passengers as a large ship like the *Lurline*. Because the plane cost only a fraction of what the ship cost and the crew-to-passenger ratio of the plane was much smaller than that of the ship, the plane fare was vastly cheaper than that of the ship.

The difference between a five-hour flight on a jet and a nine-hour flight on a propeller plane was also critical. In fact, before the jet came into service, a standard complaint of travelers to Hawaii was that the airplane was too slow and the ship was too fast. Sitting in an airplane for nine hours was a punishing experience, whereas four and a half days on a ship were not really long enough to get relaxed and into shipboard living. The jet solved the problem and with its inexpensive fares put the passenger ships out of business. It resulted, along with the publicity that Hawaii got out of statehood, in the number of visitors to Hawaii increasing from 171,000 in 1958 to 2,631,000 in 1973—a fifteenfold increase in fifteen years, averaging a solid 20 percent per year increase for a full decade and a half.[52]

This was the same annual rate of increase that tourism had registered in the prior periods (1945–49 and 1949–58) so that by 1973 Hawaii's annual count of visitors had risen by an average annual rate of 20 percent for twenty-seven years. Seldom has any industry had such a rapid and prolonged rate of growth as did Hawaii's visitor industry between 1946 and 1973. By 1973 the hotel room count had soared to over 37,000, compared with roughly 2,000 in 1949 and 6,000 in 1958.[53]

In addition to overseas investments and tourism, the Hawaiian economy was further propelled in the 1960s by a sizable buildup in the defense establishment as a result of the war in Vietnam. Although the number of servicemen stationed in Hawaii did not increase during the period, total defense expenditures for the pay of uniformed personnel, for the pay of civilian workers, and for local purchases of goods and services increased almost threefold in that fifteen-year period—from $302 million in 1958 to $841 million in 1973.[54] This was an average annual increase of more than 7 percent in current dollars, or, allowing for the modest inflation of that period, an annual increase in real spending that averaged more than 4 percent.

Given the 20 percent per year growth rate in the number of visitors, the better than 4 percent per year growth rate in constant-dollar defense spending, a huge increase in overseas investment, and some further increases in diversified agriculture and diversified manufacturing, it was inevitable that a construction boom would be generated. During the 1950s and the first half of the 1960s, the volume of construction put in place in Hawaii did not fluctuate much, providing steady employment for about 17,000 on-site construction workers. But in the last half of the 1960s the volume picked up dramatically. From 1969 through 1975, construction employment averaged above 25,000—a 50 percent increase.

Measured in constant dollars, the volume of construction put in place per year during this seven-year construction boom was more than double what it had been in the late 1950s.[55]

With a construction boom, a tourism boom, a boom in defense spending, and a boom in overseas investment, it is quite understandable that the fifteen-year period from 1958 through 1973 registered nearly a 7 percent per year growth rate. This indeed was the Great Hawaiian Boom.

MODERATE GROWTH, 1973–88

In discussing the abnormal growth of the Hawaiian economy during World War II, I stated that in normal peacetime periods for any developed national or regional economy to grow at the rate of 3 or 4 percent would be considered by most economists as being quite good. To grow at an annual rate of 6 or 7 percent would be considered too exceptional to be sustained for any extended period of time. The reasons for this are explained in section 2 of the Appendix.

Therefore, after such a long period of abnormal growth as Hawaii had from 1958 to 1973, it was no surprise to have the state economy slow down considerably in the early 1970s. Reasons for the slowdown are obvious. Tourism, which had been growing at a rate of 20 percent per year for so long, slowed to an annual average of less than 6 percent for the thirteen years from 1973 to 1986. The military establishment in Hawaii, with the end of the war in Vietnam, ceased to grow. The pineapple industry saw company after company close and its total production reduced to not much more than half what it had been in the 1950s and 1960s. And while total sugar production remained about the same as it had been, employment and acreage decreased. Growth in other areas of the economy was nowhere nearly large enough to make up for the slackening in these major industries, in part because of the depressing effect of the national energy crises of the 1970s. Hawaii's growth rate for the period 1973–88 slowed to an average annual rate of about 3 percent, as measured by constant dollar gross state product.

The most interesting and perhaps most disturbing aspect of 1973–88 Hawaii is that the "normal" annual increase in labor productivity of around 2.5 percent dropped sharply. During this period the annual rate of growth in employment was 2.7 percent, so that with total output increasing at a rate of only 3 percent, the growth in labor productivity appears to have fallen to about 0.3 percent per year. Because it is the increase in output per worker that sustains a higher standard of living, gains in the average standard of Hawaii's residents for the period 1973–88 slowed to less than 0.5 percent per year.

The most common explanation attributes this disturbing development to the growth of tourism, with its many low-productivity, low-pay jobs. Examined in the third section of Chapter 7, this explanation is found to be much exaggerated. Another is that the great increase in investments from overseas has transferred the ownership of so much of the Hawaiian economy to nonresidents that it is absentee capitalists rather than local residents who have profited. This argument is also discussed briefly in the third section of Chapter 7 and found to be without merit.

Before I suggest what I think are some of the real reasons for the dramatic reduction in the growth of output per employee, I should point out that the same thing happened contemporaneously in the national economy. Since the causes of the national slowdown in productivity growth have been analyzed in great depth, it is useful to look at the presumed causes of the national braking.

The national economy grew in the 1973–88 period at a rate of 2.6 percent per year, as measured by constant dollar gross national product. This was considerably below the long-term growth rate of nearly 4 percent per year from 1948 to 1973, but instead of the growth being based mainly on increased productivity and only secondarily on growth in employment, as in the earlier period, the relative importance of these two components was reversed. Almost all the growth in 1973–88 was due to increases in employment (2 percent per year), with productivity apparently growing at only about 0.6 percent per year—the same as in Hawaii. A drop of productivity growth rates by almost two full percentage points—from 2.5 percent (1948–73) to 0.6 percent (1973–88)—is serious. The reasons for this drop are discussed in section 5 of the Appendix.

It is unknown whether the many factors underlying the drastic decline in the growth rate of productivity in the national economy also caused the contemporaneous decline in the Hawaiian economy, but one would have to presume that many, if not most, of the national causes were also operating in Hawaii. This leads to the same conclusion for Hawaii that the experts who are quoted in the Appendix reached for the national economy: that many factors, some possibly measurable and others unmeasurable, have contributed to the decline in productivity in Hawaii since 1973. This conclusion does not diminish the seriousness of the problem. In fact, it makes the solution to the problem more difficult than if there were a single cause.

Before leaving this subject, I should comment on several developments in Hawaii in the last decade and a half that appear to have influenced the decline in its rate of productivity growth. The first is the decline in employment in some of Hawaii's most efficient industries, notably sugar and pineapple, where productivity growth in earlier years was so great, and in construction, where output per worker measured by the wage rate is about 60 percent above the average of the rest of the economy. Sugar and pineapple together constituted 25 percent of the Hawaiian economy in the 1950s but by 1988 made up less than 4 percent, and construction employment dropped nearly 15 percent from its peak in the early 1970s.

Accompanying these employment decreases in Hawaii's highly productive industries was the enormous employment increase in the least productive and lowest paid industry—retail trade. Almost one-third of the overall increase in the number of jobs in Hawaii from the early 1970s to the late 1980s occurred in retail trade, where average earnings are only about 60 percent of what all employees earn. The visitor industry, of course, contributed to this development, but it is not primarily responsible.

Developments in the Export and Import-Replacement Sectors
SUGAR

The history of the Hawaiian sugar industry since the end of World War II can best be told by reference to the major problems that the industry has faced. The first problem, which has lasted throughout the entire period, is rising costs of production. The biggest single cost of producing sugar is labor. Since the unionization of the sugar labor force in 1945 and the periodic negotiation of labor contracts with the ILWU, the price of labor has skyrocketed. In 1945 the average daily cash wage of hourly rated Hawaiian sugar workers was $5.10, to which should be added the value of perquisites (nine cents an hour or seventy-two cents a day) for a total daily wage of $5.82. In 1986 the average daily wage of these workers (cash plus fringe benefits) was $103.52—an eighteenfold increase.[56] By contrast, the Honolulu consumer price index increased only sixfold during the same period. Not only did wages skyrocket in the postwar years, but also other costs of the industry increased appreciably—such as water, land rents, taxes, fertilizers, petroleum products, and machinery.

The industry's response was to increase productivity remarkably. In 1945 it took 6,350,000 person-days of work by sugar plantation hourly rated employees to produce 821,216 tons of sugar, or 7.73 person-days per ton. In 1986 the figures were 1,290,017 person-days to produce 1,042,452 tons—or 1.24 person-days per ton.[57] This is a record sixfold increase in labor productivity, nearly 5 percent per year compounded over forty-one years. Few American industries can match this accomplishment of productivity advance. Further, more sugar has been produced on each acre of land. In 1945 each acre in cane produced an average of eight tons of raw sugar. That figure is now up to more than twelve tons, a better than 50 percent increase in land productivity.

These productivity increases have been brought about by many factors—better cane varieties, better agricultural practices, better machinery, and larger-scale production as smaller plantations merged to form larger units. In addition, there have been cost savings by using water more efficiently through drip irrigation and by shipping sugar in bulk instead of in bags. Finally, considerable income has been generated by the sale of excess bagasse-generated electricity to public utility companies.

For four decades prior to 1974 the only competition to Hawaiian sugar came from mainland beet and cane sugar producers. During this period foreign competition was of no consequence because the federal Sugar Act mandated the secretary of agriculture to limit by national quotas the amount of sugar that could be imported into the United States. The act permitted the entry of only that amount which, added to the permitted domestic production of beet and cane sugar, would result in a price that was fair both to the domestic consumer and to the domestic sugar producer. As long as Hawaii's cane could compete successfully with mainland sugar, it could remain profitable. This the Hawaiian sugar industry could do, in contrast to the Puerto Rican cane sugar industry which (after being nationalized and having its large and fairly efficient plantations broken up into small, inefficient production units) could not. Puerto Rican sugar production dropped from 1.3 million tons in 1950 to only about 250,000 tons in 1974. Since then the industry has practically gone out of business.[58]

Since congressional abandonment of the Sugar Act in 1974, Hawaiian sugar has faced competition from imports in a shrinking domestic market. To understand this development, it is necessary to consider the so-called "world sugar market," the relatively new product called high-fructose corn syrup, and the growing popularity of artificial sweeteners that are low in calories.

The "World Sugar Market." Most major countries of the world have long considered sugar to be an essential commodity. Many have striven for a degree of self-sufficiency in this product, growing cane in tropical areas and beet in temperate zones. With domestic production, they conserve their foreign exchange, improve their balance of payments, create jobs for their labor force, and are assured of some supply of sugar no matter what happens in the rest of the world. These benefits are so important to many countries that having a sugar-producing capability justifies heavy government subsidies.

Nations that cannot achieve complete self-sufficiency in sugar enter into long-term agreements with countries with surplus production to supply their remaining needs. Under such agreements, for example, specified quantities of Australian sugar are committed to the Japanese market, Jamaican sugar to the British market, and Cuban sugar to the Russian market. Approximately 80 percent of the world's sugar production is either consumed in the country in which it is raised or committed by commercial treaty to some other country, where it is marketed at a fixed price.

The uncommitted sugar of the world (the remaining 20 percent) constitutes what is called the "world sugar market." This market is the dumping ground for the homeless or surplus sugar of the world. The price that this sugar commands has been from one-third to two-thirds the going price in the stabilized sugar markets of the major industrial countries and is frequently well below the cost of production. In about one year out of eight, the demand–supply balance in sugar worldwide has been disrupted by some natural or political event, and during such periods the price of this sugar has been bid up to inflated levels—generally higher than the prices in major importing countries, where it is stabilized by long-term purchase agreements. This occurred when the Suez Canal was closed in 1956–57, when Europe lost her beet crop to frost in 1963 and 1964, when world consumption exceeded world production in 1973–75 and again in 1980.

Even during the years when the "world" price of sugar has been severely depressed below the cost of production, the price of sugar in most countries has remained well above that of the United States. This was true in the decades when the Sugar Act protected the U.S. market from being flooded by "world market" sugar, and it has been true in recent years when import quotas have similarly served. For example, in 1987, when the "world" price of sugar was about six cents a pound, the retail price of refined sugar was 67 cents in Tokyo, 43 cents in Rome and Paris, 44 cents in Stockholm, 34 cents in Buenos Aires, 36 cents in Madrid, and only 33 cents in the United States.

One might well ask, How can sugar producers sell their surplus year after year at a "world" price far below their costs of production? The answer is simple: large government subsidies make it possible. This leads to the conclusion that if the world had free trade in sugar with no subsidies and no tariffs or bilateral trade agreements, Hawaii could compete successfully in a true world sugar market. President Reagan repeatedly proposed that *all* subsidies and barriers to trade in agricultural products be eliminated on a scheduled basis by the year 2000, but he was consistently turned down by the major governments of the world. The Hawaiian sugar industry never objected to President Reagan's proposals for free and fair trade in agricultural products.

High-Fructose Corn Syrup (HFCS). A relatively new sweetener, HFCS is produced by using enzymes to convert the glucose in corn syrup into a much sweeter form of sugar called fructose. The commercial process was developed by chemists in Japan in the late 1960s and achieved major development in the United States, where corn is generally in plentiful supply. The first-generation HFCS was 42 percent fructose; but now larger portions of the glucose can be converted to fructose, making possible the production of syrup that is 90 percent fructose—twice as sweet as sugar. The standard 42 and 55 percent HFCS can be produced more cheaply than sucrose when corn prices are normal, and consequently it made heavy inroads into the U.S. sweetener market after it entered the market in 1970. From representing only 0.5 percent of the U.S. sweetener market in 1970, HFCS moved to 5 percent in 1975, to nearly 15 percent in 1980, and to over 36 percent in 1987.[59]

Although HFCS may gain a somewhat larger share of the market, it has several disadvantages that will probably keep it from expanding its share much more. It causes foods to turn brown when used in canned products; it causes the product in which it is used to absorb moisture; it lowers the freezing point in ice cream production; and, most importantly, it cannot be produced economically in a dry form and therefore can be used only where a liquid sweetener is acceptable.[60]

Diet Sweeteners. Until the mid-1970s, low-calorie artificial sweeteners supplied only about 5 percent of the U.S. sweetener market. They were consumed mainly by people who for medical reasons (for example, diabetes) had to be on a sugar-free diet. In the last decade, however, the great popularity of programs for achieving physical fitness and slimness has caused multitudes to shift to sugar substitutes and the producers of many foods and beverages to offer "diet" (nonsugar) versions of their products. As a result, the consumption of artificial sweeteners more than doubled. These products now command between 12 and 13 percent of the total U.S. sweetener market.[61]

The joint impact of HFCS and artificial sweeteners, plus the entry into the national market of subsidized foreign sugar, spelled trouble for U.S. producers. In the late 1970s, while the country was undergoing its highest peacetime inflation, the price of raw sugar in America fell to levels far too low to cover production costs—levels that were about the same as had existed a hundred years earlier at the time of the Reciprocity Treaty between Hawaii and the United States. Congress came to the rescue by adding sugar to the Farm Act, limiting imports of sugar so as to support prices at levels that would keep efficient producers in business.

The Hawaiian sugar industry, as a whole, has about broken even, with a few low-cost plantations making profits and a few high-cost plantations going out of business. Hawaii's production of sugar has been stable since 1970, at just over 1 million tons a year, because yields per acre have increased dramatically in recent years. But total land in sugar has dropped from 238,000 acres to 184,000 acres, a 27 percent decline.[62] And threats to the Hawaiian sugar industry remain.

One threat is rising costs, primarily wages, that could knock it out of competition. I see little chance that the ILWU will destroy an industry that provides jobs for so many of its members. The present union leadership subscribes to Jack Hall's statement quoted earlier: "We could bring down the temple any day, but when we do we destroy ourselves."

The second threat is that continued growth of HFCS and low-calorie sweeteners may knock sugar out of the sweetener market. Because there is no indication that HFCS can be granulated, I think its use will continue to be confined to the liquid sweeteners, and it is doubtful that

Americans will become so weight-conscious as to abandon sugar altogether.

The third threat is that subsidized foreign sugar will take over the American sweetener market. Although fights in the Congress will be intense in the years ahead, I am reasonably confident that the domestic sugar industry will be protected from this unfair competition. Sugar has generally won these congressional battles since 1934, and, with the development of HFCS, the cane and beet states have allies in the corn belt.

The fourth threat comes from a recent finding by a committee of the General Agreement on Tariffs and Trade (GATT) that U.S. sugar-import quotas unfairly restrain international trade. How this issue will be resolved is unknown, but the fact that many of the signatories of GATT also restrict the importation of subsidized foreign sugar should affect the ultimate disposition of the case.

Finally, the passage of ownership of some of the Big Five sugar agencies into foreign hands may weaken their commitment to sugar production in Hawaii, particularly if more profitable uses for their plantation lands can be found. It does not appear to me to be likely that such uses will develop on a scale that would seriously reduce sugar acreage.

For these reasons, I think that the future of the Hawaiian sugar industry, while uncertain, is on balance moderately good. By this I mean that the more efficient plantations will probably continue to produce sugar and make some profit, that plantations of average efficiency will not do much better than to survive, and that the high-cost plantations will probably go out of business as time goes by. Some decline in sugar production is probable, therefore, and so is a greater decline in acreage and in employment as both land and labor productivity continue to increase.

PINEAPPLE

Hawaii's pineapple companies emerged from World War II in an even more dominant world position than they had enjoyed in the 1930s. The economies of Malaysia, Taiwan, and the Philippines (the three largest pineapple producers after Hawaii) were all set back severely by the war, and their production immediately after the war was only about one-fifth of what it had been before. In Hawaii two more companies, Pacific Pineapple Company on Molokai and Grove Farm on Kauai, had started growing pineapple, and the older eight companies continued to increase their production. The result was that by 1950 Hawaii had expanded its output by one-third over the prewar level and accounted for almost three-fourths of the world pineapple pack.

Hawaii's production continued to expand, until it peaked in the mid-1950s at over 18 million cases of fruit. At that time, 75,000 acres were planted in pineapple. Average annual employment approximated 5,000 on the plantations and 7,500 in the canneries, but employment was much higher during the summertime harvesting and canning, and of course much lower during the rest of the year.[63]

The period of peak pineapple production in Hawaii lasted for nearly twenty years, from the mid-1950s to the early 1970s,[64] but with some decline in both acreage and employment because of rises in productivity. Meanwhile, foreign production increased by leaps and bounds. During the 1950s it rose from just over 4 million cases to well over 11 million, an increase of 175 percent. Even so, in 1960 Hawaii still packed more than half of the world's canned pineapple. During the 1960s, as Hawaiian production remained stable, foreign production more than doubled, totaling nearly 24 million cases in 1970. Foreign production costs were lower than Hawaii's, and the competition was too much for the local small companies and for one of its largest (Libby, McNeil & Libby). By 1973 only Dole, Del Monte, and Maui Pineapple Company remained in operation.

The record of world production of canned pineapple for the last half century is shown in Table 5.1. The figures presented in the table are approximate for several reasons: I had to compile them from several sources; some country figures for some years include only the part of the pack that was exported; not all countries are included for all years; and in some years some countries may have reported actual cases rather than "standard" cases—i.e., cases of 24 cans of the 2-½ can size. I converted Hawaii's actual cases for 1934–38 to standard cases by using a ratio of 75 standard cases to 100 actual cases. The table shows that Hawaii's share of the world total production of canned pineapple rose from 59 percent in the 1934–38 period to 73 percent in 1950, then gradually declined, falling to 17 percent by 1985.

It has been said that part of the foreign competition came from Hawaii's own companies, which had opened up plantations and canneries in overseas areas—Del Monte (then CalPac) in the Philippines in 1926, Dole in the Philippines in 1963, Del Monte in Kenya in 1965, and Dole in Thailand in 1966. A response for the industry was made by

Table 5.1   Approximate world production of canned pineapple, 1934–85
(In thousand cases: basis 24 2-1/2 size cans to a case)

AREA	AVERAGE, 1934-38	1950	1955	1960	1965	1970	1975	1980	1985
Australia	278	569	1,347	1,107	1,220	1,654	1,402	1,587	1,687
Ivory Coast				176	590	856	4,164	2,758	1,176
Kenya				221	445	366	984	1,884	2,181
Malaysia	3,399	734	1,220	1,919	3,840	3,484	2,205	2,096	2,146
Martinique			189	486	436	528	455	392	n.a.
Mexico		563	493	816	1,210	1,580	813	3,545	931
Okinawa				608	1,581	1,547			
Philippines	294	n.a.	n.a.	1,610	2,008	4,898	6,908	13,522	11,056
Puerto Rico	62	386	146	207	242	170			
South Africa	36	272	583	1,835	1,689	2,878	2,559	2,666	3,150
Taiwan	1,802	204	1,024	2,204	4,640	4,860	1,663	1,817	518
Thailand						900	2,033	6,393	10,680
Texas		264	217	177	185				
Hawaii	8,466	11,314	13,212	13,240	12,595	12,025	8,200	6,940	6,668
All other countries		1,147	2,083						
World total	14,337	15,453	20,516	24,606	30,681	35,746	31,386	43,600	40,193
Hawaii as % of world total	59	73	64	54	41	34	26	16	17
World total other than Hawaii	5,871	4,139	7,304	11,366	18,086	23,721	23,186	36,660	33,525

sources: Pineapple Growers Association of Hawaii, personal correspondence; Edward E. Judge & Sons, *The Almanac of the Canning, Freezing, Preserving, and Allied Industries* (Westminster, Maryland, various years).

Frank Dillard of Del Monte at a 1973 hearing held by Hawaii's congressional delegation to ascertain why so many pineapple companies had closed their Hawaii operations. Referring to the serious mealy bug infestation in the 1920s, Mr. Dillard said:

> To survive and sustain our growing domestic markets for pineapple we had to diversify our agricultural risks. This decision led to . . . the establishment of commercial operations in the Philippines. . . . Had it not been for our lower cost production base in the Philippines, Del Monte might well have been among the many companies who in recent years have been forced by rising production costs to abandon Hawaii. In effect, our lower-cost Philippines production has sustained and subsidized our overall pineapple operations, permitting us to continue Hawaiian production. . . . Over the years we have seen the emergence of foreign canning competition which enjoys the advantages of local protectionist trade barriers, lower production and distribution costs, and in some cases, government subsidies. The canner who wishes to serve these foreign markets can no longer rely on import trade alone, regardless of the quality of his product or his reputation. He must locate production facilities in areas with favorable access to his markets. It was primarily for this reason that Del Monte began commercial pineapple operations in Kenya in 1965 to serve the expanding European Economic Community.[65]

In 1973, faced with devastating foreign competition on world and U.S. canned pineapple markets, both Dole and Del Monte decided to get into the fresh fruit business in earnest. Shipments of fresh pineapple from Hawaii to the mainland quickly doubled, exceeding 50,000 tons a year.[66] Fresh fruit production rose to about 20 percent of total Hawaiian pineapple production, with shipments to the mainland in 1987 amounting to 117,000 tons. This gave Hawaii 57 percent of the total U.S. fresh pineapple market, in successful competition with Costa Rica (where Del Monte operates), Honduras (where Dole operates), the Dominican Republic (also Dole), and Mexico.[67] In 1987, canned pineapple production in Hawaii was about half of what it had been during the peak production period from the mid-1950s to the early 1970s.

Primarily because of the success of the fresh fruit business, the future of pineapple in Hawaii looks better than it has since the early 1970s. At that time most people close to the Hawaiian pineapple industry believed that pineapple's day in Hawaii was probably drawing to a close.[68] But developments since then give promise that the industry will continue in

Hawaii for a long time. A straw in the wind was the decision of the Wailuku Sugar Company in 1987 to convert some 2,500 acres of its sugar lands to growing pineapple to be packed by Maui Pineapple Co.

VISITORS

To understand the fantastic growth in Hawaii's tourism since World War II, it is necessary to look at it within the context of contemporary world-wide tourism. In addition to the modern jet, three factors have induced millions of people to take long-distance vacations. The first is the rapid postwar growth in real per capita income, which has made the average person rich by pre–World War II standards. The second is a greater knowledge of, and interest in, the world, stemming from such things as the overseas experiences of the millions of American troops serving overseas and from the proliferation of communications that occurred in recent decades. The third is the fact that most employees now are provided with two or three weeks of paid vacation every year.

Fifty years ago fewer than 400,000 Americans took long-distance overseas trips; as late as 1950 fewer than 1 million did so. By the late 1980s, more than 20 million were going to all sorts of places around the world every year.[69] Why this upsurge was economically possible is shown by a simple statistic. In the mid-1930s, when Pan American started flying from San Francisco to Hawaii, a round-trip ticket cost $720, and the U.S. average annual per capita income was barely $500; thus it would have cost the average American about one and one-half times his annual income to pay for a round-trip ticket between San Francisco and Honolulu. In 1988 a typical fare for that round trip was around $400, as against an average personal income of over $15,000, so that it cost the average American less than 3 percent of his annual income.

The same thing happened all over the developed world. Virtually no Japanese took vacation trips outside their country until the mid-1960s. By the late 1980s more than 5 million Japanese were vacationing abroad every year.

As long-distance overseas vacation travel has grown more common, tourism to Hawaii has figuratively exploded. From 15,000 overseas visitors in 1946, the number grew to 6,134,850 in 1988—at an annual average increase over those forty-two years of more than 15 percent. Over the same period total long-distance travel of the American public grew at an average rate of 10 percent. Even excluding the non-American visitors to Hawaii, the growth rate of tourism in the islands has been nearly 50 percent higher than the growth rate of total long-distance travel of Americans.

Hawaii's tourist industry has worked assiduously to capitalize on the islands' natural attractions for visitors—their salubrious climate, location between the U.S. mainland and Japan, remarkable physical beauty and diversity, and blend of Western, Polynesian, and Oriental cultures. The Hawaii Visitors Bureau, supported by continuing state subsidy as well as by industry subscription, has effectively advertised and promoted Hawaii tourism throughout the expansion of the tourist market. Special events, ranging from the now traditional Aloha Week in the early fall (a slow season in island tourism) to such sporting events as the Hawaiian Open in golf, the National Football League's annual Pro Bowl game, the annual Kona Billfish Tournament, and surfing meets—not to mention ethnic cultural events and film festivals—have provided special attractions for a variety of tourist interests.

Filmmaking in Hawaii has given worldwide publicity to its attractions. Feature films were produced in the islands as early as 1913, followed by such notable productions as *South Pacific* and *The Old Man and the Sea*. Television has supplied not only long-run series, such as *Hawaii Five-O* and *Magnum P.I.*, that display to millions of viewers the beaches and mountains of Hawaii, but also a local industry that spends some $30 million to $50 million annually in production.

Hotels and other tourist facilities were expanded to serve the rapid increase in visitors. Waikiki, scarcely a square mile of high-priced real estate, contains some 34,000 hotel and condominium rooms for transients, together with some 1,000 shops and 350 bars and night clubs. On its fringe are a large park, a public golf course, tennis courts, a zoo, and an aquarium. Crowded though it is, Waikiki remains the prime area for visitors who like it, a psychiatrist explained, because "it is not New York. It's warmer. It's exotic. . . . Just being around people is fun in Waikiki, there's a holiday mood. It's like a carnival in Rio de Janeiro, like the Mardi Gras in New Orleans. Waikiki is a parade of loud shorts and bathing suits."[70]

Tourist development in recent decades has been even more rapid on the neighbor islands as hotels—many of them financed by Japanese investors, as in Honolulu—were spread along coasts and bays hitherto off the beaten track for vacationers. Before the boom in tourism, facilities on the neighbor islands were single hotels located at points of attraction—such as Volcano House on the rim of Kilauea Crater, the Kona Inn in balmy Kona, the Naniloa Hotel on the oceanfront in Hilo, the Pioneer Inn in old Lahaina town on the west end of Maui, the Silversword Lodge on the slopes of Haleakala, and the Hotel Hana on the east end of Maui, where people like the Herbert Hoovers and the Charles Lindberghs found privacy. Few visitors then wanted to stay on any of the neighbor islands for any length of time. The typical neighbor island visit consisted of a side trip from home base in Waikiki. A favorite tour package, for example, began with a morning flight to Kauai, then on to Maui the same day for a half-day stopover to visit the summit of Haleakala, then on to the Big Island, landing at Hilo, going up to the Volcano and then on to Kona before the return to Waikiki, for a total stay of three days.

This pattern began to change around 1960, shortly after American Factors started work on its major resort development at Kaanapali on the west end of Maui. This master-planned, destination-area resort complex set the pattern for most subsequent neighbor island resort construction, and the result is that many visitors have one of the neighbor islands rather than Waikiki as their prime destination. As of the late 1980s the average length of stay has risen to five and a half days on Kauai, six and a half days on Maui, and nearly five days on Hawaii.[71] In 1960 only 15 percent of Hawaii's hotel rooms were located on the neighbor islands, but by 1989 the figure has jumped to well over 40 percent and unquestionably will continue to grow.[72]

Rural Oahu had even more difficulty than the neighbor islands in becoming a part of Hawaii's tourism picture. In my opinion, this is because vacationers in Hawaii, as in almost any other place in the world that has a metropolis, want to be either near the urban center of action or out in the country, not on the outskirts of the metropolis. Possibly this attitude of travelers and of travel agents may change over time. An indication is the success of the Kahala Hilton Hotel, located outside Waikiki beyond Diamond Head. Similarly, the Makaha Resort in West Oahu and the Turtle Bay on Oahu's north shore seem to be doing better after years of struggle. It is possible that the Ko Olina development being built at the western end of the island near Barbers Point will succeed in becoming the "second Waikiki," as its promoters predict. But like the other rural Oahu visitor facilities, it will have a big selling job to do to overcome the "either-Waikiki-or-the-neighbor-islands" orientation of travelers and travel agents.

Beginning in the 1980s a number of cruise ships have brought another variety of tourism to Hawaii by serving as floating hotels as they ply between the islands. They enable the visitor to see all the islands and to do so without the bother of repeated air flights and hotel changes.

The future of overseas, long-distance tourism, both for the world in general and for Hawaii in particular, looks good because the potential market in the developed countries has hardly been scratched. The nearly 20 million Americans who have been taking overseas and foreign trips annually in the late 1980s represent only 8 percent of the country's population, or less than 15 percent of that potential market. If those who are too young or too poor to travel are discounted, there remain some 150 million. The same situation exists in Japan, Europe, and other developed areas. Although the travel industry cannot tap all of that market or even most of it every year, it can inch up from 15 percent toward 20 percent.

Despite this vast potential, the rate of growth of long-distance vacation travel both worldwide and to Hawaii since the early 1970s has slowed. The rate of growth is likely to continue slackening, for three reasons.

First, there does not appear to be any new type of aircraft under development that could boost travel the way the big propeller plane did after World War II, the early jet did in the 1960s, and the wide-bodied jet did in the 1970s. Until there is another quantum leap in the speed, affordability, or comfort of mass air travel, there will be no more quantum leaps in the number of long-distance travelers.

The second reason is that airports and the airspace above them may not be able to accommodate further large increases in traffic. Most of America's major airports are operating at, or close to, maximum capacity. Few major cities see much possibility of increasing the capacity of existing airports or building larger ones in some other location. Public opposition to having an airport near residential neighborhoods is simply too great. For example, Honolulu badly needs a reliever general aviation airport to divert small planes from Honolulu International Airport, but every site proposed has been abandoned after local residents mounted a campaign against it.

Probably more important than airport capacity is airspace capacity. In the mid-1960s, foresighted leaders in the aviation business saw air traffic mounting at some 15 percent per year. They knew that at that rate airspace above major cities would soon be saturated. Their answer was to build larger planes so that air passenger traffic could continue to increase without a proportionate increase in the number of aircraft. This was the origin of the Boeing 747. The present crisis is much more severe than that of the 1960s. Some further increases in air traffic may be accommodated by building planes even larger than the 747, but this would aggravate already serious problems of loading time and baggage handling.

The third, and probably most important, reason why I anticipate a slower rate of growth in long-distance tourism of Americans is that the rate of growth in the real income of the American people has slowed dramatically and hence fewer and fewer people are moving into the traveling class each year.

With no new modes of air transportation scheduled to come on stream, with severe airport and airspace limitations, and with the secular rise in real income slowing, I anticipate a continuing slowdown in the rate of growth of long-distance vacation travel in the decades ahead. Nonetheless, the potential market that exists is still so great that tourism will continue to be a growth industry, both worldwide and in Hawaii, for a long time to come.

DEFENSE

As reported earlier in this chapter, nationally, the armed forces of the United States were demobilized quite rapidly after World War II, but in Hawaii the process took five years. The number of armed forces personnel stationed in Hawaii dropped from several hundred thousand in 1945 to about 68,000 in 1946 and continued to decline until 1950, when there were only 21,000. The Korean War brought a sharp reversal, as the military started a buildup in Hawaii that brought the number of personnel back to more than 50,000 by 1952. Many military personnel were joined in Hawaii by their dependents, and ever since the number of dependents has slightly exceeded the total of uniformed personnel.

Since the mid-1950s the size of the military in Hawaii has remained fairly constant at between 50,000 and 60,000 troops and between 60,000 and 70,000 civilian dependents.[73] The number of civilian employees of the defense agencies has also remained rather stable at around 20,000. On the assumption that Department of Defense civilian employees have an average of two and one-half dependents, this group adds another 50,000 people to the total number of residents in Hawaii who are dependent on the military for their livelihood. Altogether, these four categories (military and their dependents plus civilian employees and their dependents) add up to about 200,000. This number constituted about 35 percent of Hawaii's total resident population back in 1955, but as the population of the islands has grown, the percentage has drifted downward and in 1988 stood at just under 20 percent. Nevertheless, any activity that provides jobs and income to nearly a fifth of the population is of immense economic importance. In addition to the active members of the Army, Navy, Air Force, and Marine Corps, some 4,000 members of reserve units, 3,700 members of the Hawaii National Guard, nearly 1,000 members of the Coast Guard (which becomes a military unit in times of emergency), and more than 12,000 retired military drawing military pensions reside in Hawaii.

Hawaii continues to be home base for the country's largest military command, the U.S. Pacific Command. CINCPAC's mission is to maintain security in this half of the world, to defend the U.S. against attack through the Pacific Ocean area, to support the policies and interests of the United States, and to discharge all U.S. military responsibilities in the Pacific, Far East, South and Southeast Asia, and the Indian Ocean.[74] Most of the 380,000 soldiers, sailors, airmen, and marines under CINCPAC's command are stationed in Japan, South Korea, and the Philippines, others being at scattered posts around the Pacific Basin. Only about 15 percent of these troops are home-based in Hawaii; but the command headquarters for the Navy, the Army, the Air Force, and the Marine Corps components are all located in Hawaii, along with their requisite support facilities.

The main combat forces in Hawaii are the Third Fleet and the Submarine Force Pacific at Pearl Harbor, the Twenty-fifth Infantry Division (Light) at Schofield Barracks, the Fifteenth Air Base Wing at Hickam Air Force Base, and the First Marine (Expeditionary) Brigade at the Marine Corps Air Station in Kaneohe. The Naval Air Station at Barbers Point is home for several aviation units assigned to antisubmarine warfare operations.

To support the combat forces, both in Hawaii and in forward areas, the military services maintain a large number of facilities on Oahu and the neighbor islands. The following list is representative of the wide range of activities in which the services are engaged:

Training: Pohakuloa Training Area on Hawaii
Repair: Naval Shipyard, Pearl Harbor
Intelligence: Army 703d Military Intelligence Brigade, Kunia

Communications: Naval Communications Area Master Station,
   Wahiawa
Engineering and construction: Pacific Ocean Division, U.S. Army Corps
   of Engineers, Fort Shafter
Research: Pacific Missile Range Facility on Kauai
Medical facilities: Tripler Army Medical Center, Moanalua
Ammunition storage: Naval Magazine, Lualualei
Supply: Naval Supply Station, Pearl Harbor
Recreation: Hale Koa Hotel in Waikiki, Kilauea Military Camp on
   Hawaii, eight golf courses on Oahu

According to CINCPAC headquarters, the military has 506 facilities in Hawaii, with the Army having 152, the Air Force 140, the Navy 116, and the Marines 98. These facilities occupy some 265,000 acres of land, more than all of sugar and pineapple combined.

The outlook for the military in Hawaii is problematic, for no one knows what size military establishment the U.S. Pacific Command will require in the future and no one can be certain where these forces will be located. It is possible that developments in the Soviet Union in the last decade of this century will make possible a significant reduction in the strength of the military establishment in the Pacific. But since Hawaii is the core of the Pacific Command, I suspect that even if our total forces in the Pacific were cut in half, the military presence in Hawaii would not be reduced appreciably—and conceivably could even be increased as forward bases were closed.

Diversified Agriculture

The history of diversified agriculture in the modern, post–World War II Hawaiian economy is a continuation of the story that was told earlier about diversified agriculture in the pre–World War II days, consisting of efforts to produce more of the food and animal feed consumed locally, plus efforts to develop new agricultural products for export.

With respect to developing import substitutes, efforts have been about as unsuccessful as they were in prewar days, for the same reasons detailed in Chapter 3. As of 1986, Hawaii produced only 36 percent of the fresh vegetables it consumed, 31 percent of the beef, 28 percent of the fresh fruits, 23 percent of the pork, 20 percent of the chickens, and about 10 percent of the feed needed for livestock.[75] Production of canned and processed fruits, vegetables, and meats has been negligible. There have been occasional successes—for example, banana production recently staged something of a comeback—but overall the effort to achieve greater self-sufficiency in food and feed has failed.

In developing agricultural products for export, Hawaii has enjoyed some rather spectacular successes in overcoming prewar failures in such goods as rubber, sisal, and rice. In addition to coffee, which continues at about half the size of the industry in the 1960s and about one-third of its size in the 1920s, the main agricultural exports in the postwar years have been, in order of value, flowers and foliage products, macadamia nuts, papaya, seed corn, ginger root, and guava. As the following table shows, the total sales (both local and export) of these items in 1989 amounted to nearly $137 million, with most of the products being exported. By comparison, the 1980 coffee crop sold for $8.9 million.[76]

1989 market value of Hawaii's newer agricultural products

Flowers and nursery products	$62,295,000
Macadamia nuts	44,945,000
Papaya	14,380,000
Seed corn	6,120,000
Ginger root	5,827,000
Guava	3,135,000
Total	136,702,000

Another volume would be needed to tell the developmental history of all these products, but it may be instructive to consider in brief one of the biggest products (macadamia nuts) and the newest (seed corn).

The macadamia nut tree, an evergreen native to Australia, was first introduced into Hawaii in the early 1880s but was not commercially planted until the Honokaa Sugar Company at the upper end of the Hamakua Coast on the Big Island started an orchard in 1916.[77] An estimated 375 acres were planted in macadamia nuts in 1936,[78] 700 in 1952, 2,500 in 1958, 10,500 in 1973, and 21,300 in 1986,[79] almost all of them on the Big Island.

Slow growing and slow bearing, the tree takes seven or eight years to produce its first crop, not reaching full bearing until it is about fifteen years old. The macadamia tree is demanding of its environment; it cannot stand wind or frost, its sunlight and moisture requirements lie in a narrow range. Its shell is perhaps the hardest of any nut, which in early days presented a difficult processing problem. Fortunately for Hawaii, the Big Island has many areas where growing conditions are ideal, and consequently Hawaii has become the world's dominant producer of this finest nut of all.

The obvious question about the macadamia nut is whether Hawaii, having gotten the jump on the rest of the world in its production, will in time be surpassed by tropical areas where costs of production are significantly lower, as happened to the Hawaiian pineapple industry. Although this may occur, it will take a long time, and may not happen at all for reasons hinted at already. First, the slow growth of the tree means that much capital must be tied up for many years before a crop can be harvested, thus requiring a farsighted and wealthy corporation or government to embark on major macadamia nut plantings. Second, the tree's climatic demands limit to few places in the world where it will thrive. Plantings have been made in Australia, South Africa, Costa Rica, Mexico, and Guatemala; but it will be a long time before it will be known whether these or other areas can match Hawaii as the ideal site for the nut.

The seed corn industry got started in the United States in the 1920s, when it was found that the development of hybrid corn through cross-fertilization could increase yields dramatically. Before the first hybrid seeds were developed in the early 1930s, the average yield of corn per acre was about 20 bushels; by 1943 it had risen to 33 bushels, and then went up and up, reaching 47 bushels in 1956, 74 bushels in 1965, 97 bushels in 1972, 101 bushels in 1978,[80] and 119 bushels in 1986.[81]

Production of a new hybrid corn seed takes twelve generations to transfer preferred genes from one variety to another. On the mainland, where only one crop can be raised in a year, the process takes a dozen years; but it can be compressed into only four years in Hawaii, where three crops can be raised in a year. The trial was made in 1967, when a blight swept the corn belt and the firm of Holden's Foundation Seed thought of Hawaii as a place to grow corn free of the disease. By 1968, five seed corn companies were operating in the islands on some 400 acres.[82] Now there are seven companies, with nearly 800 acres in seed corn.[83]

In addition to its advantage in developing new hybrid varieties, Hawaii is ideal for producing new hybrid seeds in quantity. With three crops per year, one pound of seed of a new variety can be increased to 25,000 pounds in the course of one year, whereas it would take three years on the mainland.[84]

The rapid success of seed corn is an exception. It takes a long time to develop most new crops and to prove whether or not they will thrive economically in Hawaii. Cocoa is more typical. In 1968 a local firm started a cocoa-producing project on the Big Island and Maui in a joint venture with the Hershey Foods Corporation and Amfac. Because growing conditions in Hawaii differ markedly from those in most cocoa-producing areas (generally rain forests), it will reportedly take two human lifetimes to perfect the operation—to solve soil problems, weather and wind problems, insect problems, irrigation problems, and nutritional problems, in addition to deciding on the best varieties and seed stock to use.[85] Perhaps the length of time has been exaggerated somewhat, but a considerable period of experimentation and research will be needed. The first crop was harvested late in 1988 and was said to be remarkably mild and rich, without the harsh acidity of many chocolates.[86]

The outlook for diversified agriculture in Hawaii, perhaps predictable in the aggregate, is highly unpredictable with respect to specific products. Hawaii will continue to grow something like 25 percent of the fresh foods locally consumed and import the other 75 percent, plus practically all processed food. A half a dozen or so agricultural products will continue to be produced in Hawaii economically enough to find markets on the mainland. Although the sum of these may not equal the value of the sugar crop and could never challenge the position of the military or tourism in the economy, they will continue to make a substantial contribution to the total economy.

DIVERSIFIED MANUFACTURING

Everything manufactured in Hawaii is fabricated with tools and machinery that have been imported, except for a few machines that are custom-made locally out of imported materials. Energy that powers the machines has been imported, except for that derived from burning bagasse and a very small amount of wind, hydroelectric, solar, and geothermal power. The materials that are processed in Hawaii's manufacturing plants are all imported, except for locally grown agricultural products and a few minerals, such as rocks and limestone used in concrete products.

With these minor exceptions, it can be said that everything needed for manufacturing in Hawaii, other than the labor employed and the land that manufacturing plants are located on, must be imported. With the further disadvantage that the Hawaiian market is too small to support large-scale manufacturing operations and that overseas markets are thousands of miles away, the odds against Hawaii developing significant manufacturing activity are heavy. Indeed, as I noted earlier, prior to World War II practically all manufacturing in Hawaii was dependent in one way or another on the sugar and pineapple industries. However, despite all its disadvantages, Hawaii has recently been able to develop a moderately significant diversified manufacturing industry.

In the first few years after World War II, not much happened in diversified manufacturing, except for modest growth in the emerging garment industry. By 1950, when the Great Hawaiian Dock Strike was over and the decline of the military had stopped, the volume of diversified manufacturing in the islands was still not much larger than it had been ten years earlier before the outbreak of the war. In the field of food processing, locally raised livestock was butchered, some fresh fruits and vegetables were canned, milk from local dairies was processed, bread baked, some soft drinks and beer bottled, a few forms of pasta produced. In construction, a few concrete products were made from imported cement, a bagasse wallboard was produced called Canec, and a small amount of furniture was fabricated. Local newspapers and a magazine or two were printed locally. Local firms mixed some of the fertilizer used, formed the cans for the pineapple pack, custom-made some machinery for the plantations, and did some ship and boat repair. Aside from garment manufacturing, which had barely reached the product level of $1 million a year, and some handicrafts, that was the totality of island manufacturing. The total value of all Hawaii's diversified manufactured products in 1950 was estimated at only $65 million.[87] Employment in diversified manufacturing totaled 7,225.

During the intervening thirty-six years to 1986, employment grew by nearly two and a half times (to 17,000) and the value of all diversified manufacturing production increased to almost $2 billion a year. Some of this increase came from a greater output of the goods produced back in 1950 for local consumption—more pasteurized milk, a wider variety of bakery products, a vastly greater output of the printing and publishing industry, etc. Some of the increase came from developed or increased production, mainly of garments, for export. But most of it came from the manufacture of items for local consumption that had previously been imported. Since these latter two categories (exports and import replacements) are fundamental to the economy, they merit closer consideration.

Manufacturing for export by an economy as limited in resources as is Hawaii's is possible only when special circumstances exist. The most important special circumstance for Hawaii is its image, which has been primarily responsible for the profitable export of garments, as well as some minor items such as jewelry and perfumes. Another circumstance is the great distance to major land areas, which makes it possible for local oil refineries to sell large amounts of aviation fuel to overseas air-lines whose planes must refuel in Hawaii. Similarly, Hawaii's location in the Pacific has made it possible for local cement plants, from time to time, to ship their product to forward areas for military construction projects under "buy American" programs.

But it is Hawaii's garment industry that has provided the islands' chief manufactured export. In a sense, the industry derives its existence from early missionary influence. Local seamstresses had been making gar-ments ever since the wives of the missionaries embarked on a moral cam-paign to put clothes on native women and hand-stitched for them Mother Hubbard-type dresses which the Hawaiians called *muʻumuʻu*. (The word means "cut off" or "amputated," and the dresses were so called because they had no yoke or sleeves.)

Although a few small "factories" were making work clothes in the first decades of this century, the beginning of the modern garment industry in Hawaii dates from the mid-1930s, when a creative local Chinese named Ellery Chun developed the Aloha shirt. Chun had graduated from Yale with a degree in economics but in the social environment that then existed in Hawaii found his best employment opportunity in his father's clothing store in downtown Honolulu. Designing a silk (pongee) shirt decorated with a flower, a flying fish, or some other symbol of the islands, he called it the Aloha shirt, a name that he promptly registered as a trademark. His younger sister Ethel had studied at the Chouinard School of Art in California after completing a degree at the University of Hawaii, but again the best she could do in Hawaii's highly stratified society was to make the designs for her brother's shirts. The Chuns had their fabrics printed in Japan and the garments cut and sewn to specifi-cation by Wong's Products, a firm that had started out sewing plantation work clothes.[88]

From that modest beginning the local garment industry emerged and by the end of the 1930s was producing more than half a million dollars' worth of Aloha shirts, muumuus, beach coats, sarong dresses, etc.[89] World War II presented the industry with an augmented demand by hundreds of thousands of servicemen who wanted souvenirs from

Hawaii. After the war the industry continued to expand, with local sales being made largely to tourists, and reached a peak in the mid-1970s, when it employed some 3,500 workers. At that time, about 30 percent of the product was exported to the mainland, about two-thirds of the remaining 70 percent was sold to tourists, and one-third was bought by local residents.[90]

In the last decade the garment industry remained at about the size it reached in the mid-1970s, with employment at about 3,300. Well over 150 companies are engaged in the business, which means that the efficiencies of scale are absent in all but a few of the larger producers. Production costs tend to be higher than those of both foreign and mainland garment manufacturers. Nevertheless, the Hawaiian garment industry is noted for the high quality of its product (probably because of the expertise of local machine operators) and for its ability to stay on top of changing fashion styles in the resort and sportswear fields—whether they be traditional tropical prints or such modern fashions as Crazy Shirts and Jams. Local products carry the "Made in Hawaii" label, one more appealing to most customers than a Chicago or New Jersey label. Currently the value of garment exports from Hawaii is about $50 million a year.

The main growth in diversified manufacturing in the last third of a century has been in the import-replacement sector, a growth based on the answers to such questions as the following.

Why pay to ship air? A prime example is the local manufacture of corrugated cardboard boxes, millions of which are used annually in Hawaii by the pineapple industry alone. Corrugation of cardboard means that a good part of the product is air. The paper and glue components can be shipped much more cheaply than can the air-filled final product which, being light, carries a freight rate based on volume. Another example is plastic containers for locally produced liquid products. Shipping empty containers is a classic example of shipping air. The pineapple companies realized this some eighty years ago when they persuaded the American Can Co. to open can-making plants in Hawaii.

Why pay to ship water? Many items, soft drinks being a prime example, consist mostly of water. It is therefore more economical to ship the non-water components of the product in bulk, and then combine them with high-quality local water.

Why import reinforcing iron bars when they can be made out of local scrap metal? This is the idea behind the small steel mill on Oahu.

Why import the finished product if its components can be shipped more cheaply and made into the final product locally? This is the idea behind importing crude oil in bulk and refining it locally into its many end products. Other examples are cement making and the forming of metal doors, sashes, frames, moulding, and trim.

It is perhaps relevant to mention here that the Hawaiian sugar industry has often considered refining its raw sugar locally but has always decided against doing so, primarily because it has found it much cheaper to ship raw sugar in bulk than to ship packaged containers of the various kinds of sugar that it markets (granulated, cubed, powdered, and liquid). Moreover, for marketing reasons it is better to make the final product close to the market so that changes in demand can be adjusted to quickly.

In time other marketable import substitutes may be devised, but at this writing it appears that the list of feasible diversified manufacturing enterprises has been largely exhausted, given present levels of technology. Future growth will depend mainly on expansion of local demand, unless technological developments open up new possibilities for export. Employment in manufacturing has not increased in Hawaii in the last half dozen years, and the dollar value of all manufactures fell from a high of about $2 billion in 1981 to around $1.5 billion in 1986.[91] The main reason for this drop was the decline in the price of oil after it peaked in 1981; refined petroleum products represent a major part of the total value of diversified manufacturing in Hawaii.

The growth of diversified manufacturing since the 1940s has been aided by two factors, support from the local government and Hawaii's attractiveness as a place to live. The government of Hawaii has put considerable emphasis on encouraging manufacturing through efforts of the Economic Planning and Coordination Authority in territorial days and of the Department of Business and Economic Development since statehood. Both agencies actively promoted development of new manufactured items. Moreover, as I have already mentioned, the Hawaiian Electric Company (no doubt motivated in part by the hope of attracting more customers) in the mid-1950s engaged Stanford Research Institute to identify new industries that might succeed on Oahu. A result of the study was the establishment of Hawaii's small steel mill, which makes rebars from scrap metal.

The second and more important impetus for diversified manufacturing has been a by-product of tourism. Over the years, Hawaii has entertained as vacationers thousands of business people who undoubtedly represented every major manufacturing activity in the United States. Most of these people have a hard time getting their businesses off their minds even when on vacation. Since most of them fall in love with Hawaii, many devote part of their vacation to investigating whether their business could succeed in Hawaii. I presume the classic example of the mainland vacationer becoming a Hawaii entrepreneur was Henry J. Kaiser, but there are many others.

One is Lloyd Campbell, who had a thriving manufacturing operation in Los Angeles but in 1966 got so fed up with the smog and traffic that he and thirteen of this key employees pulled up stakes and moved the company to Hawaii. Named Camwil, the company was the oldest manufacturer of customized typewriter elements and computer print wheels in the United States and did a worldwide business. After more than twenty years of successful operation in Hawaii, the company was sold and is no longer in business.

In Campbell's case, as with some other manufacturers of products that are of high value but of low bulk and weight, being far from sources of supply and from markets is not an insurmountable disadvantage. In such cases, the attractiveness of living in Hawaii can be a prime consideration in the decision of where to locate the plant.

SCIENCE AND TECHNOLOGY

A few years ago the Arthur D. Little research firm of Cambridge, Massachusetts, won a contract with the (then) State Department of Planning and Economic Development to evaluate Hawaii's potential for developing space-related activities. Much to their surprise, they found Hawaii already heavily involved in a variety of space programs. "One of the more significant findings of this study," their report states, "has been the extent to which space-related activities are now underway in Hawaii through the efforts of the university, international astronomy teams, the military, and business."[92] Such astonishment at finding Hawaii at the cutting edge of some new scientific developments reminds me of a comment in a British publication, the *Economic Journal*, some years ago when it reviewed a collection of economic lectures that First Hawaiian Bank had sponsored and I had edited into book form.[93] "It is interesting to note that such solid fare can be absorbed in Hawaii," it stated.

Obviously, the carefully designed promotion of Hawaii as the paradise of the Pacific, where sun and fun are available at all times to all comers, had gotten through to the Bostonians and the British. What had not penetrated is that Hawaii for a century or more has been a front-runner in a number of scientific and technological fields, not only absorbing a good bit of solid intellectual fare but also creating it. Ever since the late nineteenth century, the Hawaiian sugar industry has been by far the most scientifically and technologically advanced sugar operation in the world, and the same can be said for the Hawaiian pineapple industry over its life span. Recently, Hawaii scientists were the first to succeed in generating electricity by the process of ocean thermal energy conversion, and most recently it was Hawaii scientists who developed the most advanced technique of surveying the ocean floor. These are just a few examples.

When America's space program began to get off the ground after the Soviets launched Sputnik in 1957, it became evident that Hawaii had valuable assets. For tracking and communications, it was ideally located in the vast area of the north-central Pacific Ocean. For observation, it had high mountains penetrating the air above its clean ocean environment. Furthermore, Hawaii was easily accessible with reliable air and sea transportation services. By then the Hawaiian Telephone Company was already part of the developing national satellite communications program. Consequently, when America's first spacecraft became operational, the National Aeronautical and Space Administration (NASA) established a tracking station at a 4,000-foot elevation at Kokee on Kauai. This station has participated in all the subsequent programs—Mercury, Gemini, Apollo, and the Space Shuttle.

Haleakala, on Maui, was the first mountaintop in Hawaii to be developed for scientific purposes, and in the 1960s it became known as "Science City" because of the many space-related activities located there. The U.S. Air Force has two installations, one to conduct research in electrophysics and advanced sensor technologies, and the other to track and identify space objects and to position satellites. The University of Hawaii, in conjunction with Purdue and the University of Wisconsin, operates an observatory to study the sun's activities. NASA operates a lunar ranging observatory to measure movement of the earth's surface and to keep accurate checks on time to provide global time adjustments.

In the mid-1960s all land on Mauna Kea above the 12,000-foot level was set aside by the state as a science reserve under the administration of the University of Hawaii's Institute for Astronomy. Since then eight telescopes have been installed, and two more will be completed within a few years. Support for the work of the University of Hawaii and the other sponsors of the telescopes has come from outside sources, including NASA, Canada, France, the United Kingdom, the California Institute of Technology, the National Science Foundation, the Netherlands, the University of California, and Japan. Mauna Kea was selected in 1987 as the site for the proposed 15-meter-class National New Technology Telescope (optical-red), establishing it beyond doubt as the premier site for astronomical observation anywhere in the United States, if not in the world. The installations placed on Mauna Kea so far represent a capital investment of about $100 million, have annual operating budgets of about $10 million, and employ about 130 technicians.

In the number of personnel employed—some 700—the Navy's Pacific Missile Range Facility at Barking Sands on the west end of Kauai is the largest space-related facility in Hawaii. It is a research and training center for tracking objects underwater, on the surface of the ocean, and in space out to a distance of 30,000 miles. In addition to the Navy's work, the facility is used by the National Bureau of Standards for sending out time ticks for calibration with other stations, and by the Department of Energy, which has a facility to support high-altitude nuclear testing, if that program should be revived.

In the future a major addition to Hawaii's space-related activities could be a commercial spaceport for launching small vehicles into either polar or equatorial orbit. NASA estimates that in the next ten years some 1,000 to 1,200 scientific and commercial payloads will be launched worldwide,[94] and it is thought that Hawaii's midocean location gives it an advantage over most other sites because of the safety it provides in jettisoning the launching rocket.

Hawaii's natural assets for scientific work involving the ocean are at least as great as they are for scientific work involving outer space. The islands are mountaintops rising steeply from the ocean floor, surrounded by clean, clear water that is deep close to shore and provides excellent visibility. In contrast, most ocean frontages face shallow, dirty water that may extend for hundreds of miles until the continental shelf drops off and deep water is reached. Furthermore, Hawaii's surface waters are warm, wave action is normally moderate, and the climate is remarkably benign, with cloud-free days most of the time in many areas. Because of these assets, a great deal of scientific work involving the ocean is being done locally, both deep-ocean and shallow-ocean work. Some of it is basic research, and some is applied research aimed largely at developing food sources.

Hawaii's deep-ocean research has already resulted in four developments of note, two of great potential for the future and two already of
considerable value. A potential development is the conversion into electricity of the heat from the sun's rays that is stored in the surface waters
of the ocean by a process known as ocean thermal energy conversion
(OTEC). Briefly, the process is similar to that of a steam-powered electric
generating plant. When an oil- or coal-fired furnace heats water to 212°
F, the water boils, and as it forms steam it expands to many times its liquid volume. This vapor is allowed to escape through a nozzle, and the
force of this steam jet spins a turbine to generate electricity.

Some refrigerants—ammonia and Freon are two examples—will
vaporize (or boil) at room temperature. This phenomenon can be used
to generate electricity, utilizing the temperature difference between the
warm surface water at nearly 80° F and the cold deep-ocean water.
Ammonia is circulated in a closed, pressurized pipe through a heat
exchanger—much like an automobile radiator—where it is warmed by
the surface water to its flash point, at which time it vaporizes, expands,
and is directed under pressure to drive a turbine generator. The vapor is
then collected and circulated through another heat exchanger, which is
cooled by water pumped from deep below the surface of the ocean; this
condenses it back into liquid form. The process, which can be repeated
over and over, is known as closed-cycle ocean thermal energy conversion.

An experimental OTEC plant offshore Keahole Point in west Hawaii,
financed by federal and state grants, has produced 50 kilowatts of electricity using only 40 kilowatts to operate its pumps—a 20 percent
"profit." Engineers estimate that with a full-scale plant, a 75 or even 80
percent return might be possible. Corrosion and biofouling by the seawater proved much less severe than anticipated and can be controlled by
an environmentally benign treatment process. It was also found that the
cold water pumped back into the ocean, being heavier than warm water,
immediately sank to lower levels without chilling the surface waters, so
that no ecological problems have been identified. Even so, a comprehensive monitoring program continues in force.

While oil remains available at less than about thirty dollars a barrel,
closed-cycle OTEC energy will likely sit on the shelf. But someday fossil
fuels will either be banned, because of their pollution of the atmosphere,
or they will be in such short supply that their prices will increase considerably—at which time OTEC energy will become competitive. This will

be a boon to those areas (mainly in the tropics) where the temperature difference between the ocean's surface and deep waters is as much as it is in Hawaii.

Scientists at the state's Natural Energy Laboratory are working on a 165-kilowatt generator that they hope to power with an open-cycle (OC) process, a more complex operation that was a partial vacuum to obtain steam at lower temperatures than under the system briefly described above. Once the open-cycle process is perfected, it will have the immense advantage of creating large amounts of desalinated water as a by-product. In areas of the world where both electricity and fresh water are in short supply, it is possible that the OC-OTEC system may prove to be commercially competitive, even at the present price of oil. The U.S. Department of Energy, among others, is funding OC-OTEC research at Keahole.

The second development of possibly great potential for Hawaii's economic future was the discovery some years ago of rich deposits of minerals on the deep ocean floor in the vicinity of the islands—manganese, cobalt, nickel, copper, and other minerals. These are usually found in the form of nodules, ranging from pea to potato size, that can be mined by various methods and then smelted to extract the pure metal. As long as these same minerals can be obtained less expensively by surface mining, extracting them from the seabed is an idea that will have to wait. At the rate the earth's minerals are being used up, however, the day will come (perhaps while some of us are still alive) when Hawaii will have a major mining and smelting industry.

OTEC research has demonstrated that water pumped from ocean depths near offshore is nutrient-rich and pathogen-free, and therefore much better for some types of aquaculture than the surface waters that have been used. The water is also rich in dissolved inorganic nutrients—nitrates, phosphates, and silicates. It has long been known that sea life is far more abundant in those parts of the ocean, such as off island shores, where upswellings of currents bring the nutrient-rich deep water to the surface; but until OTEC research started, no one had installed pipes and pumps deep enough in the ocean to tap this water.

At the Natural Energy Laboratory at Keahole, extensive experimental work has been done in the last few years in cultivating abalone, salmon, lobster, oysters, clams, mussels, 'opihi, trout, and various kinds of algae in this nutrient-rich deep-ocean water, which can be used cold for growing lobsters three times faster than they grow off the coast of Maine, or

used warm if that is indicated. Results there induced the state government in the early 1980s to spend $15 million in creating a 547-acre park
for commercial operations of this sort adjacent to the Natural Energy
Laboratory.[95] One seafood enterprise in the park, concentrating on abalone, oysters, salmon, and sea urchins for the U.S. mainland and Japanese markets, anticipates expanding its ponds to cover forty acres. It
seems probable that deep-ocean water aquaculture will soon overtake
traditional aquaculture in Hawaii.

Another product of deep-ocean research is technology using un-
manned miniature submarines. The University of Hawaii's Institute of
Geophysics developed a vessel for use by research geologists and ocean-
ographers in studying the ocean floor. Its sophisticated sonar equipment, which permits a wide scanning of the ocean floor even when the
vessel is in motion, also makes it valuable to telecommunications companies in laying delicate fiber optic cables across oceans. As a result, Seafloor Surveys International, Inc., was formed in 1985 by a group of University of Hawaii researchers who had worked on the project. The
company has obtained several million dollars' worth of contracts from
cable companies around the world for ocean floor mapping.[96]

The same company mapped the seafloor between the Big Island and
Maui, and then between Maui and Oahu, to determine the best route
for a proposed underwater electricity transmission cable to bring geothermal energy from the Big Island to Oahu. This project, if feasible,
would drastically reduce Oahu's dependence on oil for its electric power
—just as the production of electricity from biomass (primarily sugarcane
bagasse) has for many decades supplemented electric production from oil
on the neighbor islands: by 40 percent on Kauai, 39 percent on the Big
Island, and 23 percent on Maui.[97]

Research by the University of Hawaii into geothermal possibilities on
the Big Island has been under way for a quarter of a century. The university brought into operation the first geothermal plant in Hawaii, a 3-
megawatt facility completed in 1981. A 25-megawatt private plant is
scheduled for completion in the next few years, and it is estimated that
in time perhaps 1,000 megawatts of geothermal power can be produced
on the Big Island. Because this is about the volume of Oahu's usage, the
possibility of a deep-water transmission cable to bring the power to
Oahu is being explored.[98] The longest and deepest underwater power
transmission cable to date connects Norway and Denmark; it is 78 miles
long and 1,800 feet deep. By contrast, the Hawaii cable would be more
than twice that long and have a depth of up to 7,000 feet.[99]

Despite the fact that Hawaii has been experimenting with and operating traditional aquaculture farms for several decades, I suggested that aquaculture using deep-ocean water will possibly be more successful than traditional aquaculture. The Oceanic Institute and state and county government agencies have done intensive work on the problems of aquaculture, but the industry has not prospered and most attempts at aquaculture production have failed. Some twenty companies are engaged in fish farming, producing a variety of items from shrimp to frog legs to Malaysian freshwater prawns; but most are losing money.[100]

As a result, many people in Hawaii with aquaculture expertise have found that they can be more successful marketing their knowledge as consultants in foreign countries. In 1987 about twenty aquaculture consulting firms were operating out of Hawaii with contracts in some thirty countries, grossing over $3 million a year in revenues.[101] This activity, together with research in aquaculture, much of it federally funded, brings in more dollars than would the sale of products from aquaculture farms using surface water. Fish farming with deep-ocean water, however, is still a Hawaiian monopoly.

Since every endeavor discussed in this section has been highly technological, it is obvious that Hawaii has made considerable progress in the hi-tech field. The state has attracted more than thirty companies in electronics and software, fields that made famous Boston's Route 128 and California's Silicon Valley. Among the two dozen or so software companies operating in Hawaii is one that designs programs for computerized operations of the sugar mills, and among a dozen or so electronics companies is one that designs and manufactures air-traffic control systems for airports all over the world.

The high-technology activities that Hawaii has been able to develop, however, remain primarily in the fields of astronomy, marine sciences, alternate energy, tropical agriculture and aquaculture, and space exploration and development. These, together with the fields of electronic design, software, and biotechnology, are the areas that the state's High Technology Development Corporation was established to promote. This organization's function is to assist companies in any of the areas listed above to get organized and solve whatever problems they may have—site location, construction, and even financing through the issuance of special-purpose revenue bonds. It serves as an expediter for high-technology companies contemplating work in Hawaii. Site location, at least on Oahu, Maui, and Hawaii, is less of a problem than it used to be. Not only is there Castle & Cooke's large industrial park for high-technology companies on Oahu, but also the Maui Economic Development Board has opened a similar park on Maui and the state's Natural Energy Laboratory on the Big Island—together with an adjacent Hawaii Ocean Science and Technology Park at Keahole—provide adequate sites on those islands.

The University of Hawaii is the site of the Pacific International Center for High Technology Research, established by the state legislature in 1983. The center's budget is augmented by annual grants of $1 million from the Japanese government. In addition to conducting research, the center works to improve the flow of new technology to industry and to assist education and training in developing countries in the Pacific basin. Among other fields, it researches biotechnology—in crop improvement, insect and disease control in agriculture and aquaculture, genetic control of the fruit fly, and genetic manipulation of edible algae.

Although the new technologies discussed here will probably never play the dominant economic role that sugar and pineapple played before World War II, or that tourism and defense activities do today, they constitute a significant and sophisticated sector of the Hawaiian economy.

THE UNDERGROUND ECONOMY

To this point the only economic activities discussed have been those that are open, aboveboard, and reported. But that is not the entire story of the Hawaiian economy, nor of any other economy in a world where many economic activities are either illegal and hence hidden from the authorities, or are legal but are hidden from the tax collector and hence not reported in official figures. These hidden activities constitute what is commonly called the "underground economy."

Questions as to the size and composition of the underground economy in America were hardly raised until the early 1970s, when articles on the subject began appearing in financial journals. In 1977 the Joint Committee on the Economic Report of the U.S. Congress directed that a staff study be made of the nation's underground economy. Its report was issued in 1980. The two chief authors, Carl Simon of the University of Michigan and Ann Witte of the University of North Carolina, continued their research and in 1982 published the results in a book entitled *Beating the System: The Underground Economy.*[102]

Simon and Witte divided the underground economy into seven major sectors: income hidden to avoid income taxes; unreported income earned by avoiding excise and sales taxes; unreported income of illegal alien workers; income from illegal transfers (thievery, fraud, etc.); income from the production and distribution of illegal goods (mainly drugs); income from the production and distribution of illegal services (gambling, prostitution); and all other illegal income (hijacking, forgery, extortion, etc.). These seven major sectors were further divided into a total of twenty-five categories. The authors found that slightly over half the U.S. underground economy consisted of tax evasion, about 10 percent consisted of hidden income of illegal alien workers, and the remaining nearly 40 percent consisted of criminal activities—thievery, fraud, drugs, smuggling, gambling, prostitution, extortion, etc.

Their estimate of the total income generated by the underground economy was just under 10 percent of the total reported personal income of the nation. They admitted that they might be as much as 25 or 30 percent in error (either overestimating or underestimating) in each of the categories, but in any case this was the most comprehensive study of the subject ever attempted.

When I read this book, my question was, What is the size and composition of Hawaii's underground economy? I set out to develop the best answer to that question that I could, and this section tells the methods I used and the results I obtained.

Using the base year of 1981, I applied the Simon and Witte national findings to Hawaii to see what the dollar volume of Hawaii's underground economy would be in each of the twenty-five subsectors if Hawaii's underground economy were exactly the same fraction of total personal income as that found by Simon and Witte for the entire country. These figures are shown in column 3 of Table 5.2.

I then took each of these figures to the persons in Hawaii best qualified to judge for each category how Hawaii's actual dollar figures differed from those obtained by so applying the Simon–Witte percentages. This involved working for an extended period of time with many people from the Internal Revenue Service, the Hawaii State Tax Office, the U.S. Customs Service, the U.S. Immigration and Naturalization Service, the U.S. Bureau of Alcohol, Tobacco, and Firearms, the U.S. Secret Service, and—most importantly—the police departments of the four counties.

On the basis of all these interviews, I developed what I thought was the appropriate figure for Hawaii in each of the twenty-five subsectors. I then held a final review meeting with representatives of the above-mentioned agencies. As a result of this interdisciplinary review, I made addi-

Table 5.2 "Guesstimated" total personal income (TPI) of the underground economy: United States and Hawaii, 1981

TYPE OF INCOME	U.S. (IN BIL. $)	AS % OF U.S. TPI ($2,405.598 BIL.)	HAWAII AS SAME % OF TPI (IN MIL. $)	MY ESTIMATE FOR HAWAII (IN MIL. $)	COLUMN 4 AS % OF HAWAII TPI ($10,823 MIL.)
Income hidden to avoid taxes	124.85	5.19	561.711	503.7	4.655
Under and unreported income of legal wage earners	29.02	1.206	130.564	130.5	1.206
Under and unreported income of legal self-employed	62.33	2.591	280.428	280.4	2.591
Unreported dividend earnings	5.14	.214	23.125	15.0	.139
Unreported interest earnings	10.30	.428	46.341	46.3	.428
Unreported rents and royalties	7.61	.316	34.238	20.0	.185
Unreported estate and trust income	.55	.023	2.474	1.5	.014
Unreported corporate income	9.90	.412	44.541	10.0	.092
Unreported income earned by avoiding cigarette, alcohol, and sales taxes	.45	.019	2.025	2.1	.019
Unreported income of illegal alien workers	20.18	.839	90.792	6.0	.055
Income from illegal transfers	38.951	1.619	175.243	77.0	.711
Income to thieves and fences handling stolen goods	16.18	.673	72.795	19.8	.183
Fraud, arson	1.17	.049	5.264	5.3	.049
Other fraud (bankruptcy, check, consumer, credit card, insurance, securities)	11.15	.464	50.165	40.0	.369
Counterfeiting	.001	.000	.004	0	0
Embezzlement	.70	.029	3.149	3.1	.029
Bribery	9.75	.405	43.866	8.8	.081

Income from production and distribution of illegal

goods	30.52	1.269	137.313	394.4	3.644
Drugs	28.62	1.190	128.765	389.5	3.599
Heroin	10.93	.454	49.175	23.0	.213
Cocaine	9.26	.385	41.662	41.7	.385
Marijuana	4.83	.201	21.731	320.0	2.957
Other drugs	3.60	.150	16.197	4.8	.044
Smuggling of goods other than drugs	.25	.010	1.125	1.1	.010
Pornography	1.65	.069	7.423	3.8	.035
Income from production and distribution of illegal services	11.65	0.484	52.413	85.1	.786
Takeout from illegal gambling (sports books, horse books, numbers, sports cards, illegal casinos)	1.70	.071	7.648	34.1	.315
Loan sharking	1.70	.071	7.648	1.0	.009
Prostitution	8.25	.343	37.117	50.0	.462
Other illegal income (hijacking, forgery, protection and extortion, pirating of records and taxes)	7.50	.312	33.743	20.0	.185
Total	234.101	9.732	1,053.240	1,088.3	10.055

SOURCES: Simon and Witte, *Beating the System: The Underground Economy;* Thomas K. Hitch.

tional changes to reflect the consensus of the group. Although not everyone agreed with every figure, the consensus was that all the figures were probably a good reflection of the existing state of the underground economy in Hawaii as of 1981.

Before presenting my estimates, I should explain the income concepts involved in the study. I was trying to identify the *income to residents of Hawaii* resulting from these underground activities, and as far as possible the *net* income rather than the gross income. By this, I mean that if a marijuana grower in Hawaii, for example, has a gross income of $100,000, but spent in the open and aboveground market $10,000 on fertilizers, water, land rental, agricultural implements, etc., the hidden income would then only be the net figure of $90,000. The income to mainland importers and peddlers would not be included in the Hawaii figure.

The calculation of the appropriate income figure for illegal gambling is a bit complicated (at least for nongamblers like me). The figure includes only the "takeout" that the bookie or house retains. The takeout for legal gambling is estimated nationally at around 20 percent of the "handle" (the total amount gambled), but it is undoubtedly higher for illegal gambling. The portion of the handle that is distributed to the winners, and probably seldom if ever reported to the IRS, is not included, because for the gambling community as a whole the losses far more than balance the winnings.

In the stolen goods area, the appropriate figure is the amount the thief and the fence make from a theft, not the value of the stolen property. From national studies quoted by Simon and Witte, it would appear that, on the average, out of every $100 of thievery, $16 is in currency and $84 is in goods. Of the $84 in goods stolen, about one-fourth is recovered, nearly 60 percent is sold by the thief to the fence for resale, and a little over 15 percent is kept by the thief. The thief gets about 25 percent of the market value of the stolen goods when he sells to the fence, and this income from the sale is reduced by 10 percent to cover the thief's costs of doing business. The fence gets from 50 to 75 percent of the market value of the goods, and his gross income is reduced both by the cost of the goods and his costs of doing business. I conclude therefore that the thief receives about $11 of income out of the $84 of stolen goods and the fence receives about the same amount, for a total of $22. In addition, thieves keep a bit over 15 percent of the goods they steal. Valuing these at about 50 percent of market value and deducting 10 percent for business costs, I add another $6 to the $22. Finally, the thieves keep the $16 of the $100 that is currency, for a grand total of $44 in income to thieves and fences for every $100 of thievery. I applied this 44 percent figure to the police estimates of the value of stolen goods in Hawaii. The results of my study are shown in column 4 of Table 5.2.

My first conclusion is that plain and simple tax evasion accounts for about half of the underground economy. Nationally, it represents a little more than half; locally it appears to be slightly less than half. My second conclusion is that while the total fraction of hidden income is about the same in Hawaii and nationally (just about 10 percent of aboveground income), considerable differences are found in individual areas, as shown in columns 2 and 5 of Table 5.2.

The nine areas where law enforcement officers thought that the situation in Hawaii was consistent with the average of the entire country are: (1) under- and unreported income of legal self-employed persons, (2) under- and unreported income of legal wage earners, (3) unreported interest income, (4) income from the distribution of cocaine, (5) fraud and arson, (6) embezzlement, (7) unreported income earned by avoiding sales and excise taxes, (8) smuggling of goods other than drugs, and (9) counterfeiting.

Table 5.3 lists thirteen areas where local law enforcement officers thought that illegal income or unreported legal income was less in Hawaii than on the mainland. In the addendum to Table 5.3 I suggest reasons why Hawaii's proportion of income from those sources is likely to be lower than the national average.

Finally, Table 5.4 shows the three areas where law enforcement officers thought that Hawaii outdistanced the national averages. Income from prostitution is slightly above the national average; the takeout from illegal gambling appears to be proportionately from four to five times as great as on the mainland; and the income produced by marijuana production and distribution is about fifteen times higher than the national average.

Prostitution is somewhat above average probably because of Hawaii's large tourist population: many people will do things when on a trip that they would not do in their own hometown. I doubt that the large military population or the fact that Honolulu is a port city has much to do with it, although those factors nurtured prostitution in the islands during earlier periods of Hawaii's history—not only during the whaling era but also during World War II, when hundreds of thousands of servicemen passed through Hawaii on their way to the western Pacific.

It is common knowledge that gambling is popular in Hawaii, where it

Table 5.3   Types of illegal or unreported income proportionately smaller in Hawaii than in the nation at large

TYPE OF INCOME	U.S. (IN BIL. $)	AS % OF U.S. TPI	HAWAII (IN MIL. $)	AS % OF HAWAII TPI
Unreported income of illegal alien workers	20.18	.839	6.0	.055
Income of thieves and fences handling stolen goods	16.18	.673	19.8	.183
Fraud involving credit cards, checks, insurance, and securities	11.15	.464	40.0	.369
Income from the distribution of heroin	10.93	.454	23.0	.213
Unreported corporate income	9.90	.412	10.0	.092
Bribery	9.75	.405	8.8	.081
Unreported rents and royalties	7.61	.316	20.0	.185
Hijacking, forgery, extortion, etc.	7.50	.312	20.0	.185
Unreported dividend income	5.14	.214	15.0	.139
Income from the distribution of illegal drugs other than cocaine, heroin, and marijuana	3.60	.150	4.8	.044
Loan sharking	1.70	.071	1.0	.009
Pornography	1.65	.069	3.8	.035
Unreported estate and trust income	.55	.023	1.5	.014

SOURCES: Simon and Witte, *Beating the System: The Underground Economy;* Thomas K. Hitch.

is illegal. The time and cost of a trip to a legal gambling center probably result in more illegal gambling in the islands than would be the case if the state were conveniently close to a legal gambling spot, such as Las Vegas or Atlantic City.

It is also common knowledge that a great deal of marijuana is grown in Hawaii and a considerable amount is consumed in the state. I arrived at my own estimate, which is well below the 1982 estimates of *Newsweek* ($500 million) and of *Time* ($750 million), in the following manner.

The four county police departments, on the basis of their periodic "green harvests," estimated that the harvest value of raw, unprocessed

Addendum to Table 5.3   Probable reasons why the Hawaii ratio is smaller than the national ratio

TYPE OF INCOME	REASON
1. Unreported income of illegal alien workers	Because all aliens entering Hawaii have to pass through immigration, their presence is known. Hawaii has no open land borders for aliens to slip across.
2. Income of thieves and fences handling stolen goods	It is harder to dispose of stolen goods in a small island community than on a large continent.
3. Fraud involving credit cards, checks, insurance, and securities	Probably the same as 2 above (small island community).
4. Income from the distribution of heroin	It is more expensive and more difficult to obtain than other drugs.
5. Unreported corporate income	Corporate income is a smaller part of the total Hawaiian economy than it is of the national economy.
6. Bribery	Probably the same as 2 above (small island community).
7. Unreported rents and royalties	Many rental units are owned by out-of-state investors with management handled by a legitimate management company.
8. Hijacking, forgery, extortion, etc.	Hawaii does not have the long, open roads that lend themselves to truck hijacking.
9. Unreported dividend income	Same as 5 above.
10. Income from the distribution of illegal drugs other than cocaine, heroin, and marijuana	Marijuana dominates the Hawaiian drug market.
11. Loan sharking	Probably the same as 2 above (small island community).
12. Pornography	Most pornography in Hawaii is aboveground.
13. Unreported estate and trust income	Practically all estates and trusts are managed by trust agencies.

Table 5.4   Types of illegal or unreported income proportionately larger in
            Hawaii than in the nation at large

TYPE OF INCOME	U.S. (IN BIL. $)	AS % OF U.S. TPI	HAWAII (IN MIL. $)	AS % OF HAWAII TPI
Prostitution	8.25	.343	50.0	.462
Marijuana	4.83	.201	320.0	2.957
Takeout from illegal gambling	1.70	.071	34.1	.315

SOURCES: Simon and Witte, *Beating the System: The Underground Economy;* Thomas K.
Hitch.

marijuana grown in Hawaii in 1981 was about $125 million. Since their
harvesting raids seize many immature plants, I increased this estimate to
$150 million, and then reduced it by 10 percent to allow for the costs of
production—costs that are reported in the aboveground economy. The
wholesalers, who buy the marijuana crop for about $150 million and
probably sell it for twice that amount, derive an income of $150 million.
I then added $35 million to allow for the value added by the retailer or
distributor who sells the final product on the street in Hawaii. I arrived
at this $35 million figure by deducting half of the street value of the mar-
ijuana that I estimate is consumed in Hawaii ($70 million), on the
assumption that the retailer marks the product up 100 percent.

My estimate of $70 million as being the retail value of marijuana sold
to consumers in Hawaii is, of course, a guess. It assumes that the use of
marijuana in Hawaii is about the same as that indicated nationally from
a number of surveys. Since usage varies considerably by age, I applied
the national age-group usage figures to Hawaii's population and concluded that about 10 percent of Hawaii's population smokes marijuana
fairly regularly, and that these regulars use 23 million joints a year (240
joints per regular user per year). Assuming one gram of marijuana per
joint and assuming the street value at about $1,500 per pound, I arrived
at the $70 million figure.

To summarize my guesses about income in 1981 to residents of Hawaii
from the production and distribution of marijuana, I concluded that the
final figure of $320 million was made up of $135 million net income to
the growers, $150 million income to wholesalers, and $35 million to local
retailers. This guess of $320 million may not be out of line with
Newsweek's and *Time*'s guesses of from $500 million to $750 million if
the latter figures included the income of mainland residents that was

derived from the importation and distribution of Hawaiian *pakalolo* (*paka* meaning tobacco and *lolo* meaning crazy). *Time* and *Newsweek* did not tell their readers whether mainland income was included in their figures, however.

In my job of watching and analyzing the Hawaiian economy over the years, I became convinced that the underground economy was giving the aboveground economy a significant hidden boost. At times the official economic data would indicate that the Hawaiian economy was slowing down or even stagnating, but retail sales (particularly of such items as four-wheel-drive small trucks) would indicate the existence of more purchasing power in the market than could be explained by the official figures. This was one reason, when the opportunity presented itself with the publication of the Simon and Witte study, that I jumped at the chance to get as good a fix as I could on the size and composition of Hawaii's underground economy.

New information on Hawaii's marijuana activities that became available in the spring of 1989 made it possible to update the size of this largest single part of Hawaii's underground economy. A study of marijuana production covering the years 1980 through 1987 by Hawaii's attorney general showed a dramatic rise in the production of this crop in recent years.[103] From my base year of 1981, when 341,871 marijuana plants were confiscated by police "green harvest" operations, the number of plants so eradicated rose to 1,901,646 in 1989—nearly a sixfold increase. If some increase in price is factored in, it is plausible that as of 1987 the total income to Hawaii residents created by marijuana production and distribution amounted to somewhere in the vicinity of $2 billion, or slightly more than six times my estimate for the 1981 base year. Since total personal income in Hawaii for 1987 was about $17 billion, it would appear that the marijuana industry added about 12 percent to the official figures. This could raise the total size of Hawaii's underground economy to around 20 percent of the official open economy.

The Impact of Hawaii's State and Local Governments on the Economy

As a legacy from the days of the kingdom, Hawaii has the most highly centralized government in the Union. The state discharges many functions that in the rest of the country are generally performed by local governments, such as public education, health, welfare, and transportation (ports, harbors, airports, and roads). This limits Hawaii's local governments to what might be called housekeeping functions—public safety (police and fire protection), water supply, garbage collection, local transportation (urban buses), and recreation (parks, playgrounds, golf courses, zoos, etc.). The four counties, the sole units of local government, are limited in their taxing power largely to real-property and fuel taxes. Furthermore, whereas in most of the rest of the nation land use is regulated by local government, in Hawaii the State Land Use Commission decides the broad uses of land by zoning it as urban, agricultural, conservation, or rural; and the counties' only power is to zone urban land as between such uses as residential, commercial, industrial, or hotel.

Three basic aspects of governmental impact upon economic development are briefly considered here: taxation, land-use controls, and programs to encourage new businesses.

As a consequence of the centralization of governmental power, it is chiefly the state that impinges on economic development, as in the exercise of its taxing power. In Hawaii, the central government collects about five-sixths of state-plus-local tax revenues, as against the approximately even division to be found among most mainland states. About half of Hawaii state tax revenues come from one levy, a general excise tax on all business transactions, augmented by a special tax on transient accommodations (primarily hotel rooms). About 30 percent of the total comes from the individual income tax, and the remaining 20 percent from an array of other taxes—on corporate income, fuel, liquor, tobacco, banks and other financial institutions, insurance companies, public service companies, etc. This system effectively limits the broad impact of state tax policies on the economy to the individual income tax and to the general excise tax.

Taxation on personal income in Hawaii affects the economy in two ways, both rather minor because, although high by state standards, the state levy is low compared with the federal individual income tax. First, its progressive rates serve to redistribute wealth to a certain extent from the rich to the poor, but this redistribution is so minor as to be of no real economic consequence and is more than offset by the regressiveness of the general excise tax. Second, it raises the cost of living in Hawaii and may discourage people from moving to the state and encourage Hawaii residents to move to some less expensive location. It has probably discouraged some mainland retirees from moving to Hawaii, while causing some of Hawaii's senior citizens to leave Hawaii upon retirement. My conclusion is that the impact of the individual net income tax on the economy is very small.

The general excise, Hawaii's major revenue producer, is an unusual form of American sales tax, a percentage tax on the gross income from sales *by anyone doing any kind of business* in the state. Augmented by a companion use tax, which applies to goods brought into the state for use here, the general excise effectively covers *all* business transactions—even when only one party to the transaction is in Hawaii. Its comprehensiveness is indicated by the fact that fees paid to members of boards of directors (even of eleemosynary foundations) are taxed, because the board member is judged to be engaged in the business of selling his consulting services. Rates are 4 percent on income from retail sales of both goods and services, 0.15 percent on income of insurance solicitors, and 0.5 percent on income from all other business transactions. In addition to the normal 4 percent tax on the gross income of hotels, they pay a special 5 percent Transient Accommodations Tax, making them subject in effect to a tax of 9 percent on their income from room rentals.

The general excise tax pyramids. As an example of maximum pyramiding, a farmer's sale of fruit to a jam and jelly manufacturer is taxed at 0.5 percent; then the sale of the jelly by the manufacturer to a wholesaler is taxed at 0.5 percent; then the sale by the wholesaler to the retailer is taxed at 0.5 percent; and finally the sale by retailer to consumer is taxed at 4 percent of the retail price. This pyramids to a cumulative total of nearly 6 percent. Because mainland sales taxes generally apply only at the retail level and typically exclude food, drugs, and services from their coverage, I estimate that Hawaii's general excise tax at present rates produces about the same amount of revenue that a typical mainland sales tax of about 9 percent would generate.

The general excise may have an impact on individual businesses and on the economy. When it cannot be passed on to the buyer, it necessarily increases the cost of doing business. If the tax is passed on to the buyer, it increases the cost of living. If the tax rate is a special one for a particular industry (such as the added 5 percent tax on hotel rentals) it puts an added burden on that industry and could discourage it.

While the general excise tax undoubtedly weighs heavily on many businesses in Hawaii, it is difficult to visualize how the substantial revenues it yields could be raised by any other levy without equally adverse impacts. An obvious alternative would be to make large increases in the corporate and individual income taxes, which would probably affect business even more. For this reason, the business community over the years has generally approved of the general excise tax but has sought to modify it to eliminate its more adverse economic impacts—an effort that has been fairly successful. For example, historically sugar and pineapple were taxed at higher rates than other agriculture and manufacturing, but this differential was eliminated. Pyramiding was reduced by cutting rates at levels prior to retailing from 1 percent to 0.5 percent. Next, income to Hawaii's producers and processors from sales of their products outside the state was excluded from the tax. Finally, sales of capital goods to businesses for use in their business (such as a new boiler for a sugar mill), which used to be taxed at 4 percent because the sale was for final consumption, are now exempt. I believe that most of the more serious negative impacts of the general excise tax on the economy have been eliminated.

State land-use policies have come under attack from business primarily because of the state's insistence that agricultural land be kept in agriculture. Much time and money has been spent in trying (sometimes successfully, sometimes not) to free land zoned as agricultural for other development. This state policy is based primarily on two considerations, preserving agriculture and avoiding urban sprawl. Since the development it most curtails has been subdivision for housing, the policy has limited the amount of land available for housing and has therefore caused a greater housing shortage and higher housing prices than would otherwise have been the case. In evaluating this conflict of goals (more housing and lower housing prices versus preventing urban sprawl and preserving agricultural lands), one has to face the political reality that the people who own their homes outnumber the people who are in the market to buy one, and that those who are already housed are more interested in high home prices and open country than low home prices and new subdivisions. Homeowners control the majority of votes, and it is probably inevitable (and proper) that government policies follow the wishes of the majority.

Zoning practices of the counties have, by and large, given business little ground for complaint. When it comes to zoning land for hotels and housing, it has been my observation that the general public has been far more antidevelopment in its attitude than the zoning agencies. Generally, public opposition to hotel or housing development has been based on a desire to maintain open areas, particularly those close to beaches.

Often a public outcry has arisen *after* the zoning agency approved a project; and because county charters in Hawaii may permit initiative action to overrule the government, there have been instances in which developers have expended much time, energy, and money, only to have their preapproved project stopped in midstream. Nevertheless, I conclude that county zoning has not had a significantly adverse impact on economic development.

Appraising the effects of other governmental programs is more difficult, since almost all programs may have some impact on the economy. A good educational system helps the economy in many ways. A good transportation system is essential to the flow of commerce. A good set of civil and criminal laws that are well enforced is important to the welfare of the society and the economy. But much legislation can be (and is by interested parties) classified as being either probusiness or antibusiness. It is this type of legislation that is considered here.

Since the mid-1950s, when the Republican establishment lost control to the emerging antiestablishment Democrats, Hawaii's legislature has frequently been charged with being antibusiness and with creating what some people call a poor "business climate" in the islands. There is little doubt that in the 1950s and 1960s some legislation was antibusiness and perhaps even a bit punitive in intent. After being totally excluded from political power and then coming into power on a hate-the-boss program, labor representatives in the legislature were naturally inclined to turn the tables on the oligarchy they had upset. But those days have long since disappeared, and one is faced with the philosophical question of whether the legislature should reflect the views of an electorate that is made up primarily of workers and consumers, or reflect the views of business, which has little clout in the voting booth.

Hawaii's legislature has, by and large, given workers and consumers what they want. Hawaii's statutory employee benefit programs (unemployment insurance, workers' compensation, and temporary disability insurance) are among the most liberal in the country. Tort law, which governs the suing of people (most frequently business firms) for alleged wrongdoing, is generally considered to tip the scales in favor of the plaintiff. Under a unique statute, owners of residences on leased land are empowered to purchase the land from the owner, even if the owner does not want to sell—a clear case (to me) of condemning private property for a doubtful purpose. I say this in spite of the U.S. Supreme Court's action in upholding the constitutionality of the law. All the Court said was that if the legislature *stated* that a public purpose was being served, the Court would not challenge its wisdom. The decision was therefore basically a reaffirmation of states' rights.

How much Hawaii's prolabor and proconsumer legislation has handicapped the state economy is impossible to measure, although many business people will attest that it has hurt them. On the other hand, when most of the prolabor legislation was being passed, the Hawaiian economy was experiencing its period of greatest growth and prosperity. And during the prosperous 1960s the State Department of Planning and Economic Development appeared to be more interested in planning than in pushing economic development. Conversely, in recent years, when the legislature has been more willing to listen to business viewpoints and when the state's efforts to promote economic development have been stepped up considerably, the rate of growth of the economy has slowed measurably. Probably Hawaii's economy might have expanded a bit more rapidly in the 1950s and 1960s if the state government had been more business-oriented, and perhaps it would have slowed even more than it did in the last decade if the state government had not turned a bit more probusiness; but no one will ever know.

Both the state legislature and the county councils have been fairly liberal in funding agencies in their respective jurisdictions whose responsibility is to promote economic development. The territorial government, even before World War II, placed emphasis on expanding diversified agriculture (which then seemed the only likely area of expansion), and the state has continued this support through the University of Hawaii's agricultural programs and the Department of Agriculture. As already noted, the territorial legislature in 1949 created the Industrial Research Advisory Council, which engaged in various research and marketing programs to support diversified agriculture; and when that body was succeeded by the Economic Planning and Coordination Authority (EPCA) in 1955, programs to promote diversified manufacturing were added to the agenda. With statehood in 1959, EPCA became the State Department of Economic Development and its promotional efforts continued. In 1963 the State Department of Planning was combined with the State Department of Economic Development, and into the 1970s the department emphasized its planning and research functions—possibly because during that period the Hawaiian economy was growing so rapidly that giving it control and direction was considered more important than giving it encouragement. Nonetheless, the department was a major factor in the development of Hawaii's space-related and ocean-related scientific activities. In 1987 the planning function was shifted to the governor's office so that today the department's sole responsibility is economic development.

In the mid-1960s the state government instituted a new program for economic development, which successfully encouraged certain exports and promoted some import-replacement activities. Since then it also has lowered the cost of doing business for a large number of firms that import commodities from foreign areas. I refer to the state's active foreign trade zone program. Under federal law, selected geographic areas are designated as foreign trade zones, functioning outside the U.S. Customs Service's jurisdiction with respect to duties and quotas. In these zones, foreign and domestic merchandise can be exported or imported, stored, exhibited, manufactured or processed, assembled, and relabeled, at what are frequently considerable savings.

In 1965 the state was authorized to have Pier 39 at Honolulu Harbor designated as a foreign trade zone. Initially, the only use made of the zone was by traders who stored imports and paid no duty until the goods were removed from the pier. Later the zone moved its main facility to larger quarters at Pier 2, where some 400 firms warehouse their goods and materials.

In 1972 the independent refinery of Pacific Resources, Inc., located in the Barbers Point Industrial Park at the southwestern end of Oahu, was designated as part of Hawaii's foreign trade zone. This permitted it to import foreign crude oil duty free if the products refined from it were to be exported, thereby saving over ten cents on each barrel imported. If the products were sold domestically, the duty was only the crude oil tariff of ten cents per barrel instead of the approximately fifty-cent per barrel tariff on finished petroleum products.

The cannery of Dole Pineapple Company was added to the Hawaii foreign trade zone in 1985, enabling it to avoid payment of import duties on tinplate imported for making cans. When foreign canned pineapple enters the United States, duty is levied on the value of the fruit but not of the can itself. Domestic (Hawaiian) pineapple canned in a foreign trade zone escapes duty on the foreign tinplate used. In 1986, Maui Pineapple Company's cannery was also designated part of the foreign trade zone.

All four counties have established agencies charged with responsibility for fostering economic development, which primarily means attempting to identify business opportunities and attracting the attention of enterprises to those opportunities. Because Hawaii remains remote and little known to many mainland businesses, these efforts sometimes produce results.

My conclusion about the impact on the economy of state and local government activities is that they have not been as important—positively or negatively—as either government officials or business people think. Some government actions have been extremely irritating and perhaps even harmful to some elements in the business community, but overall the damage done has probably not had much measurable effect on the total economy. And I suspect much the same can be said about some of the probusiness activities of the government, although undoubtedly Hawaii's government has been helpful on many occasions and in many ways in promoting economic development. The economic power of state and local governments is simply not very great. Their major power is to direct economic activity to (or away from) selected geographic areas. Through state land-use controls and county zoning activities, whatever economic activity there is can be required to locate where the government wants it to go. But the government's ability to control the rate of economic growth is quite limited. A well-planned, aggressive development program can generally produce some positive results, and a weak or vacillating economic program may slow the growth rate; but basic economic forces, which government cannot control, are far more powerful than the forces that government, particularly state and local government, can mount.

In a similar fashion, economists have generally concluded that although the federal government through its monetary and fiscal powers can have a considerable influence on the level of economic activity, not even the federal government can fine-tune the economy so that it will perform precisely as desired. Even attempting such broad economic controls is entirely beyond the reach of state and local government.

The Geographic, Income, and Ethnic Distribution of Hawaii's Economic Product

Two fundamental tests of whether an economy is functioning well are the per capita product that it generates compared with that of other economies, and the extent to which this economic product is distributed in what the people consider a "fair" fashion.

Evidence presented in this book shows that Hawaii's economy has passed the first test very well. The growth in total income and product over the course of a century has generally been above the rate of growth of the United States, which over much of that time span has been the most affluent nation in the world. Furthermore, per capita personal income in Hawaii has in recent decades been at least as high as the national average, and far above that of all but a few countries in the world.

This section examines the second test against which an economy may be judged: how the total economic product is distributed among various geographic areas, income classes, and ethnic groups. An equal distribution is not to be expected, but most people want to see a distribution that is at least fair enough to avoid the divisiveness that comes from some groups being clearly favored (the "haves") and other groups being left out (the "have-nots"). If any group in society is excluded from the mainstream of economic activity, the total product that all must share is less than it otherwise would be.

Charles Reed Bishop, founder of what is now First Hawaiian Bank, put this thought well when he compared society to a field of sugarcane in his commencement address to the Punahou graduation class of 1881. "The character of the masses (not the favored few) will be the character of the nation," he said. "In a field of cane there are large hills and towering stalks scattered here and there, but the crop depends upon the average of the field and the good cultivation of the whole."[104]

Extreme maldistribution of the economic product between different areas has led to the breakup of nations and of colonial empires, as people in disadvantaged areas sought relief by severing ties with the dominant part of the nation. Extreme maldistribution by economic class, and with it the prospect of continued poverty in the face of rising aspirations, has been the basis for many of the revolutions the world has witnessed. Extreme maldistribution by ethnic group has led to immense upheavals in many lands, including the United States. Less extreme degrees of maldistribution may not cause civil wars, class wars, or racial wars, but they do lead to discontent and divisiveness. Hence the importance of the test: Is Hawaii's economic product distributed in a way that is reasonably fair?

DISTRIBUTION BY GEOGRAPHIC AREA

When I arrived in Hawaii in 1950, the entire economy was in a state of economic recession, but by comparison with Oahu the neighbor islands were deeply depressed. The difference between the level of income and the number of job opportunities on Oahu and on all the neighbor islands was so great that neighbor islanders were crying "foul." It was not fair that all the goodies were going to Oahu, while the other islands were merely being tossed scraps from the table. This condition led to an unhealthy divisiveness in Hawaii that lasted for at least another ten years before the pendulum began to swing in favor of the neighbor islands. Now they are growing economically somewhat faster than Oahu, and this trend is expected to continue for the foreseeable future.

How the neighbor islands dominated the Hawaiian economy a century ago, how they fell to a lower position than Oahu's in the mid-twentieth century, how they have regained their momentum in the last quarter of a century, and how they are projected to continue this momentum for the foreseeable future, as traced in Figure 5.3, can be explained briefly as follows.

A hundred years ago, Hawaii's economy was almost entirely agricultural, with sugar being far and away the dominant crop. Of all Hawaii's land classified as agricultural today, 84 percent is on the neighbor islands. Although the figure has varied somewhat from time to time, well over 80 percent of Hawaii's sugar has been grown on the neighbor islands. This means that a century ago a majority of jobs that existed in Hawaii (mostly agricultural and mostly in sugar) were found on the neighbor islands, and therefore that is where the bulk of the income was generated and where the most of the population (65 percent) lived.

This situation began to change after the turn of the century, when the pineapple industry got started (heavily on Oahu), when the U.S. military began its buildup in Hawaii (almost entirely on Oahu), and when tourism began to amount to something (almost entirely in Waikiki until the 1960s). But even as late as 1930 the neighbor islands were still relatively prosperous, having increased in population in the prior half century at the rapid annual rate of nearly 3 percent. Oahu, however, had grown even faster, and by 1930 had 45 percent of the total.

Sugar employment reached a peak in 1928, with more than 56,000 workers on the plantations and in the mills, and production at some 865,000 tons. For the next third of a century, until the early 1960s, production inched upward to around a million tons a year. But with increases in labor productivity, the work force declined so dramatically that by 1960 only 11,000 workers remained in sugar. Since most of this reduction was achieved by attrition instead of by layoffs, the result was that the sugar industry hired few new employees for the entire period

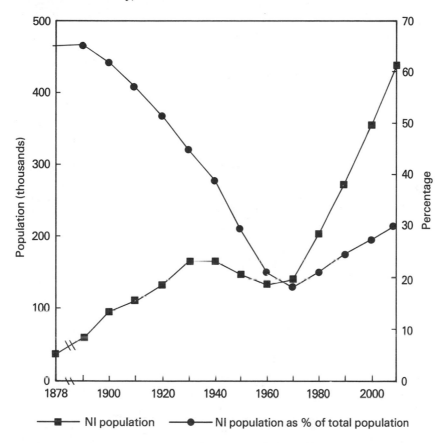

Figure 5.3 Population of the neighbor islands, 1879-1990 and projected to 2010

from 1930 to 1960. This meant that many young people growing up on the neighbor islands had to go elsewhere to find a job. That the neighbor islands had few young adults during this period is shown dramatically by the age–sex pyramid of their combined population for 1960 (Figure 5.4). Because of low birth rates in the depression years of the 1930s and in the war years 1941–45, the age groups from fifteen to thirty were rather sparsely populated throughout the country in 1960, but the situation was exaggerated on Oahu (Figure 5.5) and greatly exaggerated on the neighbor islands. (I have excluded military personnel and their dependents from the Oahu and neighbor islands pyramids because they were only temporary residents of Hawaii and their inclusion would seriously distort the pyramids.)

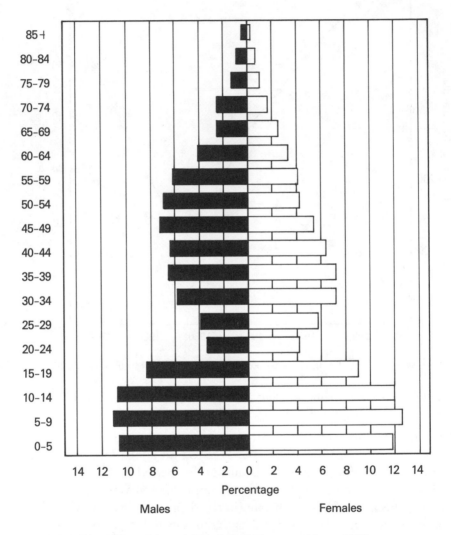

Figure 5.4 Population of the neighbor islands, by age and sex, 1960

Note: Excludes military personnel and their dependents.

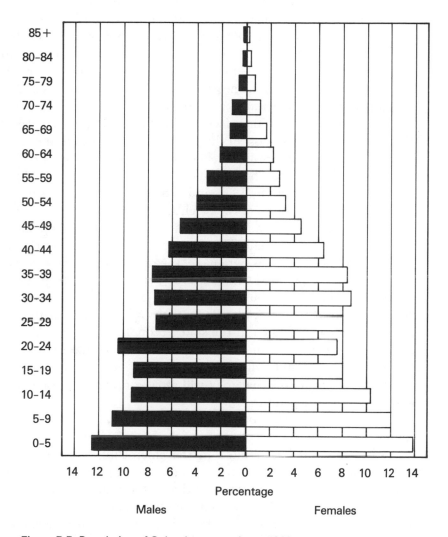

Figure 5.5 Population of Oahu, by age and sex, 1960

Note: Excludes military personnel and their dependents.

Discontent on the neighbor islands with this maldistribution of employment opportunity was so great in the 1950s that in 1954 the Honolulu Chamber of Commerce organized a series of trade-development conferences on each major island. Some 100 top business, government, and labor leaders from Oahu attended the conferences to explore specific ways that each island's economic potential could be realized. Addressing this issue in the opening sessions on each of the islands,[105] I was careful never to refer to the neighbor islands as the "outer" islands.

In the early 1960s tourism began to break out of the confines of Waikiki, and most of the tourist facilities built since then have been off Oahu, which means that most of the jobs in tourism created since then have been on the neighbor islands. The neighbor islands combined had only 15 percent of Hawaii's hotel units in 1960; but this rose to 30 percent by 1970, to 37 percent by 1980, and to over 46 percent by 1989.

Since 1970 the population of the neighbor islands has grown at a rate of 3.8 percent per year. As a result their share of the state's population has risen from 18 to 23 percent. This development has taken most of the skewedness out of the age–sex pyramid of the neighbor islands, as a comparison of the 1980 pyramid with the 1960 pyramid shows (Figures 5.4 and 5.6). In contrast, Oahu's 1980 population pyramid (Figure 5.7) reveals a large preponderance of males in their early twenties. With tourism as the main growth area in the state's economy, the State Department of Business and Economic Development projects that by the year 2010 the neighbor islands will contain nearly 30 percent of the state's population—which means that they will grow considerably faster than Oahu in the foreseeable future.

A more equal distribution of job opportunities between Oahu and the neighbor islands has been an objective of the Hawaii state plan for many years. Although this has resulted in the channeling of some capital improvement projects of the state government to the neighbor islands, the real impetus has been the efforts of the visitor industry to open new markets on the neighbor islands. But whether achieved by plan or by chance, the economies of the neighbor islands have been rejuvenated, and they have long since ceased to be the have-not areas of Hawaii. The geographic distribution of Hawaii's economic product is no longer a cause of discontent.

DISTRIBUTION BY INCOME CLASS

Analyzing the distribution of income by income class runs into such massive statistical problems that results are inconclusive. Nevertheless, it may be useful to comment briefly on the subject and to present such results as can be obtained.

Ideally, one would want to see how the various economic classes in Hawaii have fared over, say, the last fifty years, comparing the plantation era with today. Was the spread between the rich and the poor greater then than now, or vice versa? Unfortunately, there is no answer to a question like that. We know that the average sugar wage has risen from $2.38 a day in 1939 to $103.52 in 1986, both figures including the value of fringe benefits. And we know, therefore, that sugar workers' incomes have increased much more than the cost of living, so that there has been an improvement in the level of living of such employees. But the question is, Have the workers' incomes improved relative to the plantation managers', whose salaries and benefits have not been recorded nearly so well? And it is not just the issue of the plantation workers versus the plantation managers. The issue is the entirety of the lower-income groups versus the middle- and higher-income groups, and here the data simply do not exist.

The U.S. decennial census did not elicit detailed information about income until 1950, by which time most of Hawaii's Asian immigrants had already been residents a long time. Individual income tax data are of no use because most people did not file a return before World War II, and in any case the income inclusions and exclusions have changed so drastically that comparisons are virtually impossible. We simply have to forego comparing changes in income distribution over time, from the plantation era to the modern era.

The only useful comparison is between Hawaii and the nation at large, as disclosed by the 1980 census. The same questions about personal income were asked across the entire country in 1979, yielding data that indicated whether incomes in Hawaii were more concentrated or more evenly spread out than for the country as a whole. Taking as the universe all families and unrelated individuals (227,000 in Hawaii and 64 million for the entire country), we find the following: a smaller proportion of the population in the lower and lower-middle income brackets (under $25,000 a year) in Hawaii than for the country as a whole; about the same proportion in the upper-middle income brackets ($25,000 to $35,000); and a considerably larger portion in the upper income brackets above $35,000 (Figure 5.8). This results in a median family income in Hawaii that was somewhat higher than for the nation as a whole—$22,750 versus $19,587.

One may conclude from these limited data that, as of 1979, the poor in

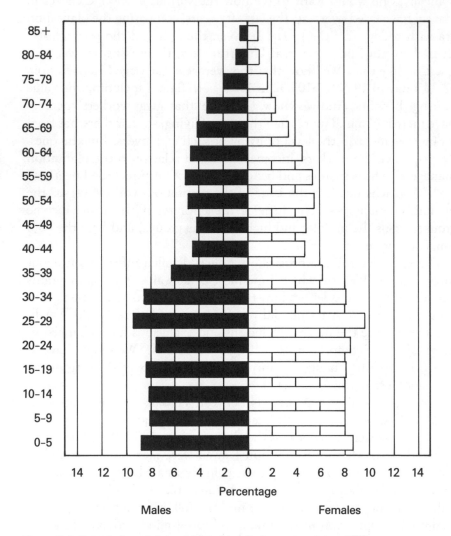

Figure 5.6 Population of the neighbor islands, by age and sex, 1980

Note: Excludes military personnel and their dependents.

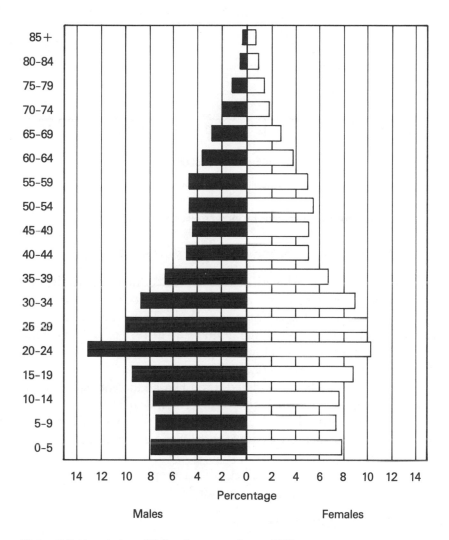

Figure 5.7 Population of Oahu, by age and sex, 1980

Note: Excludes military personnel and their dependents.

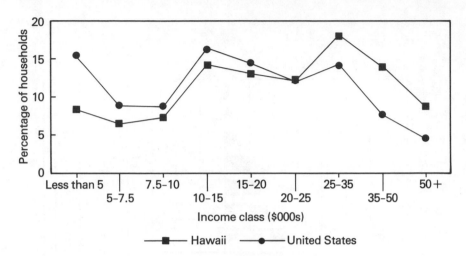

Figure 5.8 Distribution of households by income class: Hawaii and the United States, 1979

Source: U.S. Census Bureau, *Statistical Abstract of the United States.*

Hawaii were about as far below the rich as in the country as a whole, but that Hawaii had relatively fewer families who were poor and more families who were rich than the country as a whole. This conclusion is substantiated by the 1980 census, which found that in 1979 only 9.9 percent of Hawaii's population was below the poverty line as contrasted with 11.7 percent for the entire country.

This conclusion would be modified if the Hawaii income figures were reduced to compensate for a higher cost of living in Hawaii than the average for the country. However, as discussed in section 4 of Chapter 7, no reliable statistical measure exists of the difference in the cost of living between Hawaii and the mainland. Even if one did, there would be no way of knowing how many families would drop out of each income bracket if appropriate adjustments were made.

DISTRIBUTION BY ETHNIC GROUP

Hawaii is famous for the upward mobility of the many races and nationalities that have come to the islands. Wave after wave of immigrants have started at the bottom, as plantation workers or in later years as busboys or dishwashers, and have climbed up the occupational, economic, and social ladders to establish themselves on a level of equality with other ethnic or national groups. How much of this perception of upward mobility is fact and how much is fiction?

For the purpose of this analysis, the best evidence is a combination of U.S. decennial census data and data from the periodic surveys of the Hawaii State Department of Health called the Hawaii Health Surveillance Surveys (HHSS). We are fortunate to have the HHSS because for this purpose the decennial census has a fatal flaw: it does not disaggregate the military and their dependents (all of whom are visitors to Hawaii on a two- or three-year assignment) from the local resident population, the group of interest here. (Because the income of military families is slightly lower than that of civilian families, including them would reduce income levels somewhat, but quite differently for individual ethnic groups, depending upon their numbers. Eliminating the military and their dependents removes about 30 percent of the whites, over two-thirds of the blacks, and one-third of the American Indians, but only a tiny fraction of the Japanese, Chinese, and Filipinos.)

The last published HHSS was made in 1983 and gives some clues to ethnic income levels. Unfortunately, it was conducted with too small a sample (about 1.5 percent of the population) to calculate data for the smaller ethnic groups. The only ethnic groups for which the data are statistically reliable are Caucasians, Japanese, Chinese, Filipinos, and Hawaiians. For other ethnic groups it is necessary to rely upon U.S. census data. Such data may not be too inaccurate for this purpose because some of the minor ethnic groups, such as Samoans and Vietnamese, most of whom are recent arrivals, are not generally represented in the armed forces.

With all these caveats, what the data reveal about differences in economic status by ethnic group is shown in Tables 5.5 and 5.6. Table 5.5, from the Hawaii Health Surveillance Survey of 1983, is the primary table. It shows that among resident civilian families in Hawaii the median family income in 1983 was $26,100, with Chinese families ranking highest ($31,400), Japanese second ($30,500), Caucasians third ($29,500), Filipinos fourth ($22,400), and Hawaiians fifth ($20,900). Clearly the Chinese, now mostly in their third and fourth or later generations in Hawaii, and the Japanese, mostly in their second and third generations, have climbed the economic ladder and in fact are a rung or two above the Caucasians. Equally clearly, the Filipinos, many of whom immigrated in recent years, have not. Nor has the Hawaiian group, although they have of course been here much longer than anybody else.

The income status of smaller ethnic groups is shown in Table 5.6, derived from the 1980 U.S. census. It indicates that the Vietnamese and Samoans were toward the bottom of the family income array, which is

Table 5.5   Median annual money income of Hawaii families and unrelated individuals, by ethnic stock, 1983

| ETHNIC STOCK[a] | CIVILIAN FAMILIES[b] | |
	NUMBER (1,000)	MEDIAN INCOME ($1,000)
All groups	226.7	26.1
Unmixed		
Caucasian	55.1	29.5
Japanese	67.0	30.5
Chinese	15.4	31.4
Filipino	26.3	22.4
Hawaiian	3.0	20.9
Korean	2.6	*
Black	1.0	*
Puerto Rican	1.8	*
Samoan	2.6	*
Other unmixed[c]	2.3	*
Mixed		
Part-Hawaiian	35.1	19.9
Non-Hawaiian	14.4	23.3

SOURCE: Department of Health, Hawaii Health Surveillance Program, special tabulation published in *The State of Hawaii Data Book 1984,* table 391.

NOTES: Excludes persons in institutions or military barracks, on Niihau, or in Kalawao. Based on a sample survey of 3,987 families and 1,317 unrelated individuals.

*   Base figure too small for calculation or reliable median.

a. Definitions used in this table differ from those in reports of the U.S. Census Bureau. Persons of mixed race are shown separately in this table but in 1980 census tabulations are assigned to one of the unmixed groups on the basis of self-identification or race of mother.

b. By ethnic stock of family head.

c. Includes persons not reporting ethnic stock.

not surprising since most members of these groups came to Hawaii recently. Koreans were at about the same level as the Filipinos, both groups having many members who recently migrated to Hawaii. Including all part-Hawaiians with the full-blooded Hawaiians does not much change the rank of that group.

Table 5.6 Median income of Hawaii households and families, by race of householder, 1979 (Based on a 15.7 % sample)

	FAMILIES	
RACE	NUMBER	MEDIAN INCOME (dollars)
All races	227,974	22,750
White	80,824	20,792
Black	3,774	12,764
American Indian, Eskimo, Aleut	712	13,114
American Indian	692	13,246
Eskimo[a]	—	—
Aleut[a]	20	8,500
Asian and Pacific Islander	138,359	24,680
Japanese	62,500	29,215
Chinese	14,580	28,433
Filipino	28,153	20,519
Korean	3,996	19,463
Asian Indian[a]	161	28,854
Vietnamese	574	8,018
Hawaiian	24,296	19,824
Guamanian[a]	349	15,477
Samoan	2,481	10,662
Other	1,269	12,668
Race, n.e.c.	4,305	14,053

SOURCE: U.S. Census Bureau, *1980 Census of Population, General Social and Economic Characteristics, Hawaii,* PC80-C-1-13 (Washington, D.C.: Government Printing Office, June 1983), tables 71, 81, and 97.

n.e.c.—not elsewhere calculated.
a. Sampling variation is particularly serious for these small groups.

The reasons why the Filipino and Hawaiian groups lag behind the others are too numerous and too complex for me to analyze. Table 5.7, however, seems to disclose the primary reason—a relatively low level of educational achievement. Over 80 percent of the Chinese, Japanese, and Caucasians finish high school, against fewer than 60 percent of the Filipinos and Hawaiians. Differences in higher education are even greater: over one-third of the Chinese and Caucasians and nearly one-fourth of the Japanese finish college, but only 10 percent of the Filipinos and only

Table 5.7   Years of school completed by persons in Hawaii 25 years old and
over, by ethnic stock, 1983

| | | YEARS OF SCHOOL COMPLETED (%)[b] | | |
ETHNIC STOCK[a]	PERSONS 25 YEARS AND OVER	8 YEARS OR LESS	12 YEARS OR MORE	16 YEARS OR MORE
All groups	568,457	11.3	81.1	21.8
Unmixed				
Caucasian	159,965	4.1	90.4	33.5
Japanese	164,308	13.1	80.5	22.2
Chinese	33,361	12.4	81.5	34.4
Filipino	65,736	32.4	59.3	10.0
Hawaiian	6,568	26.1	55.2	2.4
Korean	9,664	17.0	77.0	19.0
Black	7,332	0.9	98.1	11.7
Puerto Rican	4,535	24.8	64.9	2.2
Samoan	4,486	16.8	61.1	3.6
Other unmixed[c]	5,248	19.2	58.3	10.8
Mixed				
Part-Hawaiian	72,118	4.6	82.2	9.3
Non-Hawaiian	35,135	3.4	88.1	15.0

SOURCE: Hawaii State Department of Health, Hawaii Health Surveillance Program, special tabulation published in *The State of Hawaii Data Book 1984,* table 126.

NOTES: Excludes persons in institutions or military barracks, on Niihau, or in Kalawao. Based on
a sample survey of 8,999 persons 25 years old and over.

a. Definitions of ethnic stock used in this table differ from those in reports of the U.S. Census
Bureau. Persons of mixed race are shown separately in this table but in 1980 census tabulations are assigned to one of the unmixed groups on the basis of self-identification or race of
mother.

b. Based on number reporting years of school.

c. Includes persons not reporting ethnic stock.

2.4 percent of the Hawaiians do so. The Samoans, who rank close to the
bottom of the economic ladder, are also close to the bottom of the educational ladder.

These data are confirmed by the literacy status of Hawaii's adult population. For the total adult population, the average rate of functional illit-
eracy is just under 20 percent (about the national average), but for
Hawaiians it is 30 percent and for Filipinos over 40 percent.[106]

I come to three conclusions from this exercise. First, the popular view
that Hawaii is a place where migrants of any race or nationality can
climb the economic ladder to the top is valid. Second, the correlation

between the amount of education and the level of income is so clear that every possible effort should be made to improve the education of Hawaiians, of Samoans, of Filipinos, and in fact of all lagging ethnic groups. Third, with 28 percent of Hawaii's civilian population already of mixed ethnicity, and with well over half of all civilian births in Hawaii being of mixed ancestry, it will not be long before we can forget the issue of the ethnic differences between people and simply consider ourselves members of one race—the human race. This might not work everywhere, but it would in Hawaii.

CHAPTER 6

Economic Lessons from the Past and Questions about Hawaii's Economic Future

Economic Lessons from the Past

THE FIRST and most obvious lesson to be learned from the economic changes that have taken place in Hawaii is that, as John Donne wrote a century and a half before Captain Cook took his ships into the Pacific, "No man is an island, entire of itself; every man is a piece of the continent, a part of the main." When Cook sighted Kauai on the morning of 18 January 1778, Hawaii ceased to be a group of islands entire of itself; it became a part of the main. As such, its destiny—economically, politically, and socially—has been determined as much by world events as by its own initiative. There is no way this could have been avoided, and those who think it could have been avoided or that the clock can be turned back two hundred years are living in a fool's paradise.

When the early explorers introduced guns, the old system of local chieftainships gave way to an all-powerful alii nui. When the sea captains in the China fur trade discovered Hawaii's great stands of sandalwood, the whole thrust of economic activity changed. When the American Board of Commissioners for Foreign Missions in Boston decided in 1819 to send the first company of missionaries to Hawaii, the basis was laid for a total reconstruction of Hawaiian society, government, and economy. When the New England whalers shifted their hunt from the Atlantic to the Pacific, Hawaii's society and economy underwent another transformation. When President Theodore Roosevelt, under pressure from American labor unions, got the Japanese government to stop the migration of Japanese laborers to America, Hawaii's sugar industry faced a momentous crisis. When Franklin Roosevelt's New Deal produced the Wagner Act, the foundations of Hawaii's plantation

oligarchy were undermined. And, of course, when the Japanese government decided to take on the United States in its drive to establish a New
Order in Asia, Hawaii's economy and society were drastically transformed again.

In more modern times, distant events have continued to affect Hawaii
profoundly. Without the work of engineers and scientists around the
world in developing aviation and telecommunications systems, Hawaii
would still be relatively isolated from the rest of the world, tucked away
in the vast reaches of the north-central Pacific with probably only a
handful of hotels and a few thousand visitors annually. If the tropical
countries of the world had not decided to grow pineapple, Hawaii would
still pack most of the world's pineapple. If Congress had not decided in
1974 to abandon the forty-year-old Sugar Act, Hawaiian sugar would
have been spared a major crisis. If Japanese scientists had not discovered
how to convert the glucose in corn syrup into fructose, cane might still
be king. If the Japanese had not been so successful in remaking their
economy after World War II, Hawaii's largest foreign trade connection
would never have developed.

The list could go on, but it should suffice to demonstrate that most of
the momentous changes that have taken place in the Hawaiian economy
have been initiated by political, social, military, technological, and other
developments in other parts of the world, beyond the power of Hawaii
to control.

This leads to the second great lesson: a society must make the best of
whatever situation it is faced with. The government of Kamehameha III
rightfully decided that if Hawaii could not successfully resist the West
(which it could not), it might as well join 'em. Later Hawaiian governments, as they watched the islands of the Pacific being gobbled up by
imperialist powers, concluded that Hawaii should be part of the United
States economically, and under Kalakaua finally achieved the Reciprocity Treaty. If American laws would not let Chinese enter Hawaii after it
became part of the United States, and if Theodore Roosevelt's agreement with Japan barred the entrance of Japanese after 1907, Hawaii
would look to the Philippines for labor. When it became obvious that
the airplane could bring millions of people to Hawaii annually on vacation, Hawaii's government and business community joined hands to create what is probably the world's best tourist infrastructure. When
Hawaii lost its dominance in the world pineapple market, its agricultur-
alists developed replacement exports such as papaya, macadamia nuts,

flowers, and foliage. When the Wagner Act made unionization of the labor force inevitable, Hawaii's employers adopted entirely new approaches to their labor relations problems.

The third lesson is that in reacting to changes in the economic environment, there is no substitute for an intelligent, scientific, thoughtful, research-oriented approach. The way the sugar industry coped with problems involving water, insects, markets, and a host of other issues is a good example. The same goes for pineapple, for Hawaii's development of tourism, and for diversified agricultural exports, which finally succeeded after nearly every food plant that grows anywhere in the world had been tried in the islands. Other examples of intelligent response are the way Hawaii faced the grim realities of World War II; how its employers sought the best help they could find when they were faced with union problems they could not solve by themselves; how its business and government leaders attracted billions of dollars of investment capital needed to sustain economic growth; how the Hawaii Visitors Bureau set up the best market-research program when it realized how competitive the world visitor market was; how the ILWU leadership gave up its class-war stance when it realized that the community, including even its own members, would not accept it; how the state promoted research in both outer space (sky) and inner space (ocean) when it became evident that man would no longer confine his activities to the surface of the earth. The list could go on, but it is obvious that if we had approached our problems by relying on instincts, by making snap judgments, we would have floundered.

The fourth lesson is that in a world where all geographic areas are a part of the main, each will have a higher standard of living if it engages in those economic activities in which it has some comparative advantage. If an area is cut off from the world as precontact Hawaii was, it *has* to be self-sufficient and can produce a standard of living that is in the range of only a few hundred dollars per person per year. Postcontact Hawaii found a higher standard by functioning within the national and world economies, by growing sugar and a few other crops as well as or better than anywhere else, by providing the U.S. Defense Department with the best site for its command headquarters in the whole Pacific, and by giving vacationers a more satisfying vacation experience than almost any other place in the world. In modern times, we have discovered that we can do other things quite well compared with the rest of the world (such as looking at space from atop Mauna Kea) and have seen some economic diversification beyond the old Big Four activities of sugar, pineapple, visitors, and defense. One thing Hawaii cannot do is to grow many foods as inexpensively as other parts of the world can do it for us.

A fifth lesson to be learned from the changes that have taken place in the Hawaiian economy is that it is not good to have too much power concentrated in any one group. Educated people will not stand for such a situation, will resent it, oppose it, and sooner or later depose it. Kaahumanu and her cohorts resented, opposed, and—upon the death of Kamehameha I—overthrew the kapu system, which they felt unjustly infringed on their rights. But if more than the elite are to be involved in this process, a universal system of liberal education is a prime requisite. What the original (generally uneducated) immigrant plantation workers put up with was something their children, educated in an American school system that stressed freedom, equality of opportunity, and human rights, would not. As a result, the oligarchic plantation system was brought to an end.

Similarly, most of the people in Hawaii resented the autocratic rule of the Army under martial law in World War II, particularly after the Allies' victory in the Battle of Midway had removed its only excuse. So they opposed it and succeeded in having it modified and then abolished nearly a year before the war was over.

One response that the autocratic military rule, together with the autocratic plantation rule, called forth was a mass unionization of the labor force as the war was drawing to a close. This put labor unions, particularly the ILWU, in such a powerful economic position that they too came to be resented, opposed, and reduced to appropriate size.

One by one, the power centers of the economy were enfeebled. At present, there appears to be no new center of power on the rise in what is now a pluralistic economy and society. It is to be hoped that no group will attempt to become the power center—but if it does, its days will surely be numbered.

The sixth lesson from Hawaii's economic history is that upward mobility hinges to a large degree on good education. Wave after wave of generally uneducated immigrant laborers have come to Hawaii, started at the bottom of the economic and social ladder, and then climbed that ladder to achieve social and economic equality with those who were the elite. Although many factors were required for success, clearly those groups who put strong emphasis on education did best and those who did not fared worst. Seldom in history have so many people in such a short time started so low and risen so high as did the immigrant laborers and their children who came to Hawaii and took advantage of the educational opportunities. They stand in sharp contrast to the small minority who saw no point in educational achievement.

A final lesson from Hawaii's economic history is that the development of a new industry takes an immense amount of time, effort, enterprise, money, and sometimes luck. It took sugar a half century to amount to much. Pineapple developed faster, but it still took thirty years from the time the first pineapple in Hawaii was canned until the industry reached an output of a million cases a year—which was less than one-tenth its later size. Papayas have been grown commercially in Hawaii for seventy-five years, but only in the last few decades have they become a significant crop. The same can be said of macadamia nuts; commercial plantings go back only about half a century. From the decision to make Pearl Harbor America's main naval base in the Pacific, it was twenty years before even a dry dock was built. The flower and foliage business that has now grown quite large was half a century in the making. And it took nearly thirty years from the time the predecessor of the Hawaii Visitors Bureau was organized until tourism grew to the magnificent total of 25,000 visitors a year. And how long has Hawaii been researching and experimenting with aquaculture, which someday may outgrow its infancy?

This last point is important because many people concerned with economic development seem to think that if an older industry falls by the wayside, an inventory of viable replacements sits ready on the shelf from which selection can be made. Such false optimism about how quick and easy economic development can be achieved breeds a lack of concern for maintaining existing economic activities when there seems to be doubt about their future. I would estimate that at least half of the people in Hawaii today, including some business leaders and economists who should know better, think that the "old" sugar industry is on its way out and the sooner it folds up and makes way for some new industry, the better. The facts are that Hawaii still produces about as much sugar as it ever did and that the roughly 50,000 acres of former sugar land that have gone out of production (with 180,000 productive acres still in cane) lie largely fallow. Under the most favorable of scenarios it will probably be a generation or more before those lands get back into productive use.

This last "lesson of history" has the moral that to maintain a growing and thriving economy, economic developments of all kinds must be pursued in the hope that out of the many attempts made, some one or two or three may *in the distant future* amount to something. Meanwhile, preserving what we have that has taken us so long to develop is the path of wisdom.

Questions about Hawaii's Economic Future

In considering Hawaii's long-term economic future, it is necessary to make assumptions about what will *not* happen, to keep the subject matter manageable. Looking ahead first a quarter of a century and then a full century, I assume that civilization will not be destroyed by nuclear or chemical warfare and that emissions of carbon dioxide will not so blanket the earth as to cause temperatures to rise and melt the polar ice caps, thereby inundating coastal areas of the world (including many major cities)—assumptions that are perhaps rashly optimistic. I even assume that developments of a less catastrophic nature will not change the direction of Hawaii's economy as in the last fifty years the Wagner Act, World War II, statehood, and the jet airplane changed it. This is, of course, a rash assumption. In short, to avoid much unproductive speculation, I assume that Hawaii will not suffer (or benefit) from any major world developments beyond its control. If it does, I hope that the state will be able to cope with them as well as it has coped in the past.

WHAT WILL BE THE MOST PROBABLE ECONOMIC DEVELOPMENTS IN THE NEXT QUARTER CENTURY?

The last chapter demonstrated that the Hawaiian economy since World War II went through four distinct periods: rapid contraction after the war in the late 1940s, substantial growth in the 1950s, a great economic boom beginning in the 1960s and continuing into the early 1970s, and for the next fifteen years a modest average growth rate of around 3 percent per year.

What is most probable for the next twenty-five years is a period characterized by a somewhat slower growth rate—with annual growth in the number of visitors at about 2.5 percent, in employment at about 1 percent, in population at about 0.8 percent, and in gross state product of about 2 percent. A 2 percent growth in real gross state product with a 1 percent growth in employment implies some improvement in the rate of labor productivity growth over that experienced in the last fifteen years.

Looking in turn at each major sector of the Hawaiian economy, I offer the following justification for my forecast.

The Visitor Industry. Starting from a modest base in 1946, the number of visitors coming to Hawaii grew at an average annual rate of 20 percent during the late 1940s and throughout the 1950s, as the airplane replaced the ship and made long-distance travel possible for multitudes. It continued to grow at that rate during the 1960s, as jet aircraft replaced propeller planes and as people around the world heard about Hawaii after it achieved statehood. Tourism also got a lift in the 1960s when Japan relaxed its foreign-exchange controls and permitted its nationals to travel abroad.

By the early 1970s the number of visitors coming to Hawaii had risen to 2 million a year, and to maintain a 20 percent growth rate on that base was beyond expectation. With the advent of the wide-bodied jet and its less expensive fares, however, the number of visitors to Hawaii did increase at an average annual rate of 10 percent through the 1970s. By 1980 the annual visitor count reached nearly 4 million, so that maintaining even a 10 percent annual rate of increase was not realistic. From this peak, the cumulative growth in tourism in the 1980s declined to less than 6 percent per year but in absolute numbers continued to climb.

This slowing of the rate of growth of tourism to Hawaii is best viewed by looking at Hawaii's original market, westbound visitors coming primarily from the U.S. mainland and Canada. The Hawaii Visitors Bureau began separating its count of eastbound and westbound visitors in 1951. From 1952 to 1969 the westbound visitor count increased by an annual average of 20 percent. For the next nine years (1969–78) the increase averaged 11 percent; from 1978 to 1988 it averaged 3.5 percent.

The eastbound market is newer and still being developed. Fewer than 100,000 eastbound visitors per year came to Hawaii until the 1960s, but since then that market has grown to more than 1.5 million. Once Hawaii loses its novelty, however, this rate of growth will taper off. A straw in the wind: Hawaii no longer is the prime honeymoon spot for young Japanese.

In the light of these trends—and considering that no new types of airplane are likely to be coming into use soon, that more transpacific routes are overflying Hawaii, and that the growth in real income in America has slowed drastically—I conclude that the growth in tourism to Hawaii will continue to slow, dropping for the next twenty-five years to an average of about 2.5 percent per year. This will yield slightly more than 10 million visitors in 2010 compared with 5 million in 1988, provided that Hawaii's visitor promotion will continue to be as effective in the future as it has been in the past.

Defense. The size of the defense establishment in Hawaii has been relatively stable for thirty years or more, with uniformed personnel numbering between 50,000 and 60,000 and their civilian dependents numbering between 60,000 and 70,000. It is always possible that some development could change this, such as the closure of some U.S. military bases in the western Pacific and the transfer of their personnel to Hawaii, or alternatively having the Soviet Union's apparent change in attitude toward the West during the last few years turn out to be for real, permitting a major reduction in U.S. defense forces. But it seems to me most probable that the defense establishment in Hawaii will continue at about its present size, with defense agency pay rates for both military and civilian personnel keeping a bit ahead of inflation so that there will be a modest real growth in defense expenditures here.

Sugar. Since America's domestic sugar industry has been able for practically all of the last half century to persuade Congress to protect it from the subsidized surplus foreign sugars that flood the so-called "world sugar market," and since it appears unlikely that high-fructose corn syrup will be producible in crystalline form, I think that there will still be a U.S. market for some 6 to 7 million tons per year of domestically produced beet and cane sugar in the years ahead. This means that Hawaii plantations can survive if they can continue to contain their costs to meet the competition from mainland sugar producers. I think that most of them will be able to do this, although some that have been marginal for years will probably be closed and others will reduce their production by eliminating their least productive acreage. An average decline of about 1 percent per year in Hawaiian sugar production over the next few decades—down from a million tons a year to perhaps 750,000 tons by 2010—seems a reasonable assumption.

Pineapple. Hawaii's two remaining pineapple companies have survived all the difficulties the industry confronted in past decades and they appear to be economically viable for the foreseeable future. Dole is strongly established in the fresh fruit market and Maui Pineapple Co. is expanding its production. A reasonable assumption is that Hawaii's pineapple industry will be stabilized at about its present level for the indefinite future.

Other Export Enterprises. The other export sectors—diversified agriculture, diversified manufacturing, and space- and ocean-related activities —are not likely either to grow or to decline enough to have a major impact on the total economy. Tourism will continue to diversify, however, in the sense that Hawaii will develop new attractions that will bring new classes of visitors to the islands for purposes other than rest and recreation.

On the basis of the above assumptions, I think the most probable development for the Hawaiian economy for the next quarter century will be a modest growth in total real gross state product of about 2 percent per year, or roughly two-thirds of the rate experienced during the last decade and a half. This forecast is fairly close to the projections developed in 1988 by the State Department of Business and Economic Development.[1] The DBED report, however, assumes that the number of visitors to Hawaii will increase at an average rate over the next twenty-five years of 3.5 percent, whereas I am more inclined to think that an average rate of about 2.5 percent is more likely, for reasons already enumerated.

With tourism the prime factor in the growth of the total Hawaiian economy, my forecast of the rate of growth in tourism can be translated into indications of the rate of growth in total employment and population. In the 1973–86 period, tourism grew at 6 percent per year and employment grew at 2.5 percent, or 40 percent of the rate of tourism. In the DBED projections to the year 2010, tourism is projected to grow at 3.5 percent per year and employment at 1.5 percent, again a ratio of 40 percent. It follows that my projection of a 2.5 percent growth rate in tourism implies about a 1 percent growth rate in employment (.40 × 2.5 percent = 1 percent).

Similarly, the relationship between increases in employment and population is relatively stable. From 1973 to 1986, as employment increased at an annual rate of 2.5 percent, the resident population increased at a rate of 1.72 percent; that is, population increased at about 70 percent of the rate of employment increase. The DBED projection for the next twenty-five years has a ratio of population-to-employment growth of 80 percent. Thus if employment increases in the next twenty-five years at the 1 percent per year rate that I suggest, Hawaii's population should increase at about 0.8 percent per year. The DBED in its long-range projections estimates that the "natural" rate of increase in Hawaii's population (the excess of births over deaths) for the next few decades will be slightly above 0.6 percent per year. My own forecast implies a modest amount of net in-migration.*

Is Hawaii's Economy Growing Too Fast, and Should the State Try to Control Its Growth?

Concern about Hawaii's rapid growth is recent. No one thought that Hawaii was growing too fast prior to World War II. During most of the nineteenth century the critical social problem was to repopulate Hawaii, as the native Hawaiians were thought to be a dying race. During World War II, when Hawaii grew phenomenally, the compelling thought was to win the war. Immediately after the war, when the economy and the population were both contracting drastically, there were certainly no cries of overpopulation. Even during the 1950s, as Hawaii began to regain economic strength, there was no expressed concern about growing too fast; the problem was to grow at all.

Only since the great boom that started in the late 1950s has Hawaii grown so fast as to cause concern about the islands becoming overpopulated. This worry developed in Hawaii at about the same time that a concern that the entire world was overpopulated became widespread. In 1968 Dr. Paul Ehrlich of Stanford University published his best seller, *The Population Bomb*, in which he correctly concluded that the world faced a situation in which "hundreds of millions of people are going to starve to death in spite of any crash programs embarked upon now" and that in the less developed countries "the birth rate must be brought into balance with the death rate, or mankind will breed itself into oblivion."[2] Shortly thereafter the Club of Rome produced its best seller, *The Limits to Growth*, in which it concluded, probably correctly, that "if the present growth trends in world population, industrialization, pollution, food

*EDITOR'S NOTE: A natural growth rate of 0.6 percent is based on the assumption that the annual number of visitors to Hawaii would be constant at 4,357,000 to the year 2005. Assuming that the visitor count rises to 8 million by 2005, the DBED population growth rate projection is double—1.2 percent per year over the period 1980–2005. Alternatively assuming (as does the author) a visitor count of "slightly more than 10 million," the DBED projection of population growth rate goes even higher. See Eleanor C. Nordyke, *The Peopling of Hawaii* (Honolulu: University of Hawaii Press, 1991, 2d edition), Table 5–1, State Population and Economic Projections (and footnotes).

production, and resource depletion continue unchanged, the limits to growth on this planet will be reached sometime within the next one hundred years. The most probable result will be a sudden and uncontrollable decline in both population and industrial capacity."[3]

These and many similar reports in the late 1960s and the 1970s focused both professional and popular attention on population control and on protecting the environment. In most developed countries, population growth was so slight that primary attention was devoted to environmental protection, and it is from this period that most laws aimed at controlling air and water pollution derive. The population explosion in many less developed countries has continued practically undiminished, with most programs of population control failing to check the surge. Starvation continues rampant in many parts of the world.

Hawaii's response to this worldwide concern with overpopulation and a deteriorating environment was to strengthen its own environmental protection legislation and to focus on the problem of future overpopulation in the islands. In the latter area, there was a flurry of activity in the late 1960s and throughout the 1970s. The legislature created a temporary Commission on Population Stabilization, and then gave it a higher status by making it the Commission on Population and the Hawaiian Future. In 1974 the state adopted a "State of Hawaii Growth Policies Plan," calling for a reduction in the birth rate and in the volume of inmigration. But even these "slowed growth" proposals, by expert opinion, constituted "reckless courses which a finite environment cannot endure."[4] Local chapters of national organizations, such as Zero Population Growth and the Sierra Club, and local groups, such as Life of the Land and Save the Surf, spoke out strongly against the "insidious cancer" of increasing population.[5] Gavan Daws of the University of Hawaii made what was probably the strongest statement when he stated in 1974 that "we are an island community gone mad, behaving like a limitless continent in a world that has already turned into a crowded, strained island."[6] There was talk in high political circles of trying to get the U.S. Constitution amended to permit the state to limit migration into Hawaii.

All this amounted to a great flow of rhetoric and the drafting of many plans that had no possibility of implementation. About the only tangible action was the passage of a statute legalizing abortion, the first in the nation, which has contributed to lowering further what was already a low birth rate. As the 1970s gave way to the 1980s, most of the steam went out of this movement, and readers of the daily newspapers in Hawaii in the past several years have seen little about the issue. It is hard to maintain excitement about an ill-defined calamity that may or may not occur sometime in the distant future, with no clear course of preventative action evident.

But the issue is not dead and should not be dead; it is only sleeping. If Hawaii were to grow in the next one hundred years as it has in the past, these islands would become so crowded as to make impossible the achievement of a good life. A few examples may illustrate the point. With residents numbered at 1,098,200 in 1988, if Hawaii's population were to increase for the next one hundred years as it has for the last century (at 2.6 percent per year), it would exceed 14 million in 2088. If the population were to grow at the rate recorded since the end of the postwar contraction in 1949 (2.0 percent per year), it would amount to nearly 8 million in 2088. If it were to grow at what I have called the "moderate" growth rate of the 1973–86 period (1.7 percent per year), it would reach nearly 6 million people by 2088. And if it were to grow at the even slower annual rate projected by the State Department of Business and Economic Development for the next twenty-five years (1.25 percent), the state's population in 2088 would be 3.8 million—well over three times the 1989 population. A few pages back, I suggested a population growth rate of 0.8 percent per year for the next twenty-five years, which if extended for another seventy-five years would raise the state's population to approximately 2.5 million people.

Undoubtedly, nearly anyone living in Hawaii would be aghast to contemplate any one of these projections—even a population of 2.5 million by 2088, let alone one of 14 million. In fact, back in 1977 a Commission on Population and the Hawaiian Future did a survey on all islands to measure public opinion on population issues. It found that 89 percent of the respondents believed the state was growing too fast and that 80 percent were convinced there were already enough people living in Hawaii.[7] The results of this survey could have been predicted because, except in rare circumstances, few want to see more people move into their community. To be "crowded" is a relative concept. To most people adding any more to the present population threatens to create a crowded condition.

On the other hand, most people adjust to living in towns instead of in the country, in cities instead of in towns, and in metropolitan areas instead of in cities. I doubt that any more people would say today that enough people are living in Hawaii than the 80 percent who said it when surveyed a decade ago, yet the population has increased by 15 percent in the meantime. The present number of people tends to be about the "right" number. Although many grow sentimental about the charms of a rustic life, the wider range of choices open to them in a developed community has great appeal.

I speak from experience. When I arrived in the islands in 1950, Oahu, which constitutes less than 10 percent of the land in Hawaii, had 80 percent of the territorial population. By neighbor island standards, Oahu was already heavily populated, but in the next thirty-six years (to 1986) Oahu's population increased nearly two and a half times—from 353,000 to 817,000. I consider today's "overpopulated" Oahu a much better place in which to live than it was in 1950, on a number of scores. Bad as traffic congestion is now, it was worse then. It took longer to get to work downtown from Koko Head than it does today, because we had only one lane of traffic all the way to Kaimuki, at which point the traffic merged with city traffic on Waialae Avenue. People living on the windward side of the island had the treacherous trip over the Pali with no tunnel, and a trip out to Wahiawa or Waipahu was much more time-consuming than it is today.

In those days, I and many others had cesspools instead of sewers, as we sometimes regretted when we had prolonged heavy rains. As for places to eat, Waikiki had only four major hotels with dining rooms and a couple of restaurants, in contrast to the hundreds of good restaurants of all types today. Downtown Honolulu had no open space like Tamarind Park, and the area Ewa (west) of Bethel Street was essentially a dilapidated shambles where few felt safe on the streets at night. Everybody's Super Market near the corner of Kapiolani and McCully was the only one in town, and the choice of retail stores was a tiny fraction of what it is today. The area that is now the Ala Moana Shopping Center was a wasteland of coral heaps and scrub vegetation. Where I lived on Portlock Road, the closest restaurant was three miles away and the closest drug store was six miles distant in Kaimuki. What is now the Hawaii Kai area housed a good many piggeries, which bred flies by the millions; and the area had a lot of wasteland, which bred mosquitoes by the millions. Now I hardly ever see a fly or a mosquito.

The point of such comparison is obvious. To me, at least, Honolulu is more attractive today than it was in 1950, mainly because of what it has been able to do with more people and more money. Real per capita income in Hawaii today is more than twice what it was in 1950. This

growing affluence made it possible for the territorial and state governments, the county governments, and private businesses to effect the
many improvements that have been made. I do not know what the real
per capita income of Hawaii would be if a halt had been called to all economic development back in 1950, but it surely would be far below what
it is today. With declining employment that was experienced anyway in
sugar and pineapple, the overall rate of unemployment would probably
have been very high.

With that thought, let me select a population target (not a forecast)
for one hundred years from now that I consider the most probable of the
various population projections discussed above—a 0.8 percent per year
increase to 2086 which would result in a total statewide population of
2,436,000. I think that Hawaii could accommodate that number of people with no deterioration in the quality of life.

Because Oahu, with limited water supplies, is already heavily populated, this accommodation would dictate that practically all population
growth occur on the neighbor islands, as has been the intent of the
Hawaii State Plan for many years. This would raise the density of population on the neighbor islands to about one-third of what it is today on
Oahu and would occur so gradually that the present generation would
hardly notice it. Their grandchildren and great grandchildren would
have grown up with it, probably marveling that their ancestors led such
primitive lives, as we sometimes marvel about our ancestors.

In considering the land-use consequences of a population increase of
the magnitude I have projected, it is important to remember that all land
in Hawaii is classified by the state as urban, agricultural, or conservation
(except for a few acres of low-density "rural" land on the neighbor
islands which can be disregarded in this calculation). In this scenario I
leave conservation land untouched, since it consists primarily of rugged,
mountainous land kept intact to protect the water supply. Some scenic
and historic lands are also classified as "conservation." This leaves for
development only urban and agricultural land, which for this purpose I
call nonconservation land.

Oahu has 231,385 acres of nonconservation land: 90,320 acres classified as urban and the rest agricultural. This makes Oahu 39 percent
urbanized. With a population (in 1986) of 816,700, the density is 9.04
persons per acre of urban land.

The neighbor islands combined have 1,913,363 acres of nonconservation land, with 74,845 acres classified as urban, making them 3.9 percent

urbanized. With a (1986) population of 245,600, the density is 3.28 people per acre of urban land.

The state's 1988 resident population was 1,098,200. The "target" population I have selected for 2086 is 2,436,000, which assumes a 0.8 percent growth rate per year over the next century. The population increase would therefore be 1,337,800. (I include in this calculation only the resident population, not the *de facto* population, which includes tourists. Visitors are excluded from this scenario because they use so little of the resources that ultimately limit population—land and water.[8])

If the neighbor islands were to add 1,337,000 people to their present population of 245,600, their total population would be 1,582,600. If urban land on the neighbor islands were populated at the Oahu density rate of nine persons per acre, this would require a total of 175,933 acres of urban land. As noted above, the neighbor islands already have 74,845 acres of urban land, so the required addition would be 101,088 acres. This would somewhat more than double the amount of urban land on the neighbor islands and would reduce the amount of agricultural land by about 5 percent. Total urban land on the neighbor islands would then amount to about 9 percent of all nonconservation land, in contrast to Oahu's present 39 percent. This increase would result in a population density less than Oahu had in 1940. It would certainly not cover the neighbor islands with concrete, but rather leave them more rural than Oahu.

If the state government were serious about directing the future growth of Hawaii's population to the neighbor islands (which is what I am suggesting and which has been the state's unimplemented plan for years), it could make a start by taking two actions. First, it could severely limit hotel construction on Oahu so that practically all growth of tourism would be on the neighbor islands, where most of it will be in any case. Second, it could take major steps to decentralize the state government out of Honolulu and to the neighbor islands.

Another action necessary for this scenario to work satisfactorily would be for the neighbor islands to continue the policy that most of them have followed for the last twenty-five years or more by confining urban development to existing urban areas until additional city space is clearly necessary. This avoids urban sprawl.

Finally, something would have to be done to keep people looking for sun and not for jobs from descending on Hawaii, whether they be retirees, playboys, or just drifters. This could probably be accomplished in the future, as it has been rather successfully in the past, by restrictive land-use policies that keep the price of housing high. The state and the counties can continue to provide subsidized housing for low-income families resident in the state; but if low-cost housing were generally available, hordes of sun-seeking people would be encouraged to settle in Hawaii.

This leaves as the only source of excessive population the increased immigration from foreign countries, which in recent decades has been substantial. Short of persuading the U.S. government to adopt a more restrictive immigration policy, I see no way that this influx of people to Hawaii can be stemmed. Even without jobs, most of the immigrants would be better off here than in their home countries. But my employment and population forecasts assume some net immigration, and persons from low-income areas may be the best source of that immigration because the future Hawaii economy will continue to have many jobs requiring minimum skills that local residents are disinclined to fill.

But what if my assumption of an average 0.8 percent annual increase in population for the next hundred years turns out to be seriously underestimated, as could easily happen? If population growth rates turn out to be 1.5 percent per year, or even 2 percent or more, Hawaii's population a century hence would be perhaps 6 million instead of 3 million, or even 10 million or more. That would require all islands in the state to be as densely populated as Oahu is today, and Oahu would be largely covered with concrete. Most agriculture would be wiped out, so that such a population could only be supported if tourism continued to grow indefinitely in the future as it has in the past—which I think is probably out of the question.

Gross overpopulation is among those improbable calamities that, if they were to happen, would occur only in the far distant future after all people now living are dead. For that reason it probably does not command serious attention now. If at some future time overpopulation begins to occur, I hope that our best minds then can think of some solution that is better than the only one suggested so far by those who think such a calamity is inevitable—to have the state adopt a policy of discouraging or even prohibiting economic development. Even the federal government, with broad monetary and fiscal powers infinitely greater than any controls available to a state, has not been very successful in "fine-tuning" the growth of the economy to a desired rate.

Hawaii's state and local governments, by land-use policy, can direct economic growth toward or away from selected geographic areas—as I am suggesting that they do; but attempting to limit the size of the state population by controlling economic growth could easily stultify the economy, particularly because in Hawaii negative actions would inevitably be directed against the visitor industry. That industry is fragile and flighty, tourists readily discerning when they are unwelcome. Were that to happen, Hawaii would be in a more serious mess than the mess created by a population grown so large that it somehow detracts from the quality of life.

As George Chaplin said in 1975, when addressing a conference on alternative economic futures for Hawaii: "We cannot think about human values without thinking of an economic base. A sound economy doesn't assure a high quality of life, but a shaky or failing economy almost certainly precludes it."[9] Let us hope that the Hawaiian economy will be as sound in the future as it has been in the past, and that it will grow in the future, as I have forecast, at a rate that will provide for the employment needs of local people but not at a rate that will eventually result in overpopulation.

CHAPTER 7

Epilogue: Economic Issues of the Present

How Sensitive Is the Hawaiian Economy to the National Business Cycle?

PRIOR TO the early 1970s, without question the Hawaiian economy was insensitive to the national business cycle—a cycle of oscillation between what are generally short periods of recession and longer periods of prosperity.[1] Even the deep and prolonged Great Depression of the 1930s affected Hawaii far less than most of the country, as indicated by the fact that in 1935 only 7 percent of Hawaii's population was on relief as contrasted with 13.8 percent on the mainland.[2] Nor were the moderate recessions of the first twenty-five years after World War II transmitted to Hawaii. Similarly, prosperity of the national economy was no guarantee that the Hawaiian economy would be prosperous. Hawaii seemed to go its own way economically.

Hawaii's insensitivity to the business cycle during this period was documented by a U.S. Department of Commerce report published in 1973.[3] The study found that during the five recessions between the end of World War II and 1972, forty-two states were more sensitive to the national business cycle than Hawaii and only seven were less responsive. Highly industrialized Michigan ranked first in sensitivity. At the other extreme were the two Dakotas, which actually had a record of being prosperous during periods of national recession and being depressed when the nation was prosperous—that is, having countercyclical economies. Hawaii's economy was simply neutral, being neither cyclical nor countercyclical.

Hawaii had a number of poor years during the postwar period. One of these (1949) happened to coincide with a national recession year, but only by accident. Bad times for the islands resulted from long strikes in major local industries, from West Coast dock and maritime strikes, which prevented shipping to Hawaii, and from several serious cutbacks in military spending in the territory.

Hawaii's insensitivity to the national business cycle stemmed from the fact that none of the three prime bases of the Hawaiian economy was sensitive. The size of the military presence in Hawaii hinged on national defense needs in the Pacific. Sugar prices depended on world sugar production to some extent, but mainly on sugar legislation of the U.S. Congress. Moreover, sugar requires generally six years from planting to replanting, and hence production and employment are not influenced by adverse economic conditions that last only a year or two. Pineapple prices depended partly on foreign supplies in the U.S. market, but mainly on the volume of peaches and citrus fruits, rather than on the level of aggregate national demand. And, like sugar, pineapple requires several years from planting to replanting, generally three.

The industrial composition of the Hawaiian economy has changed since those days, however, because of the rapid growth of the visitor industry. Whereas tourism generated less than 3 percent of Hawaii's total income in 1949 and less than 7 percent in 1958, by 1973 it accounted for more than 20 percent and currently accounts for about one-third. This greater dependency on tourism is considered by some to increase Hawaii's sensitivity to the national business cycle because they think that tourism itself is extremely sensitive, an economically "fragile" industry. This issue must be addressed.

"Tourism" covers a wide range of activities, from driving to a lake, mountain, or resort a short distance from home, to flying around the world. Hawaii's tourism is intermediate between these two extremes, since most of its visitors fly from 2,000 to 6,000 miles to reach the islands. This class of tourism has been monitored by the U.S. government for many decades in the statistical series called U.S. Travel to Overseas Foreign Countries. If one adds to the number of American travelers who go to overseas foreign destinations those who take trips to Mexico (foreign but not overseas) and those who take trips to Hawaii (overseas but not foreign), the result is a comprehensive measure of the long-distance travel market of the U.S. that is relevant to Hawaii's visitor industry. The number of such long-distance American travelers increased from 473,000 in 1946 to 16,638,000 in 1983.

Figure 7.1 plots this trend against the eight periods of recession in the United States since World War II. It is evident that the 1949 recession did not slow the growth of American long-distance travel, but growth of such travel did slow in 1951, a year of prosperity, probably because the war in Korea kept many Americans at home. The 1953–54 recession did not slow the growth of American long-distance travel at all, but that of 1957–58 apparently did depress this class of travel. The 1960 recession may have had a slightly depressing effect. Long-distance travel did grow in 1960 during the recession but fell off in 1961, the year of the Bay of Pigs invasion. I would guess that the fear of imminent war with the Soviet Union caused by the Bay of Pigs incident did more to keep Americans at home in 1961 than did the prior year's recession.

The 1970 recession had no effect on the growth of long-distance travel. The 1973–75 recession appears to have had a depressing impact, although long-distance travel growth had already slowed in 1973 prior to the recession, for reasons addressed below. The 1980 recession apparently had no effect, whereas the severe recession that started in July 1981 appears to have had a depressing affect in that year. But during 1982, when the recession was at its worst, it had no impact at all.[4] In fact, 1982, the year of the worst recession since the 1930s, was a time of great growth in long-distance travel.

When one compares long-distance travel with durable-goods manufacturing, an industry that is quite sensitive to the business cycle, it becomes clear that long-distance travel is insensitive (Table 7.1). Recessions *always* hurt durable-goods manufacturing and hurt it severely, whereas recessions hurt long-distance tourism sometimes, have no affect at other times, and actually seem to help it sometimes.

What I conclude from this analysis is that national recessions have no predictable impact on long-distance travel: they may or may not affect long-distance travel adversely. The recession of 1957–58 appears to have hurt the industry, and the recessions of 1960–61, 1973–75, and 1981 may have. But the recessions of 1949, 1953–54, 1970, 1980, and 1982 did not. This analysis also indicates that international disturbances may or may not adversely affect the market. The Korean War and the Bay of Pigs incident apparently did, but the Vietnam War apparently did not. From this analysis, I would not want to bet on what sort of impact either recession or war has on the American long-distance tourism market.

In addition to recessions and international disturbances, another factor that can affect any area that heavily depends on long-distance travel is the share of the market it is able to attract. This could be the most important factor of all. Hawaii is only one of thousands of vacation areas around the world that compete vigorously with one another. How well

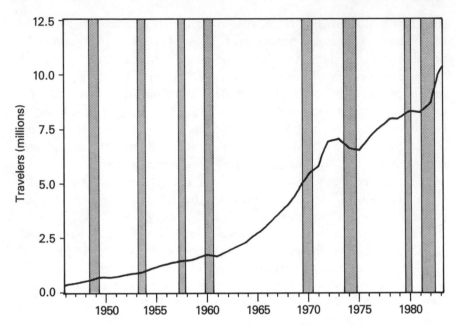

Figure 7.1 Number of U.S. long-distance travelers during eight recessions

Note: Periods of recession are shaded in gray.

any of them does depends more on how well they satisfy the visitor and how well they promote themselves than on minor changes in the total travel market.

A final consideration with respect to the sensitivity of long-distance travel to the national business cycle is that not all of Hawaii's long-distance travelers originate in the United States. One-third of them come from abroad, so that whatever adverse impact a national recession may have on the American travel market would not necessarily affect one-third of the Hawaii trade.

To summarize, the Hawaii visitor industry is not cyclically sensitive, although some national recessions probably affect it to some extent. Other factors, such as international disturbances and Hawaii's ability to compete for the long-distance traveler with other vacation areas, are more important than the business cycle in determining how well the visitor industry will do.

Clear as it is that Hawaii does not move in economic lockstep, the notion that "the Hawaiian economy follows the national economy with a six months' lag" has nevertheless been widely held for so long in the

Table 7.1 Impact of recessions on durable-goods manufacturing and on long-distance U.S. travel, 1949 to 1981–82

RECESSION PERIOD	ANNUAL % GROWTH RATE FOR DURABLE-GOODS MANUFACTURING			ANNUAL % GROWTH RATE FOR TRAVEL		
	PRIOR TO RECESSION (1)	DURING RECESSION (2)	DIFFERENCE BETWEEN 1 & 2 (3)	PRIOR TO RECESSION (4)	DURING RECESSION (5)	DIFFERENCE BETWEEN 4 & 5 (6)
1949	+4	–9	–13	+13	+13	0
1953–54	+13	–12	–25	+10	+10	0
1957–58	+6	–12	–18	–14	+2	–12
1960–61	+15	0	–15	+11	–3	–14
1970	+8	–7	–15	–14	+15	+1
1971–75	+6	–12	–18	–12	–2	–14
1980	+8	–7	–15	+6.5	+2.5	–4
1981–82	+3	–11	–14	0	+9	+9
Average			–17			–4

SOURCE: U.S. Commerce Department.

islands that I am compelled to remind the reader how diverse the national economy is, and how at any one time most parts of the country are either much more or much less prosperous than the average of them all. In calculating rates of change, the "national economy" is the weighted average of fifty state economies. As already demonstrated, that average may differ markedly from Hawaii's, and there is no set pattern of lag to rely on in predicting swings of the business cycle in this—or any other—state.[5]

There are, however, two economic functions that have demonstrated a causal relationship between Hawaii and the nation at large. One is interest rates, which show a close relationship; the other is consumer prices, which do not always have a close relationship to the Hawaiian economy and never have a predictable effect on it.

As to interest rates, at any one time a vast array is being charged and paid across America, ranging from what a well-financed municipal government pays on tax-free bonds to what a poor derelict pays when he pawns his overcoat. Rates charged by lending institutions vary according to the size, duration, and purpose of the loan and the perceived risk of default. Rates paid by financial institutions also vary according to the amount of deposit, its duration, and the purpose to which the institution will put the money. Checking accounts usually draw minimum interest, savings accounts more, and long-term certificates of deposit still more. Thrift institutions that use deposited money for second mortgages pay higher rates than banks that primarily make commercial loans.

In this kaleidoscope of interest rates there is order. The prime rate charged to low-risk major corporations is substantially identical across the nation at any one time. Mortgage loan rates for the same types of mortgages are nearly identical, and the same is true of municipal bond rates for a given grade of bond. The reason for such consistency is that money can move instantly from place to place at little cost and therefore knows no state boundaries. Every major bank makes loans all over the country and every major corporation shops all the money markets, so that for the same type of loan to the same type of borrower, interest rates are virtually identical across the nation. Regional variations, if they exist, seldom exceed a fraction of a percent. Consequently, when money-market conditions call for a rise or fall in interest rates, response throughout the nation is essentially the same. Interest-rate changes on the mainland are reflected almost instantly in Hawaii.

The general level of consumer prices also responds nationally. Prices rose all over the country (though in varying amounts) after the two oil-price shocks of the 1970s, and the slowing of inflation in the 1980s was experienced in all parts of the United States. The record shows, however, that year-to-year consumer price movements in Hawaii have not closely tracked the national average. For example, in the fourteen years between 1967 and 1980 the Honolulu consumer price index (CPI) rose at a slower rate than did the national CPI in eleven years, at the same rate in two, and faster in one year. By contrast, in the early 1960s and the 1980s, prices in Hawaii rose somewhat faster than did the national index. The difference in the rate of change in the two indexes was as much as two percentage points in 1981. To generalize, price movements in Hawaii and on the mainland are generally in the same direction but seldom in the same amount, and without any predictable lag.

Is Foreign Investment a Threat to Hawaii? What about Mainland Investment?

Twice in recent times, opposition to foreign investment has been widely expressed in Hawaii, first in the mid-1970s and again in the mid-1980s. Both times the resented interloper was Japan. With many large investments in Hawaii made by Japanese during these two periods, and with extensive press coverage of this activity, some people began to wonder if Honolulu was destined to become a little Tokyo. Honolulu's mayor proposed putting restrictions on Japanese investments in the state.

To gain perspective on this issue, it is well to go back in history a few decades. Prior to the early 1950s, Hawaii had been able by and large to supply its capital needs from local sources. A 1950 study showed that corporations and individuals resident in Hawaii in 1949 owned slightly more capital assets overseas than overseas investors owned in Hawaii.[6] This was possible because the capital needs of the sugar and pineapple industries were largely met from their retained earnings. The capital needs of other local industries were modest, and the people of Hawaii apparently saved a substantial amount of their income and invested a good bit of it overseas.

When Hawaii's economy began to grow in the late 1950s and particularly in the 1960s, capital needs far exceeded the capacity of the local economy to generate savings. Furthermore, by then most savings of individuals were institutionalized; and the stocks, bonds, mutual funds, pension plans, and insurance policies that people put their savings into were largely located on the mainland. Enterprises had to go outside Hawaii to get funds needed to finance economic growth. Much time and effort were spent by government, private organizations, and many individuals in trying to attract outside capital. Fortunately, we were quite successful; if we had failed the Hawaiian economy would have stagnated instead of leading the nation in its growth rate. In addition to investment capital from the mainland, over the years Hawaii attracted investments from many foreign countries—mainly Canada, Britain, Australia, Hong Kong, and Japan. But by far the largest volume of investments has come from Japan (three-fourths of the total through 1986), and it is only Japanese investments that local public opinion seems to think pose a threat.

The first wave of Japanese investment in Hawaii, in the early and mid-1970s, came when Japanese controls on foreign exchange were relaxed. Over $300 million flowed into Hawaii for the purchase of existing properties and for the construction of new enterprises—mainly in the visitor and visitor-related areas of hotels, restaurants, golf courses, and retail stores. The second wave came in the mid-1980s, when the yen appreciated dramatically. In 1986 and 1987 more than a billion dollars of Japanese investments was made in Hawaii.[7] One difference between the two periods (in addition to the magnitude of investment) was that in the latter period a considerable amount was spent for the purchase of residential properties, with some Japanese purchasing large numbers of houses in the more fashionable areas of Honolulu, presumably for the purpose of renting them to others rather than for personal occupancy.

Before examining whether this kind of massive Japanese investment constitutes a threat to Hawaii, it is useful to identify the reasons why the Japanese have invested so much money abroad, particularly in the United States and especially in Hawaii. The first reason is that they have had an economic surplus to invest abroad. The post–World War II Japanese economy has been remarkably prosperous. For years Japan has run a massive trade surplus, giving it an immense amount of foreign currency (particularly U.S. dollars) which could readily be invested abroad. These monies could, of course, have been frittered away in high and riotous living, but the Japanese in recent decades have saved large portions of their incomes (especially compared with Americans), accumulating great amounts for investment.

The second reason is that, with the depreciation of the dollar and the appreciation of the yen, property prices in the United States looked incredibly attractive to the Japanese. When exchange rates were stabilized after World War II, the yen/dollar ratio was pegged at 360/1. In the early 1970s, when exchange rates were permitted to fluctuate, the dollar began to depreciate in relation to the yen. Despite the drop, in 1985 the major countries of the world agreed with the United States that the dollar was still badly overvalued; the yen/dollar exchange rate fell to 195/1 in 1986 and kept falling all the way to a low of 120/1 in early 1988. At this time of writing (mid-1989), it is back up to about 140, but even at 180/1 the yen could buy twice as much in the United States as when it was at 360/1. At 120/1 it could buy three times as much. If one considers that, even at 360/1, properties in the United States looked inexpensive to the Japanese compared with the prices of properties in Japan, the exchange rates of recent years made American properties irresistibly affordable.

But why did the Japanese concentrate so much of their purchases of real property, as distinct from stock and bonds, in Hawaii instead of the other states? I think there are three reasons.

First, the Japanese know Hawaii much better than any other U.S. state. Ever since 1965, when new currency regulations permitted Japanese to travel abroad, between 15 and 20 percent of all Japanese who take trips abroad have made Hawaii their destination, even though it is much farther away than such vacation alternatives as Saipan, Guam, Hong Kong, Taiwan, or Okinawa. By the mid-1970s, nearly half a million Japanese were vacationing in Hawaii every year, and the figure now exceeds a million.

Tourism paves the way for investment. Before World War II the economic growth of both Florida and California was spurred by tourism—rich businessmen from the north going there for vacations, liking the place, and deciding that they should do some business there, if only for the purpose of taking company-paid trips. In postwar years tourism has spurred the economic development of places like Arizona and Hawaii for the same reason: business people are more inclined to invest in a place they know and like than one they have never seen. Frequently I have said that from a strictly economic viewpoint the investment side-benefit of tourism is about as important as the dollars or yen tourists spend in Hawaii while on vacation.

Second, the Japanese undoubtedly feel more comfortable in Hawaii than in any other part of the United States. The Oriental composition of Hawaii's population makes them feel far more at ease than they would be in a place populated mainly by Caucasians, with African Americans and Hispanics as the other main ethnic groups. Where else would they find a state where a large percentage of the top government, business, and professional leaders are of Asian, primarily Japanese ancestry, where Japanese is commonly spoken by employees of the hotels and restaurants they patronize, and where there are even local Japanese-language newspapers?

Third, Hawaii has for many decades been heaven on earth to the Japanese, their idea of a real paradise. As a result, many of them would love to own a piece of it. I remember on my first trip to Japan in 1960, before Japanese were permitted to travel outside the country, finding that Hawaii even then had this reputation. On that trip I was able to visit many rural areas and found there, as well as in the cities, that Hawaii had an appeal that no other place in the world came close to. Most impressive to me was the fact that in public parks, where music was broadcast by an outdoor loudspeaker, more often than not the music would be Hawaiian. What would give a person more esteem than to be able to say "I own property in Hawaii"?

So Japanese real-property investors moved in on a big scale and now own two-thirds of Hawaii's major hotel properties, a large portion of the golf courses, an interest in the largest interisland airline, and a large number of apartment houses, retail stores, restaurants, and other diversified businesses. In addition, as I have already mentioned, during the last few years the Japanese have purchased several hundred single-family residential homes of high quality.

So, to the main question: What threat, if any, does this investment pose for Hawaii? I can visualize six conceivable threats that local residents might fear, but I believe that all but one of them are groundless.

THREAT TO THE CONTROL OF HAWAII'S POLITICAL INSTITUTIONS

This is almost too farfetched to merit attention. Ownership of businesses or property in a democracy like Hawaii does not give the owner political power. The Big Five discovered that forty years ago. In addition, under U.S. law, political contributions by foreign nationals are illegal.

THREAT TO THE CONTROL OF HAWAII'S ECONOMIC INSTITUTIONS

This is equally farfetched. There is too much local pride and spirit in Hawaii for any foreign group to elect the governing bodies of such organizations as the Hawaii Visitors Bureau, the Chamber of Commerce, or the Better Business Bureau.

THREAT OF TAKING JOBS AWAY FROM LOCAL PEOPLE

This is almost equally farfetched. In the hotel business, where the Japanese penetration has been the most extensive, there are tens of thousands of jobs that immigration laws, if nothing else, would keep from being filled by Japanese nationals. Of course, in the Japanese-owned companies, some of the management jobs will be occupied by Japanese nationals, but the number is minuscule.

THREAT OF AN OUTFLOW OF MONEY FROM HAWAII BY THE RETURN OF PROFITS TO JAPAN

Here we get to an area that has a little—but very little—substance. In the first place, profits as a percentage of sales in most businesses seldom exceed about 5, and in practice only about half the profits earned are paid out in dividends to the owners, with the remainder being reinvested. Therefore the outflow of funds is minimal compared with the other ways in which a company's gross income is distributed—in wages, salaries, local purchase of goods and services, payment of local and federal taxes, etc. When a Japanese firm bought the Royal Hawaiian Hotel, for example, the ownership simply moved from Boston to Tokyo. When a Japanese firm builds a new hotel, such as the Mauna Lani, or reconstructs an old hotel, such as the Halekulani, it creates much more local income than will be repatriated in profits for decades.

It is important to note that over the years the flow of funds into Hawaii from the overseas investments of Hawaii's residents has been closely in balance with the flow of funds out of Hawaii to overseas owners of assets in Hawaii. I noted earlier that the two flows were approximately in balance in 1949 when the subject was first examined. Since 1958 the State Department of Business and Economic Development has constructed gross state product accounts and has developed estimates of these two money flows.[8] These data show that in 1958 the outflow of earnings was about $40 million and the inflow about $30 million. Since then the outflow has remained larger than the inflow every year, but only by modest margins. In 1965 the outflow was $120 million and the inflow $114 million; in 1975 the figures were $531 million and $385 million; and in 1985 $1,509 million versus $1,421 million. The upsurge of

Japanese investment in the last few years has probably widened the gap
a bit.

Threat of a Lack of Concern for the Welfare of the Local Community

This possible threat probably bothers more thinking people in Hawaii
than any of the prior four, but a number of considerations keep it from
being a serious concern. First, as noted earlier, the Japanese have
invested heavily in Hawaii in most instances because they love and
admire the place, and they generally plan to at least visit regularly.
There have been few get-rich-quick artists among them. Second, as foreigners they are invited guests who are subject to having their invitation
revoked. This consideration puts foreign investors in a category totally
different from out-of-state domestic investors and therefore deserves
attention.

Under the U.S. Constitution, states have power to control the investment of foreigners in almost all ways except to prohibit the purchase of
residential property for owner-occupancy. Twenty or more states have
placed limits of one kind or another on foreign purchases of assets under
their jurisdiction. If Hawaii chose to clamp down on foreign investors
because they behaved improperly (or for any other reason), it could do
so. Therefore, every foreign investor knows that if his behavior is considered by Hawaii's state government to be detrimental to the interests
of the community, he may jeopardize the right of all foreign investors to
purchase assets in the state. In short, he has to be on much better behavior than he would have to be at home.

For this reason, many of the Japanese investments in Hawaii have
been joint ventures with local firms, and in most cases Japanese firms
doing business in Hawaii have retained local advisers to steer them clear
of making mistakes. In addition, in the early 1970s John Bellinger, president of First Hawaiian Bank, organized the Japan–Hawaii Economic
Council, composed of top business and government leaders from both
Hawaii and Japan. The council, rotating its annual meetings between
Japan and Hawaii, has been a top-level forum for discussion of problems
involving the two areas, including Japanese investment in Hawaii. Talk
at these meetings has been frank, and the Japanese participants have
generally incorporated the information that was exchanged into their
investment ventures.

As a result of these several considerations, it has been my observation that of all the overseas investors in Hawaii (including those from the U.S. mainland), the Japanese have probably tried hardest to be good citizens. Where they have failed, it has mainly been through ignorance, although no group will ever be completely free of unprincipled members.

The Hawaii State governor's office recently issued a set of guidelines for investors, telling them what kinds of investments we want and what kinds we do not want.[9] While these are only guidelines, foreign investors are thereby put on notice that if they do not heed our wishes they will receive a lot of bad publicity—at least.

THREAT OF INFLATIONARY INCREASES IN REAL-PROPERTY VALUES AND RESULTING HIGHER REAL-PROPERTY TAXES

Here is the prime public relations problem the Japanese have had in Hawaii since the mid-1980s and in my opinion the basis for most of the public concern about Japanese investments. As of late 1988, some 350 single-family residences on Oahu had been sold to Japanese purchasers in the previous eighteen months.[10] One Japanese investor announced that he planned to purchase as many as a thousand homes, as long-term investments in rental housing. Most purchases were in upscale neighborhoods at high prices. In fact, the nub of the problem is that the Japanese purchasers of residential properties appear willing to pay prices well above the current market, starting what many residents see as an inflationary spiral.

A personal example may illustrate the problem. I sold my home on Portlock Road in 1983 for $440,000, as good a price as I could get on the market at that time. The residential market on Portlock Road did not change materially until the Japanese discovered the neighborhood. In 1987 a Japanese bought a house next door to my old home for $1.3 million—a much older and inferior house, but with a better location by virtue of being on the beach instead of next to it. Shortly thereafter, the purchaser of my house put it on the market for $1.35 million. The neighbors were greatly exercised because real-property tax assessments are based on current sales in the area. They foresaw their assessments rising not by 10 percent but probably by 100 percent or more.

This sort of thing happened in a number of neighborhoods in Honolulu. Consequently, there has been strong pressure on the city and state governments to legislate, either to stop foreign purchases of residential property or to provide some kind of real-property tax relief for residents in affected neighborhoods. Because of public criticism, Japanese investment in residential property has slowed considerably and will probably cease to be an issue soon. Recently the largest Japanese purchaser of residential properties in Hawaii announced that he was tired of the publicity he had gotten and was pulling out. My former house is still on the market.

My conclusion is that Japanese (and other foreign) investment does not constitute a threat to Hawaii, but that the small fraction going into residential properties has sometimes been spent as if money were going out of style, has inflated prices in a few residential areas, and has legitimately irritated residents in those neighborhoods. The larger part that has gone into commercial and industrial ventures has been helpful to the economy, although too much has been spent for the purchase of existing properties and too little for starting new enterprises.

But what about mainland investments, which over the years have been much larger than Japanese investments? Here there is reason for concern because the mainland investor is not the "invited guest" subject to having his "invitation" revoked, as is the foreign investor. There is no pressing reason for him to worry about public opinion. This distinction can be crucial in a company's decision whether or not to try hard to be a good corporate citizen.

The real determinant of whether absentee ownership is good or bad is whether the absentee owner acts in a good or bad manner. Foreign investors have a greater incentive to take local concerns into consideration than do mainland investors. For example, several Japanese investors in Hawaii have been persuaded by the Japan–Hawaii Economic Council and by their local advisers and joint-venture partners to make sizable contributions to charitable and other community activities in Hawaii on a scale that few mainland companies have come close to matching. In addition, the Japanese have established three colleges and one advanced management training institute in Hawaii—the Kansai Gaidai College, the Tokai University Pacific Center, the Waseda Hawaii International College, and the Japan–America Institute of Management Sciences.

Is Tourism Turning Hawaii into a Low-Income Service Economy?

Conventional wisdom holds that tourism is turning Hawaii into a low-income service economy. It is evident that many jobs in the visitor industry are low-skill and low-pay—such as those of dishwasher, chambermaid, waiter and waitress, bellboy, laundry worker, and retail clerk. With more than one-third of all civilian employment in Hawaii generated by visitor spending, the depressing impact on average income seems readily apparent.

This view tends to be confirmed by a casual look at the data. Each year the State Department of Labor and Industrial Relations publishes the average annual earnings of workers in Hawaii by industry classification, so that we have statistics giving a rough measure of the depressing impact of the low-wage industries. In 1987 the average annual earnings of all employed persons in private industry in the state was $18,010. But in hotels, where tourists spend 35 percent of their money, the average was only $15,782; in restaurants (recipients of 25 percent of tourists' money) it was only $8,812; in retail stores (22 percent) it was about $12,000; and in amusement and entertainment establishments (6 percent) it was also about $12,000. Only in transportation (12 percent) were average earnings larger than the all-industry average, $21,539.[11]

The average of the above annual earnings, when weighted by the volume of tourist expenditures in each category, is $13,530. A quick calculation shows that if the average annual wage of the entire labor force is $18,010 and if one-third of it earns only $13,530, the other two-thirds must have annual earnings of $20,261. Since $20,261 is about 12 percent higher than $18,010, one may be tempted to conclude that the one-third of the labor force whose jobs depend on visitor spending is pulling down the average wage of the entire work force by about 12 percent. But this conclusion is greatly exaggerated, for three reasons.

First, more than half the employment created by visitor spending is in industrial sectors other than hotels, restaurants, retail stores, etc., where the visitors spend their money. Hotels, for example, distribute about half the money they receive from visitors to their employees in the form of wages and salaries; this represents the *direct* impact of visitor spending on employment. The other half is spent for a vast array of goods and services that hotels need to operate, and the companies that supply these goods and services then distribute some of the money they receive from the hotels to their employees. These wages represent the *indirect* impact on employment of visitor spending. Finally, when the hotels' employees and the suppliers' employees spend their income, they create more jobs throughout the entire economy; this is the *multiplier* effect. My point is that jobs created by the indirect and multiplier effects of visitor spending are at least as numerous as the jobs created directly. Since these jobs are in all industries in the state and presumably provide earnings approximately equal to the average of all nonvisitor-industry employees, the result is that only one-sixth of the jobs attributable to tourism pull down the average earnings of the other five-sixths, instead of one-third pulling down the average earnings of the other two-thirds. This cuts the 12 percent figure to around 6 percent.

Second, the annual earnings of many who work in hotels, restaurants, etc., are considerably higher than the annual earnings reported by the State Department of Labor because many jobs in those industries are part-time, held by people who hold more than one job. When Joe Blow works in a filling station for six hours a day and then waits on table in a hotel dining room for four hours in the evening, only his pay by the hotel is reported in the hotel-industry figures. His actual earnings may be twice what the hotel reports to the Labor Department. This factor is important in the hotel and restaurant industries, where moonlighting is common. In the only study of this subject in Hawaii I know of, it was found that in Waikiki hotels 42 percent of all male employees had a job in addition to their hotel employment, and 29 percent of all female employees were moonlighting.[12] This factor could well reduce the 6 percent depressant figure calculated above to 4 percent or lower.

Third, many employees who work in establishments where visitors spend their money—waiters, waitresses, doormen, chambermaids, valet parking attendants, taxi drivers, bellboys, etc.—receive tips. An unpublished study made a few years ago[13] found that waiters and waitresses in Waikiki eating establishments were generally paid only the minimum wage (hence the low annual earnings in the restaurant industry reported to the Department of Labor), but that their income from unreported tips was three times the minimum wage. Further, it found that 25 percent of all workers employed directly in the visitor industry received tips. When this substantial amount of income is added to reported earnings, the 12 percent differential I started with a few paragraphs back has probably disappeared.

The conclusion from this analysis has to be that the visitor industry is not turning Hawaii into a low-income economy. Whatever downward pull it has on average income in Hawaii is very small.

Before leaving this subject, it is necessary to discuss another statistic that is sometimes used to show that tourism is turning Hawaii into a low-income economy. In the early 1970s, when tourism accounted for about 16 percent of the total Hawaiian economy, Hawaii's per capita personal income averaged about 17 percent above the national average. Since then it has dropped back to about 3 percent above the national average, and it is easy to conclude that the reason is that tourism grew from 16 percent of the state's economy to more than one-third during that time. But if this were the cause, how does one explain that Hawaii's per capita personal income rose from well below the national average in the early 1950s to well above the national average in the late 1960s, during a period when tourism was growing from less than 3 percent of the Hawaii economy to around 16 percent?

To my knowledge, no one knows for certain the answer to this statistical riddle. Probably it is because there are many factors that influence the average level of per capita personal income, besides the distribution of the work force between high-wage and low-wage industries. Other major factors are the percentage of the population that is in the labor force, the percentage of the labor force that is at work, the productivity of the labor force, the rate of wage inflation taking place, and the general profitability of business. All these factors fluctuate from time to time and move at different rates in different parts of the country—hence the constant change in the ranking of the states with respect to the level of average personal income. Perhaps more of these factors were working in Hawaii's favor in the late 1960s and early 1970s, when Hawaii was having its greatest economic boom, than in the 1950s and the 1980s. Certainly one factor, and probably the most important, was the size of the labor force relative to the total population. With the armed forces included in both the labor force and the population, the ratio of labor force to population in 1970 was 52 percent for Hawaii and 42 percent for the nation.[14] But by 1985, with many youths and women entering the labor force on the mainland, as they had earlier in Hawaii, the nation's ratio had jumped to 49 percent while Hawaii's had dropped to 51 percent.[15] In the light of these developments, it is easy to see why per capita personal income in the nation increased over that span of time much faster than it did in Hawaii.

It is sometimes said that Hawaii would have been better off economically if we had developed such high-pay industries as manufacturing instead of low-pay tourism. While the comparison I am about to make is subject to all the qualifications concerning statistical comparisons that I have just mentioned, the fact is that today (1988 figures) Hawaii's per capita personal income is higher than that of major manufacturing states. Our per capita personal income is 103 percent of the national average, whereas Michigan's is 100 percent, Pennsylvania's is 98 percent, Ohio's is 94 percent, and Indiana's is 90 percent. Hawaii's per capita income is high in spite of the fact that we have a large military population, whose family incomes fall somewhat below the civilian average.[16] The conclusion must be that an economy based on tourism is not necessarily a low-income economy.

In fact, an economy based largely on tourism has a number of significant advantages. One, which I hesitate to mention because it could easily be misinterpreted, is that it creates *some* low-skill, low-pay jobs— which is a plus instead of a minus. Today, unfortunately, a full 20 percent of the adults in the labor force are functionally illiterate and can perform satisfactorily only in jobs that do not require the ability to read and write. Without jobs such as dishwasher and chambermaid, most of these people would be unemployable.

To its other positive features, it should be added that tourism does not pollute inland or coastal waters as many manufacturing industries do, and air pollution produced by tour buses is minimal compared with total air pollution. Tourism is not highly sensitive to the business cycle, as is manufacturing. Tourism usually takes up little space; our present 65,000 hotel rooms occupy less than four hundreths of 1 percent of Hawaii's land area. It does not take much water; less than 1 percent of the state's water supply is used by tourists.[17] Tourism has resulted in Hawaii having a proliferation of fine stores and shops that would otherwise not exist. The same goes for restaurants of all sorts, for golf courses, for tennis courts, for the large number of scheduled air flights between the islands and on transpacific routes, and for the wide range of entertainment activities that are largely supported by visitors but available to local residents as well.

A case can even be made for the view that many of our people, whose work brings them into contact with visitors, have a broader view of the world and are less provincial than they would be without this contact. The opposite side of this coin is that some of Hawaii probably rubs off on some of our visitors, and they leave with a better feeling about race relations and humanity in general than when they came.

How High Is the Cost of Living in Hawaii and Why Is It High?

At the outset it should be made clear that there is no numerical answer to the first question and that the answer to the second question is highly speculative. A discussion of this subject is necessary, however, because these are probably the questions most frequently asked about the Hawaiian economy. It is better to know that there is no precise answer (and why) than to believe a wrong answer. In addition, a discussion of the subject serves the purpose of giving the reader an understanding of some aspects of Hawaii's economy not touched on elsewhere.

Until fairly recently (1981 in one case and 1986 in the other), two federal agencies made annual studies of the cost of living in Hawaii for certain classes of people and compared them with living costs for similar groups in certain parts of the mainland. One set of studies, which dates back to 1949, was made for the Federal Civil Service Commission (now renamed the Office of Personnel Management and hereafter referred to as OPM). It was made to determine how much the cost-of-living allowance (COLA) that is paid to white-collar federal employees should be in Hawaii. The comparison in this case was between such workers in Hawaii and their counterparts in Washington, D.C. The COLA levels set as a result of these studies are shown in Table 7.2.

As discussed in Chapter 4, during World War II the federal government found it necessary, in order to recruit people for service in forward areas, to pay recruitment or incentive differentials above the regular pay for federal white-collar jobs. These were paid to mainland civil recruits sent out to forward areas, such as Hawaii, Alaska, and American Samoa. While the war was still on, a ruling of the comptroller general

Table 7.2   Cost-of-living allowance
for Oahu, 1949–88

YEAR	RATE (%)
1949	25
1950–54	20
1955–59	20
1960–61	17.5
1962–74	15.0
1975	12.5
1976–77	17.5
1978–80	15.0
1981	17.5
1982	20.0
1983–85	22.5
1986–present	22.5

SOURCE: Office of Personnel Management.

resulted in this added allowance being paid to all federal employees in those areas, not just to those recruited on the mainland. The standard differential paid was the maximum permitted by law, 25 percent. When the war ended, this differential was continued, but it needed some justification. This was provided by Presidential Executive Order 10,000 of 16 September 1948, which converted the wartime recruitment differential into a "post" differential for certain areas deemed to have extraordinarily difficult living conditions, notably unhealthful conditions, or excessive physical hardship. These areas are currently American Samoa, Canton Island, Christmas Island, Johnston and Sand Islands, Midway Islands, Wake Island, and Guam. The wartime recruitment differential was converted into a "cost-of-living" allowance for Hawaii, Alaska, Puerto Rico, Guam, and the Virgin Islands. As a result of the prescribed diffferentials and allowances, it became necessary to determine the extent to which each of these areas met the criteria for the payment of a "post" differential or a cost-of-living allowance.

The other set of studies, which dates back to 1967, was conducted by the U.S. Bureau of Labor Statistics (hereafter referred to as the BLS). It was an expansion of several onetime studies of intercity differentials in living costs of workers' families in various metropolitan areas. A new series of indexes was started in 1967, which priced the budgets of an urban family of four people at three standards of living (lower, intermediate, and higher) in thirty-nine metropolitan areas—including Honolulu—and certain nonmetropolitan areas. These studies were discontinued in 1981 for lack of federal funds. Honolulu's budget costs as a percentage of the national average are shown in Table 7.3.

The data in Table 7.2 indicate that the cost of living of white-collar federal workers in recent years has been approximately 20 percent higher in Honolulu than in Washington, D.C. Since the BLS studies show the cost of living in Washington for the three urban family budgets to be slightly above the national average, one may conclude that the Honolulu differential of somewhere around 20 percent over relatively expensive Washington would convert to a differential of somewhere around 25 percent over the national average. Table 7.3 indicates that the budget for a family of four with a moderate or intermediate standard of living is somewhere around 25 percent higher in Honolulu than the average of the country. The lower and higher budgets have an even greater differential—more like 30 percent.

Both the OPM and the BLS explicitly state that their data apply only

Table 7.3 Honolulu urban family budgets as a percentage of U.S. urban family budgets, 1967–81

SEASON AND YEAR	LOWER BUDGET	INTERMEDIATE BUDGET	HIGHER BUDGET
Spring			
1967	122.5	120.1	123.2
1969	124.3	120.4	125.7
1970	123.5	119.8	124.5
Autumn			
1971	124.6	119.5	123.9
1972	123.4	119.0	124.3
1973	121.3	118.3	120.3
1974	123.8	118.7	123.1
1975	127.5	122.0	126.9
1976	126.6	120.9	126.6
1977	126.7	122.1	126.6
1978	128.8	124.0	129.8
1979	131.2	125.7	130.9
1980	131.6	123.1	129.0
1981	132.6	125.5	132.2

SOURCE: U.S. Bureau of Labor Statistics data; calculated by (Hawaii)
Department of Planning and Economic Development.

to the particular budgets studied and should not be used to generalize
about the cost of living for all people or for other groups of people in any
area. But these caveats generally go unheeded. Thus, when the OPM
reports that it costs something like 22.5 percent more for a white-collar
federal worker to live in Hawaii than to live in Washington, that is to
most people an adequate answer to the question of how high the cost of
living generally is in Hawaii compared with the mainland. And when
the BLS states that it costs about 25 percent more for a family of four to
purchase the items in an intermediate budget in Honolulu than it costs,
on the average, on the mainland, that is also taken as a general answer
to the question. The BLS has been fighting this battle of misinterpreta-
tion with no success during the seventy-five years it has been compiling
the consumer price index. When the CPI goes up, say, 5 percent, people
almost universally conclude that *their* cost of living has gone up 5 percent, whereas the figure applies only to those people whose consumption
pattern exactly matches the market basket of goods and services that is
priced to compute the index—and there are few if any in that category.

For all those with different budgets, prices may actually have risen by more than 5 percent or less than 5 percent, or may even have fallen. Nevertheless, with the OPM and the BLS studies both showing about a 25 percent differential in living costs between certain classes of people in Hawaii and their counterparts in certain parts of the mainland, that appears to most people to constitute a reasonable measure of how high the cost of living in Hawaii is compared with the mainland average.

But measuring differences in the cost of living in different places can be tricky, particularly if consumption patterns in the two places differ. In fact, this measurement may be the most difficult statistical job faced by economists. "The problem of how we are to compare purchasing powers . . . is one of great difficulty," John Maynard Keynes wrote. "It has been a stumbling block in the way of a clear treatment of the whole subject of purchasing power."[18] The BLS stated years ago that the issue "involves many technical problems," adding that "consequently, very few empirical comparisons of this kind have been made."[19] Therefore one should not accept the OPM and the BLS conclusions unless the methods they use in making their cost-of-living studies are examined and found to be valid.

Basically, both the OPM and the BLS use mainland patterns of consumption to determine the market-basket items to be priced in all geographical areas. They also use mainland patterns to calculate the weights to be assigned to those items. The OPM takes as its base the consumption pattern of families in Washington and then prices this market basket of goods and services in both Washington and the comparison cities, including Honolulu. It adopted this methodology from the U.S. State Department, which for many years has made cost-of-living studies in all places around the world where State Department employees are stationed. The State Department uses Washington as the standard because Americans sent abroad are expected to maintain their American pattern of consumption relatively intact, not forced to start living like the natives in the posts to which they are assigned. The problem of applying this comparison locally is that most federal employees in Hawaii are local people who are themselves "natives."

The BLS used for its intercity cost-of-living surveys a market basket of goods and services constructed for each of the three levels of living, on the basis of what the average family in the United States consumes at each of those three levels of living. It is not the Washington pattern of consumption. Rather, it is a composite pattern thought to represent the expenditure pattern of the average American family at each of the three income levels. The only modification in the market basket that is priced in Honolulu and other cities is to relate heating and cooling costs to local temperature conditions.

These methodologies would be appropriate for comparing the cost of living in Honolulu with Washington (OPM) or with a group of mainland cities (BLS) if the pattern of consumption of families in Honolulu was the same as that in Washington (OPM) or in the average U.S. city (BLS). But if these patterns for Honolulu differed in any considerable degree from Washington or the average U.S. city, then the methodologies would not be appropriate.

Economists, statisticians, and mathematicians differ on many issues on the question of how to measure differences in the cost of living in places where the patterns of consumption vary, but they all agree that it is improper to take the pattern of consumption in one place and then price it in another place being compared with the first. Richard Ruggles put it this way: "Prices and quantities [of goods and services purchased by consumers] tend to be inversely correlated, so that there is a systematic substitution of low-priced goods for high-priced goods in the consumption of each country. It is therefore always less expensive to buy what is actually consumed in any country than to buy any other market basket."[20] The validity of this statement has been demonstrated by many studies. I will cite only three.

First, in 1931 the International Labour Office (ILO), on request from the Ford Motor Company (which wanted to know how much to pay its employees in Europe so that they would have the same purchasing power as its employees in Detroit), priced the Detroit worker's pattern of consumption in fourteen European cities. In every case it cost more to buy the Detroit market basket in the European cities than it did in Detroit. The ILO then reversed the process and priced the pattern of consumption of workers of those European cities in Detroit, and found that it cost more to buy the European market basket in Detroit than it did at home in Europe.[21]

Second, around 1950 the BLS priced the Washington, D.C., pattern of consumption of transportation and food in San Juan, Puerto Rico. It found that the Washington type of transportation would cost 13 percent more in San Juan than in Washington and that the Washington type of food would cost 32 percent more. It then priced San Juan patterns in Washington and found that the San Juan type of transportation and food respectively cost 23 and 27 pecent less in San Juan than they would in Washington.[22]

Third, in 1960–61 the Economic Commission for Latin America studied price differentials in nineteen Latin American countries. Ruggles reports one finding of the study as follows: "Comparing Haiti with Argentina as the base, the Argentine basket of goods would cost in Haiti 175 percent of what it would cost in Argentina: 75 percent more. But if the Haitian market basket were purchased in both Argentina and Haiti, the cost in Haiti would be only 79 percent of what it would be in Argentina: 21 percent less."[23] Other country comparisons, with the Argentina pattern of consumption as the base for the first measurement and the pattern of consumption in the comparison country as base for the second measurement, developed the following contradictory figures: Bolivia, 136 percent and 89 percent; Brazil, 115 and 85 percent; Ecuador, 139 and 87 percent; Mexico, 139 and 96 percent; Paraguay, 119 and 78 percent; Peru, 123 and 94 percent; and Uraguay, 105 and 85 percent.[24] As Ruggles asserted, it is always less expensive to buy what is actually consumed in any place than to buy any other market basket.

The reader may wonder whether it is not possible to arrive at a good measure of the difference in the cost of living in two places, such as in the examples above, by splitting the difference between the contradictory findings. According to the ILO, in practice an average can be taken of the two values, but its significance will be purely conventional. Commenting on Irving Fisher's efforts to find the best way of determining where between the two values the true value lay, John Maynard Keynes wrote: "We can concoct all sorts of algebraic functions of p and q as determining the point's position, and there will be not a penny to choose between them,"—p being the price, say, of a Washington unit of consumption in San Juan, and q being the price of a San Juan unit of consumption in Washington.[25]

We come then to the crucial question: Is the pattern of consumption of residents of Honolulu different in any considerable degree from the pattern of consumption of residents of mainland cities, including Washington, D.C.? If it is, then the OPM method of measuring the difference in the cost of living for federal white-collar workers is not valid and overstates the cost of living in Honolulu. If there are considerable differences beyond those in heating and cooling expenditures, then the BLS method used in their three budget-level studies also is invalid and likewise overstates the cost of living in Honolulu.

In my opinion, there are many reasons to believe that people in Hawaii have a life-style different in many ways from that of people generally on the mainland. It is therefore reasonable to assume that their patterns of consumption are also considerably different.

To begin with, Hawaii is more than 2,000 miles out in the Pacific Ocean, on the edge of the tropics, with a Polynesian tradition, and with vastly different demographics from the rest of the country. The mainland population is composed almost entirely of Caucasians, African Americans, Hispanics, and Native Americans. These four groups constitute less than one-third of Hawaii's resident, nonmilitary population. More than two-thirds is made up of a great mixture of many races and nationalities, with Japanese the largest, Hawaiian and part-Hawaiian next, then Filipinos, and Chinese. (The military population is omitted from this calculation because military personnel are temporary residents who generally live on base or in government housing and can buy at commissaries.)

Hawaii has perpetual summer except at high altitudes, where relatively few people live. We do not heat our houses, and, because summers are cool compared with most parts of the mainland, few single-family homes have air conditioning. We do not need a winter wardrobe and our children often go to school barefoot until they enter the seventh grade.

Hawaii's life-styles are informal compared with most mainland standards. Slacks and Aloha shirts for men and informal dresses for women are almost universal, even for parties, weddings, and funerals. Even stuffy bankers do not wear a coat and tie more often than a few times a year.

Distances are short on all islands except the Big Island. There is no need for big cars; the driver is seldom on the road for more than an hour at a time. The typical car owner has a hard time putting more than about 10,000 miles a year on his car.

Many food habits are different in Hawaii. Although most of Hawaii's non-Caucasian population is Americanized, tea frequently replaces coffee, rice replaces potatoes, shoyu replaces standard American seasonings, papayas replace oranges, and so on. Many tropical and Oriental foods that are seldom seen on the mainland are common diet items in Hawaii.

Recreation tends to be outdoors. Many people in Hawaii of course play golf and pay green fees and many go to commercial bowling alleys.

But for large segments of the population, recreation consists of going to the beach to swim or surf, jogging, fishing, or hiking in the mountains.

Finally, and this is most important, the relative prices of various consumer items are frequently different in one place from those in another. Everyone who has changed his residence knows that his pattern of consumption changes somewhat because price relationships vary in different localities, frequently for obscure or inexplicable reasons, and each person tries to maximize his consumption by buying the less expensive items that provide the same utility. As Ruggles stated, it is always less expensive to buy what is actually consumed in any country than to buy any other market basket.

Not only do I think that patterns of consumption in Hawaii are probably different in many respects from those on the mainland, but the OPM and the BLS also apparently thought so in the early 1950s. When required by Executive Order of the President 10,000 in 1948 to determine the cost-of-living differentials between certain areas of the country (including Hawaii) and Washington, D.C., the Civil Service Commission (OPM) contracted with the BLS to do the required studies. The BLS decided (presumably with OPM concurrence) that the economic, demographic, and cultural characteristics that existed in Hawaii were so different from those in Washington that some method of measuring the cost-of-living differences between the two places other than merely comparing prices of some market basket of goods and services had to be developed.

The methodology the BLS developed in the early 1950s to measure the difference in the cost of living in Hawaii and Puerto Rico as compared with Washington, D.C., was based on Engels's law, which states that the higher one's income, the more one spends on luxuries and the less (percentagewise) one spends on necessities.[26] It follows that if a, say, $5,000 a year income in Washington permits the consumption of more luxuries than a $5,000 a year income in Hawaii, then Washington costs are lower than Hawaii's. I always felt that the problem with this approach was the imprecision of defining the dividing line between luxuries and necessities—particularly in two different cultures—yet the results of the study hinge entirely on where this line is drawn. In any case, the OPM dropped its contract with the BLS after a few years and, unfortunately in my opinion, adopted the U.S. State Department's methodology.

I conclude that, because the patterns of consumption in Honolulu differ considerably from those in mainland cities, and because both the OPM and the BLS use mainland patterns of consumption as their base for the market basket that is priced to determine the cost of living in Honolulu, they both overstate the cost of living in Honolulu. In their defense, I would say that for them to do the job right (assuming there is any right way, which most economists qualified in this field doubt) would require so much manpower and money for field work, and would involve so many judgments about which commodities in one place give satisfaction equivalent to other commodities in other places, that they probably have had no alternative to doing what they have done. Federal budgets for this sort of work have become so tight that the BLS has even had to drop its studies of intercity differences in costs of living (a relatively inexpensive project because it involved simply pricing standard budgets); and federal agencies do not like to make judgments that affect allowances paid to federal employees out of fear of court suits challenging those judgements—as OPM well knows from the class-action suit that stopped its studies of cost-of-living differentials. It is not a happy situation, but it is probably inevitable.

Assuming that the OPM and BLS studies both overstate Hawaii's cost of living, how much is the overstatement and what is the correct figure? Neither I nor anybody else knows the answer to this question, assuming that there is an answer. All I can conclude is that Hawaii's living costs for most people would probably be lower than Alaska's, probably not much higher than in some high-cost cities, such as Boston, and a great deal higher than in some low-cost cities, such as Austin, Texas.

Now I come to the second question posed: Why is the cost of living high in Hawaii? Since the million people living here could probably give hundreds of answers to this question and since even an expensive study might not develop a satisfactory answer for even a single homogeneous income group, I will simply comment on the three reasons that I think are the most important.

First are the land-use policies of the State government that limit the amount of land available for housing, which in turn limits the total amount of housing, which in turn causes extremely high housing prices for home owners and extremely high rentals for home renters. Practically all surveys of housing prices in metropolitan areas of the United States over the last few decades have shown that Honolulu's housing prices are extraordinarily high—about twice the national average and according to most surveys higher than in any mainland city.

Contrary to popular opinion, Honolulu's high housing prices are not caused by the high cost of residential land. Most new housing on Oahu in recent decades has been built on leased land, where the only immediate land cost is for site development; or on land owned for an extended period of time by the developer, which has an inconsequential book value; or on land purchased in a large tract by the developer, the cost per lot of which is usually not exorbitant. In none of these three situations does the price of land greatly push up the cost of housing. Practically no housing has been built on individual lots because few individual lots are available—so few that Honolulu is not listed in national surveys of the price of residential lots.

Also contrary to popular belief, Honolulu's high housing prices are not due primarily to high costs of house construction. McGraw-Hill's *Housing Magazine* periodically surveys the cost of materials and labor for the construction of a standard 1,500 sq. ft. ranch-style house in about 100 cities. It finds that in Honolulu materials cost about 20 percent and labor about 4 percent above the national average, making local construction costs somewhat higher but well below the costs in some cities on the mainland.

The practice of requiring a developer to pay for on-site improvements, such as roads and sewers, plus requiring him to construct a specified number of units for sale at low prices to low-income families, does increase construction costs; but these are now common practices across the country. And Hawaii's 4 percent general excise tax on the sale of houses adds another 4 percent to the final price, but these factors are not sufficient to explain the immense difference between housing costs in Hawaii and in most of the nation.

The primary reason for Honolulu's high housing prices is simply an imbalance between supply and demand. Prior to the passage of the state's land-use law in the early 1960s, the price of housing in Hawaii was not particularly out of line with the rest of the country, but since then the construction of so few residences has been authorized and so many families have entered the housing market that the supply has simply not been able to keep up with demand and prices have soared. In broad outline, the problem is that simple.

Since the early 1960s the policies of Hawaii's state and county governments with respect to land use have been to (1) keep agricultural land in agriculture, (2) maintain open space and avoid urban sprawl, (3) accommodate population growth in compact urban centers to save energy and infrastructure costs, and (4) restrict growth on Oahu to encourage a more even distribution of population among the islands. I once documented these policies with statements taken from the state constitution, from "state of the state" gubernatorial addresses to the legislature, from the land-use law, from the state's general plan and its various functional plans, and from the counties' general and development plans. In those documents I found eighty-three declarations that supported the four policies just listed. With these policies so firmly imbedded in laws and regulations, it is no wonder that it has been extremely difficult to get agricultural land reclassified for residential use. Since it has not been possible for existing urban areas to accommodate the housing needs of a growing population, demand has badly outstripped supply. David Callies quotes land-use expert Richard Babcock as concluding that in Hawaii these land-use restrictions "have contributed to one of the nation's most appalling shortages of housing and a substantial increase in the cost of what housing there is."[27]

One geographic exception to this rule may serve to prove the points I have made. Back in the 1950s, before these restrictive land-use policies were adopted, a large number of residential subdivisions were laid out in the Hilo area of the Big Island with the purpose of selling them mainly to nonresidents, who might not build on them but who could have the satisfaction, at a modest cost, of owning some land in Hawaii. This sales gimmick was successful; thousands of residential lots were laid out and sold, but few were built upon. Consequently, in the Hilo area, unlike the rest of Hawaii, a large number of residential lots remain on the market (some perhaps lacking utility services) at reasonable prices. Anyone wanting a home in that area has the option of buying a lot and building a home on it. The result is that the last time I made a comparison of housing prices in the Hilo area with the Honolulu area (in 1982) I found that the average sales price of a single family home in Hilo was $71,871, contrasted to $174,173 in Honolulu, and the average price of a condominium in Hilo was $36,133, contrasted to $102,515 in Honolulu. The Hilo area beat the gun and developed a massive inventory of residential lots before Hawaii's restrictive land-use policies came into being. As a result, housing there is at least 50 percent cheaper than in the rest of Hawaii.

I trust that the reader will notice that I have simply explained why housing prices in Hawaii (except for the Hilo area) are so high. I have not passed judgment on the merit of these land-use policies, which have had the beneficial result of drastically curtailing urban sprawl, nor have I passed judgment on the actions of some get-rich-quick developers in the Hilo area back in the 1950s who, when carving out so many subdivisions, inadvertently laid the basis for low housing costs in the Hilo area.

The second reason why the cost of living in Hawaii is high is that on a per capita basis taxes exceed those in most of the other forty-nine states and are especially high on consumer incomes and purchases. Hawaii's tax laws also make the cost of unemployment insurance, workers' compensation, temporary disability insurance, and tort insurance very high, thereby increasing the cost of doing business. Those costs, of course, are passed on to the consumer whenever possible.

State and local taxes combined, in 1988 the average per capita tax burden in Hawaii was $2,326, contrasted with $1,768 for the average of the fifty states and the District of Columbia.[28] This made Hawaii's state and local taxes 31 percent higher than the national average. The fact that visitors pay the retail excise tax on their purchases and overseas-based airlines pay aviation fuel taxes and airport use taxes reduces this figure somewhat but still leaves Hawaii well above the national average.

The impact of taxes on the cost of living is probably greater than these figures suggest because, as already noted, Hawaii relies heavily on its general excise tax. As I have already discussed, this tax adds a minimum of 4 percent on every retail sale (of all goods and services) and may pyramid to nearly 6 percent because of the 0.5 percent excise tax on producing, processing, and wholesaling. Furthermore, Hawaii taxes personal income at relatively high rates, and personal income taxes are a component of the cost of living. As of 1989, eight states had no net income tax, and only three had maximum rates higher than Hawaii's top 10 percent rate.[29] A system of credits against the income tax offsets the burden of consumption taxes on lower-income households, but only in part.

The third cause of the high cost of living in this state is Hawaii's great distance from the source of supply of so many of the commodities consumed here. Most of our food, clothing, furniture, and building supplies and practically all mechanical items come from a minimum of over 2,000 miles away and some from much farther.

This distance from the market adds to the prices at which items sell for three reasons. The first and most obvious is the cost of ocean freight, which the Jones Act requires to be carried in U.S. bottoms between the mainland and Hawaii. With the efficiency of ocean freight movement made possible by containerization, shipping rates are lower than many people think. I compared ocean-freight rates between the West Coast and Hawaii with the retail prices of imported commodities in Hawaii and conclude that *on the average* freight charges add about 4 to 5 percent to the cost of imported merchandise, regardless of whether the merchandise is food, soft goods, or hard goods. Items that come by air freight, of course, bear heavier transportation costs. The second reason why distance from sources of supply adds to the cost of merchandise is that, in addition to the ocean-freight charges, at least two additional handlings of the merchandise are required to move it to the dock and from the dock to its final destination. The final cost factor arises from the fact that business firms in Hawaii generally have to maintain considerably larger inventories of stocks than would be the case if they were close to their sources of supply and had frequent train and truck service. I do not know how much these latter two cost factors add to the price of merchandise sold in Hawaii, but it is certainly not inconsequential.

To summarize the cost-of-living issue: First, there is no way to develop a numerical measure of the difference between the cost of living *generally* for people living in Hawaii and people *generally* in any other place. The BLS and the OPM know this, and their measures are confined to clearly identified groups in Hawaii and in the comparison areas. Second, the BLS and the OPM both have overstated the Hawaii differential in living costs for the groups identified by using mainland patterns of consumption as the basis for the market baskets that they have priced both in Hawaii and in the comparison areas. Such a procedure always overstates the differential, but no one knows by how much. Third, nonetheless all evidence indicates that the cost of living for most people in Hawaii is probably a good bit higher than it is for most people in most parts of the country, although the difference between Hawaii and some of the high-cost cities on the mainland is probably not very great. Finally, the primary reasons for Hawaii's high cost of living are high housing costs, high taxes, and the vast distance from the source of so many of the items that people in Hawaii consume. The magnitude and relative importance of these three prime causal factors are not known.

Can the Hawaiian Economy Ever Become Largely Diversified?

The object of economic diversification is to develop new export or import-replacement industries, not merely to attract new specialty retail shops or other enterprises oriented strictly to the local market. This means that in considering areas of possible diversification one can drop more than half the industrial classifications contained in the federal *Standard Industrial Classification Manual*[30]—including construction; transportation, communications, gas, and sanitary services; wholesale and retail trade; finance, insurance, and real estate; all services except those that can be exported; and government functions, except federal defense and other activities that might be located in Hawaii.

This leaves as theoretically conceivable areas for diversification the following: agriculture, forestry, fishing, mining, manufacturing, electric energy services, exportable services, and federal government programs. To answer the question of whether Hawaii can ever become largely diversified, it is necessary to look at each of these areas and determine what Hawaii's comparative advantages are. In one way or another, I have done much of this examination in earlier parts of this book and will touch on most of it lightly here.

FURTHER DIVERSIFICATION OF AGRICULTURE

Diversification of agriculture breaks down into production for export and production for replacing imports. Both activities have already been explored rather thoroughly, with the conclusion that Hawaii is unlikely in the future to produce more of its own food and feed. Chances are good, however, that exports of diversified agricultural products will continue to increase, macadamia nuts, flowers and foliage, and papayas being the big items, but also with future possibilities for such items as cacao, new varieties of coffee, oil from the Chinese tallow tree, and whatever else agricultural scientists may be able to develop.

FORESTRY AND LUMBER PRODUCTS

Although able to harvest a few trees each year, Hawaii lacks stands of timber that could serve as the basis for any significant industry. Besides, it must retain watershed areas, where most of the forests are located, in vegetation cover to retain rain water.

FISHING

I have not discussed commercial fishing because Hawaii has little of it— and less today than it used to have. The ocean surrounding the islands is deep and hence (except for the reef areas) has only pelagic fish, of which tuna is the main commercial variety in this part of the ocean. Most fishing industries are based on large populations of fish in the relatively shallow waters over a continental shelf, or on the return of deep-sea fish to where they were spawned, as with salmon. Lacking a continental shelf and homing fish, any Hawaii fishing industry has to be based either on deep-sea fish (primarily tuna) or on fish farming.

The local tuna industry did moderately well for several decades, with its main packing plant (Hawaiian Tuna Packers) in Honolulu and a smaller one with a shorter life span on Kauai. These packing plants have gone the way of all but one small tuna packer on the mainland—put out of business by foreign competition. Japan, Taiwan, South Korea, and, most importantly in recent years, Thailand have taken over the tuna-packing business from the continental United States and Hawaii. Some American packers still operate in Puerto Rico and American Samoa, where cheap labor makes the operation sustainable.

Since Hawaii's reef fish are in such short supply that they cannot meet even the local demand, the only possibility for a Hawaiian export fish industry is in aquaculture. I have discussed this potential already, concluding that not much can be expected in traditional aquaculture that uses surface water, but that an aquaculture based on using nutrient-rich water from the ocean depths may develop into a significant industry in the future.

MINING

Since Hawaii almost totally lacks mineral deposits, mining is not an area of possible diversification. Some years ago it was thought that local bauxite deposits might be exploitable, but that was not the case. The only conceivable area for development would be the deep-sea mining of mineral nodules, which contain manganese, cobalt, copper, etc. This possibility has been under intensive study and development for many years. Perhaps, when land-based minerals approach exhaustion, expensive, deep-sea mining will come of age. Present thinking is that Hawaii would certainly play a role in such a development, but possibly only as a support base for mining ships rather than as a processing site for the recovered ore. In any event, this possible development seems to be rather far down the road.

MANUFACTURING

In earlier chapters I concluded that the possibility of Hawaii's developing anything of consequence in the manufacturing field beyond what has already been done looks rather slim. What seems most likely is some expansion of assembly work in some scientific fields, based both on local scientific work and on the desire of the processors to locate their plants in the islands. Something special has to be going for a manufacturer to locate in Hawaii. We probably have done about as much in replacing imported manufactured goods with locally produced manufactured goods as we can at the present stage of technology. Undoubtedly more import-replacement manufacturing will be developed in the future, but at present Hawaii certainly does not need any more oil refineries, cement plants, or steel mills.

ELECTRIC SERVICES

As discussed earlier, Hawaii's extensive work in finding alternative energy sources has included the development of geothermal energy on the Big Island. Current plans call for the generation of about 1,000 megawatts of geothermal power on the Big Island and transporting it to Oahu by cable. If this large project can be brought to fruition, a new industry of significant size would come into being and Hawaii's balance of payments with the rest of the world would be improved by a major reduction in oil imports.

EXPORTABLE SERVICES

Services can be exported in two ways. The first is to go abroad, provide a service to whoever wants it in his homeland, and then return to Hawaii with the proceeds of sale. The second is to have the person who wants the service come to Hawaii and have it provided locally. International consulting service is a prime example of the first. Tourism and sales to the military are prime examples of the second. Some see the possibility of Hawaiian firms processing paperwork for East Coast banks, insurance companies, and legal firms during Hawaii's daylight hours (their night), a service made feasible by the speed and low cost of data transmittal by telecommunications. I have my doubts.

Hawaii's activities in the international consulting field have already been discussed. Despite the hopes (and perhaps dreams) of some analysts who expected this activity to become a mainstay of the Hawaiian economy, this has not happened, nor does it give any promise of ever happening. We will probably continue to do some international consulting in the fields of sugar production and milling, in aquaculture, and in diversified tropical agriculture; and undoubtedly other consulting activities will emerge from time to time. But it is difficult to see how these activities will ever become a significant part of the Hawaiian economy.

Aside from tourism and sales to the military, the major exportable services that Hawaii residents can sell locally to overseas-based organizations currently are, and probably in the future will continue to be, in the educational and scientific fields. Space-related and ocean-related scientific activities have already brought large amounts of overseas money into Hawaii, and these fields give every promise of growing. As noted earlier, we already have four Japanese institutions of higher learning. The most likely addition to scientific facilities in the near future is a rocket site on the Big Island for the launching of small payloads into either equatorial or polar orbit. But while these types of activities add a new and exciting dimension to the economy, it seems improbable that they will come close to achieving the economic importance that sugar and pineapple used to have and that tourism and the military have today.

FEDERAL GOVERNMENT PROGRAMS

The main federal government programs outside the Washington, D.C., area that create income in other regions of the country are the purchase of supplies, mainly items of defense; the purchase of services, mainly of a research nature; regional headquarters for federal civil administration; and military bases.

The first category is obviously not relevant to Hawaii's economic future. Hawaii is not and never will be a significant manufacturer of the civilian or military supplies the federal government purchases. In the second category Hawaii has done modestly well and undoubtedly will continue to do so. The NASA telescope on Mauna Kea, the Air Force electrophysics research on Haleakala, and the Navy Pacific Missile Range Facility on Kauai are good examples. The University of Hawaii has a policy of not accepting classified research contracts from the government, but individual faculty members may, as private consultants, accept such work and some have done so. There has also been considerable federal funding of research work in astronomy, ocean and geophysical sciences, biomedical sciences, and tropical agriculture. The total expenditures of all this is modest compared with what the federal government spends in some states but a great deal more than in many others.

Historically, Hawaii has been the regional headquarters in the Pacific for the administration of some federal nondefense programs and can expect to continue that role, but this is not a likely growth area. Providing sites for military bases, however, now constitutes the second major component of the Hawaiian economy and will undoubtedly continue to do so. The most likely possibility of any major expansion of the military in Hawaii (short of a drastic deterioration of international relations in the Pacific) would be for some of our allies in forward areas, such as Japan, South Korea, or the Philippines, to decide that they did not want U.S. military personnel stationed on their soil—in which case some military strength might be pulled back to Hawaii.

From this analysis, I must conclude that the chances of the Hawaiian economy ever becoming largely diversified are nil. Nevertheless, by virtue of its numerous agricultural industries, diversified tourism, defense establishments, and the many minor sectors of the economy that have developed in the post–World War II years, such as ocean-related and space-related activities, Hawaii's economy is already moderately well diversified—certainly more so than the economies of such states as Nebraska and South Dakota, which are still almost exclusively dependent on agriculture, or Rhode Island, Connecticut, and New Hampshire, which are heavily dependent on manufacturing. And compared with seventy-five years ago, when Hawaii had little economic activity other than sugar and pineapple, the Hawaiian economy is not narrowly concentrated.

What is Hawaii's Economic Role in the Pacific Basin?

Aside from serving as the most important vacation area in the entire Pacific and also as headquarters for all U.S. military activity in this half of the world, Hawaii's economic role in the Pacific has been rather modest. Nonetheless, there has been a long search for the major role that many people have thought Hawaii is destined to have in the great and developing area of the Pacific Basin.

The first economic role Hawaii played in the world economy was supplying China with sandalwood. That trade, minor for China but major for Hawaii, lasted during the first four decades of the nineteenth century until the sandalwood forests had been destroyed.

The second role, that of refitting the Pacific whaling fleet and providing rest and recreation for the crews, lasted for a half century, from around 1820, when the Atlantic fleet began moving into the Pacific for the hunt, until about 1870, when the discovery of petroleum in America drastically reduced the importance of whale oil. The whaling trade was an "invisible" export—selling goods and services in Hawaii to foreigners for money that originated overseas.

The third role, that of serving as the legendary crossroads of the Pacific, started when ships in large numbers began crisscrossing the northern Pacific in the last half of the nineteenth century. This role lasted until World War II, when all civilian traffic in the Pacific was stopped and after which the big, long-distance airplane put passenger ships out of business and containerization of surface freight cargo put freighters on a direct-haul, quick-turnaround basis.

Before that war Hawaii was not only the crossroads of the Pacific for ships but also for airplanes, cables, and radio. The early transpacific airplanes flying west from San Francisco made Hawaii their first stop on the way out and their last stop on the way back. All the telegraph cables laid west from North America came to Hawaii and then went on to their final destinations. In the early days of radio communications, the lack of long-distance transmitting power also made Hawaii the crossroads for Pacific wireless communications. But now many large jets overfly Hawaii, and voices and data are usually beamed to the Pacific via the satellite that looks down on Hawaii from its position 22,300 miles up in space. Technology has largely eliminated the roads that used to cross in Hawaii.

A fourth pre–World War II activity that was oriented to the Pacific basin and had some economic spin-off for Hawaii was an international movement that spawned two organizations of some importance, the Pan-Pacific Union and the Institute of Pacific Relations. The economic spin-off for Hawaii came from the fact that these two organizations brought many people to Hawaii for conferences and meetings and thereby contributed to the growth of tourism in the islands. In fact, the Pan-Pacific Union was essentially an outgrowth of the tourist-promotion activities of its founder, Alexander Hume Ford. Ford had been active with the original Hawaii Promotional Committee in the early years of the twentieth century. In 1907 he tried to persuade the Australian government to join with Hawaii in forming a Pan-Pacific Tourist and Information Bureau. He was also instrumental in organizing the Outrigger

Canoe Club in 1908 to revive the sport of surfing, and in 1911 he formed an international organization called Hands-Around-The-Pacific Club, which in 1917 adopted the name Pan-Pacific Union.[31]

The Pan-Pacific Union published a major quarterly journal and during the 1920s organized ten international conferences that met in Hawaii. The first, in 1920, was the Pan-Pacific Science Conference, and the last, in 1929, was the Pan-Pacific Surgical Conference. Other major conferences were on education (three), on women (two), and on food, commerce, and the press.[32] The Pan-Pacific Union died in the 1930s partly as a result of the Depression, which reduced support for its program of international conferences, and also as a result of Japan's expansionist activities, which made the work of a cooperative international organization in the Pacific impossible.

The founder of the Institute of Pacific Relations was Frank C. Atherton, president of Castle & Cooke. Atherton's father was a founder of the Honolulu Young Men's Christian Association in 1869, and Frank followed in his father's footsteps by organizing YMCAs on the neighbor islands and by helping to form the racially integrated Nuuanu YMCA in Honolulu. In 1916 he became a member of the national YMCA committee responsible for handling the organization's international activities. The YMCA planned a Pacific basin leadership conference and put Atherton in charge of organizing it. Out of it in 1925 came the formation of the Institute of Pacific Relations. The IPR, with its secretariat in Honolulu, had participation from Australia, Canada, China, Hawaii, Japan, Korea, New Zealand, the Philippines, and the United States. Ray Lyman Wilbur, president of Stanford University, was chairman; Atherton was vice-chairman.[33]

The IPR's initial mission was to improve international relations in the Pacific through forums directed to promoting better understanding among Pacific nations. But within a few years, against Atherton's wishes, it changed its focus to become a research and publications-oriented organization. Its research office was moved to the mainland in 1930 and for the next quarter of a century it was a major publisher of studies of conditions in the Pacific, issuing some 1,500 titles by 1952—many by outstanding scholars of the time.[34] It also published the quarterly journal *Pacific Affairs*.

In 1936 the secretariat was moved to New York and after that the Hawaii people who had been active in the IPR "seemed to forget their once soaring vision of the role the Islands might play in Pacific and world affairs. Virtually all talk of Hawaii's special destiny as a model and a leader ceased after the mid-1930s and was never again revived."[35] Perhaps the blunt language used by Edwin C. Carter, general secretary of the IPR, when he moved the secretariat to New York had something to do with this. He charged that Hawaii, "far from being an inspirational social model as the local internationalists believed, was much too provincial to play host to such an organization."[36] In Carter's words, "Honolulu has no culture; no facilities for world news; and is so tropical that no one can think of doing serious work."[37]

The IPR ran into serious trouble just before the war by being charged with pro-Japanese leanings, and it became a major target of the McCarthyites after the war for its alleged and unsubstantiated pro-Communist sympathies. It was dissolved in 1961.

After World War II Hawaii was too busy for at least a decade with its own internal economic problems to give thought to its role in the Pacific, but by the late 1950s this had changed. The first postwar move to establish Hawaii's role in the Pacific was instituted by, of all people, a Texan. Lyndon B. Johnson, then majority leader in the U.S. Senate, in 1959 proposed that the federal government establish an international university in Hawaii "as a meeting place for the intellectuals of the East and the West [because] for too many years we have neglected the simple things that would break down barriers between ourselves and people who should be our friends."[38] No one will ever know whether Johnson had in mind repaying Texas's debt to the 442d Regimental Combat Team from Hawaii for rescuing the Texan "Lost Battalion" in southern France in October 1944. In any case, with enthusiastic support from his friend Jack Burns, Hawaii's future governor, and from the local community in Hawaii, the Center for Technical and Cultural Interchange Between East and West (commonly called the East–West Center) was established in 1960 on the campus of the University of Hawaii. Since then many thousands of scholars and students have been in residence and hundreds of millions of dollars have been spent by the Congress on its support. It has undoubtedly benefited Hawaii in unmeasurable ways because so many of the business, government, and cultural leaders of the nations in the Pacific Basin have attended the center.

The second postwar effort to establish a role for Hawaii in the Pacific, strictly economic, was pushed by William Quinn, Hawaii's last territorial and first state governor. Quinn's idea was that with millions of tons of cargo worth billions of dollars passing by Hawaii, each ship headed for various destinations around the Pacific rim, why not have them all come to Hawaii, unload their cargoes, and then fill each ship with cargo that was headed for a given destination? Each ship would leave its home port in Asia or America laden with cargo headed for many destinations to be off-loaded at Hawaii. In Hawaii it would pick up a load of cargo all destined for its home port. According to a study of this subject by the Bureau of Business Research of the University of Hawaii, "The premise of the plan is that the cost of cargo movement across the Pacific can be reduced by grouping large lots of freight in Hawaii according to the port of destination on the Mainland, in South America, or in the Far East."[39] Benefits to Hawaii would be immense, according to Quinn, who said that "in time, if fortune smiles upon us, Hawaii will be the entrepot of the Pacific and the commercial center of the Pacific world."[40] He was never able to get the many shipping lines operating in the Pacific to accept this idea, in part because the great circle route across the northern Pacific misses Hawaii by several hundred miles and in part because it would have upset the system of conference ocean shipping rates that had been worked out over a long period of time. The proposal died a quiet death after Quinn was defeated for reelection.

In 1969 Governor Burns launched a major project, funded by the legislature, to set goals for Hawaii to achieve in the next thirty years—by the year 2000. Numerous study groups ("task forces") were appointed, and their reports constituted the subject of a Governor's Conference on the Year 2000 held in 1970. The economics task force on "Hawaii and the Pacific Community" concluded that "Hawaii's transition from a goods to a service economy will be virtually complete in 2000. . . .

> A major factor in this evolution to a service economy undoubtedly will be a decision by the major agribusiness firms to make domestic agricultural production, especially sugar and pineapple, ancillary to their international operations. This will leave only a few enterprises producing goods. . . . Even our primary industries, limited to marine exploitation and diversified agriculture by 2000, would still be heavily committed to service in the form of research and development. . . . For Hawaii's service economy to prosper, it will need to expand its markets—and expansion will take place mainly in the Pacific basin because the people are there. . . . Hawaii's future commerce, therefore, will be almost exclusively in exporting skills and know-how to Pacific and world markets.[41]

This 1970 vision of a Hawaiian economy based by the year 2000 almost exclusively on the export of skills and know-how to countries in the Pacific basin shows how attractive, and yet how elusive, is the dream that it is Hawaii's economic destiny to be, somehow, the hub of the great Pacific wheel.

The next major economic role envisaged for Hawaii emerged in the mid-1970s, during the administration of Governor Ariyoshi, when David Heenan, dean of the College of Business Administration at the University of Hawaii, persuaded the legislature to appropriate funds to be used to induce multinational corporations doing business in the Pacific to establish their regional headquarters in Hawaii. At that time about half a dozen multinational corporations had Pacific regional headquarters in Hawaii. Through the work of a "Governor's Committee for Hawaii as a Regional Center for the Pacific," which had a staff of two traveling sales representatives, that number was expanded to around twenty by the late 1970s. One of the biggest fish netted was the International Telephone and Telegraph Company—which shortly after getting established in Hawaii changed its mind and centralized all operations in New York.

After this effort had been left unfunded for several years, in 1988 the legislature appropriated $550,000 for it and a number of other promotional programs to be operated as joint projects by the state government and the Chamber of Commerce of Hawaii. Results of this second effort are not in yet.

These efforts at finding *the* great economic role for Hawaii to play in the Pacific have been more frustrating than productive. The frustration stems from the fact that it seems so obvious that Hawaii should be a major player. Over the last two millennia the economic center of the world has shifted westward from the eastern Mediterranean to the central Mediterranean, then to the Atlantic coast of Europe, then to the Atlantic coast of America, and now to the Pacific, where Japan has become America's chief trading partner after Canada, where the "four tigers" (South Korea, Hong Kong, Taiwan, and Singapore) are on the prowl, and where most of the other Asian economies are moving ahead faster than the rest of the world. Hawaii, with more than half of its population of Asian ancestry, seems ideally located in the middle of all this action.

Governor Jack Burns enunciated the perception of Hawaii that comes from this happy set of circumstances more vividly than any other spokesman, as the following selection of his comments illustrates.[42] Hawaii is "the hub of the great wheel of the Pacific." Island people are "the greatest ambassadors on the face of the earth." People from the islands will spearhead "a dramatic upsurge in Pacific trade . . . commerce . . . understanding . . . trust . . . [and] good intent." "It is increasingly clear that Hawaii's economic prosperity is increasingly tied to commerce in the Pacific." "We in Hawaii are in the Center of the Sea, in the quiet vastness of the awesome Pacific, geographically unique."

> We in Hawaii yearn for, and work for, the development of a spirit of community in the Pacific Basin. We seek to inspire and promote a Pacific Community of Nations, a spiritual unity of people of diverse ethnic origins. We see this as our special role and duty and destiny by reason of the precious gift of American freedom given to us, by reason of our unique geographical location, by reason of our total blending of the cultures of East and West in our interracial unity and harmony, by reason of our extraordinary prosperity and attractive physical and social environment, and by reason of our proven history of dedication to man's highest ideals.

While much of the above can be dismissed as political rhetoric, there is no doubt that Burns spoke for many hopeful people when he expressed a view of Hawaii's manifest destiny—that somehow, sometime, by some means, Hawaii's unique attributes of location and multiracial population will give it an important economic role to play in the Pacific. In response to such visions, skeptics point out that, Hawaii's location notwithstanding, modern technology has evolved most commerce, financial transactions, and communications between America and Asia to pass around or above Hawaii. They have no more reason to stop in Hawaii than their Atlantic counterparts would have reason to stop in Bermuda if it were located in the middle of the Atlantic halfway between America and Europe. As for Hawaii's multiracial population, they point to the observation of Derek Davies, editor of the *Far Eastern Economic Review,* who said that most of Hawaii's Asian Americans have become 100 percent American in viewpoint, have lost touch with their Oriental roots, see Asia as it used to be rather than as it is today, and have a mind-set more suited to Kansas City or Boston than to the Orient.[43]

While I tend to share these skeptical views of Hawaii's ever playing a major role in the Pacific other than for tourism and the military, Hawaii can expand its modest success in developing several economic activities of significance to the Pacific basin. The state has had a moderate amount of trade with other Pacific areas, but aside from refined petroleum products, practically all its exports have been reexports of items that originated on the mainland.[44] The Pacific regional headquarters of a number of major multinational corporations are located here. Some of our companies have expanded their activities to include many Pacific areas. We give, and sometimes sell, technical aid in many fields to the less developed nations in the Pacific. Hawaii's educational institutions attract large numbers of students from Pacific and Asian countries. Activities of this sort are to be encouraged and expanded wherever possible, but they should not be viewed as having the potential to challenge tourism or services to the U.S. defense agencies as a major base for the Hawaiian economy.

The conclusion of this discussion is that Hawaii's economic role in the Pacific basically is, and has been for a good many generations, primarily twofold. The first is to be the most attractive spot in the world for the people of the Pacific to visit for rejuvenation—not only vacationers seeking Hawaii's superb subtropical environment, but also athletes and sports enthusiasts who participate in the many sporting events held here and people attracted by Hawaii's cultural activities or by the many scientific and intellectual meetings that Hawaii hosts. Perhaps most importantly, Hawaii is a place for the youth of the Pacific basin to gain an education. This was essentially what Alexander Hume Ford had in mind when he formed the Hands-Around-The-Pacific Club in 1911.

Hawaii's second role is to serve as headquarters of the United States military in the half of the world that, stretching between the poles, encompasses the Pacific and Indian oceans. Major General John M. Schofield spent two months of 1873 reconnoitering the islands to evaluate Hawaii's military utility to the United States.[45] He reported to Secretary of War Belknap that Pearl Harbor was potentially the most important port in the entire northern Pacific, and from that time America's interest in Hawaii has been based primarily on the crucial role the islands play in the defense of the nation.

Hawaii's two great economic roles in the Pacific have thus been clearly identified for several generations. These two activities are so important that they have directly or indirectly created between a third and a half of Hawaii's total income each year over the past half century. We have over the years expanded our economic activities in the Pacific in many ways and will undoubtedly continue to do so. But the idea that there is some stellar economic role for Hawaii to play in the Pacific, other than in the fields of tourism and defense, is based more on hope than on reality.

Appendix: Comments

1. **It is possible to develop a statistical measure of the relative importance of Hawaii's major export industries.** This is done by using a methodology I developed in 1960 and which is explained in detail in a First Hawaiian Bank publication entitled *The Impact of Exports on Income in Hawaii.*

I can best explain this methodology by using the sugar industry as an example. In 1960 the sugar industry received gross revenues of approximately $144 million. About 40 percent of this amount was distributed *directly* to persons in Hawaii in the form of wages, salaries, and dividends. A little more than half of the remaining 60 percent was spent for goods and services produced in Hawaii—rents, telephone services, legal fees, local taxes, construction work, etc.—and much of this *indirectly* became income to residents of Hawaii. The remainder leaked out of Hawaii in the purchase of fertilizer, trucks, etc. Thus I found for the Hawaiian sugar industry that of the $144 million it received in 1960, it distributed 67 percent to persons in Hawaii, or a total of $96 million. The remaining 33 percent leaked out of Hawaii and created income to people in other parts of the world.

Local recipients of the $96 million created additional income when they spent it, and the recipients of this new income created still more income when they respent it in turn. At each stage of spending there is a leakage of a little over one-half (savings and leakages out of Hawaii), so that after four or five rounds the new money brought into Hawaii by the export of sugar has almost all leaked out of the state's economy. But before this happens, each dollar of export-generated income to residents of Hawaii has created, through the multiplier, another 72 cents for the residents of the state. This process is shown in Table A.1.

If one adds to the $96 million of personal income created directly and

Table A.1   The income multiplier for Hawaii

| | | | EXPENDITURE | | |
TRANSACTION	INCOME	FEDERAL INCOME TAXES AND SAVINGS	TOTAL	INCOME REMAINING IN HAWAII	VALUE OF IMPORTS
1st round	1.00	.16	.84	.42	.42
2nd round	.42	.067	.353	.176	.176
3rd round	.176	.028	.148	.074	.074
Etc.	.	.	.	.	.
	.	.	.	.	.
	.	.	.	.	.
Etc.	.	.	.	.	.
Total	1.724	.276	1.448	.724	.724

indirectly by sugar another 72 percent for the new income created through the multiplier effect, one arrives at a figure of $165 million. Thus, if the sugar industry brings into Hawaii $144 million from the sale of its products overseas, that will create about $165 million of personal income in Hawaii.

The percentage of pineapple revenues that results in personal income in Hawaii directly and indirectly is much lower than sugar's 67 percent because—at least until recently—most pineapple had been canned and all the material for tin cans is imported, thereby creating an immense leakage that does not exist in sugar. For pineapple, the figure I found for personal income created directly and indirectly was 53 percent, compared with sugar's 67 percent. (This percentage would be higher for today's pineapple industry in Hawaii, which exports so much more fresh fruit than when the preceding estimation was made.)

A much larger percentage of defense-agency spending results in personal income to Hawaii residents because most of it is in the form of wages and salaries. The figure I found was 79 percent.

The figure for visitor expenditures was low, 54 percent, because outside of expenditures for hotel rooms and such things as tips, many of the things tourists spend their money on are imported from overseas.

Using these ratios for years other than 1960 (as I have done in Chapters 4 and 5) reduces the accuracy of the measurement because industry patterns of expenditure change over time; but I think the measure is still fairly reliable for other years, and in any case it is the only measure available. I should note that for the visitor industry in 1988 (shown in Figure 5.2) I dropped the percentage figure for direct and indirect impacts from 54 to 49. The reason for this arbitrary adjustment is that expenditures by Japanese visitors for imported luxury items, such as Scotch liquors, exquisite luggage, and superior leather goods, had increased dramatically and thereby created larger leakages than before.

2. Growth rate figures for Hawaii's economy are only approxima-tions. In describing the four postwar economic periods, I have rounded the percentage growth rate figures for each of the periods and called them approximate. I have done so for several reasons.

First, although economic data are now vastly superior to what they were before World War II and much better than several decades ago, they are still far from perfect. This is admitted by the data compilers, who first report a "preliminary" figure or two before releasing a "final" figure. And over the months and years the "final" figure may be revised many times. In 1988, for example, I received from the U.S. Commerce Department a revision of state personal income data that contained sizable corrections going all the way back to 1929 nearly sixty years ear-lier! So when I use current data to calculate a growth rate of, say, 3.1 percent for some previous period, I do not think there is any basis for being more precise than to conclude that the growth rate was probably about 3 percent.

Second, there is no ideal single data series for measuring the growth of the Hawaiian economy back to the end of World War II. The gross state product series, the best to use, goes back only to 1958.[1] The total personal income series goes back all the way to 1939, however, so that it is available for the period 1939–57. What I have done for the 1939–57 period is to use total personal-income figures, as developed for Hawaii by the U.S. Commerce Department, and put these figures on a constant dollar basis by using the Honolulu consumer-price index as a deflator. This is a reasonable procedure, because nearly 85 percent of Hawaii's gross state product consists of personal income and because the CPI is a fair measure of the changing value of personal income. But these figures at best are only good approximations.

Finally, any clever person can make figures lie, just as people who are not so clever can inadvertently lie with figures by misusing data. For example, I can produce quite different growth rates for the immediate postwar period by using 1946 as the starting date instead of 1945, or by using 1950 as the ending date instead of 1949. The same goes for all the other periods I have identified. This is a third good reason why I label the growth rates for these periods as being "approximate."

3. The dollar volume of miscellaneous exports is difficult to calculate. It is so for both conceptual and statistical reasons. One of the conceptual problems is that the Hawaii Visitors Bureau counts (properly, I think) all people from overseas who come to Hawaii as "visitors" (a term that most people assume to be synonymous with "tourists"), even though some come here for reasons unrelated to recreation. Should people who come to Hawaii to make movies, to look at the planetary system through immense telescopes, or to run in the Honolulu Marathon be counted as visitors and the money they spend counted as visitor expenditures, or should these areas of activity be considered separate export activities and included in the "all other" classification? For the purpose of Figure 5.2, which shows changes in the industrial composition of the economy, I have considered them as new export activities and put them in the "other" category.

Another conceptual problem arises in connection with the petroleum refining industry. If one of Hawaii's refineries sells aviation fuel to an overseas-based airline that refuels in Honolulu, how should the sale be classified? Insofar as the travelers on the airplane are visitors to Hawaii (as most of them tend to be), the sale should be credited to the visitor industry. But insofar as the travelers are local residents, the sale is conceptually a part of the internal economy, like selling them gasoline for their cars. And insofar as the travelers are in-transit passengers headed for some destination other than Hawaii, it is as truly an export sale as would be a sale to an airline flying between Singapore and Hong Kong.

Even if I had the time and patience to sort out all these issues, it would not be possible statistically for several reasons, the chief being that sales by Hawaii's two refineries (to airlines or to anybody else) are confidential. For industries with many producing units, total industry sales are public information; but when there are only two companies in an industry, no information can be published because it would disclose the accounts of each company to the other.

Another statistical problem comes from trying to separate total sales of an industry (such as flowers and foliage, or papayas) into local sales and export sales. This breakdown is seldom reported and consequently some guessing is involved in making the separation.

Despite all these problems and the consequent qualifications about accuracy, I have tried to identify gross revenues from export sales of all the industries in the "other" category for 1939, 1949, and 1988 and then converted the gross revenue figure into a personal-income figure, using the methodology explained in the first section of this appendix.

4. A convenient way to analyze the causes of economic growth in an area is to think of them as being the product of the total amount of labor input and the productivity of that labor. An economy "grows" when its total output of goods and services increases. Basically, there are only two ways for an economy to grow. One is to have more people working (or working longer hours). This leads to an increase in "labor input." The other way is for the productivity of the work force to increase, so that on the average each worker produces more per hour than he or she did before. This leads to an increase in "labor productivity," or output per unit of labor input.

Growth of the economy is therefore the product of increases in labor input *and* in labor productivity. A 1 percent increase in labor input (from 1.00 to 1.01) and a 2 percent increase in labor productivity (from 1.00 to 1.02) will result in slightly better than a 3 percent increase in the output of the economy ($1.01 \times 1.02 = 1.0302$). When the percentage increases are small, the difference between multiplying and adding the two numbers is inconsequential.

Increasing labor input is a readily understandable concept, but increasing labor productivity is not. Numerous studies have been made of how labor-productivity increases come about.[2] Without getting into technical analysis, it can be said that many factors are usually responsible—simply working harder and more diligently being only one. Major factors are more and better tools and machines, the substitution of mechanical power for human and animal power, a better-educated work force that can work more intelligently and efficiently, better management skills that organize the work process more effectively, advancement of knowledge that leads to the development of more productive methods and materials, the substitution of large-scale for small-scale production, and shifting production from low- to high-productivity industries. These and other factors undoubtedly play different roles in each gain in productivity.

At times some industries register remarkable increases in productivity with the introduction of new machines or new technologies, while other industries and occupations show little or no increase—particularly the service industries. For example, barbers still take about as much time to cut a person's hair as they did fifty years ago, and hotel chambermaids still clean about the same number of rooms per day as their predecessors did. On the other hand, in a few service industries, such as telecommunications and air transportation, where better machines and equipment have been developed, productivity increases have been great.

As an example of how the two growth factors work, consider the expansion of the American economy in the first couple of decades after World War II. From 1948 to 1973 employment increased at an average annual rate of 1.5 percent and the gross national product (i.e., the total output of goods and services) in constant dollars increased at an average annual rate of 3.8 percent—implying that the average increase in labor productivity of the entire economy was about 2.3 percent per year (3.8 minus 1.5 equals 2.3). This is a rough and ready measure, but according to Edward Denison's comprehensive studies of productivity changes in the American economy, during that period the increase in productivity per employee was about 2.45 percent per year on the average.[3] This leads me to the conclusion that a good norm for productivity growth over the long run is around 2 to 2.5 percent per year. With the labor force increasing at about 1.5 percent per year, this pegs the growth of the economy at somewhere between 3 and 4 percent annually when the economy is achieving good growth. Anything above that rate would mean that employment would be increasing abnormally fast or productivity increasing abnormally fast, or both.

What happened in Hawaii during the great boom from 1958 to 1973 was that employment increased at the exceptionally fast rate of 4.2 percent per year owing to a large amount of in-migration and a rapid increase in female labor force participation rates.[4] With constant-dollar gross state product increasing at about 6.8 percent per year, the productivity of the labor force apparently rose at the "normal" rate of about 2.5 percent per year.[5]

5. The growth in productivity of the U.S. economy as measured by output per unit of labor input began to slow dramatically in the early 1970s, for numerous reasons. Edward Denison of the Brookings Institution, a foremost expert in the field, in 1985 published a study that analyzed this slowdown in productivity growth. He estimated that for the national economy, productivity per hour worked dropped by 1.92 percent between the periods 1948–73 and 1973–82.[6] This drop is almost identical to the two percentage point fall suggested by my rough calculation in Chapter 5.

Denison attributes about 40 percent of the drop to the following group of causal factors, which he calls "measurable determinants" because he believes that he can measure statistically how much each factor contributed to the total decline in productivity: a slightly less productive labor force because of the large numbers of young people and women who entered it during the period; an increase in government employment, which is generally less productive than work in the private sector; the diversion of a substantial volume of productive resources to pollution control; the diversion of a considerable volume of productive resources to improved health and safety programs on the job; and increases in the costs of dishonesty and crime in the workplace.

The other 60 percent of the drop in growth in labor productivity he assigns to a slowdown in the "advance of knowledge" and to a group of miscellaneous, unmeasurable determinants. The knowledge he refers to is knowledge of how to produce at constantly lowered costs, that is, more efficiently. This includes technical and organizational knowledge. It therefore encompasses many fields such as basic research, applied research, and industrial psychology. Denison identifies advances in knowledge as the major factor in the rapid growth of productivity in the 1948–73 period.

The miscellaneous unmeasurable determinants are such things as misallocation of labor because of poor job placement arising from governmental restrictions on the use of tests for job placement purposes and governmental requirements to employ minority groups; misallocation of capital because of efforts to minimize corporate and individual income taxes; increased barriers to international trade, which channel resources into high-cost and less productive uses; increases in energy prices; and more governmental requirements for data and information and for compliance with regulations, all of which use productive resources for purposes that do not increase the output of the nation.

Denison's conclusion is obvious: there has been no single major cause of the slowdown in productivity in the national economy since 1973, but rather a whole host of minor causes. "Nearly all measurable determinants contributed to the lowering of the growth rate of output per person employed," he states, and there were "small to moderate adverse changes in many of the unmeasurable output determinants."[7]

A more recent study of the causes of the slow growth in labor productivity in the United States in the 1970s and 1980s was made by three professors at the Massachusetts Institute of Technology.[8] This analysis considers numerous factors involved in the slowdown, including the new one of corporations' excessive concern with short-term profits. The concern, arising from the threat of hostile takeover, stimulates the taking of profits at the expense of investments that might not pay off for several years but would have raised productivity. The authors conclude that unless many things are done to reverse this trend, the nation will become progressively more impoverished in relative terms.

Notes

Chapter 1

1. Douglas L. Oliver, *The Pacific Islands* (3d ed., Honolulu: University of Hawaii Press, 1989), 17.

2. Cecilia Kapua Lindo and Nancy Alpert Mower, *Polynesian Seafaring Heritage* (Honolulu: Kamehameha Schools Press, 1980), 19.

3. This section draws upon information in Kamehameha Schools, Hawaiian Studies Institute, *The Ahupua'a* (Honolulu: Kamehameha Schools Press, 1982), 20–26.

4. Peter Buck, *Vikings of the Sunrise* (New York: Stokes, 1938), 313–316.

5. Tommy Holmes, *The Hawaiian Canoe* (Hanalei, Hawaii: Editions Limited, 1981), 8–9.

6. Ibid., 9–10.

7. Herb Kane, *Voyage* (Honolulu: Island Heritage, 1976), 103.

8. C[harles] S. Stewart, *Journal of a Residence in the Sandwich Islands during the Years 1823–25* (Honolulu: University of Hawaii Press, 1970), 139–140.

9. Theodore Morgan, *Hawaii: A Century of Economic Change, 1778–1876* (Cambridge, Mass: Harvard University Press, 1948), 17.

10. E. S. Craighill Handy and Elizabeth Green Handy, *Native Planters in Old Hawaii* (Honolulu: Bishop Museum Press, 1972), 287–288.

11. David Malo, *Hawaiian Antiquities* (Honolulu: Bishop Museum Press, 1957), 60.

12. Handy and Handy, 74.

13. Holmes, 20, 27.

14. Ibid., 109.

15. Emma M. Beckley, *Hawaiian Fisheries and Methods of Fishing* (Honolulu: Advertiser Steam Press, 1883), 1–21. See also Samuel M. Kamakau, *The Works of the People of Old* (Honolulu: Bishop Museum Press, 1976), 59–81.

16. Catherine Summers, *Hawaiian Fishponds* (Honolulu: Bishop Museum Press, 1964).

17. Samuel M. Kamakau, *The People of Old* (Honolulu: Bishop Museum Press, 1964), 3.

18. Peter H. Buck, "Polynesian Migration," chapter 2 in E. S. Craighill Handy et

al., *Ancient Hawaiian Civilization* (Rutland, Vt., and Tokyo: Charles E. Tuttle, 1965), 33.

19. Lindo and Mower, 21.

20. Ben R. Finney, *Polynesian Peasants and Proletarians* (Cambridge, Mass.: Schenkman Publishing Co., 1973), 13–14.

21. Patrick Vinton Kirch, *Feathered Gods and Fishhooks* (Honolulu: University of Hawaii Press, 1985), 66.

22. Irving Goldman, *Ancient Polynesian Society* (Chicago: University of Chicago Press, 1970), 211.

23. George Hu'eu Sanford Kanahele, *Ku Kanaka: Stand Tall* (Honolulu: University of Hawaii Press, 1986), 352.

24. Oliver, 567.

25. For a range of population estimates, see Edward Joesting, *Hawaii: An Uncommon History* (New York: W. W. Norton, 1972), 18; Handy and Handy, 326; Ralph S. Kuykendall, *The Hawaiian Kingdom*, 3 vols. (Honolulu: University of Hawaii Press, 1938–67), 1:270; Morgan 25.

26. Serano Bishop, *Reminiscences of Old Hawaii* (Honolulu: Hawaiian Gazette Co., 1916), 14.

27. Kuykendall, 1:270.

28. Edward D. Beechert, *Working in Hawaii* (Honolulu: University of Hawaii Press, 1985), 10.

29. Felix M. Keesing, *Modern Samoa* (London: George Allen & Unwin, 1934), 291.

30. Charles E. Snow, *Early Hawaiians* (Lexington, Ky.: University Press of Kentucky, 1974).

Chapter 2

1. Archibald Campbell, *A Voyage round the World from 1806 to 1812* (Honolulu: University of Hawaii Press, 1967), 118.

2. Abraham Fornander, *An Account of the Polynesian Race*, 3 vols. (Rutland, Vt., and Tokyo: Charles E. Tuttle, 1969), 1:113.

3. Helen Gay Pratt, *In Hawaii a Hundred Years* (New York: Scribner's Sons, 1939), 92, 94.

4. Ibid., 92.

5. Ross H. Gast, *Don Francisco de Paula Marin* (Honolulu: University of Hawaii Press, 1973), 50.

6. Robert L. Cushing, "The Beginnings of Sugar Production in Hawaii," *Hawaiian Journal of History* 19 (1985), 30.

7. Kuykendall, 1:176.

8. Ibid.

9. Ibid., 153.

10. Sumner J. La Croix and James Roumasset, "The Evolution of Private Property in Nineteenth-Century Hawaii," *Journal of Economic History* 50, no. 4 (1990): 829–852.

11. Kuykendall, 1:133–136.

12. Ibid., 154.

13. Ibid., quoting Richard's letter of 8 November 1836 to Chapman.

14. Ibid., 154.

15. Ruth Tabrah, *Hawaii: A History* (New York: W. W. Norton, 1984), 52–53.

16. Kuykendall, 1:168–169.

17. Ibid., 1:267–298; Morgan, 130–136.

18. Gavan Daws, *Shoal of Time: A History of the Hawaiian Islands* (New York: Macmillan Co., 1968), 126. See also Lilikala Dorton, "Land and the Promise of Capitalism: A Dilemma for the Hawaiian Chiefs of the 1848 Mahele," Ph.D. dissertation, University of Hawaii, 1986, for a critical analysis of how the land was divided.

19. John J. Chinen, *The Great Mahele* (Honolulu: University of Hawaii Press, 1958), 31.

20. Kuykendall, 1:294.

21. Thomas H. Creighton, *The Lands of Hawaii* (Honolulu: University of Hawaii Press, 1978), 48.

22. Joseph W. Ellison, *Opening and Penetration of Foreign Influence in Samoa to 1880* (Corvallis, Oreg.: Oregon State College, 1938), 7–8.

23. Kuykendall, 1:41.

24. Ibid., 77.

25. Ibid., 79.

26. Ibid., 56–59.

27. Robert H. Stauffer, "The Hawai'i–United States Treaty of 1826," *Hawaiian Journal of History* 17 (1983): 55–58.

28. Letter from J. C. Jones and John Meek to Captain W. B. Finch of the USS *Vincennes* in 1829, quoted by Kuykendall, 1:435.

29. Kuykendall, 1:165–167.

30. Ibid., 206–221.

31. Ibid., 392–397.

32. Robert C. Schmitt, *Historical Statistics of Hawaii* (Honolulu: University of Hawaii Press, 1977), 25.

33. Kuykendall, 1:331–332.

34. Ibid., 1:423.

35. Ibid., 2:45.

36. Ibid., 203–219.

37. Ibid., 254.

38. Ibid., 3:17–30.

39. Ibid., 27.

40. Morgan, 212.

41. Kuykendall, 1:85–86.

42. Morgan, 62.

43. Ibid., 67.

44. Quoted by Kuykendall, 1:89.

45. Pratt, 94.

46. Kuykendall, 1:434–436.

47. Ibid., 92.

48. Ibid.

49. Quoted by Kuykendall, 1:90.

50. Kuykendall, 1:309.

51. Morgan, 75–76.

52. Kuykendall, 1:93; Morgan, 77.

53. Joesting, *Hawaii: An Uncommon History*, 93.

54. Morgan, 76.

55. Kuykendall, 1:307.

56. Quoted by Kuykendall, 1:310.

57. Ibid., 307.

58. "Personal Recollections of Hawaii," quoted by Joesting, *Hawaii: An Uncommon History*, 93.

59. Cushing, "The Beginnings of Sugar Production in Hawaii," 17–34.

60. Kuykendall, 1:175.

61. Morgan, 175.

62. Kuykendall, 1:315.

63. Ibid., 2:141.

64. Ibid., 143.

65. Morgan, 164–168, 227–228.

66. Ibid., 161–164, 227–228.

67. Ibid., 59, 96–97, 227–228.

68. Ibid., 168–172, 227–228.

69. Ibid., 172, 227–228.

70. Ibid., 97.

71. Ibid., 159–160.

72. L. J. Crampon, "Hawaii's Visitor Industry," *Journal of Travel Research* 13, no. 2 (1974), 25.

73. Robert Crichton Wyllie, "On Capital and Banking," *Transactions of the Royal Hawaiian Agricultural Society* 1, no. 3 (1852), 41.

74. Kuykendall, 1:95.

75. Ibid., 176.

76. Ibid., 3:87.

77. Ibid., 90; also Jacob Adler, *Claus Spreckels: The Sugar King in Hawaii* (Honolulu: University of Hawaii Press, 1966), 131–147.

78. Arthur C. Alexander, *Koloa Plantation, 1835–1935: A History of the Oldest Hawaiian Sugar Plantation* (Honolulu: Honolulu Star-Bulletin, 1937), 4.

79. Ibid., 5.

80. Ibid., 19–20.

81. Ibid., 21.

82. Ibid., 10.

83. Ibid., 22.

84. Ibid., 6.

85. Schmitt, *Historical Statistics of Hawaii*, 7.

86. Dr. Noa Emmett Aluli, as quoted in the *Honolulu Star-Bulletin*, 17 February 1987, 85.

Chapter 3

1. U.S. Census Bureau, *Historical Statistics of the United States* (Washington, D.C.: U.S. Government Printing Office, 1975), 8; Schmitt, *Historical Statistics of Hawaii*, 9–10.

2. U.S. Commerce Department, *Income of Hawaii*, Supplement to *Survey of Current Business* (Washington, D.C.: U.S. Government Printing Office, 1953), 18.

3. Schmitt, *Historical Statistics of Hawaii*, 334–336.

4. U.S. Commerce Department, *Income of Hawaii*.

5. Schmitt, *Historical Statistics of Hawaii*, 335, 338, 412, 419.

6. Robert L. Cushing, "Energy Conversion—Sunlight to Sucrose," paper presented to the Social Science Association of Honolulu, 2 October 1972; U.S. Census Bureau, *Historical Statistics of the United States*, 1106.

7. Morgan, 180.

8. Hawaiian Sugar Planters' Association (HSPA), *The Story of Sugar in Hawaii* (Honolulu, 1926), 48.

9. John W. Vandercook, *King Cane* (New York and London: Harper and Brothers, 1939), 145–146.

10. Morgan, 177.

11. Kuykendall, 3:52.

12. Beechert, 24.

13. Morgan, 103.

14. Sanford L. Platt, "Immigration and Emigration in the Hawaiian Sugar Industry," paper presented to the Industrial Relations Section, Hawaiian Sugar Technologists, Honolulu, T.H., 15 November 1950. See this paper for a full record of the organized importation of labor into Hawaii.

15. 31 Stat. 143: 48 U.S.C. 504.

16. Platt, 11.

17. Ibid., 12–13.

18. Ibid., 12.

19. 48 Stat. 456: U.S.C. 1238.

20. Kuykendall, 1:328.

21. Beechert, 42.

22. U.S. Bureau of Labor, *Labor Conditions in Hawaii, 1902*, (Washington, D.C.: U.S. Government Printing Office), 13–15.

23. Beechert, 97.

24. Ibid.

25. Ibid., 48.

26. Ibid., 49.

27. Ibid., 97, quoting Bureau of Immigration, *Report 1886*, 39.

28. Ibid., 97.

29. Ibid., 98.

30. U.S. Bureau of Labor, *Labor Conditions in Hawaii, 1903*, 19–20.

31. Beechert, 19.

32. Ibid., 47, 48.

33. Ibid., 67.

34. Ibid., 87.

35. Ibid.

36. Ibid., 123.

37. Ibid.

38. U.S. Bureau of Labor, *Labor Conditions in Hawaii, 1903*, 36.

39. U.S. Bureau of Labor, *Labor Conditions in Hawaii, 1911*, 685.

40. Alexander, 38.

41. Schmitt, *Historical Statistics of Hawaii*, 359.

42. Ibid., 360.

43. Department of Planning and Economic Development (DPED), *State of Hawaii Data Book 1986* (Honolulu, 1986), 339, 590.

44. Ibid., 591; Schmitt, *Historical Statistics of Hawaii*, 360.

45. U.S. Commerce Department, *The Cane Sugar Industry*, Msc. series, no. 53 (Washington, D.C., 1917).

46. Letter to the HSPA from the U.S. Department of Agriculture dated 27 June 1967.

47. Morgan, 178.

48. Josephine Sullivan, *A History of C. Brewer & Company* (Boston: Walton Advertising & Printing Company, 1926), 105.

49. Vandercook, 128.

50. Morgan, 154.

51. Vandercook, 114.

52. Morgan, 182.

53. HSPA, *The Story of Sugar*, April 1929.

54. Ibid., 54–67.

55. Vandercook, 128–134.

56. Ibid., 124–142.

57. Arthur L. Dean, *Alexander & Baldwin, Ltd. and the Predecessor Partnerships* (Honolulu: Alexander & Baldwin, 1950), 13–19.

58. Vandercook, 69.

59. Kuykendall, 3:65.

60. Pratt, 272.

61. Ibid., 275.

62. Lee Meriwether, "A Plantation in Hawaii," *Harper's Weekly*, 10 November 1888, reprinted in Alexander & Baldwin's house organ, *Ampersand*, Fall 1988, 20–21.

63. U.S. Bureau of Labor Statistics, *Labor Conditions in Hawaii, 1939*, 19.

64. Vandercook, 29.

65. U.S. Bureau of Labor Statistics, *Labor Conditions in Hawaii, 1939*, 19.

66. Beechert, 281.

67. U.S. Bureau of Labor Statistics, *Labor Conditions in Hawaii, 1939*, 73.

68. Schmitt, *Historical Statistics of Hawaii*, 359–360; U.S. Census Bureau, *Historical Statistics of the United States*, 468.

69. U.S. Census Bureau, *Statistical Abstract of the United States, 1986*, 654.

70. U.S. Bureau of Labor Statistics, *Labor Conditions in Hawaii, 1939*, 74–78.

71. Kuykendall, 2:145.

72. Ibid., 147.

73. Edward Joesting, *Tides of Commerce* (Honolulu: First Hawaiian, Inc., 1983), 96–97.

74. Kuykendall, 2:146.

75. Vandercook, 158.

76. All of these companies have published corporate biographies, as follows: Josephine Sullivan, *A History of C. Brewer & Company* (Boston: Walton Advertising and Printing, 1926); Edwin P. Hoyt, *Davies: The Inside Story of a British-American Family in the Pacific and Its Business Enterprises* (Honolulu: Topgallant Publishing Co., 1983); Frederick Simpich, Jr., *Dynasty in the Pacific* [American Factors], (New York: McGraw-Hill, 1974); Frank J.Tayler, Earl M. Welty, and David W. Eyre, *From Land and Sea: The Story of Castle & Cooke of Hawaii* (San Francisco: Chronicle Books, 1976); Arthur L. Dean, *Alexander & Baldwin, Ltd. and the Predecessor Partnerships* (Honolulu: Alexander & Baldwin, Ltd., 1950). In addition to the above full-scale corporate biographies, American Factors issued a 105-page booklet in 1949 telling the first 100 years of its history (William A. Simonds, *Kamaaina: A Century in Hawaii*) and Castle & Cooke did the same in 1951 with a 61-page booklet (A. G. Budge, *The First 100 Years*).

77. Budge, 10.

78. Ibid., 17.

79. Morgan, 175.

80. Kuykendall, 2:146.

81. Adler, 22.

82. Kuykendall, 2:147.

83. Adler, 23.

84. Ibid., 203.

85. Dean, 34.

86. Ibid., 72–73.

87. Ibid., 92–93.

88. Adler, 103.

89. HSPA, *The Story of Sugar,* 78.

90. Vandercook, 159.

91. HSPA, *Sugar Manual, 1976.*

92. Kuykendall, 3:53.

93. Schmitt, *Historical Statistics of Hawaii,* 619.

94. Kuykendall, 3:54–55.

95. Richard Daniel Weigle, "The Sugar Interests and American Diplomacy in Hawaii and Cuba, 1893–1903," Ph.D. dissertation, Yale University, 1939, 57.

96. Alexander, 36.

97. Kuykendall, 3:147.

98. Sullivan, 130.

99. Kuykendall, 3:56–57.

100. Sullivan, 174, 181.

101. Vandercook, 165.

102. Gast, 209.

103. Ibid., 19.

104. Forest B. H. Brown, *Flora of Southern Polynesia*, Bishop Museum Bulletin no. 84, (Honolulu: 1931), 137.

105. E. C. Auchter, "People, Research, and Social Significance of the Pineapple Industry of Hawaii" (manuscript, Pineapple Growers Association of Hawaii, Honolulu, June 1950), 6.

106. Ibid., 6–7.

107. Gus M. Oehm, "By Nature Crowned: King of Fruits: Pineapple in Hawaii" (manuscript, University of Hawaii, Honolulu, circa 1951), 41.

108. Ibid., 33.

109. David Livingston Crawford, *Hawaii's Crop Parade: A Review of Useful Products Derived from the Soil in the Hawaiian Islands, Past and Present* (Honolulu: Advertiser Publishing Co., 1937), 199.

110. Oehm, 41.

111. Ibid., 50.

112. Ibid., 65.

113. Ibid., 90.

114. Auchter, "People, Research, and Social Significance," 19.

115. Oehm, 18.

116. Ibid., 113.

117. Crawford, *Hawaii's Crop Parade*, 200.

118. Schmitt, *Historical Statistics of Hawaii*, 414.

119. Crawford, *Hawaii's Crop Parade*, 201.

120. Joseph King Goodrich, *The Coming Hawaii* (Chicago: A. C. McClurg, 1914), 107.

121. E. C. Auchter, "The Pineapple Industry: A Brief Review of Its History, Research Achievements, and War Job," testimony presented before the Congressional Hearing on Statehood for Hawaii, Honolulu, T.H., 8 January 1946, 8–23.

122. Nell B. Elder, *Pineapple in Hawaii* (Honolulu: Hawaii Department of Public Instruction, circa 1956), 10.

123. Oehm, 124–125.

124. Maxwell O. Johnson, *The Pineapple* (Honolulu: Paradise of the Pacific Press, 1935), 245.

125. Elder, 10.

126. Auchter, "The Pineapple Industry," 21, 22.

127. Ann Rayson, *Modern Hawaiian History* (Honolulu: Bess Press, 1984), 105.

128. Taylor et al., 165.

129. Oehm, 128–129.

130. Ibid., 130.

131. Ibid., 23.

132. Schmitt, *Historical Statistics of Hawaii*, 360, 417.

133. Rayson, 9.

134. Auchter, "The Pineapple Industry," 26.

135. Oehm, 143.

136. Ibid., 144–146.

137. Taylor et al., 164.

138. Johnson, 240–242.

139. Auchter, "The Pineapple Industry," 28.

140. Ibid., 28.

141. Johnson, 40–43.

142. Ibid., 111–132.

143. Auchter, "The Pineapple Industry," 32.

144. Ibid., 31–32.

145. Oehm, 165.

146. U.S. Bureau of Labor Statistics, *Labor Conditions in Hawaii, 1939*, 88.

147. Ibid.

148. Auchter, "The Pineapple Industry," 16.

149. Taylor et al., 169–170.

150. Henry A. Walker Jr., "The Decline and Fall of the Big 5," address to the Rotary International, District 500 Conference, Hilo, Hawaii, 4 May 1979.

151. Dean, 167–180, 197, 212, 233.

152. Crawford, *Hawaii's Crop Parade*, 48–50.

153. Sullivan, 105.

154. Crawford, *Hawaii's Crop Parade*, 3, 18.

155. Ibid., 21.

156. Ibid.

157. Crawford, *Hawaii's Crop Parade*.

158. Ibid., 170.

159. Schmitt, *Historical Statistics of Hawaii*, 419, 547.

160. Crawford, *Hawaii's Crop Parade*, 54, 66, 100.

161. Perry F. Philipp, *Diversified Agriculture in Hawaii* (Honolulu: University of Hawaii Press, 1953), 174, 175, 210.

162. David Livingston Crawford, *Paradox in Hawaii: An Examination of Industry and Education and the Paradox They Represent.* (Boston: The Stratford Co., 1933), 133–137.

163. Ibid., 182.

164. Quoted by Stanley D. Porteus, *And Blow Not the Trumpet* (Palo Alto: Pacific Books, 1947), 108.

165. Ibid.

166. Philipp, 126.

167. Ibid., 127.

168. Schmitt, *Historical Statistics of Hawaii*, 334.

169. Crawford, *Hawaii's Crop Parade*, 93.

170. Ibid., 94.

171. Ibid., 100.

172. Ibid., 93.

173. Ibid., 97.

174. Ibid., 222.

175. Ibid., 234.

176. Ibid., 184.

177. Crampon, 25.

178. Edward B. Scott, *The Saga of the Sandwich Islands* (Crystal Bay, Nev.: Sierra-Tahoe Publishing Co., 1968), 611.

179. U.S. Census Bureau, *Historical Statistics of the United States*, 25, 33, 36.

180. Adler, 104, 109.

181. Ibid., 104.

182. Ibid., 126–127.

183. Kuykendall, 1:20–23, 175.

184. Ibid., 2:171; 3:104.

185. Ibid., 2:173–174.

186. Thomas K. Hitch and Mary I. Kuramoto, *Waialae Country Club: The First Half Century* (Honolulu: Waialae Country Club, 1981), 167.

187. Hawaii Visitors Bureau, "Profile of the Hawaii Visitors Bureau," mimeo., June 1991, 1.

188. Ibid., 1–2.

189. William L. Worden, *Cargoes: Matson's First Century in the Pacific* (Honolulu: University of Hawaii Press, 1981), 36.

190. Ibid., 163.

191. Scott, 601.

192. Ibid., 623.

193. Hitch and Kuramoto, 167.

194. Scott, 406.

195. Ibid., 579.

196. Hitch and Kuramoto, 5.

197. Robert C. Schmitt, *Origins of the Hawaii Visitors Bureau Research Program, 1911–1950*, Occasional Paper No. 7 (Honolulu: University of Hawaii School of Travel Industry Management, 1984), 16–17.

198. Hitch and Kuramoto, 5–11.

199. Taylor et al., 153.

200. Worden, 84.

201. Pan-Pacific Union, *Pan-Pacific*, January–March 1937, 17–18.

202. Kuykendall 3:387.

203. Ibid., 396.

204. Ralph S. Kuykendall and A. Grove Day, *Hawaii, a History* (Englewood Cliffs, N.J.: Prentice-Hall, 1976), 215.

205. Erwin N. Thompson, *Pacific Ocean Engineers, 1905–1980* (Honolulu: U.S. Army Corps of Engineers, Pacific Ocean Division, circa 1985), 23–24.

206. Rayson, 31.

207. Paul T. Yardley, *Millstones and Milestones: The Career of B. F. Dillingham* (Honolulu: University of Hawaii Press, 1981), 262.

208. U.S. Navy Department, Pearl Harbor Naval Shipyard, "A Brief Summary of the Diplomatic History between the U.S. and Hawaii, with Yearly Historical Sketches of the Years 1901–1941," unpublished manuscript, code 160, 4.

209. Scott, 661.

210. Rayson, 34.

211. U.S. Navy Department, Pearl Harbor Naval Shipyard, 6, 14.

212. Kuykendall and Day, 215.

213. U.S. Navy Department, Pearl Harbor Naval Shipyard, 6–8.

214. Fred A. Stindt, *Matson's Century of Ships* (Kelseyville, Cal.: Fred A. Stindt, 1982), 29.

215. Ibid., 34.

216. Schmitt, *Historical Statistics of Hawaii*, 10.

217. U.S. Commerce Department, *Income of Hawaii*, 20.

218. Robert M. Kamins, *The Tax System of Hawaii* (Honolulu: University of Hawaii Press, 1952), 179.

219. Ibid., 168.

220. Beechert, 150; U.S. Bureau of Labor Statistics, *Labor Conditions in Hawaii, 1906*, 130.

221. U.S. Bureau of Labor Statistics, *Labor Conditions in Hawaii, 1929–30*, 117.

222. Schmitt, *Historical Statistics of Hawaii*, 138.

223. Beechert, 165–219.

224. Ibid., 155–156.

225. Ibid., 196, 260.

226. Ibid., 260.

227. Ibid., 256, 261, 281.

228. Ibid., 274.

229. Ibid., 277.

230. Ibid., 281.

231. Ibid., 290.

232. This analysis has been made possible by the large volume of statistical data for that period unearthed and compiled in recent decades. Chief contributor is the U.S. Commerce Department, which in the early 1950s added Hawaii (then still a territory) to its state personal income series, and did so retroactively to 1939 in *Income of Hawaii*. Other organizations, notably the Hawaii State Department of Planning and Economic Development, the University of Hawaii, and the research departments of First Hawaiian Bank and the Bank of Hawaii, all made major contributions.

233. U.S. Commerce Department, *Income of Hawaii*, 31–32.

234. First Hawaiian Bank, *The Impact of Exports on Income in Hawaii* (Honolulu, 1962).

Chapter 4

1. Schmitt, *Historical Statistics of Hawaii*, 167–168; U.S. Commerce Department, *Income of Hawaii*, 18.

2. U.S. Census Bureau, *Historical Statistics of the United States*, 224.

3. U.S. Commerce Department, *Income of Hawaii*, 20.

4. Ibid.

5. Schmitt, *Historical Statistics of Hawaii*, 10.

6. Gwenfread Allen, *Hawaii's War Years, 1941–1945* (Honolulu: Advertiser Publishing Co., 1950), 370–371.

7. U.S. Commerce Department, *Income of Hawaii*, 20.

8. Allen, 282.

9. Ibid., 356–357.

10. Ibid., 357.

11. Ibid., 80.

12. Ibid., 35; also conversation with Ernest Kai, who was then Hawaii's attorney general and was present in Governor Poindexter's office when these events took place.

13. Ibid., 171–172, 175–176.

14. Ibid., 300.

15. Ibid.

16. Ibid.

17. Ibid., 300–301.

18. Ibid., 402.

19. Ibid., 303.

20. Ibid., 311, 316.

21. Beechert, 286.

22. Allen, 310.

23. Ibid., 306, 307.

24. Ibid., 324.

25. Ibid.

26. Ibid., 325.

27. Ibid.

28. Ibid., 289.

29. Auchter, "The Pineapple Industry."

30. Allen, 310.

31. U.S. Commerce Department, Income of Hawaii, 20.

32. HSPA, "HSPA Statement of the War Record of Civilian and Industrial Hawaii," for the Joint Congressional Committee to Investigate the Pearl Harbor Attack, Honolulu, 20 February 1946.

33. Allen, 285.

34. HSPA, Hawaiian Sugar Manual, 1988, 10–11.

35. Allen, 309.

36. U.S. Commerce Department, Income of Hawaii, 23.

37. Schmitt, Historical Statistics of Hawaii, 414.

38. Allen, 67.

39. Ibid., 152.

40. Ibid., 153.

41. Porteus, And Blow Not the Trumpet, 176.

42. Allen, 158.

43. Ibid., 156.

44. R. H. Lodge, Waipahu at War (Honolulu: Oahu Sugar Co., no date).

45. Allen, 157.

46. J. Garner Anthony, Hawaii under Army Rule (Honolulu: University Press of Hawaii, 1975), 38.

47. Allen, 157.

48. Simonds, 4.

49. Beechert, 231.

50. *Honolulu Star-Bulletin & Advertiser*, 4 December 1985, 51.

51. Porteus, *And Blow Not the Trumpet*, 235.

52. Allen, 283.

53. Ibid.

54. *Hawaii Business*, January 1988, 18–26.

55. Beechert, 287.

56. Ibid., 291.

57. Bernard W. Stern, *Rutledge Unionism* (Honolulu: University of Hawaii Center for Labor Education Research, 1986), 1–14.

58. U.S. Bureau of Labor Statistics, *Labor Conditions in Hawaii, 1947*, 185.

59. Allen, 310–311.

60. Ibid., 26.

61. Beechert, 274.

62. Lawrence H. Fuchs, *Hawaii Pono: A Social History* (New York: Harcourt, Brace & World, 1961) 269.

63. Ibid.

64. The wording of these three clauses is contained in Commerce Clearing House, *Labor Law Reports* (Riverwoods, Ill., 2 September 1948), paragraph 8065; also in P. F. Brissenden, "The 'Three Clauses' in Hawaii Labor Agreements," *Political Science Quarterly* 68, no. 1 (1953), 92.

Chapter 5

1. Thomas K. Hitch, *Hawaii: The Most Vulnerable State in the Nation* (Honolulu: First Hawaiian Bank, 1973), 38.

2. Paul F. Brissenden, "The Great Hawaiian Dock Strike," *Labor Law Journal* 4, no. 4 (1953), 231.

3. Sanford Zalburg, *A Spark is Struck! Jack Hall and the ILWU in Hawaii* (Honolulu: University Press of Hawaii, 1979), 495.

4. Fuchs, 311, 320.

5. Ibid., 357.

6. Ibid., 312.

7. Personal correspondence with Judge Mau.

8. Fuchs, 312.

9. Ibid., 361.

10. Ibid.

11. Ibid., 305.

12. Ibid., 362.

13. Ibid., 366.

14. Ibid., 373.

15. Ibid., 368.

16. Edward Johannessen, *The Hawaiian Labor Movement: A Brief History* (Boston: Bruce Humphries, 1956), 153.

17. Zalburg, 398.

18. Ibid., 435–436.

19. According to Henry Walker, former president of Amfac, Inc.

20. Allen, 107.

21. Fuchs, 360.

22. Hitch, *Hawaii: The Most Vulnerable State in the Nation*, 39–40.

23. Ibid.

24. Personal correspondence from the Pacific Maritime Association, 31 October 1988.

25. Fuchs, 313.

26. Noel J. Kent, *Hawaii: Islands under the Influence* (New York and London: Monthly Review Press, 1983), 136.

27. Department of Labor and Industrial Relations, *Labor Organizations and Affiliates, 1987–1988* (Honolulu, 1988); U.S. Census Bureau, *Statistical Abstract of the United States, 1986*, 424.

28. U.S. Census Bureau, ibid.

29. Department of Labor and Industrial Relations, *Labor Organizations and Affiliates, 1987–1988*, 24.

30. Ibid.; U.S. Census Bureau, *Statistical Abstract of the United States, 1986*, 424.

31. Department of Labor and Industrial Relations, ibid., 57.

32. Ibid., 26.

33. U.S. Commerce Department, "Sensitivity of State and Regional Income to National Business Cycles," *Survey of Current Business*, April 1973, 22.

34. Schmitt, *Historical Statistics of Hawaii*, 125.

35. Ibid., 165.

36. U.S. Commerce Department, *Income of Hawaii*, 20.

37. Ibid., 20.

38. Ibid.

39. Schmitt, *Historical Statistics of Hawaii*, 120.

40. Thomas K. Hitch, "Mid-1950 Review of Hawaiian Economic Conditions," unpublished report to the Board of Governors of the Hawaii Employers Council, Honolulu, 1950.

41. Ibid.

42. U.S. Bureau of Labor Statistics, *Labor Conditions in Hawaii, 1947*, 210–214.

43. Schmitt, *Historical Statistics of Hawaii*, 107.

44. Hawaii Visitors Bureau, *Annual Research Report on Visitors to Hawaii*, 1950–59.

45. Ibid.

46. Ibid.

47. Schmitt, *Historical Statistics of Hawaii*, 661.

48. Ibid., 415–416.

49. Stanford Research Institute, *A Study of Industrial Development Opportunities on Oahu* (Honolulu: Hawaiian Electric Co., 1955).

50. Thomas K. Hitch, "What Can We Do to Assure Hawaii's Economic Future?" In *Highlights of Trade Development Conferences with the Chambers of Commerce on Kauai, Maui, Hawaii, and Molokai, July through November 1954*, (Honolulu: Chamber of Commerce, 1954).

51. Thomas K. Hitch, *A Brief Political, Social, and Economic History of Hawaii* (Honolulu: First Hawaiian Bank, 1971), 15.

52. Hawaii Visitors Bureau, *Annual Research Report*, 1959–74.

53. Ibid.

54. Schmitt, *Historical Statistics of Hawaii*, 165.

55. DPED, *The Hawaii State Plan: The Economy* (Honolulu, 1984), 40.

56. HSPA, *Hawaiian Sugar Manual*, 1987, 7.

57. Ibid, 10–11.

58. *Hawaiian Sugar Manual*, 1975, 24.

59. Ibid.

60. Donald E. Nordland, "High Fructose: The Competition to Sugar," address to the International Society of Sugar Cane Technologists, Manila, February 1980.

61. HSPA, *Sugar Manual*, various years.

62. Ibid.

63. Schmitt, *Historical Statistics of Hawaii*, 343, 417.

64. Ibid., 475–476.

65. Frank E. Dillard Jr., testimony before Hawaii's congressional delegation, Honolulu, 20 October 1973.

66. U.S. Agriculture Department, *Federal–State Market News*, weekly (Washington, D.C., December 1977).

67. U.S. Commerce Department and U.S. Agriculture Department, "U.S. Imports: Fresh Pineapple, Calendar Year 1987" (Washington, D.C., 26 February 1988).

68. Pineapple Growers Association of Hawaii, *Present Problems and Future Production of Pineapple in Hawaii* (Honolulu, 1973).

69. U.S. Census Bureau, *Statistical Abstract of the United States, 1988*, 227.

70. *Honolulu Advertiser*, 26 April 1988, quoting Dr. Mark Stitham, a recent president of the Hawaii Psychiatric Association.

71. Hawaii Visitors Bureau, *1989 Annual Research Report*, 7.

72. Ibid.; *Annual Research Report*, 1961, 13.

73. Schmitt, *Historical Statistics of Hawaii*, 661; DPED, *Data Book*, 1987, 13.

74. CINCPAC Public Affairs Office, "U.S. Pacific Command at a Glance." U.S. Pacific Command Fact Sheet. Camp Smith, Oahu: March 1991.

75. Hawaii Agricultural Statistics Service, *Statistics of Hawaiian Agriculture, 1986* (Honolulu).

76. Ibid.

77. First Hawaiian Bank, *Economic Indicators*, March 1986.

78. Crawford, 163.

79. Hawaii Agricultural Statistics Service, various years.

80. First Hawaiian Bank, *Economic Indicators*, October 1979.

81. U.S. Census Bureau, *Statistical Abstract of the United States, 1988*, 629.

82. First Hawaiian Bank, *Economic Indicators*, October 1979.

83. Hawaii Agricultural Statistics Service, *Statistics of Hawaiian Agriculture, 1986*.

84. First Hawaiian Bank, *Economic Indicators*, October 1979.

85. *Honolulu Star-Bulletin & Advertiser*, 24 July 1988, B4.

86. *Honolulu Star-Bulletin*, 21 December 1988.

87. Bank of Hawaii, *Annual Economic Report*, 1951.

88. *Honolulu Advertiser*, 6 October 1987, B1.

89. First Hawaiian Bank, *Economic Indicators*, June 1978.

90. DPED, *Garment Manufacturing in Hawaii* (Honolulu, 1979).

91. Bank of Hawaii, *Economic Report,* various years.

92. Arthur D. Little, Inc., *Evaluation of the Potential for Space-Related Activities in the State of Hawaii,* report prepared for the Hawaii State Department of Business and Economic Development (Cambridge, Mass.: 1987), 27.

93. Thomas K. Hitch (comp.), *Economics for the 1960's* (Honolulu: First Hawaiian Bank, 1961).

94. *Hawaii Business,* November 1987, 56.

95. *Hawaii High Tech Journal* 4, no. 1 (1988), 6–10.

96. *Honolulu Star-Bulletin,* 26 May 1988, D1.

97. First Hawaiian Bank, *Economic Indicators,* September/October 1986.

98. Ibid., September/October 1987.

99. Ibid., March 1982.

100. *Honolulu Star-Bulletin & Advertiser,* 14 August 1988, A8.

101. Ibid., A9.

102. Carl P. Simon and Ann D. Witte, *Beating the System: The Underground Economy* (Boston: Auburn House, 1982).

103. Department of the Attorney General, *A Survey of Hawaii's War on Drugs* (Honolulu, February 1989), 26.

104. Quoted by Harold Winfield Kent, *Charles Reed Bishop: Man of Hawaii* (Palo Alto: Pacific Books, 1965), 244.

105. Hitch, "What Can We Do to Assure Hawaii's Economic Future?"

106. *Honolulu Star-Bulletin,* 15 March 1989, 1.

Chapter 6

1. DBED, *Revised Long-Range Economic and Population Projections, for State of Hawaii to 2010—Series M–K* (Honolulu, January 1988).

2. Paul R. Ehrlich, *The Population Bomb* (New York: Ballantine Books, 1968), 11.

3. Club of Rome (Donella H. Meadows, Dennis L. Meadows, Jørgen Randers, and William W. Behrens III), *The Limits to Growth* (New York: New American Library, 1972), 29.

4. Nordyke, 1st edition, 124.

5. Ibid., 119.

6. Quoted by Nordyke, ibid., 122.

7. Commission on Population and the Hawaiian Future, *Population Growth* (Honolulu: Office of the Governor, 1977).

8. DPED, *Proceedings: Governor's Tourism Congress, December 10 and 11, 1984* (Honolulu: 1985), 71.

9. George Chaplin and Herbert C. Cornuelle, "A Conference on Alternative Economic Futures for Hawaii" (mimeo., Honolulu, 25 July 1975), 7.

Chapter 7

1. Some of this chapter appeared in a study I did for the State Department of Planning and Economic Development in 1985. See Coopers & Lybrand, *Model and*

Implementation Framework for Monitoring the Impacts of Tourism in Hawaii (Honolulu: DPED, 1986), chapter 6, 6-31 to 6-43.

2. Territorial Planning Board, *First Progress Report: An Historic Inventory of the Physical, Social and Economic and Industrial Resources of the Territory of Hawaii* (Honolulu: February 1939), 37.

3. U.S. Commerce Department, "Sensitivity of State and Regional Income to National Business Cycles," 22–27.

4. John E. Connaughton and Ronald A. Madsen, "State and Regional Impact of the 1981–1982 Recession," *Growth and Change: A Journal of Public, Urban, and Regional Policy* 16, no. 3 (1985), 1–10.

5. Joel Garreau, *The Nine Nations of North America* (Boston: Houghton Mifflin Co., 1981), xiv–xv. Mr. Garreau was then senior editor of the *Washington Post*.

6. Bank of Hawaii, *Economic Report*, 1950.

7. DBED, International Services Branch, *A Listing of Foreign Investments in Hawaii* (Honolulu: 31 December 1987), 65.

8. DBED, *Hawaii Gross State Product Accounts, 1958–1985* (Honolulu, 1988), 158–161.

9. *Honolulu Star-Bulletin*, 11 February 1989, A3.

10. Information from Michael Sklarz, research director, Locations, Inc., Honolulu.

11. Department of Labor and Industrial Relations, *Employment and Payrolls in Hawaii, 1987* (Honolulu: 1988), 5, 6.

12. Estelle Hepton, *Moonlighting in Waikiki* (Honolulu: University of Hawaii Industrial Relations Center, 1961).

13. By Bruce Plasch, economic consultant, Honolulu.

14. Schmitt, *Historical Statistics of Hawaii*, 10, 120; U.S. Census Bureau, *Statistical Abstract of the United States, 1986*, 26, 34, 391.

15. Schmitt, ibid., 14, 327; U.S. Census Bureau, *Statistical Abstract of the United States, 1988*, 13, 322, 366.

16. DBED, *Data Book, 1988*, 48.

17. Kent M. Keith, "The Right Role for Tourism in Hawaii," talk presented at Governor's Tourism Congress, Honolulu, 10–11 December 1984.

18. John Maynard Keynes, *A Treatise on Money*. Vol. 5, *The Pure Theory of Money* (London: Macmillan Press, 1971), 86.

19. Eleanor M. Snyder, "Technical Note: Measuring Comparable Living Costs in Cities of Diverse Characteristics," *Monthly Labor Review* 79, no. 10 (October 1956), 1187.

20. Richard Ruggles, "Price Indexes and International Price Comparisons," in *Ten Economic Studies in the Tradition of Irving Fisher* (New York: John Wiley & Sons, 1967), 187.

21. International Labour Office (ILO), *An International Enquiry into Costs of Living: A Comparison of Workers' Living Costs in Detroit (USA) and Fourteen European Cities* (Geneva: 1931).

22. Snyder, 1188.

23. Ruggles, 187.

24. Ibid., 186.

25. Keynes, 100.

26. Snyder, 1187–1190.

27. David L. Callies, *Regulating Paradise: Land Use Controls in Hawaii* (Honolulu: University of Hawaii Press, 1984), 173.

28. Tax Foundation of Hawaii, *Government in Hawaii, 1990*, 13.

29. Ibid., 26.

30. U.S. Office of Management and Budget, *Standard Industrial Classification Manual* (Washington, D.C.: Government Printing Office, 1972).

31. Paul F. Hooper, *Elusive Destiny: The International Movement in Modern Hawaii* (Honolulu: University of Hawaii Press, 1980), 101–104.

32. Ibid., 89–91.

33. Ibid., 107–114.

34. Ibid., 118.

35. Ibid., 124.

36. Ibid., 121.

37. Ibid.

38. Ibid., 148.

39. University of Hawaii, Bureau of Business Research, "A Transshipment Center for Hawaii," mimeographed report, 15 June 1962, 2.

40. Address to the annual meeting of the Hawaiian Sugar Planters' Association, 5 December 1961.

41. George Chaplin and Glenn Paige, ed., *Hawaii 2000* (Honolulu: University of Hawaii Press, 1973), 346–348.

42. Quoted by Hooper, 159–162.

43. *Honolulu Star-Bulletin & Advertiser*, 30 October 1988, B3.

44. DPED, *Hawaii's Trade with the Pacific Islands, 1980–1985*, Trade Report no. 67 (Honolulu, 1987).

45. Kuykendall, 2:248–249.

Appendix

1. DBED, *Hawaii Gross State Product Accounts, 1958–1985* (Honolulu, June 1989).

2. See John W. Kendrick, *Productivity Trends in the United States* (Princeton: Princeton University Press, 1961) and *Postwar Productivity Trends in the United States, 1948–1969* (New York: National Bureau of Economic Research, 1973); Edward F. Denison, *Accounting for U.S. Economic Growth, 1929–1969* (Washington, D.C.: The Brookings Institution, 1974) and *Trends in American Economic Growth, 1929–1982* (Washington, D.C.: The Brookings Institution, 1985).

3. Denison, *Trends in American Economic Growth, 1929–1982*, 33.

4. Schmitt, *Historical Statistics of Hawaii*, 118.

5. DBED, *Hawaii Gross State Product Accounts, 1958–1985*.

6. Denison, *Trends in American Economic Growth, 1929–82*, 33.

7. Ibid., 56.

8. Robert Solow, Michael Dertouzos, and Richard Lester, *Made in America* (Cambridge: MIT Press, 1989).

References

(All government agencies are Hawaiian unless otherwise noted.)

Adler, Jacob. *Claus Spreckels: The Sugar King in Hawaii.* Honolulu: University of Hawaii Press, 1966.

Alexander, Arthur C. *Koloa Plantation, 1835–1935: A History of the Oldest Hawaiian Sugar Plantation.* Honolulu: Honolulu Star-Bulletin, 1937.

Allen, Gwenfread. *Hawaii's War Years, 1940–1945.* Honolulu: Advertiser Publishing Co., 1950.

Aller, Curtis. *Labor Relations in the Hawaiian Sugar Industry.* Berkeley: University of California Institute of Industrial Relations, 1957.

Anthony, J. Garner. *Hawaii under Army Rule.* Honolulu: University Press of Hawaii, 1975.

Arthur D. Little, Inc. *Evaluation of the Potential for Space-Related Activities in the State of Hawaii.* Cambridge, Mass.: 1987.

Auchter, E. C. "The Pineapple Industry: A Brief Review of Its History, Research Achievements, and War Job." Testimony presented before the Congressional Hearing on Statehood for Hawaii, Honolulu, T.H., 8 January 1946.

———. "People, Research, and Social Significance of the Pineapple Industry of Hawaii." Manuscript, Pineapple Growers Association of Hawaii, Honolulu, June 1950.

Bank of Hawaii. *Annual Economic Report.* Honolulu, various years.

Barber, Joseph, Jr. *Hawaii: Restless Rampart.* New York: Bobbs-Merrill Co., 1941.

Beckley, Emma M. *Hawaiian Fisheries and Methods of Fishing.* Honolulu: Advertiser Steam Press, 1883.

Beechert, Edward D. *Working in Hawaii.* Honolulu: University of Hawaii Press, 1985.

Bishop, Serano. *Reminiscences of Old Hawaii.* Honolulu: Hawaiian Gazette, Co., 1916.

Brissenden, Paul F. "The 'Three Clauses' in Hawaiian Labor Agreements." *Political Science Quarterly* 68, no. 1 (1953): 89–108.

———. "The Great Hawaiian Dock Strike." *Labor Law Journal* 4, no.4 (1953): 231–279.

Brown, Forest B. H. *Flora of Southern Polynesia.* Bishop Museum Bulletin no. 84. Honolulu, 1931.

Buck, Peter. *Arts and Crafts of Hawaii.* Honolulu: Bishop Museum Press, 1957.

———. "Polynesian Migration," Chapter 2 in E. S. Craighill Handy et al., *Ancient Hawaiian Civilization.* Rutland, Vt., and Tokyo: Charles E. Tuttle, 1965.

———. *Vikings of the Sunrise.* New York: Stokes, 1938.

Budge, A. G. *The First 100 Years: A Report on the Operations of Castle & Cooke for the Years 1851–1951.* Honolulu: Castle & Cooke, 1951.

Callies, David L. *Regulating Paradise: Land Use Controls in Hawaii.* Honolulu: University of Hawaii Press, 1984.

Campbell, Archibald. *A Voyage round the World from 1806 to 1812.* Honolulu: University of Hawaii Press, 1967.

Chaplin, George, and Glenn Paige, eds. *Hawaii 2000.* Honolulu: University of Hawaii Press, 1973.

Chaplin, George, and Herbert C. Cornuelle, eds. "A Conference on Alternative Economic Futures." Mimeo., Honolulu, 25 July 1975.

Chinen, John J. *The Great Mahele.* Honolulu: University of Hawaii Press, 1958.

CINCPAC Public Affairs Office. "U.S. Pacific Command at a Glance." Honolulu, U.S. Pacific Command Fact Sheet. Camp Smith, Oahu, March 1991.

Club of Rome (Donella H. Meadows, Dennis L. Meadows, Jørgen Randers, and William W. Behrens III). *Limits to Growth.* New York: New American Library, 1972.

Commerce Clearing House. *Labor Law Reports.* Riverwoods, Ill., various years.

Commission on Population and the Hawaiian Future. *Population Growth.* Honolulu: Office of the Governor, 1977.

Connaughton, John E., and Ronald A. Madsen. "State and Regional Impact of the 1981–1982 Recession." *Growth and Change: A Journal of Public, Urban, and Regional Policy* 16, no. 3 (1985) 1–10.

Coopers & Lybrand. *Model and Implementation Framework for Monitoring the Impacts of Tourism in Hawaii.* Honolulu: DPED, 1986.

Crampon, L. J. "Hawaii's Visitor Industry." *Journal of Travel Research* 13, no. 2 (1974).

Crawford, David Livingston. *Hawaii's Crop Parade: A Review of Useful Products Derived from the Soil in the Hawaiian Islands, Past and Present.* Honolulu: Advertiser Publishing Co., 1937.

———. *Paradox in Hawaii: An Examination of Industry and Education and the Paradox They Represent.* Boston: The Stratford Co., 1933.

Creighton, Thomas H. *The Lands of Hawaii.* Honolulu: University of Hawaii Press, 1978.

Cushing, Robert L. "The Beginnings of Sugar Production in Hawaii." *Hawaiian Journal of History* 19 (1985): 17–34.

———. "Energy Conversion—Sunlight to Sucrose." Paper presented to the Social Science Association of Honolulu, 2 October 1972.

Daws, Gavan. *Shoal of Time: A History of the Hawaiian Islands.* New York: Macmillan Co., 1968.

Dean, Arthur L. *Alexander & Baldwin, Ltd. and the Predecessor Partnerships.* Honolulu: Alexander & Baldwin, Ltd., 1950.

Denison, Edward F. *Accounting for U.S. Economic Growth, 1929–1969*. Washington, D.C.: The Brookings Institution, 1974.

————. *Trends in American Economic Growth, 1929–1982*. Washington, D.C.: The Brookings Institution, 1985.

Department of the Attorney General. *A Survey of Hawaii's War on Drugs*. Honolulu, February 1989.

Department of Business and Economic Development (DBED). *Hawaii Gross State Product Accounts, 1958–1985*. Honolulu, June 1989.

————. *Revised Long-Range Economic and Population Projections for the State of Hawaii to 2010*. Series M–K. Honolulu, January 1988.

Department of Business and Economic Development (DBED), International Services Branch. *A Listing of Foreign Investments in Hawaii*. Honolulu, 31 December 1987.

Department of Health, Hawaii Health Surveillance Program. *The State of Hawaii Data Book*. Annual. Honolulu.

Department of Labor and Industrial Relations. *Labor Organizations and Affiliates, 1987–1988*. Honolulu, 1988.

————. *Employment and Payrolls in Hawaii, 1987*. Honolulu, 1988.

Department of Planning and Economic Development (DPED) [later Department of Business and Economic Development (DBED)]. *Garment Manufacturing in Hawaii*. Honolulu, 1979.

————. *The Hawaii State Plan: The Economy*. Honolulu, 1984.

————. *Hawaii's Trade with the Pacific Islands, 1980–1985*. Trade Report no. 67. Honolulu, 1987.

————. *Proceedings: Governor's Tourism Congress, December 10 and 11, 1984*. Honolulu, 1985.

————. *State of Hawaii Data Book*. Annual. Honolulu, various years.

Dillard, Frank E., Jr. Testimony before Hawaii's Congressional Delegation, Honolulu, 20 October 1973.

Dorton, Lilikala. "Land and the Promise of Capitalism: A Dilemma for the Hawaiian Chiefs of the 1848 Mahele. Ph.D. dissertation, University of Hawaii, 1986.

Duus, Masayo U. *Unlikely Liberators: The Men of the 100th and 442nd*. Honolulu: University of Hawaii Press, 1987.

Edward E. Judge & Sons. *The Almanac of the Canning, Freezing, Preserving, and Allied Industries*. Annual. Westminster, Md.

Ehrlich, Paul R. *The Population Bomb*. New York: Ballantine Books, 1968.

Elder, Nell B. *Pineapple in Hawaii*. Honolulu: Hawaii Dept. of Public Instruction, circa 1956.

Ellison, Joseph W. *Opening and Penetration of Foreign Influence in Samoa to 1880*. Corvallis, Oreg.: Oregon State College, 1938.

Finney, Ben R. *Polynesian Peasants and Proletarians*. Cambridge, Mass.: Schenkman Publishing Co., 1973.

First Hawaiian Bank. *The Impact of Exports on Income in Hawaii*. Honolulu, 1962.

————. *Economic Indicators*. Published bi-monthly. Honolulu.

Fornander, Abraham. *An Account of the Polynesian Race*. 3 vols. Rutland, Vt., and Tokyo: Charles E. Tuttle, 1969.

Fuchs, Lawrence H. *Hawaii Pono: A Social History*. New York: Harcourt, Brace & World, 1961.

Fujiyama, Wallace. "Japanese Investments in Hawaii: Being a Part of the Hawaii Culture." In *Proceedings of the 16th General Meeting of the Japan–Hawaii Economic Council, Kohala, Hawaii, July 16–18, 1987*, pp. 47–49.

Garreau, Joel. *The Nine Nations of North America*. Boston: Houghton Mifflin Co., 1981.

Gast, Ross H. *Don Francisco de Paula Marin*. Honolulu: University of Hawaii Press, 1971.

Goldman, Irving. *Ancient Polynesian Society*. Chicago: University of Chicago Press, 1970.

Goodrich, Joseph King. *The Coming Hawaii*. Chicago: A. C. McClurg, 1914.

Handy, E. S. Craighill, and Elizabeth Green Handy. *Native Planters in Old Hawaii*. Honolulu: Bishop Museum Press, 1972.

Handy, E. S. Craighill et al. *Ancient Hawaiian Civilization*. Rutland, Vt., and Tokyo: Charles E. Tuttle Co., 1965.

Hawaii Agriculture Statistics Service. *Statistics of Hawaiian Agriculture*. Honolulu, annual.

Hawaii Business. Monthly periodical. Honolulu: Hawaii Business Publishing Corporation.

Hawaii Employers Council. *Research Reports*. Honolulu, various years.

Hawaii High Tech Journal. Quarterly. Honolulu: East West Magazine Company.

Hawaiian Sugar Planters' Association (HSPA). *The Story of Sugar in Hawaii*. Honolulu, 1929.

———. *Sugar Manual*. Honolulu, annual.

———. "HSPA Statement of the War Record of Civilian and Industrial Hawaii." Statement for the Joint Congressional Committee to Investigate the Pearl Harbor Attack, Honolulu, 20 February 1946.

———. *The Hawaii Plantation Record*. Periodical. Honolulu.

———. *Plantation News*. Monthly. Honolulu.

Hawaii Visitors Bureau. *Annual Research Report on Visitors to Hawaii*. Annual. Honolulu.

———. "Profile of the Hawaii Visitors Bureau." Unpublished and undated manuscript, Honolulu.

Hepton, Estelle. *Moonlighting in Waikiki*. Honolulu: University of Hawaii Industrial Relations Center, 1961.

Herschler, L. H. *Fifty Years of Water Service*. Honolulu: Waiahole Water Company, 1966.

Hitch, Thomas K. *A Brief Political, Social, and Economic History of Hawaii*. Honolulu: First Hawaiian Bank, 1971.

———. *Hawaii: The Most Vulnerable State in the Nation*. Honolulu: First Hawaiian Bank, 1973.

———. "Mid-1950 Review of Hawaiian Economic Conditions." Report to the Board of Governors of the Hawaii Employers Council, Honolulu.

———. "What Can We Do to Assure Hawaii's Economic Future?" In *Highlights of Trade Development Conferences with the Chambers of Commerce of Kauai, Maui*,

Hawaii, and Molokai, July through November 1954. Honolulu: Chamber of Commerce, 1954.

————, comp., *Economics for the 1960's*. Honolulu: First Hawaiian Bank, 1961.

Hitch, Thomas K., and John A. Davis. "Wages and Productivity." *Review of Economics and Statistics* 31, no. 4 (November 1949): 292–298.

Hitch, Thomas K., and Mary I. Kuramoto. *Waialae Country Club: The First Half Century*. Honolulu: Waialae Country Club, 1981.

Hobbs, Jean. *Hawaii, A Pageant of the Soil*. Stanford: Stanford University Press, 1935.

Holmes, Tommy. *The Hawaiian Canoe*. Hanalei, Hawaii: Editions Limited, 1981.

Hooper, Paul F. *Elusive Destiny: The International Movement in Modern Hawaii*. Honolulu: University of Hawaii Press, 1980.

Hoyt, Edwin P. *Davies: The Inside Story of a British-American Family in the Pacific and Its Business Enterprises*. Honolulu: Topgallant Publishing Co., 1983.

International Labour Office (ILO). *An International Enquiry into Costs of Living: A Comparison of Workers' Living Costs in Detroit (USA) and Fourteen European Cities*. Geneva, 1931.

Joesting, Edward. *Hawaii: An Uncommon History*. New York: W. W. Norton, 1972.

————. *Tides of Commerce*. Honolulu: First Hawaiian, Inc., 1983.

Johannessen, Edward. *The Hawaiian Labor Movement: A Brief History*. Boston: Bruce Humphries, 1956.

Johnson, Maxwell O. *The Pineapple*. Honolulu: Paradise of the Pacific Press, 1935.

Judd, Gerrit P. *Hawaii: An Informal History*. New York: Macmillan Publishing Company, 1961.

Kamakau, Samuel M. *The People of Old*. Honolulu: Bishop Museum Press, 1964.

————. *The Works of the People of Old*. Honolulu: Bishop Museum Press, 1976.

Kamehameha Schools, Hawaiian Studies Institute. *The Ahupua'a*. Honolulu: Kamehameha Schools Press, 1962.

Kamins, Robert M. *The Tax System of Hawaii*. Honolulu: University of Hawaii Press, 1952.

Kanahele, George Hu'eu Sanford. *Ku Kanaka: Stand Tall*. Honolulu: University of Hawaii Press, 1986.

Kane, Herb. *Voyage*. Honolulu: Island Heritage, 1976.

Keesing, Felix Maxwell. *Modern Samoa*. London: George Allen & Unwin, 1934.

Keith, Kent M. "The Right Role for Tourism in Hawaii." Talk presented at Governor's Tourism Congress. Honolulu, 10–11 December 1984.

Kendrick, John W. *Postwar Productivity Trends in the United States, 1948–1969*. New York: National Bureau of Economic Research, 1973.

————. *Productivity Trends in the United States*. Princeton: Princeton University Press, 1961.

Kennedy, Stanley C. "Air Lanes Across the Pacific." *Pan-Pacific*, January–March 1937.

Kent, Harold Winfield. *Charles Reed Bishop: Man of Hawaii*. Palo Alto: Pacific Books, 1965.

Kent, Noel J. *Hawaii: Islands under the Influence*. New York and London: Monthly Review Press, 1983.

Keynes, John Maynard. *A Treatise on Money.* Vol. 5, *The Pure Theory of Money.* London: Macmillan Press, 1971.

Kikuchi, William K. "The Fishponds of Kauai." *Archeology on Kauai* 14, no. 1, issue 32 (March 1987).

Kirch, Patrick Vinton. *Feathered Gods and Fishhooks: An Introduction to Hawaiian Archeaology and Prehistory.* Honolulu: University of Hawaii Press, 1985.

Kuykendall, Ralph S. *The Hawaiian Kingdom.* 3 vols. Honolulu: University of Hawaii Press, 1938–67.

Kuykendall, Ralph S., and Herbert S. Gregory. *A History of Hawaii.* New York: Macmillan Publishing Co., 1927.

Kuykendall, Ralph S., and A. Grove Day. *Hawaii: A History.* Englewood Cliffs, N.J.: Prentice-Hall, 1976.

La Croix, Sumner J., and James Roumasset. "The Evolution of Private Property in Nineteenth-Century Hawaii." *Journal of Economic History* 50, no. 4 (1990): 829–852.

Lihue Sugar Company. *Annual Report 1960.* Lihue.

Lind, Andrew. *Hawaii's People.* Honolulu: University of Hawaii Press, 1980.

Lindo, Cecilia Kapua, and Nancy Alpert Mower. *Polynesian Seafaring Heritage.* Honolulu: Kamehameha Schools Press, 1980.

Lodge, R. H. *Waipahu at War.* Honolulu: Oahu Sugar Co., n.d.

Luomala, Katherine. *Voices in the Wind.* Honolulu: Bishop Museum Press, 1955.

Malo, David. *Hawaiian Antiquities.* Honolulu: Hawaiian Gazette, 1903. Reprint. Honolulu: Bishop Museum Press, 1957.

McGee, Robert T. "State Unemployment Rates: What explains the differences?" *Quarterly Review* of the Federal Reserve Bank of New York (Spring 1985): 28–35.

Meriwether, Lee. "A Plantation in Hawaii." *Harper's Weekly,* 10 November 1888. (Reprinted in Alexander & Baldwin's house organ, *Ampersand,* Fall 1988.)

Morgan, Theodore. *Hawaii: A Century of Economic Change, 1778–1876.* Cambridge, Mass.: Harvard University Press, 1948.

Nagahata, Utaka, and Ralph Toyota. "VVV: A Social Movement." *Social Process in Hawaii* 8 (November 1943): 29–35.

Nordland, Donald E. "High Fructose: The Competition to Sugar." Address to the International Society of Sugar Cane Technologists, Manila, February 1980.

Nordyke, Eleanor C. *The Peopling of Hawaii.* Honolulu: University of Hawaii Press, 1977. 2d edition, 1991.

Oehm, Gus M. "By Nature Crowned: King of Fruits: Pineapple in Hawaii." Manuscript, University of Hawaii, Honolulu, circa 1951.

Oliver, Douglas L. *The Pacific Islands.* 3d ed. Honolulu: University of Hawaii Press, 1989.

Pan-Pacific Union. *Pan-Pacific.* Quarterly.

Philipp, Perry F. *Diversified Agriculture in Hawaii.* Honolulu: University of Hawaii Press, 1953.

Pineapple Growers Association of Hawaii. *Present Problems and Future Production of Pineapple in Hawaii.* Honolulu, 1973.

Platt, Sanford L. "Immigration and Emigration in the Hawaiian Sugar Industry."

Paper presented to the Industrial Relations Section, Hawaiian Sugar Technologists, Honolulu, T.H., 15 November 1950.

Porteus, Stanley D. *And Blow Not the Trumpet*. Palo Alto: Pacific Books, 1947.

———. *A Century of Social Thinking in Hawaii*. Palo Alto: Pacific Books, 1962.

Pratt, Helen Gay. *In Hawaii a Hundred Years*. New York: Charles Scribner's Sons, 1939.

Rayson, Ann. *Modern Hawaiian History*. Honolulu: Bess Press, 1984.

Richards, Mary Atherton. *Amos Starr Cooke and Juliette Montague Cooke*. Honolulu: Daughters of Hawaii, 1987.

Ruggles, Richard. "Price Indexes and International Price Comparisons." In *Ten Economic Studies in the Tradition of Irving Fisher*. New York: John Wiley & Sons, 1967.

Schmitt, Robert C. *Historical Statistics of Hawaii*. Honolulu: University of Hawaii Press, 1977.

———. *Origins of the Hawaii Visitors Bureau Research Program, 1911–1950*. Occasional Paper no. 7. Honolulu: University of Hawaii School of Travel Industry Management, 1984.

Scott, Edward B. *The Saga of the Sandwich Islands*. Crystal Bay, Nev.: Sierra-Tahoe Publishing Co., 1968.

Simon, Carl P., and Ann D. Witte. *Beating the System: The Underground Economy*. Boston: Auburn House, 1982.

Simonds, William A. *Kama'aina: A Century in Hawaii*. Honolulu: American Factors, 1949.

Simpich, Frederick, Jr. *Dynasty in the Pacific*. New York: McGraw-Hill, 1974.

Snow, Charles E. *Early Hawaiians*. Lexington, Ky.: University Press of Kentucky, 1974.

Snyder, Eleanor M. "Technical Note: Measuring Comparable Living Costs in Cities of Diverse Characteristics." *Monthly Labor Review* 79, no. 10 (October 1956): 1187–1190.

Solow, Robert, Michael Dertouzos, and Richard Lester. *Made in America*. Cambridge, Mass.: MIT Press, 1989.

Spears, John R. *The Story of the New England Whalers*. New York: Macmillan Publishing Co., 1908.

Stanford Research Institute. *A Study of Industrial Development Opportunities on Oahu*. Honolulu: Hawaiian Electric Co., 1955.

Stannard, David E. *Before the Horror: The Population of Hawaii on the Eve of Western Contact*. Honolulu: University of Hawaii Press, 1989.

Stauffer, Robert H. "The Tragic Maturing of Hawaii's Economy." *Social Process in Hawaii* 31 (1984–85): 1–24.

———. "The Hawai'i–United States Treaty of 1826." *The Hawaiian Journal of History* 17 (1983): 55–58.

Stewart, C. S. *Journal of a Residence in the Sandwich Islands during the Years 1823–25*. Honolulu: University of Hawaii Press, 1970.

Stindt, Fred A. *Matson's Century of Ships*. Kelseyville, Cal.: Fred A. Stindt, 1982.

Stern, Bernard W. *Rutledge Unionism*. Honolulu: University of Hawaii Center for Labor Education Research, 1986.

Sullivan, Josephine. *A History of C. Brewer & Company*. Boston: Walton Advertising & Printing Company, 1926.

Summers, Catherine. *Hawaiian Fishponds*. Honolulu: Bishop Museum Press, 1964.

Tabrah, Ruth. *Hawaii: A History*. New York: W. W. Norton, 1984.

Tax Foundation of Hawaii. *Government in Hawaii*. Annual. Honolulu.

Taylor, Frank J., Earl M. Welty, and David W. Eyre. *From Land and Sea: The Story of Castle & Cooke of Hawaii*. San Francisco: Chronicle Books, 1976.

Territorial Planning Board. *First Progress Report: An Historic Inventory of the Physical, Social and Economic and Industrial Resources of the Territory of Hawaii*. Honolulu, 8 February 1939.

Thompson, Erwin N. *Pacific Ocean Engineers, 1905–1980*. Honolulu: U.S. Army Corps of Engineers, Pacific Ocean Division, circa 1985.

Todaro, Tony. *Tony Todaro Presents: The Golden Years of Hawaiian Entertainment, 1874–1974*. Honolulu: Tony Todaro Publishing Co., 1974.

U.S. Agriculture Department. *Federal–State Market News Service*. Weekly. Washington, D.C.

———. *Yearbook of Agriculture*. Annual. Washington, D.C.

U.S. Bureau of Labor. *Labor Conditions in Hawaii*. Washington, D.C.: U.S. Government Printing Office, 1901, 1903, 1906, 1911.

U.S. Bureau of Labor Statistics. *Labor Conditions in Hawaii*. Washington, D.C.: U.S. Government Printing Office, 1906, 1929–30, 1939, 1947.

U.S. Census Bureau. *Historical Statistics of the United States*. 2 vols. Washington, D.C.: U.S. Government Printing Office, 1975.

———. *1980 Census of Population, General Social and Economic Characteristics, Hawaii*. PC80–C–1–13. Washington, D.C.: Government Printing Office, June 1983.

———. *Statistical Abstract of the United States*. Annual. Washington, D.C.

U.S. Commerce Department. *The Cane Sugar Industry*. Msc. series, no. 53. Washington, D.C., 1917.

———. *Income of Hawaii*. Supplement to *Survey of Current Business*. Washington, D.C.: U.S. Government Printing Office, 1953.

———. "Sensitivity of State and Regional Income to National Business Cycles," *Survey of Current Business*, April 1973.

U.S. Commerce Department and U.S. Agriculture Department. "U.S. Imports: Fresh Pineapple, Calendar Year 1987." Washington, D.C., 26 February 1988.

U.S. Navy Department, Pearl Harbor Naval Shipyard. "A Brief Summary of the Diplomatic History between the U.S. and Hawaii, with Yearly Historical Sketches of the Years 1901–1941." Unpublished manuscript, code 160.

U.S. Office of Management and Budget. *Standard Industrial Classification Manual*. Washington, D.C.: U.S. Government Printing Office, 1972.

University of Hawaii, Bureau of Business Research. "A Transshipment Center for Hawaii." Mimeographed report, 15 June 1962.

Vandercook, John W. *King Cane*. New York and London: Harper and Brothers, 1939.

Walker, Henry A., Jr. "The Decline and Fall of the Big 5." Address to Rotary International, District 500 Conference, Hilo, Hawaii, 4 May 1979.

Weigle, Richard Daniel. "The Sugar Interests and American Diplomacy in Hawaii and Cuba, 1893–1903." Ph.D. dissertation, Yale University, 1939.

Worden, William L. *Cargoes: Matson's First Century in the Pacific.* Honolulu: University of Hawaii Press, 1981.

Wyllie, Robert Chrichton. "On Capital and Banking." In *Transactions of the Royal Hawaiian Agricultural Society* 1, no. 3 (1852): 41–53.

Yardley, Paul T. *Millstones and Milestones: The Career of B. F. Dillingham.* Honolulu: University of Hawaii Press, 1981.

Zalburg, Sanford. *A Spark is Struck! Jack Hall and the ILWU in Hawaii.* Honolulu: University Press of Hawaii, 1979.

Zillgitt, Constance Elaine. *The Blue Book of Hawaii Nei.* Honolulu: Blue Book Publishing Company and Bureau, 1941.

Index